FOAL

# RECLAIMING
# AMERICAN
# VIRTUE

# RECLAIMING AMERICAN VIRTUE

## THE HUMAN RIGHTS REVOLUTION

## OF THE 1970S

Barbara J. Keys

Harvard University Press

Cambridge, Massachusetts, and London, England

2014

Library of Congress Cataloging-in-Publication Data

Keys, Barbara J.
Reclaiming American virtue : the human rights revolution of the 1970s / Barbara J. Keys.
pages cm
Includes bibliographical references and index.
ISBN 978-0-674-72485-3
1. Human rights—Government policy—United States.    2. Human rights advocacy—
United States.    3. United States—Foreign relations—20th century.    I. Title.
JC599.U5K49  2014
323.0973'09047—dc23          2013015286

# Contents

Introduction: Enter Human Rights     1

1.  The Postwar Marginality of
    Universal Human Rights     15

2.  Managing Civil Rights at Home     32

3.  The Trauma of the Vietnam War     48

4.  The Liberal Critique of
    Right-Wing Dictatorships     75

5.  The Anticommunist Embrace
    of Human Rights     103

6.  A New Calculus Emerges     127

7.  Insurgency on Capitol Hill     153

8.  The Human Rights Lobby     178

9.  A Moralist Campaigns for President     214

10. "We Want to Be Proud Again"     242

Conclusion: Universal Human Rights
in American Foreign Policy     269

Abbreviations     279
Notes     283
Bibliographical Essay     339
Acknowledgments     347
Index     351

# Introduction

## *Enter Human Rights*

O F THE CAUSES that fire the human imagination today, the idea of human rights has few rivals in its power to inspire and to mobilize. As a language of idealism, it now encompasses almost every aspiration for human betterment, so much so that it exerts an almost irresistible gravitational pull on the way we frame our pursuit of the good life. In Milan Kundera's well-known parody, even a parking spot on a crowded Paris street becomes a human right.[1] It would take a sizeable forest's worth of paper pulp to print the proliferating treaties, conventions, covenants, declarations, and case law that comprise today's enormous body of international human rights law, and a small city to house the hundreds of thousands of advocates in tens of thousands of organizations across the globe who labor to bring force to literally hundreds of distinct, codified rights. Foundations, think tanks, universities, and foreign ministries employ an army of human rights experts; politicians of every stripe profess fealty to human rights. Cynicism, criticism, and charges of cultural imperialism abound, but have not dislodged human rights from their privileged place in our moral lexicon.

This idealism attained its global stature in the 1970s, thanks in large part to its embrace by Jimmy Carter. By giving the idea the backing of a global superpower, he propelled it to extraordinary heights of recognition

*1*

and popularity around the world. The same was true at home, where international human rights, before Carter gave them the presidential touch, had been a minor issue on the national stage. The reasons for this fateful shift, so consequential for America and the world, are little understood. Too often it is explained as a natural recalibration of American moral standards after the aberrational Realpolitik of the Nixon and Ford administrations and the weakening of Cold War anticommunism in the wake of the Vietnam War. In fact it was almost accidental, and human rights moved slowly and fitfully from backstage to center stage because to contemporaries there was nothing obvious about them. The concept's utility as an answer to pressing questions had to be tested, its contours molded into politically useful forms, and other solutions found wanting before human rights were anointed as a new foreign policy paradigm.

When human rights became an American rallying cry and a global sensation in 1977, it was a transformation that seemed as sudden as it was surprising. For decades advocates of international human rights had toiled in obscurity, stalking the musty corridors of impotent United Nations commissions, publishing pamphlets read only by fellow initiates, and lamenting their lack of real-world influence. Suddenly they found themselves in an exhilarating new environment. Government officials avidly read their reports; journalists called them for statements on current events; academic and philanthropic organizations flooded them with invitations to proliferating conferences and symposia. Their activities made headlines and were lauded in editorials. "These are heady times," one of them noted, not without a sense of disorientation.[2]

When Carter proclaimed a profound moral commitment to human rights on taking office in 1977, he became the first leader of a major country to elevate the international promotion of human rights to a central role in foreign policy. Fueled by Carter's embrace of the concept, U.S. print and television news media used the term roughly five to ten times as often in 1977 as in earlier years.[3] Amnesty International, a London-based human rights organization that had recently gained a measure of global renown thanks to its campaigns against torture, won the Nobel Peace Prize. The award brought international fame and prestige to the movement and signaled the new success of human rights as a grassroots endeavor, no longer confined to elite lobbying. Amnesty's

U.S. section was so strained by the pressures of its dizzying recent growth that its leadership talked about dampening the intake of new members.[4] Other organizations devoted to promoting human rights abroad grew at spectacular rates, and it seemed that all sides of the political spectrum hailed their work as admirable and inspiring. Journalist Ronald Steel likened human rights to motherhood and apple pie: "beyond partisanship and beyond attack."[5]

This book explains why so many Americans embraced the cause of international human rights with such enthusiasm at this moment in time, and why and how promotion of human rights became a central aspiration of U.S. foreign policy. Human rights were far more than a slogan, and they had relevance far beyond purely diplomatic concerns. They helped redefine America to Americans, for they were about American identity even more than they were about foreign policy. They emerged from a struggle for the soul of the country, for principles to define not only America's international behavior but its character in a world shaped by new power relations—above all by its loss in the Vietnam War and all the soul-searching that entailed. As Americans entered the 1970s, many felt that they were standing on quicksand. Old certainties, beliefs, and standards—about America's role in the world and the nature of the world at large—had crumbled. The promotion of international human rights was one of the ideas that helped Americans make sense of the new global terrain. Crucially, it served not as a means of coming to terms with the Vietnam War but as a means of moving past it. Human rights became a way to heal the country by taming the legacy of Vietnam.

Human rights promotion was an antidote to shame and guilt. The popularity of human rights in the 1970s was a function of their capacity to shift attention and blame away from the trauma of the Vietnam War and the embarrassments and self-criticism of the civil rights movement and Watergate. For a group of conservatives who felt that the war had been a just and necessary cause, human rights were a way to reassert the fundamental immorality of communism, to revive Cold War priorities, and to position the United States once again on the side of both right and might. For moderate liberals who had come to see the war as immoral and a stain on the country's honor, promoting human rights in America's right-wing allies spotlighted evil abroad and offered a way to distance the

United States from it, alleviating their sense of responsibility. The two sides had divergent views of what had gone wrong in Vietnam, but both felt a deep need to reclaim the moral high ground in the war's wake.

Conservative Democrats were the first to use human rights as the moral underpinning of a post-Vietnam War foreign policy. They directed the concept against the Soviet bloc, first centering their attention on emigration of Soviet Jews and then more broadly on Soviet-bloc repression of dissidents. This was the camp of Democratic hawks, unrepentant Cold Warriors like Senator Henry Jackson who feared the country had lost its nerve after the Vietnam War. They were, as one journalist aptly put it, the reaction to the reaction to the Vietnam War, fretting over every sign of liberal guilt, renewed isolationism, or accommodation with adversaries, always seeing a slippery slope leading to a global communist victory.[6] They spoke of regenerating the American will, and of human rights as a means to that end. Many of the neoconservatives who drove the strategy of George W. Bush's administration after 9/11 had their roots in this group; before then they influenced Reagan's human rights program. They were the first to propound an American vision of international human rights promotion for a national audience, but when Carter came to office they lost the first round of the definitional battles. Later they would have their chance to rewrite the lexicon.

On the other side were proponents of a liberal version of human rights. They were mostly former supporters of peace candidate George McGovern, who in 1972 had sought a "new morality" to replace the Cold War ideology that had produced a brutal and mistaken war. Influenced by the New Left even though they largely avoided its anti-imperialist bent, these mainstream liberals found, once freed of the war itself, that promoting international human rights offered a path to ending, once and for all, the country's entanglement with the problematic South Vietnamese dictatorship and to dissociating the United States from other repressive allies. Their conservative antagonists repeatedly accused them of succumbing to liberal guilt, and a feeling of culpability for the repressive actions of U.S. allies was central to their worldview. Yet their attraction to human rights and their choices of particular avenues for human rights promotion were in important ways much more about feeling good than about feeling guilty. In the words of their leading congressional proponent, Donald Fraser, human rights provided a way for "the United States [to] feel better about itself" after "the trauma of the Vietnam War."[7]

The liberal human rights ideas that slowly trickled into U.S. foreign policy in the mid-1970s were tightly circumscribed to fit a new era of limited resources and distaste for intervention. Their dollar cost was minimal, but they provided enough substance to allow the United States to reclaim the mantle of virtuous nation. At a time when American opinion had turned decisively against the idea of acting as a global policeman, the promotion of human rights offered a limited program that left solutions largely in the hands of foreigners. To a considerable degree, the message was that it was enough that Americans not be part of the problem. Human rights were also appealing because they had international origins and legitimacy, yet seemed consonant with American ideals. The country could push the world in Americanizing directions even while spreading ostensibly international norms with the support of international bodies.

Both words and their definitions matter. The struggle for improving the human condition is as old as humanity, but it matters which banners are waved and which slogans inspire. Not every struggle for justice and freedom is a human rights movement, nor is every cause ever fought under the flag of human rights recognizable as such by today's definitions. Charting the rise of contemporary understandings of human rights requires careful attention to the use of the term and its core post-1948 referents: the idea of universalism, deference to the UN and its Universal Declaration of Human Rights (UDHR), and the seeking of legitimacy and redress through international law and international opinion. Americans have a long history of espousing freedom and democracy, at home and abroad, and the rise of human rights in the 1970s is part of this longer history. At the same time, developments in the 1970s represent a notably new variant of these longer-term impulses, one that was not simply inevitable. Understanding the causes and consequences of the specific outcomes produced in the 1970s requires attending to the vocabulary and the arguments made in those years.[8] Nothing underscores the novelty of human rights in the American foreign policy firmament more than the Carter administration's profound confusion over what human rights promotion meant in practice. Although quick to assert continuities with American tradition, administration officials could not turn to the policies of previous administrations for guidance. They felt as though they were making it up, and they were.

It was not just any scheme of universal justice or freedom that Americans espoused in the 1970s. The human rights ideals pressed in the later 1970s were legitimized with reference to the United Nations UDHR. The declaration's twentieth anniversary in 1968 had occasioned among Americans a collective yawn or puzzled shrug, when it was noticed at all. In the 1970s Americans dusted it off and raised it as a new standard. At first its new fans stumbled over the details. What exactly was it called? Was it a "treaty"? Had it been "ratified" by the United States? (It was not a treaty, and the country had simply signed it.) Soon nearly everyone was staking claims and counterclaims in its name.

A rough guide to the changing meaning of the term "human rights" in the United States is provided by the indexers of the *New York Times*. Human rights made its first appearance as a heading in 1935. By 1946, the heading referred readers to "civil liberties." In 1951 the heading became "freedom and human rights," still listing articles concerned predominantly with civil liberties.[9] In 1965 the indexers noted that the heading dealt with "the concept of freedom in general and . . . general trends within US." For "civil rights as a matter of racial equality," it referred readers to the heading "Negroes (in US)." The articles listed were primarily on civil liberties topics, with a few references to UN activities. A key shift, one that suggests the mental universe associated with the term had fundamentally changed, occurred in 1976. Instead of merely instructing readers interested in "freedom and human rights" outside the United States to look at relevant geographic headings, the entry listed articles about foreign countries by name. Although throughout the 1970s the indexers continued to link human rights with the more general concept of freedom, in 1976 the term took on a distinctly foreign flavor. Argentina, Chile, China, Czechoslovakia, France, Hungary, India, Northern Ireland, Italy, the Middle East, Paraguay, Poland, South Korea, the Soviet bloc, Spain, Thailand, Uruguay, Vietnam, and Yugoslavia were all mentioned, crowding out the civil liberties issues—privacy, search and seizure—that had previously been the exclusive "see also" focus.[10] Human rights had become a topic about *there*, even more than about here.

The rise of human rights was inextricably tied to the legacy of the 1960s, a tumultuous decade whose meaning and legacy remain contested a half-century later. Despite important continuities, the embrace of universal rights in the 1970s was less a logical follow-through from the civil rights activism of the sixties than a rupture that entailed fundamental redirection. Many white, centrist liberals who adopted human rights as the new paradigm in the 1970s had marched in protests for African American civil rights in the 1960s, and their involvement in campaigns for civil rights at home and human rights abroad drew on similar impulses, including a commitment to social justice and empathy for the suffering of others. But what was most important about human rights, as distinct from civil rights, was that it shifted the focus from problems at home to problems abroad. The few Americans who in the 1960s had talked about the universal human rights of the UN's Universal Declaration had talked about human rights in the United States first, with elsewhere coming in a distant second. In the 1970s, human rights became a way of directing attention elsewhere—a program for improving the rest of the world rather than rectifying deficiencies at home. Although Carter and many others who embraced international human rights in these years spoke of domestic reform as necessary and linked to external efforts, human rights campaigns in these years were overwhelmingly focused on distant injustice. Their popularity derived in significant measure from their capacity to function as a distraction from problems at home, allowing Americans to move beyond the now-tiresome self-criticism of the sixties.

The new projection of international human rights as America's key message for the rest of the world represented a revolutionary shift in foreign policy. Despite its apparent links to long-held notions of American exceptionalism and Wilsonian idealism, the reframing of U.S. foreign policy to prioritize universal human rights developed at the United Nations marked a dramatic break with the Cold War verities that had guided policy-making since the late 1940s. The new emphasis entailed redefining the world's core problems and the appropriate responses to them. It signaled a qualitatively new level of concern with the lives of peoples far removed from North America, but it was also founded on a West-knows-best attitude that some critics saw as a return to imperialism. Because the Vietnam War had left a distaste for interventionism of all kinds, action against abuse revolved around scolding and punishing rather than aiding and fixing. Instead of seeking fundamental structural change in conditions that produced searing inequality and injustice, mainstream human rights campaigns in the 1970s conveyed the notion that the problem lay in individual evil perpetrated by small numbers of wrongdoers, rather than fundamental injustices in which Americans, too, were implicated.

Larger changes in the international system and the influence of external events—most significantly, the rise of Soviet dissidence—helped make human rights one possible answer to America's quest for renewal after the Vietnam War, but more than anything else, what propelled this new outward-looking search for global justice were the emotions aroused by that deeply divisive, traumatic war. At its core the human rights revolution of the 1970s was an emotional response to the trauma of the Vietnam War. This was particularly true for the liberals who became the most ardent proselytizers for human rights, for whom U.S. involvement in Vietnam was a tragedy, one that left them feeling embittered, excluded, and embarrassed. By the war's final years, liberals saw it as an endless stalemate that rained down death and destruction upon the South Vietnamese people, at painfully high cost in American dollars and lives and at the expense of the good opinion of much of the world. That it was conducted without clear congressional sanction, in the face of the most widespread protests in the nation's history, and through presidential deception and secrecy magnified their frustration and anger. For liberals in Congress the desire to reclaim a voice in the conduct of foreign affairs would become a powerful motivating factor in the human rights surge.

Children napalmed, villages burned, civilians massacred, prisoners tortured, vast stretches of countryside decimated by bombing: for some Americans, these were the images conjured up by the mere utterance of "Vietnam," and for them it was a given that atrocities and war crimes were part of the conflict. In the 1960s and 1970s, such images produced powerful currents of opposition to the war, but not opposition framed in terms of human rights. Antiwar activists considered the war immoral and often objected vehemently to the war's brutality. Yet very few raised objections in terms of international human rights norms. It would have been surprising if they had, for international human rights were little-known standards that were globally ignored (self-determination being the one exception in an era of decolonization). To the world of the 1960s, they carried little moral force and virtually no legal weight. Moral feeling undergirded much of the opposition to the war, but it was not the only grounds for antipathy. The cost to American taxpayers, the deaths of tens of thousands of American soldiers, the class and racial inequalities manifested in the draft, the extent of deception and secrecy practiced by successive presidential administrations in waging the war, and the tarnishing of the American image abroad all weighed heavily, quite apart from misgivings about the war's brutality. Nor did most Americans or even most of those who opposed the war accept that atrocity and racism were woven into the fabric of the war. Revelations in 1969 about the My Lai massacre, reports in the early 1970s about assassinations carried out as part of the Phoenix program, and photographs of South Vietnamese political prisoners housed in "tiger cages" were shrugged off by most Americans. Media attention aroused temporary ire, but the most common long-term reactions were to disbelieve reports as propaganda or to downplay them as aberrant. For those for whom morality *was* the defining aspect of the war, at stake was a fundamental human morality, not obscure human rights standards proclaimed by an ineffective international organization of governments.

The Vietnam War, then, did not serve as an incubator of ideas of human rights. The war's role was crucial in a quite different sense. Among the core group of congressional liberals and activists who would generate the momentum for integrating liberal human rights considerations into foreign policy, the war generated a deep sense of shame and embarrassment, feelings of guilt that cried for expiation, and a profound desire to return to normalcy—feelings that sometimes worked at cross-purposes and led to no single, obvious remedy except a strong antipathy to military intervention. Anger and frustration at the sense of having been excluded from having a say in the war would generate among certain congressmen and activists a keen determination to exercise a greater voice in foreign policy-making. For congressional conservatives who tried to resurrect a Cold War consensus in part through notions of human rights, anger at congressional exclusion from policy-making also played a pivotal role, but in their case it was driven by fear that the war had produced a loss of faith and feelings of weakness that could fatally undermine the struggle against communism.

In the end, after fits and starts, human rights became the new mantra because the concept resonated with extraordinary power among a public eager to reclaim American virtue. By focusing attention on abuses elsewhere, conservatives found a potent tool to resurrect anticommunism and liberals found a way to restore their faith in America's fundamental benevolence. International human rights promotion offered a new calculus, according to which the abuses that deserved the world's attention were not associated with America's own mass bombing and napalming of civilians but with Soviet totalitarianism that stamped out freedom for its subjects or with Third World dictators who inflicted barbarous tortures on their own people.

If the ascendancy of human rights was not the inevitable offspring of the civil rights and antiwar movements, neither did it emerge out of nowhere. It was influenced by global developments during a time when the international order fundamentally changed.[11] Détente loosened the hold of Cold War fears on the public imagination, opening up political space for new concerns. The breakdown of the Bretton Woods international monetary system, the oil shock of 1973, and Third World demands for a new international economic order portended a new economic landscape. What we now call globalization took off in the 1970s: growing world markets, tighter international monetary links, and rapid cultural exchange.

Technological and communications advances created new perspectives on what seemed to be a growing list of global problems requiring global solutions. It became possible to collect information about victims of repression abroad more cheaply, easily, and rapidly than before. Television's ability to capture events with an immediacy and directness gave news reports of abuses more power. Satellite broadcasting began in 1964; by the early 1970s, color television had become widely available, beaming in vivid detail the far corners of the world into American living rooms on a nightly basis. "We have suddenly been swept into a whole new electronic grid and lashed to international girders, one with mankind," commented one political analyst in 1971.[12] Also enhanced were the means to use new communications technologies to generate action. Letter-writing, direct-mail fund-raising, and petition campaigns burgeoned with the popularity of xerographic technology. Increases in jet travel played a role, too: as travel became cheaper and quicker, international links became easier to forge. As scientists and scholars began routinely to jet around the world to international conferences, they became more aware of and responsive to abuses of their peers in the world. America's youth had a new, conscious relationship with other cultures and societies, one undergirded by unprecedented levels of exchange among young activists of the world and by a sense of a common humanity that transcended nation-states. One commentator suggested in 1971 that "being more concerned with people than with nations," the younger generation would require "new rationales for American foreign policy."[13]

Changes in the way people perceived the world fueled the new activism, not least the sense that the planet and its problems were ever more interlinked. Everywhere in the 1970s people began to speak and write of a new transnational era. Interdependence was the buzzword. The world seemed to shrink to a global village or a Spaceship Earth. Photographs of the earth from space that made it look like a tiny blue marble reinforced the sensibility that the planet was a single unit. "You don't look down at the world as an American," an Apollo X astronaut said, "but as a human being." Many of those who watched the astonishing new feats in space felt echoes of the feelings space flight was said to give astronauts: "an instant global consciousness, a people orientation, an intense dissatisfaction with the state of the world and a compulsion to do something about it."[14] Wedded to rising Holocaust awareness, the feeling of interdependence helped generate a belief that injustice mattered even in far-flung parts of the world and that silence in the face of abuses amounted to complicity.[15]

The 1970s offered activists a lengthy and compelling list of abuses to combat. In 1973 a military coup in Chile overthrew a democratically elected socialist government that had awakened enthusiasm around the world and replaced it with a repressive dictatorship that suspended civil liberties and tortured and killed thousands of political opponents. Chile generated more global outrage than any other single country, but brutality and repression were widespread across Latin America in these years. Gruesome tales of torture and political imprisonment seemed to pour out from all corners of the world, from South Korea to Indonesia to Greece. Burundi and Uganda were the sites of large-scale massacres. Critics accused Pakistan of genocide in the war that led to the creation of Bangladesh. A brutal civil war in Nigeria triggered by a Biafran secessionist movement reanimated humanitarianism in the late 1960s. Yet despite the litany of crimes, earlier decades had seen their share of repression, brutality, and disasters—and of humanitarian responses as well.[16] No doubt activists genuinely perceived an increase in repression. But it is fairer to say that people in the 1970s saw new things because they put on new lenses.

In the context of these broader developments, some options seemed to make more sense than others. Liberals in the late 1960s and early 1970s tentatively began to appropriate and recast the language and ideas of human rights that handfuls of international lawyers and church groups had used since the 1940s. For small groups of Quakers, Methodists, Catholics, and others, the UDHR had served as a referent in activism for social justice at home and abroad. These groups had worked with small numbers of international lawyers and activists in organizations like the International League for Human Rights, founded in the 1940s and until 1978 the only general human rights organization headquartered in the United States. The achievement of human rights liberals in the 1970s was to extricate international human rights lawyers from their obsession with petitioning the ineffectual United Nations, to popularize for more secular audiences the human rights talk of religious groups, and to generate out of these antecedents a new program for U.S. international involvement to replace the old Cold War consensus that had been fractured by the Vietnam War.

The genealogy of the conservative strand of human rights thinking was quite different.[17] It began, too, with the Universal Declaration, but as transmitted by American Jewish groups and Soviet and Eastern European dissidents. In the first half of the 1970s, Soviet dissidents such as Andrei Sakharov and Aleksandr Solzhenitsyn became international heroes of a self-styled human rights movement that legitimized itself in part through appeals to the Universal Declaration. They became moral icons in the West, and the dissident movement offered conservatives a discourse about human rights that reaffirmed the preeminence of the struggle against communism. Conservatives who disliked détente and wanted to return to the simple verities of Cold War anticommunism found in the dissident movement a powerful critique of Nixon's accommodation with communist powers. The dissident strand of human rights talk intertwined with the language of American Jewish groups who used human rights appeals to anchor their antidiscrimination campaigns and, beginning in the late 1960s, their activism on behalf of Soviet Jews.

Both of these were human rights movements. Their synchronicity and overlap in referents ensured that they were partly entwined. Liberals who wanted to overturn the Cold War framework sympathized with and were influenced by the Soviet-bloc dissident movement. Conservative Democrats who directed their ire toward the communist world's human rights abuses sometimes acknowledged that America's right-wing allies also committed atrocities that deserved attention and action. Both strands of thinking prioritized civil and political rights over economic and social rights, though conservatives emphasized freedom of religion, movement, and speech, while liberals were exercised most of all by torture and arbitrary imprisonment. In their genealogies and their core impetus—whether to continue the Cold War or to move beyond it—they were sharply different. In the Carter years, after some confusion, the liberal version came to define human rights. But Carter did not settle the conflict over what human rights meant; he merely inflamed the contest.

Every president since Carter has grappled with human rights. As a slogan, "human rights" offers little real guidance to the questions it raises: the term is so capacious as to provide scope for almost any program of human betterment. Is it about eradicating hunger? Banning torture? Increasing emigration? Fighting terrorism? Building democracies? The phrase alone can mean all of these things, or none. Endless arguments have been waged about which rights matter most. Do democracy and civil liberties provide the strongest guarantee against repression, or do the needs for adequate food and shelter come first? Where does morality fit relative to traditional economic and security interests, and how can policies that necessarily balance a variety of interests avoid appearing selective or hypocritical? Once goals are identified, what costs should be borne in order to achieve them, and how should they be pursued: by quietly lobbying other governments behind the scenes, publicly shaming them, putting in place sanctions, providing incentives, or—perhaps—even going to war?

These questions point to the fundamental truth that morality in foreign policy is simply politics by other means. The human rights idea became popular because it offered a sense of purity and transcendence of politics, but it was at heart a political language. The Carter administration failed to paper over the fissure between liberal and neoconservative answers to these questions—to address the key issue of what kind of politics human rights should promote. Much of the U.S. engagement with human rights policies and rhetoric in subsequent decades represented a playing out of the conflict between these two visions. The division engendered in the rise of human rights in the 1970s would continue to shape American engagement with the world in fateful ways into the twenty-first century.

## CHAPTER 1

# The Postwar Marginality of
# Universal Human Rights

W HEN JIMMY CARTER put human rights at the center of his foreign
policy, he said he was merely restoring morality to its rightful
place after its anomalous demotion under Nixon and Ford. Carter's invocation of a moral agenda was not new to American foreign policy, nor to
foreign relations in general. All empires have cloaked their rule in moralistic garb, and even the consummate realists Nixon and Kissinger spoke
of their foreign policy as designed to serve moral ends—in their case, the
creation of a stable international order and a secure peace. Elements of
the Wilsonian tradition of promoting democracy appeared in Carter's
human rights program, giving his foreign policy ideas a potentially long
genealogy. Yet it is anachronistic to suggest that human rights promotion
has always been embedded in U.S. foreign policy or that the human
rights programs of the 1970s were merely a reversion to tradition. The
Roosevelt and Truman administrations ensured that universal human
rights became part of the United Nations' mandate at the end of the
Second World War, but the early history of American engagement with
this creation shows just how unconvincing most Americans found it.
International human rights enjoyed a brief fluorescence at the end of the
war, but for most of the 1950s and 1960s, Americans mostly ignored UN

human rights. When the subject was in the news, it was often regarded as alien, un-American, or irrelevant.

With the rise of human rights as a moral lingua franca after the end of the Cold War, observers began to read human rights back in anachronistic ways. A recent survey of U.S. foreign relations, for example, sees human rights as a major element in American thinking in the nineteenth century, calling social reformer Jane Addams a "human rights advocate" and claiming that the U.S. government pressured Russia "on issues of human rights" in the 1880s and private American groups urged "their own government and others to protect human rights in countries where they were threatened."[1] These descriptions conflate a post–World War II system and definitions with differently grounded and articulated notions of justice and rights. Before the twentieth century, Americans spoke most often not of human rights but of natural, civil, political, social, or constitutional rights.[2] Such rights, along with Christian values, the notion of civilization, and ideals such as freedom, republicanism, and democracy, were part of a distinctive idiom of international idealism in the nineteenth century. In the early twentieth century, American conceptions of human rights were often defined in economic terms, especially after the devastating effects of the Great Depression. In the 1930s, drawing on a tradition of Populist backing for the "human rights" of workers in the contest between labor and capital, the demagogic Catholic "radio priest" Father Charles Coughlin (before he turned to anti-Semitism and fascism) inspired millions of listeners in part by calling for tax cuts and living wages for workers on the grounds that the "sanctity of human rights" for the poor should supersede the "sanctity of property."[3] When President Franklin Roosevelt proposed a second bill of rights in 1944, it focused on economic rights and implied a diminishment of individual liberties in the form of property rights. These were features of rights that did not assume prominence in the postwar years.

The commonly held view that universal human rights are the contemporary articulation of deep ethical and religious impulses (for just rule, respect for the human person, avoidance of suffering) is a truism that obscures the postwar system's unique features.[4] It is too easy to assume that the rise of universal human rights after the Second World War was logical and inevitable and to look for antecedents that allow us to tell a story of continuities, in which ideas experience temporary setbacks but break through eventually due to their inherent appeal.[5] In this version the 1940s set out a vision that was temporarily frozen by the Cold War but eventually triumphed, first tentatively in the 1970s, with piecemeal efforts to enforce the human rights ideals laid out after 1945, and then more vigorously in the 1990s after the constraints of the Cold War disappeared. In reality the links from the 1940s to the 1970s to the 1990s are less linear and more contingent and divergent than this story allows. In the United States, within a few years of their enunciation, the new rights ideas generated the most vigorous and energetic response not in the form of enthusiastic embrace but of attack from enraged conservatives.

The Roosevelt and Truman administrations were instrumental in inserting "human rights and fundamental freedoms" into the United Nations Charter, just as they orchestrated virtually all other aspects of the document. The Truman administration was later a key player in the drafting of the UDHR—by a commission chaired by the late President Roosevelt's wife. Yet there is little evidence that the resulting acknowledgments of human rights were intended as anything more than "inspirational fiction."[6] Even to the women's, Christian, Jewish, and African American organizations that lobbied for them, they were not the main prize; it was enough that an international organization dedicated to securing the peace was formed, even if it was predicated not on genuinely new visions of global governance or morality but was designed as a great power condominium.[7]

In the war's early years, appeals to human rights were a way to inspire public enthusiasm for the war effort. When the conflict's outcome seemed to hang in the balance, the Roosevelt administration invoked ideals to assure people that.the enormously costly war was not merely another round in an endless contest of power politics, but a worthy struggle that would secure a better world and a lasting peace. In his January 1941 State of the Union address, even before the United States was drawn into the war, President Roosevelt proclaimed that an enduring peace required "a world founded upon four essential freedoms": freedom of speech, freedom of worship, freedom from want, and freedom from fear of aggression. "Freedom means the supremacy of human rights every-where," he declared.[8] Crucially, the Four Freedoms encompassed New Deal–style economic and social justice, rather than merely civil and political rights. These broad sets of rights would make their way into the UDHR after the war, but economic and social rights would never have the same resonance for most Americans as the more familiar political freedoms, and in some quarters would evoke a deep-seated fear of socialism.

At Roosevelt's initiative, a throwaway line was inserted in a 1942 dec-laration by allied and associated powers signaling their intent "to pre-serve human rights and justice in their own lands as well as in other lands."[9] The wording signaled that the goal was merely preserving the status quo, not extending rights to new areas or creating new rights. Soon after the declaration was made public, Roosevelt ordered the internment of Japanese Americans on the West Coast.[10]

Even rhetorical obeisance to human rights was lacking in the Atlantic Charter, the joint statement of war aims that Roosevelt and Churchill drafted in August 1941, before the United States was a party to the war. The charter's most heralded provision was a statement in favor of self-determination, but it was hardly a paean to the self-governing capacities of colonial peoples. Churchill insisted that it applied only to areas under Nazi control, not to the British Empire. For Roosevelt's advisers, antico-lonialism was a means of extending U.S. economic power by acquiring access to new markets and raw materials. The crux of the negotiations about the content of the declaration was not over what both sides regarded as purely aspirational rhetoric but rather over trade issues and a possible future international organization, issues with clear economic and secu-rity repercussions. As critics noted at the time, the charter failed to men-tion civil and political rights. Initially included by the British Foreign Office, a reference to defense of "the rights of freedom of speech and thought" was deleted by Under Secretary of State Sumner Welles on the grounds that a still heavily isolationist Congress might balk at a commit-ment to defend rights that, because they were abrogated in every Axis country, could pull America into the war. Although Welles added a ref-erence to a peace that included "freedom from fear and want," the charter did not hint at international protection of human rights.[11] It has even been suggested that when human rights were eventually inserted in the United Nations Charter, it was "a kind of consolation prize" offered in place of the Atlantic Charter's promise of self-determination, which would eventually be deemed too dangerous and taken off the postwar agenda.[12]

Hesitancy and ambivalence characterized the American approach to international human rights throughout the war, especially when it came to actions that might have tangible effects. In late 1944, the Big Three initially excluded human rights from a draft of what would become the United Nations Charter. Although State Department planners considered including an international bill of human rights as part of the future United Nations and a subcommittee of legal experts even wrote a draft bill of rights in 1942, the idea was eventually dropped. Still, the U.S. delegation at the Dumbarton Oaks meetings that wrote the first version of the UN Charter pressed for some mention of promotion of human rights in the document, and the British and Soviets reluctantly agreed. The result was a deliberately weak and ambiguous formulation of a goal to "promote respect for human rights and fundamental freedoms."[13]

Tepid as it was, wartime rhetoric about human rights was partly a response to a groundswell of organizing and agitating among religious, women's, and labor groups in the United States and many other countries. Statements of faith in human rights ideals and proposals for bills of rights proliferated. Enthusiasts embraced rights not in order to prevent recurrence of the Holocaust, which as yet only barely penetrated public consciousness, but because curbing the power of dictatorships to trample on individual rights seemed a way to reduce the chances of a future war.[14] Many were also attracted to individual rights as an alternative to the now-discredited minorities rights structures embedded in the League of Nations, whose charter had placed the rights of specific groups in Eastern Europe under international protection but had made no mention of individual human rights.[15]

Recognizing the powerful resonance of the idea, the Roosevelt administration accredited nearly four dozen nongovernmental organizations as official consultants to the U.S. delegation sent to write the final UN Charter at the 1945 San Francisco Conference. The administration's aim was to enlist these organizations—groups such as the National Peace

Conference, the American Federation of Labor, the National Association for the Advancement of Colored People (NAACP), and the American Jewish Congress—as public advocates of the new organization, selling the public on a more internationalist role for the United States.[16] Wilson's failure to gain U.S. admission to the League of Nations was a lesson in what to avoid; this time around, public support was to be carefully culti- vated. Some of the nongovernmental organizations' representatives came away feeling that it was their pressure that put human rights on the agenda, but it is more likely that the administration was already con- vinced of the public relations value of paying lip service to human rights ideals.[17]

The San Francisco Conference was an American show, and while the major powers fought battles on controversial issues such as veto power in the Security Council, when it came to human rights, the United States held the reins. The reference to "fundamental human rights" in the char- ter's preamble was adopted from a South African proposal written by segregationist Jan Smuts, but the nature and thrust of the human rights references in the UN Charter are above all a product of American influ- ence, for better or for worse.[18] The charter includes several mentions of the aspiration to "promote" and "encourage respect for" human rights and fundamental freedoms; stronger verbs such as "assure" or "protect" were rejected. American officials believed that encouragement of rights could be an international concern, but protection remained the concern of states unless violations of rights were so extreme or extensive that they threatened the peace.[19] Article 1, setting forth the principal purposes of the organization, included "international cooperation in . . . promoting and encouraging respect for human rights and for fundamental freedoms for all." Articles 55 and 56 committed members to take "joint and sepa- rate action" to promote "universal respect for, and observance of, human rights and fundamental freedoms."[20] The charter thus became the first international treaty to refer to human rights in general, rather than to the rights of specific groups.[21] These aspirational references, however, were deliberately curtailed by affirmation of the principle of state sovereignty in Article 2(7), which reads: "Nothing contained in the present Charter shall authorize the United Nations to intervene in matters which are essentially within the domestic jurisdiction of any State. . . ."[22] Nothing about the framing of the references to human rights or their elaboration in the subsequent drafting process suggests that they were intended to undermine the bedrock principle of national sovereignty.

The charter did not define or enumerate "human rights and fundamental freedoms," leaving the meaning of the two terms and their relationship to one another deliberately vague. (It is an open question as to why "fundamental freedoms," included by rote in references to the UN system into the 1970s, eventually dropped out of usage.) Acting Secretary of State Edward Stettinius, for one, merely sputtered that they were the same human rights and fundamental freedoms "for which great intellectual leaders of mankind have struggled since the ancient beginnings of Athens, Jerusalem and Rome."[23]

At American instigation, human rights made it into the 1947 Paris Peace Treaties with Bulgaria, Finland, Hungary, Italy, and Romania, with greater effort at definition. Each treaty included a pledge to "take all measures necessary to secure to all persons . . . without distinction as to race, sex, language or religion, the enjoyment of human rights and of the fundamental freedoms, including freedom of expression, of press and publication of religious worship, of political opinion and of public meeting."[24] It was on grounds of failure to adhere to these conditions, freedom of religion above all, that communist satellites Bulgaria, Hungary, and Romania were delayed entry to the UN until the 1950s, and on these grounds that the United States and other Western countries set in motion International Court of Justice rulings on adherence to the peace treaties. The individual "human rights" case that garnered the most attention in the early Cold War was the 1948 arrest and subsequent trial and imprisonment of Hungary's Catholic archbishop József Mindszenty, who was hailed as a fearless hero and martyr for human rights—a sort of Solzhenitsyn of the early Cold War. Much of the ensuing outrage in the United States was couched in terms of the defense of "Christian American democracy" against "anti-Christian tyranny," with the peace treaties rather than the UN Charter or the Universal Declaration of Human Rights as the most frequently cited legal grounds for objection.[25]

The task of giving concrete expression to the UN's still vague invocations of ideals was left to its Commission on Human Rights, a body created at U.S. initiative. Led by Eleanor Roosevelt, the U.S. representatives played a key role in drafting the UDHR, but also in ensuring that it lacked enforcement provisions. Human rights advocates within the United Nations first intended to write a legally binding international bill of human rights. Like Stalin, however, Truman had no desire for a document with enforcement powers that could constrain American power.[26] The relative ease with which the various delegations hammered out the declaration reflected how little was at stake in the creation of a document that was intended to be a beacon, not a guide to actual behavior.[27]

Signed in 1948 in the shadow of the Eiffel Tower in Paris and then passed by the UN General Assembly in New York, the declaration is the foundational document of the postwar human rights regime and a reference point for all subsequent discussions of human rights. Billed as "a common standard of achievement for all peoples and all nations," it announces in its first article that "[a]ll human beings are born free and equal in dignity and rights. They are endowed with reason and conscience and should act towards one another in a spirit of brotherhood." Its subsequent thirty articles enumerate civil and political rights—such as the right to life, liberty, and security of the person, to fair trial, property, and freedom of movement and religion, and prohibitions on slavery, torture, and arbitrary arrest—as well as economic and social rights, including the right to work, to education, to an adequate standard of living, and to "a social and international order in which the rights and freedoms in this Declaration can be fully realized."[28]

The Soviet Union abstained from the vote on the UDHR, opposing it on the grounds that it undercut the principle of state sovereignty.[29] In the Soviet conception, in which the interests of state and individual were coterminous, liberal Western notions of rights as a protection from state power made no sense. Rights did not inhere in individuals by virtue of their humanity but derived from the state and reflected its stage of development.[30] Andrei Vyshinsky, the veteran prosecutor of the Stalinist show trials, lectured the UN that rights "could not be conceived outside the state."[31] As internal repression moderated after Stalin's death in 1953, however, the Soviet Union came to see benefits in the propaganda value of embracing elements of the UN human rights program.[32] The Soviets since the 1920s had held up the depredations of American racism to ridicule and condemnation; the declaration provided an irresistible tool for further attacks. If its own record of civil and political rights was hard to defend except on purely fictional grounds, the Kremlin had greater credibility when it crowed about its achievements in economic and social rights.

Many American conservatives found the declaration as ideologically alien as did Stalin and Vyshinsky, racing into battle even as the document was being drafted. Conservative lawyer Frank Holman used his presidency of the American Bar Association in 1948 to launch an attack on treaty law—"the greatest threat to human freedom"—and on the UN's "so-called human rights" instruments in particular.[33] In a blaze of speeches, articles, and pamphlets, he vilified UN human rights initiatives as instruments of great potential danger that would supersede U.S. law, rewrite the U.S. Constitution, and possibly even "destroy . . . our form of government."[34] The economic and social rights in the forthcoming Universal Declaration, he thundered, were an effort to "adopt the New Deal on an international scale" through paternalistic government that would promote "state socialism, if not communism, throughout the world."[35] He warned that new UN powers would mean that complaints lodged by the Soviets could compel Americans to be brought before international courts and possibly punished with death.[36] The UN Convention against Genocide, drafted alongside the Universal Declaration, was even more dangerous. Its powers were so sweeping, Holman claimed, that a white motorist who accidentally struck and killed a black child could be hauled off to The Hague to stand trial for genocide.[37]

Although officials in the Eisenhower administration would later deride such concerns as absurd, Holman and others could point to Supreme Court decisions and comments by John Foster Dulles before he became secretary of state that supported their claims.[38] In a much-cited 1952 speech, Dulles said that the executive branch's power to make treaties was "liable to abuse" and could "take powers away from Congress and give them to the President" as well as "cut across" constitutional rights.[39] In 1950 a California district court ruled that the UN Charter's human rights provisions were "superior" to a state law that barred Japanese noncitizens from owning land. The reasoning of the decision was overturned on appeal, but in the meantime the *Wall Street Journal* charged that the district court's conclusion that "the United Nations

Charter has become the supreme law of the land" were "the twelve most ominous words of legal meaning uttered in our time!"[40] At the federal level, some Justice Department officials and members of Congress suggested that the UN Charter could be used as a basis for antilynching legislation.[41] Many conservatives saw such statements as evidence that the UN human rights program was but one prong of an effort to create a world government that would trample American liberties.

The resulting conflict between Congress and the executive branch was a kind of mirror image of the conflict that erupted in the 1970s. Both owed much to congressional rage at what was seen as years of presidential usurpation of congressional powers. Holman was animated by a deep-seated hatred of Roosevelt and fear of the power of central government, just as many liberals would later be inspired by hatred of Nixon and centralized foreign policy. The difference was that in the 1970s the object was to press for greater action on human rights, while in the 1950s Congress forced the president into inaction.

Senator John Bricker, drawing on the ideas of the American Bar Association, spearheaded the campaign to contain the UN threat through a constitutional amendment to limit the potential domestic repercussions of international treaties. A conservative Ohio Republican who had been Thomas Dewey's running mate in the 1944 presidential campaign, Bricker was the kind of Republican who loudly denounced FDR as a tool of a worldwide communist conspiracy.[42] Said to be so conscious of the stately requirements of the Senate that he walked as if someone were carrying a full-length mirror in front of him, he typified the reactionary Old Guard Republican: a supporter of Red-baiting Senator Joe McCarthy, an admirer of isolationist Senator Robert Taft, and "a fervent hater of foreign aid, the United Nations, and all those he lumped with Eleanor Roosevelt under the contemptuous designation 'One Worlders.' "[43] Like many Republicans, he saw the New Deal's expansion of federal government authority as a threat to American liberties and resented FDR's unilateral foreign policy decisions. Among the Senate's most conservative members, he was also one of its least respected on a national level, winning the rating of worst senator in a 1949 poll of journalists.[44] One critic described his intellect as "like interstellar space—a vast vacuum occasionally crossed by homeless, wandering clichés."[45]

In 1951 Bricker proposed a resolution that would have required the president to withdraw from participation in UN human rights initiatives. He called the human rights covenant then being drafted "a Covenant on Human Slavery" that "would destroy our cherished freedoms."[46] Brickerism is sometimes described as springing from Southern fears that racial segregation would be imperiled by human rights treaties, and such fears undoubtedly underpinned much congressional support for the amendment. Bricker and Holman, however, were animated most of all by fear that economic and social rights provided a cover for a New Deal agenda to institute socialism at home.[47] Holman suggested that the Universal Declaration's guarantee of a right to "social security" could be interpreted to mean that the United States was "to provide, or in a large part provide, social security for all the rest of the world."[48] These were mainstream ideas at the time. Journalist William Fitzpatrick, who would later win a Pulitzer Prize for a toned-down expression of his anti–human rights invective, wrote in the *New Orleans States* in 1948 that the UDHR would institute "a world-wide social and economic system with Uncle Sam paying the bills" and "an International Court of Human Rights to which every one of us may be held responsible." An opponent of civil rights laws, Fitzgerald warned that the declaration would undermine rights to choose "intimates and fellow workers." It would weaken immigration law, take aim at religion, override many states' laws, ignore American customs, and, as in Nazi Germany and the Soviet Union, attack the institution of marriage. He condemned it as "a far-reaching, revolutionary document which could easily drive this country to the poorhouse and its people to totalitarianism."[49]

Bricker's anti–UN human rights resolution brought him into contact with the American Bar Association, which convinced him that a constitutional amendment offered the surest way to deter the UN threat.[50] A few months later Bricker launched a new assault on the internationalism that underpinned the human rights system. What became known as the Bricker Amendment was a series of proposed constitutional amendments introduced in the years 1951–1954, all designed to limit treaty-making power in order to defend the United States against the threats posed by the UN covenants on genocide, women's rights, and human rights. In its various iterations the amendment would have required that any treaty or executive agreement take effect only through legislation, or in other words, that treaties would not be the "supreme law of the land" unless and until Congress wrote enabling legislation.[51] Drawing on Holman's arguments, Bricker charged that without his amendment, UN human rights treaties would take precedence over the U.S. Constitution.[52] The "basic human rights" of Americans were in danger of being "supervised or controlled by international agencies over which they have no control," he warned.[53]

By the early 1950s, as the Cold War flared into hot war in Korea, Americans had grown disenchanted with many UN activities, which seemed too often to offer cover for communist anti-American propaganda. In 1952 a large cohort of Republicans swept into Congress, riding on Eisenhower's coattails, dissatisfaction with the stalemate in the Korean War, and McCarthyite hysteria over communist influence in the Truman administration. When Bricker reintroduced his amendment at the beginning of 1953, he had sixty-one cosponsors. Like the foreign aid cutoffs of the 1970s, the measure united a diverse group of legislators, from die-hard conservatives to Southern Democrats determined to maintain segregation to some who simply wanted to signal disapproval of UN activities.[54] In mid-1953 proponents of the measure mounted a wide-ranging public campaign that included radio broadcasts, full-page advertisements in the *Wall Street Journal*, and millions of letters and telegrams to politicians and businessmen across the country. The Vigilant Women for the Bricker Amendment presented Bricker with petitions signed by over three hundred thousand people, neatly tied in red, white, and blue ribbons.[55] Outside a core of dedicated conservatives, however, the issue had only modest resonance: a poll in early 1954, at the peak of the controversy, indicated that 28 percent of respondents had heard or read about the Bricker Amendment, and opinion seems to have been evenly divided in favor and against.[56]

The Eisenhower administration strongly opposed the amendment, worrying that the measure would "cripple" executive power and render it "helpless in world affairs."[57] In 1953 Dulles tried to head off Senate insurrection by withdrawing from drafting the UN covenants and promising not to sign them. The ACLU, B'nai B'rith, the American Jewish Congress, and the American Federation of Labor weighed in against the amendment. Even so, a watered-down version of the Bricker Amendment was defeated in February 1954 by only a single vote, one cast by a liberal Southern Democrat who arrived late to register the deciding "no"—according to lore, after having been dragged, drunk or hung over, from a nearby tavern.[58]

A chastened administration stuck to its promise not to participate in the UN covenant process. Although the General Assembly did not approve the results of the covenant-drafting process until 1966—the International Covenant on Civil and Political Rights and the International Covenant on Economic, Social, and Cultural Rights—much of the texts had been drafted before the Eisenhower pullout. The U.S. imprint mattered in some important ways, including the decision to write two separate covenants, a move that in the view of many observers relegated social and economic rights to secondary status.[59] After 1953, however, the U.S. refrained from further involvement. The U.S. delegation to the Third Committee, the body responsible for human rights issues, now had one of the most boring jobs on earth, ordered to sit in silence during human rights debates and to raise their hands in votes only to abstain.[60]

The UN Convention against Genocide, submitted to the Senate for ratification in 1949, also fell victim to Brickerism. Many religious, women's, civil rights, and labor groups supported ratification, but the convention was a lightning rod for the extreme right. Constituents flooded their congressmen with warnings of the dire consequences that would befall the country should it sign on to this toothless effort to prevent mass murder. Not until Nixon in 1970 did another president attempt to put it before the Senate, and then he was excoriated by the far right for falling for a "communist hoax." "Apparently Kissinger hasn't told Nixon," charged one anti-Semitic group, that if the convention were in force, the president could "be hauled off to a foreign country for trial and execution if found 'guilty' of alleged 'war crimes' in Vietnam!"[61] It would not be ratified until 1986.

U.S. noninvolvement after 1953 had little practical effects on real-world events, for UN human rights efforts were undertaken only in the abstract. Even as thousands of complaints from individuals alleging violations of human rights streamed in to the United Nations from across the world, the UN Human Rights Commission in 1947, urged on by Eleanor Roosevelt, formally renounced any power to investigate the correspondence, creating instead a system for filing complaints that John Humphrey, head of the UN Secretariat's Human Rights Division, called "the most elaborate wastepaper basket ever created."[62] This refusal even to investigate, much less to act on violations, remained in place until the second half of the 1960s, when Third World states, whose numbers in the UN grew at a rapid rate after decolonization, provided the impetus for a nominally more active approach. Petition systems were put in place in forums of Third World interest—first racial discrimination, then apartheid and colonialism—and then expanded to allow the study of all petitions that could be shown to "reveal a consistent pattern of violations of human rights."[63] With such a vague standard for measuring when human rights reached the threshold for international efforts, the petition clauses were used in practice only in a handful of cases against countries without Third World friends.

Before the 1970s, women's, peace, labor, and religious groups with long-standing internationalist agendas were the main guardians of a discourse of international human rights, though it was a discourse that did little to penetrate the consciousness of most Americans. Jewish social justice groups, liberal Protestant denominations, and Catholic groups inspired by Vatican II reforms were among the few nongovernmental organizations that gave international human rights and UN human rights in particular an institutional home between the end of the Second World War and the 1970s. The American Jewish Committee commissioned legal scholar Hersch Lauterpacht's 1942 study of an international bill of rights, participated in the San Francisco Conference, worked for the adoption of the Universal Declaration, and pushed for enforcement mechanisms. From the Roosevelt era through the 1960s, the committee aligned its interests with ending discrimination against both blacks and Jews, forming an active part of the "liberal-labor-Negro coalition" that undergirded the civil rights movement. It promoted ratification of the two primary covenants as well as other human rights conventions and advocated creation of a UN High Commissioner for Human Rights.[64] In the sixties growing Holocaust awareness spurred Jewish groups to press for U.S. ratification of the UN Genocide Treaty. In 1964 the Jewish Labor

Committee funded an Ad Hoc Committee on the Human Rights and Genocide Treaties, but despite letterhead support from a range of civil liberties, religious, and labor bodies, including the ACLU, the NAACP, and the American Friends Service Committee, its influence remained marginal and efforts to secure ratification went nowhere.[65]

For some Christian groups, too, international human rights seemed a promising means toward a better world. The Catholic hierarchy, especially after the ground-shifting Second Vatican Council of 1962–1965, gave human rights new prominence in its efforts to pursue international peace and social justice.[66] Liberation theology, with its focus on social justice and helping the poor, and a novel doctrinal embrace of religious freedom, were among the factors spurring what one scholar calls the "Catholic human rights revolution."[67] Pope John XXIII, in the 1963 encyclical *Pacem in Terris*—which constitutes the Church's preeminent example of rights-based arguments—wrote that the world community must aim at "the recognition, respect, safeguarding and promotion of the rights of the human person." He called the UDHR "a step in the right direction" and urged the UN to become more effective in guaranteeing human rights.[68] His successor, Pope Paul VI, named January 1, 1969, the World Day of Peace with the theme "Promotion of Human Rights—The Way to Peace."[69] The language became a standard referent: when Johnson briefly terminated air strikes on North Vietnam, for example, the pope telegraphed to express his hope for "justice, brotherhood and due respect for the human rights of the inhabitants of that troubled area."[70]

Liberal Protestant denominations, mostly those associated with the National Council of the Churches of Christ of the U.S.A. (NCC), were active in the civil rights movement and linked their concerns to issues of poverty and social justice abroad.[71] O. Frederick Nolde, representing the NCC's predecessor, the Federal Council of Churches, had played a role in pressing the U.S. delegation in San Francisco to include religious freedom and other human rights in the UN Charter. Although its vision of a just social order derived from religious principles, the NCC accepted the UN human rights system as providing the most authoritative and legitimate definition of rights in the international system.[72] In the 1950s NCC resolutions deplored violations of religious liberty and other rights in the Soviet Union and Eastern Europe. The mainstream ecumenical

World Council of Churches, which had early on pushed for the inclusion of freedom of religion in the UN covenants, in 1968 issued a statement saying that human rights were "a common concern" and nations could not therefore regard such concern as "unwarranted interference."[73] The American Friends Service Committee, an independent Quaker organization dedicated to pacifism and humanitarianism, developed a strong interest in international human rights as an outgrowth of its larger mission. Among religious organizations with human rights programs, the committee was rare in the emphasis it accorded to economic and social rights relative to civil and political rights.[74]

In these years the only U.S.-based nongovernmental organization dedicated explicitly to human rights was the International League for the Rights of Man (ILRM), formed in 1942 by Roger Baldwin (one of the founders of the ACLU) along with international collaborators. In the 1950s and 1960s, the organization consisted of a small group of international lawyers with an even smaller staff and a tiny budget. From the beginning it regarded the UDHR and the UN's human rights covenants as the authoritative definitions of human rights and worked primarily by lobbying UN agencies to improve their implementation of human rights. Its efforts to alleviate specific human rights violations focused on civil and political rights. It sent fact-finding missions, observed trials, supported victims, and published reports.[75] Freedom House, founded in 1941, would become a major player in human rights debates in the late 1970s, but the group always focused its efforts on "freedom," a concept it repeatedly said was not identical to human rights. Its priority was free elections and it worked to focus attention on political rights, but in its view the legitimacy of efforts to promote freedom did not derive from UN documents, nor were those efforts best pursued through UN agencies. Its lack of interest in international law and its avoidance of a human rights label mean that it should not be considered a human rights organization in these years, even if some of its activities focused on concerns that overlapped with human rights.[76]

For a few brief years during and immediately after the war, international human rights norms were the subject of an idealistic public campaign and a cynical great power appropriation. Then the attention of the public and the great powers waned. The post-1948 years have a well-deserved reputation as a period of relative inactivity in U.S. promotion of international human rights. Human rights became one more tool in an anticommunist propaganda kit, used in the rarified world of the UN but with nearly undetectable resonance in the real world, and one of diminishing utility once mounting civil rights protests in the 1950s vividly exposed America's Achilles' heel.[77] There are few more telling indicators of the marginality of the UN human rights program in the eyes of American leaders than the fact that in the first decades of the Cold War, women were assigned to oversee it. As U.S. representative to the UN Commission on Human Rights, Eleanor Roosevelt was succeeded by Mary Lord, Marietta Tree, and Rita Hauser. (Morris Abram provided a brief male interlude in the late 1960s.) The Universal Declaration was adopted, and then largely ignored. The internationalization the new ideals implied called forth fear and opposition; and then the whole issue was subsumed under the pressing demands of homegrown human rights problems.

## CHAPTER 2

# Managing Civil Rights at Home

IN THE SUMMER of 1964, a Cornell University student named David Hawk set off for Mississippi along with hundreds of other middle-class white college students swept up by the drama and idealism of the civil rights movement. Hawk and his fellow Freedom Summer volunteers were taking part in a voter-registration campaign that aimed to redress the astonishing fact that, thanks to harassment, poll taxes, and spurious literacy tests, only about 5 percent of Mississippi's voting-age blacks were registered—the lowest rate in the country. The students, mostly white and venturing into the South for the first time, faced arrest and beatings from hostile white locals. Three participants were murdered. It was an eye-opening, life-changing experience for Hawk, exposing him at first hand to shocking levels of injustice and poverty. Two summers later, Hawk participated in a similar program known as the Southwest Georgia Project, but by 1967, as the civil rights movement grew more radical and whites were squeezed out, Hawk turned to the growing movement against the Vietnam War.[1]

In the mid-1970s Hawk became executive director of Amnesty International's American section, and he would later say that the moral concerns that animated his activism in the 1960s flowed naturally into his human rights work: having fought against injustice at home, "it seemed logical to work for the same thing abroad."[2] It is tempting to see the leap from advocating rights at home to pressing for rights abroad as a logical progression and to give the civil rights movement credit for laying the seeds for the later flowering of international human rights. Yet there were strong elements of discontinuity. The end of major civil rights mobilizing in the late 1960s and the advent of a mass movement under the banner of international human rights in the late 1970s left too substantial a gap to suggest that one flowed into the other. It is true that many civil rights activists of the 1960s joined human rights campaigns in the 1970s, but even more did not. Many civil rights veterans showed little interest in human rights issues, and none more so than African Americans. Apartheid in South Africa was the only issue with significant resonance for blacks, and despite minority recruitment efforts and campaigns directed at African issues, groups like Amnesty in the 1970s frequently lamented their failure to attract African American members.[3]

Above all, the two movements drew on distinctly different sources of inspiration and were linked to very different visions of problems and solutions. Civil rights activists saw the movement at home as linked to struggles for justice elsewhere, but those struggles were framed as collective struggles against colonialism and white supremacy, for self-determination and civil rights, with the state as the guarantor of liberty and equality. In contrast, the human rights movement of the 1970s sought legitimacy and solutions in international law resting above the authority of the nation-state.[4] As Rita Hauser, Nixon's representative to the UN Human Rights Commission, would later put it, civil rights and universal human rights rested on "different concepts and different documents and ran on separate tracks."[5] The shift from looking inward to looking outward was also momentous. When Americans turned to human rights, after a decade when lecturing to others on human rights seemed ludicrously at odds with the country's profound failures to guarantee basic rights to many of its own citizens, it was partly a declaration that America had put its own house in order and could now turn to righting wrongs elsewhere.

While the painful and sometimes violent struggle for racial equality preoccupied the country in the 1950s and 1960s, the civil rights movement monopolized the terrain of rights talk. For Americans in those years, human rights were a familiar component of the discourse of civil rights. The term lacked the ubiquity it gained in the 1990s, but politicians, the media, and private organizations wielded it in the context of domestic struggles often enough for it to seem routine. It was an auxiliary of civil rights, invoked in the natural law tradition of the rights of man. It denoted above all the civil and political rights of African Americans but sometimes also included economic and social rights and the rights of other minority groups and women. In the decade before 1973, the *New York Times* used the term civil rights four times as often as human rights and often employed the latter as a loose synonym for civil rights. As interest in international human rights took off after 1973, however, frequency of use and meaning shifted. In the decade after 1973, usage of the two terms in the country's newspaper of record drew even, and human rights became more often a referent to international rather than domestic issues.[6] As international issues came to colonize the term, it began to conjure up not the rights of Americans guaranteed by domestic law but the rights of foreigners as delineated in UN documents.


The civil rights movement had internationalist concerns: African American leaders saw links between subjugation at home and colonialism abroad, between the racism they experienced at home and the racism that fueled the Vietnam War, between their struggle and the struggles of black Africans fighting white supremacy. The primary focus of the movement, however, was the effort to wring greater protections from the federal government. It was above all about seeking American remedies to American injustice.

In a brief window after the Second World War, civil rights activists had looked with hope to the UN and invoked the Universal Declaration of Human Rights in criticizing America's record on race, but when the advent of the Cold War made this approach seem subversive, it was abandoned. In 1946 the NAACP drafted an appeal that internationalized the concerns of black Americans. Titled "An Appeal to the World: A Statement on the Denial of Human Rights in the Case of Citizens of Negro Descent in the United States of America and an Appeal to the United Nations for Redress," the document declared that America's treatment of its black citizens was "not merely an internal question . . . but a basic problem of humanity."[7] The brainchild of W. E. B. Du Bois, the eminent African American thinker and advocate, the appeal documented lynching, segregation, denial of voting rights, and other inequities. When the NAACP attempted to present the appeal to the UN Human Rights Commission in 1947, Eleanor Roosevelt angrily charged the group with making propaganda for the Soviets. She threatened to resign from the NAACP board, a move that would have been a sharp blow to the organization. She was persuaded to stay, but NAACP head Walter White forsook appeals to universal human rights as a tool for reform.[8] The civil rights movement poured its energies into appealing to whites at home, to the constitutional ideals and traditions of the nation, and to the federal government as the key to action. Even for Du Bois, the appeal to UN human rights was an anomaly. He was not interested in the Universal Declaration when it was adopted in 1948, and after the failure of his appeal he returned to long-standing interests far removed from the particular internationalism of universal human rights.[9]

Keeping their focus resolutely on issues at home, advocates of civil rights sometimes invoked human rights to link the cause to the American tradition of natural rights. It was in this sense that Johnson's future vice president, Hubert Humphrey, used the term in his famous 1948 speech urging the Democratic Party to back an African American civil rights plank. "To those who say, this civil rights program is an infringement on states' rights, I say: . . . walk forthrightly into the bright sunshine of human rights!" Humphrey declaimed in an oft-cited line.[10] He was speaking about African American rights: antidiscrimination and antilynching laws, desegregation of the armed forces, and voting rights; "human rights" linked these issues to American tradition. The Minnesota liberal was aware of internationally defined human rights, for in the 1950s he swam against the Brickerite tide in favoring engagement with the UN's human rights treaties, but America's key task, as he saw it, was to solve domestic problems by enforcing the nation's own laws. For Humphrey, as for other liberals in the 1950s, the promotion of human rights meant focusing inward. The crux of the issue, Humphrey said in 1959, was "the moral and constitutional duty of the State to protect and to guarantee the rights of its citizens." Introducing a package of civil rights bills in 1959 that he called the Omnibus Human Rights Act, he cited human rights as a means of situating civil rights within the American tradition of natural rights, calling the nation to make good the principles of the Declaration of Independence and the Constitution.[11]

Alongside catchall terms such as freedom, justice, equality, and brotherhood, human rights was a frequent referent for the civil rights movement. The boundaries between civil and human rights were rarely rigidly drawn. Sometimes activists grasped human rights concepts in part by serendipity or accident, though there was a general trend to speak of human rights as a gesture of inclusivity, using the broader term to connote aims beyond rights for blacks or to convey the message that securing rights for some did not come at the expense of rights for others. This was Fred Shuttlesworth's aim in 1956 when he named his Birmingham civil rights group the Alabama Christian Movement for Human Rights, without giving much thought to whether civil and human rights differed.[12] The group of health-care workers who banded together in 1964 to provide medical assistance to Mississippi Freedom Summer volunteers called themselves the Medical Committee for Human Rights partly because a similarly named committee for civil rights had just folded.[13] Because civil rights seemed identified with the South, those who wanted to signify that racism was a national problem sometimes used the broader moniker. In 1959, for example, a radical youth group in Ann Arbor held a conference on racial discrimination under the heading "Human Rights in the North."[14] State and local agencies with a mandate to fight racial discrimination in housing and employment were often rebranded as human rights bodies when, as so often happens with bureaucracies, their briefs expanded. In 1962 New York's State Commission against Discrimination became the Commission for Human Rights.[15] The analogous agency in New York City, formed in reaction to the Harlem riots of 1943, had started out as the Unity Committee in 1943; in 1955 it became the Commission on Intergroup Relations; in 1961 it was renamed the Commission on Human Rights.[16] Such examples could be multiplied indefinitely.

The movement's single most widely publicized use of the language of human rights fit this pattern. In 1967, when sociologist Harry Edwards started an effort to convince African American athletes to boycott the

U.S. Olympic team, he named his group the Olympic Project for Human Rights. It was not a call to international human rights: his manifesto to the American public spoke only of the injustices suffered by African Americans, and it was only later and at the suggestion of a South African activist that he added exclusion of South Africa from the Olympics to his list of demands. He hoped the broader label would elicit support from other oppressed groups in the United States and project a moderate image at a time when "civil rights" was beginning to conjure up the militant radicalism of Black Power and the Black Panthers.[17] He failed, as the signature achievement of the Olympic Project—the black-gloved, raised-fist salutes offered by sprinters John Carlos and Tommie Smith as they stood on the winner's podium at the 1968 Olympic Games—raised a firestorm of white anger back home.[18]

Television news programming reflected both the elasticity and domestic focus of understandings of human rights. A 1969 CBS report on a massive oil spill off the coast of California quoted a local politician stressing the importance of placing the "human rights" of local residents above the profits of oil companies. In 1970 ABC reported that Myrlie Evers, the widow of slain civil rights leader Medgar Evers, was running for Congress on "a human rights platform." Supporting Ralph Nader's campaign for privacy protections in the new computer age, a Columbia University professor warned that computer data could undermine "human rights."[19]

As Americans entered the 1970s, their understanding of human rights was tied to domestic issues. Student radicals in the early 1970s organized the Human Rights Party in Michigan, which focused on domestic issues, defining human rights as "housing, health care, child care, education, transportation, food and clothing." Its foreign policy plank was anti-militarist and stressed the "need for planetary survival through unity," but made no mention of any universal human right except for self-determination.[20] The section called "Human Rights" in the Democratic Party handbook prepared for the 1970 congressional elections was devoted to domestic civil and economic rights: employment discrimination, "black capitalism," voting rights, and desegregation.[21] When the American Bar Association's individual rights section started up a journal entitled *Human Rights* in 1970, section chairman Jerome Shestack justified it by invoking threats to domestic civil liberties.[22] Under Kennedy,

Johnson, and Nixon, the White House's central filing system included a subject category for human rights; what was filed there related almost exclusively to domestic civil rights concerns, with a small smattering of UN issues.[23]

The contrasting uses of *human rights* by Martin Luther King, Jr., and Malcolm X point to the fluidity of a term that could be defined in multiple ways. King described the civil rights struggle as part of an international human rights movement, often linking the fight for civil rights at home to African struggles against white supremacy. The struggle for freedom is global, he said in a speech decrying global poverty and U.S. support for the apartheid regime in South Africa.[24] His was a vision of human rights that had little to do with the Universal Declaration, international law, and individual liberties. Instead it was inspired by a mixture of Christian faith, socialist internationalism, and African American social gospel, and it was a language he turned to as he tried to shift the civil rights struggle from the domain of political rights to new economic demands.[25] At a Southern Christian Leadership Council retreat in 1967, he told his colleagues, "we have moved from the era of civil rights to the era of human rights," from a "reform movement" to "an era of revolution." What he meant by human rights was a radical redistribution of wealth, not only in the United States but around the world.[26] Coinciding with his outspoken denunciation of the Vietnam War, King's talk of human rights increased his marginalization, as many Americans came to see him as a dangerous radical.

Before his assassination in early 1965, Malcolm X was almost alone in calling for the UN's international human rights system to be used as a forum for civil rights action. In 1964 the black nationalist told African Americans to stop seeing their problems as simply domestic matters and instead to raise the struggle to a "higher level—to the level of human rights." Atrocities all over the world were brought before the United Nations, Malcolm X charged, but a "conspiracy" was keeping African American suffering out of the international sphere. "Civil rights means you're asking Uncle Sam to treat you right," he explained. "Human rights are something you were born with. Human rights are your God-given rights. Human rights are the rights that are recognized by all nations of this earth."[27] Scoffing at U.S. criticism of the Soviet Union's treatment of its Jewish citizens, he said, "Imagine this. I haven't got anything against Jews, but that's their problem. How in the world are you going to cry about problems on the other side of the world when you haven't got the problems straightened out here?"[28] At the time of his death, he was developing plans to charge the United States at the UN with genocide against its African American citizens, drawing on articles in the UDHR and the Genocide Convention.[29] Spurred by Malcolm X's writings, the Student Non-violent Coordinating Committee (SNCC) adopted a resolution in 1967 proclaiming itself a human rights organization that worked not only for the liberation of black Americans but against "colonialism, racism and economic exploitation" elsewhere, especially in the Third World. To work toward these ends, SNCC created an International Affairs Commission and authorized an application for nongovernmental organization status with the UN's Economic and Security Council.[30]

Malcolm X and SNCC, however, were a radical fringe in a fragmenting civil rights movement confronting an energized white backlash. With their fervid denunciations of whites as devils and murderers and calls for blacks to rise up against their oppressors, their embrace of an internationalist conception of human rights served to underline how far removed it was from the mainstream. For most Americans, human rights remained contained in an American framework.

In the fifties and sixties, as decolonization made anticolonialism and racism global preoccupations, the foreign media turned the spotlight on racial discrimination in the United States. From Truman on, successive administrations worried about the damage done to America's image by televised images of racial violence and endless stories about racism and segregation. Third World diplomats assigned to the United States came home with tales of harassment, unequal treatment, and disrespect when they tried to get a cup of coffee, even in places like New York City.[31] In charting the lines of influence between civil rights efforts at home and global forces, the more powerful trajectory went from outside in: the civil rights agenda at home played a part in spawning a global human rights movement, but even more pronounced were the changes that the world, looking in, spurred in the United States.

By the 1960s, as Brickerism receded and Congress assumed a more deferential position toward the executive branch, the Kennedy and Johnson administrations quietly reengaged with the UN human rights program. Antiracism and self-determination, rather than human rights per se, were the preeminent slogans. The types of human rights violations that would compel attention in the 1970s—especially torture, political imprisonment, and mass killings—occurred in the 1960s but were hardly noticed, and they were not the subject of concerted international action before 1967.

In 1963 President Kennedy ended the decade-long moratorium on U.S. engagement with UN human rights covenants by asking the Senate to approve UN conventions on the political rights of women and the abolition of slavery and forced labor. Kennedy noted that the rights in these treaties were already assured by the Constitution, but that the country should not "stand aloof from documents which project our own heritage on an international scale." Addressing the UN General Assembly two months later, he said the United States was as concerned with ending discrimination abroad as it was with ending it at home and that violations of human rights anywhere in the world were a matter of American concern.[32] Yet Kennedy put little political capital behind ratification, and the Senate approved only the Supplementary Slavery Convention— the only one supported by the American Bar Association and the one dealing with an issue Americans felt was long in their own past.[33] The other two, alongside the Genocide Convention moldering there since 1949, stalled in the Senate Foreign Relations Committee, which saw no domestic constituency for human rights treaties to offset the very vocal and energetic opposition the right could muster.

The Kennedy administration's embrace of economic development and the Alliance for Progress in Latin America are sometimes cited as evidence of its commitment to foster international human rights, but these initiatives were aimed at fostering economic growth, not promoting rights; they did not appeal to international law, nor were they legitimized with rights talk. In the administration's few efforts explicitly designed to foster human rights awareness, domestic civil rights problems left little room for discussion of the problems of foreigners. In 1962, for example, the U.S. National Commission for UNESCO brought together a small group of nongovernmental organizations—the American Jewish Committee, the Methodist Church Board of Missions, the NAACP, and a few others—to help create a "guide for community action" on human rights. It provided a detailed history of the human rights accomplishments of the UDHR and the UN ("more rights, fewer wrongs"). Its instructions for local activities revolved entirely around issues of discrimination in employment, education, and housing. When it came time to celebrate Human Rights Day, the pamphlet instructed, the keynote speaker should discuss the difficulties of combating discrimination, but should also highlight achievements: "We have already come far. . . . More important, we have the right to correct our faults." The only intimation that the American human rights project might have international ramifications came at the end, when the authors wrote that every success at the community level, every school integrated, "contributes to the chain reaction building up for human rights the world over."[34]

The Johnson administration's limited international human rights activities reflected its civil rights agenda at home. In 1966 Johnson signed the Convention for the Elimination of All Forms of Racial Discrimination and submitted it to the Senate for ratification. When the administration set up a commission to promote observance of the twentieth anniversary of the Universal Declaration, dubbed Human Rights Year, its efforts reflected the dominance of civil rights concerns. When one commission member raised racism in South Africa at an early planning meeting, member Bruno Bitker said the group's mandate was "not to deal with issues abroad," and the rest of the group concurred. As another participant explained, the U.S. government's concern with human rights elsewhere was merely "tangential"; the focus had to be on rights at home. At another meeting, Chairman Averell Harriman said it would be unwise to "point a finger" at other countries, which might point back at America's own failures. When the devastating famine in Biafra came up, one participant commented that "human rights in this country should be the greatest concern," and Atlanta *Constitution* publisher Ralph McGill argued against a resolution calling for Biafran relief, saying "the United States Government could get in trouble with its friends."[35]

The commission's outputs reflected the overriding influence of domestic concerns. Its publications, including three hundred thousand leaflet-posters placing the UDHR next to the Bill of Rights and a booklet titled *Human Rights: Unfolding of the American Tradition*, aimed at Americanizing UN human rights as a counter to lingering Brickeritis. In a move that would be unthinkable for official publications just a decade later, it also put out a detailed volume surveying how well the United States upheld each of the thirty articles of the UDHR. The commission devoted special attention to racism at home, holding a conference on racial discrimination in American education and sponsoring a Smithsonian exhibit on human rights that gave pride of place to the Emancipation Proclamation.[36]

Perhaps reflecting its own lack of enthusiasm, the commission found that the UN human rights program had little resonance among Americans. The program of a primary school's commemoration of Human Rights Day suggests the very loose vernacular connotations of human rights: the schoolchildren sang songs such as "Born Free" and dressed up as Aristotle, Benjamin Franklin, Thomas Jefferson, and "Justice," carrying sword and scales.[37] The commission's planning report emphasized the "need to popularize the concept of human rights—human rights as a coherent, unified approach to the work of government covering the areas of civil rights, administration of justice, health, education, labor, housing, social security, etc."[38] Its final report's recommendations included centralizing human rights considerations in the State Department but focused on domestic issues such as education and housing. The recommendation to provide "increased attention" to international human rights came in last, after the observation that "all countries are violating human rights." It was described as something that "will demand greater understanding and compassion from the American people," who would need to be educated about the pragmatic as well as moral benefits of such a posture.[39]

Despite the money and resources put into the effort, celebration of Human Rights Year had virtually no public significance. With the country facing civil rights fatigue, the media mustered no interest in appeals to UN human rights. "Human rights events . . . lack drama and tend to require a background and understanding not readily available to press, television, and radio reporters and commentators," the commission's final report lamented. Human rights might get the attention they deserve, the report said, if only the media had a greater sense of public service.[40] In an internal report, a participant judged Human Rights Year "a dismal failure." The commission's activities never got more than nominal support from a handful of national groups and were ignored by the major religious denominations. "The impact was just about zero," and "all over the land . . . there was a marked apathy."[41]

Meanwhile, at the UN, the growing ranks of newly decolonized nations ensured that in the General Assembly and its organs, including the Human Rights Commission, the concerns of the Third World were at the top of the agenda.[42] Portugal's continuing stand against self-determination in its colonies, a whites-only government in Southern Rhodesia after 1965, and apartheid in South Africa were the targets of endless resolutions, reports, and denunciations. In 1962 the General Assembly called apartheid in South Africa a threat to peace and called for economic sanctions. In 1965 the General Assembly began declaring racial discrimination a "crime against humanity." By the end of 1968, the General Assembly had adopted about thirty-five resolutions on South Africa alone. Denunciations of racism and colonialism were endlessly reiterated.[43]

In this context, U.S. foreign policy had an anticolonial component, but observers in the 1960s would not have described it as a human rights program: the terminology is anachronistic. Morris Abram recalled that in 1968 when he exceeded his instructions at the UN Commission on Human Rights by proposing to look into "some particularly glaring examples of . . . consistent patterns of violation of human rights" in Greece and Haiti, "all hell broke loose." It was as though he "had committed some grievous crime," he recalled, judging from the State Department's heated reaction to his suggestion that U.S. allies could be criticized on human rights grounds.[44] American diplomats did not speak of universal human rights nor did Foggy Bottom see the promotion of international rights as an appropriate goal of foreign policy. To the extent U.S. diplomacy aligned itself with anticolonialism, self-determination, and antiracism, it did so not as part of an overt scheme to promote human rights but to promote friendly relations with newly independent African countries.

U.S. policy toward southern Africa highlights the predominance of the language of antiracism and anticolonialism. Specifically human rights–based appeals occasionally made an appearance, but the global struggle of the 1960s was about collective self-determination more than individual rights.[45] In the case of South Africa, few Americans knew or cared much about apartheid except when crises such as the 1960 Sharpeville massacre drew headlines. African Americans were preoccupied with domestic civil rights, and Martin Luther King's calls for a South African boycott and the protest efforts of groups such as the American Committee on Africa made almost no headway in making apartheid an issue of grassroots concern. The committee networked with many groups that included activism against apartheid on their crowded agendas—the National Council of Churches, New Left and civil rights groups, Americans for Democratic Action—but until the mid-1970s none of the agitating translated into noticeable media or public interest. The Kennedy administration had supported a UN arms embargo on South Africa, with mostly symbolic effects. The Johnson administration was concerned enough to send an observer to the 1964 trial that awarded a life sentence to Nelson Mandela, but the observer concluded that the proceedings had been fair and that Mandela had been engaged in revolutionary activity. Economic and security interests prevailed in a climate that offered little pressure for strong antiapartheid action.[46]

Southern Rhodesia was a partial exception to this trend. It was of less strategic value in the eyes of American policy-makers, who were willing in this case to take their cue from the British. In 1965 a whites-only government headed by Ian Smith unilaterally declared independence from Britain and established a white-supremacist government that disenfranchised nearly 95 percent of the population. At Britain's initiative, the Security Council ruled that the situation was a threat to international security and for the first time ordered mandatory economic sanctions. Pressing the administration to support sanctions, American civil rights groups framed the issue as one of racial discrimination, without casting it as a general human rights issue. Roy Wilkins of the NAACP urged the Johnson administration to do everything possible to prevent the emergence of another apartheid government. The United States must "ally itself with the cause of racial equality in Africa, as it is doing at home," he wrote; it "can have no part in abetting the ugly business of racism."[47]

Internal administration memos also did not cast it as an issue of human rights.[48] When former secretary of state Dean Acheson decried the Rhodesian sanctions as "barefaced aggression, unprovoked and unjustified by a single legal or moral principle," and targeting a state that had threatened no one, Johnson's UN ambassador, Arthur Goldberg, responded with arguments centered on security interests, buttressed by morality.[49] In a public appeal he defended sanctions as a "moral" issue, noting that it would constitute a "double standard" to deny racial equality abroad while on a nationwide campaign to bring the benefits of equality to American blacks. Goldberg cited human rights obligations imposed by the UN Charter, but only as a peripheral supporting point and without mentioning the UDHR or other UN human rights documents.[50] As the exchange suggests, the impetus for U.S. support of economic sanctions arose as part of an anticolonial posture and was an offshoot of antiracism policies at home, not a general human rights initiative. Until Congress overturned the sanctions in 1971, by far the strongest rhetoric on Rhodesia came from anticommunists on the right, not from advocates of antiracism on the left, who were preoccupied with the war in Vietnam.[51]

The Johnson administration did not sell its policies in international human rights terms, and internal correspondence suggests officials rarely saw their own efforts in that light. A 1966 Department of State report on the "foreign policy ideas developed during the Johnson Administration" included forty-four items, with an emphasis on development aid, population control, and health and food aid, but no mention of human rights.[52] A memo on the administration's major accomplishments in the UN could find only one to cite under the heading of human rights: signing the convention on racial discrimination.[53]

The predominance of domestic civil rights considerations was everywhere in evidence. Celebrating Human Rights Day in 1969, a group affiliated with the Ad Hoc Committee chose Southern Christian Leadership Conference leader Jesse Jackson as keynote speaker.[54] For the UN's Teheran Conference marking the twentieth anniversary of the UDHR, the Johnson administration chose the NAACP's Roy Wilkins as head of the U.S. delegation. His presence was intended to head off attacks on racism in America, especially in the aftermath of King's assassination. Wilkins did his job admirably. In the words of one internal report, Wilkins's key speech was a success in that it "highlighted broad American unity in facing up to admitted US race problems."[55]

Civil rights progress at home was the face of America's human rights program abroad. Lawyer Morris Abram was both cochairman of the White House Commission on Civil Rights and U.S. representative to the UN Human Rights Commission; it was the latter position that flowed from the former, rather than the reverse.[56] Abram wrote in 1968 that Johnson's main achievement in the field of international human rights was his civil rights program at home. "For the first time in the history of the Commission," he wrote, "the men and women who speak for America no longer needed to apologize for or equivocate about our national policy in matters of race."[57] It was not that racial problems had vanished— indeed, race riots erupted across the country with ferocity in the summer of 1968—but rather, Abram commented, that the country was now honest about its shortcomings and determined to remedy them. Even so, he concluded in an assessment that painted the UN's human rights program as little more than moral suasion, "We who are still grasping so desperately for implementation of the protections guaranteed to all citizens in the United States Constitution can hardly be impatient with the UN's progress."[58]

In 1968, Anna Roosevelt Halsted took the United States to task for lagging in the fight for human rights. The daughter of Franklin and Eleanor Roosevelt and the vice chairman of President Johnson's Commission for the Observance of Human Rights Year, Halsted told a meeting of nongovernmental organizations that the United States had failed to secure rights for African Americans at home. As to the American role in promoting human rights abroad, Halsted said only that the United States should ratify the UN covenants on human rights. She said nothing about a U.S. responsibility to work toward mitigating human rights abuses abroad.[59] For most Americans at that time, the stricture against interference in other countries' internal affairs remained a stark barrier to such thinking. But a mere seven years later, observers assessing the "American human rights record" would take a very different tack. Liberal columnist Anthony Lewis, writing in late 1975, took this topic to mean not the record of rights promotion at home but of rights promotion abroad. On the question of "official attitudes toward human rights, the recent American record is dismal," he wrote. "In Chile, in Brazil, in the Soviet Union and South Korea and many other places the American Government has appeared insensitive to the grossest inhumanity—in strange contrast to our feelings and legal standards at home."[60] In a few short years, the locus of human rights activity shifted from home to abroad.

Only as civil rights problems faded from the national agenda could Americans credibly invest human rights with a different meaning. For nearly two decades, internal struggles for justice and rights preoccupied the country. America's representatives in international forums continued to invoke freedom and democracy in the propaganda war against the Soviets, but a mass movement on behalf of rights elsewhere had to await the expiration of the great convulsion over rights at home. When the new movement came, it would be less about extending the battles of the sixties than about declaring them over and searching for foreign rather than homegrown monsters to slay. Until then, Abram's 1969 assessment remained valid: "Most people are not strongly motivated by deprivations of human rights in other lands, unless they identify with the victims for reasons of family, race, religion or national origins; their concern is also limited by the feeling that 'we have troubles enough of our own.'"[61]

## CHAPTER 3

# The Trauma of the Vietnam War

O N JUNE 8, 1972, a South Vietnamese plane dropped napalm on the village of Trang Bang, South Vietnam, setting huts and people aflame. As the villagers fled their homes, Associated Press photographer Huynh Cong "Nick" Ut snapped rolls of photographs. One of them, appearing the next day on the front pages of almost every major newspaper in the United States, showed five children running down a road, crying. In the center was a nine-year-old girl whose clothes had been burned off, her face a grimace of pain and fear. Ut's photo would become an iconic image of the war, visual shorthand for the suffering the war was inflicting on South Vietnamese civilians. Ut won a Pulitzer Prize. Phan Thj Kim Phúc spent fourteen months in the hospital and would suffer a lifetime of complications from her burns.[1]

Nixon suspected the photograph had been staged. In a private conversation caught on the White House taping system, he told his chief of staff, "I wonder if that was a fix." His Democratic challenger in the presidential election, George McGovern, had no such doubts: the photo literally moved him to tears. It "ought to break the heart of every American," he told voters during his campaign. "How can we rest with the grim knowledge that the burning napalm that splashed over little Kim and countless thousands of other children was dropped in the name of America?"[2] "Too many seem indifferent to death among the Vietnamese," he chided.[3]

The divergent reactions of Nixon and McGovern reveal the fault line in the genealogy of international human rights in the United States. For those who saw the war as a just cause, even if one gone awry in the execution, the human suffering the war produced was understandable. War was war, and suffering was inevitable in war. Some of those in this camp would take up with alacrity the cause of human rights in the Soviet Union. Moralizing against Soviet abuses served as a remedy for what they saw as excessive American self-criticism over failures in Vietnam and a reminder that communism, not American imperialism, was the real evil. For others who saw the war as an indelible blot on the American conscience, the crimes committed in its prosecution could not be excused. For these people, human rights provided a way to move past the Vietnam War and to try to offset its terrible mistakes. For them, however, the target would be not communist countries but unsavory dictatorships of the right.

While the war dragged on, Americans rarely made explicit appeals to international human rights. Many on the left saw the war as a product of colonialism and racism—the same evils that preoccupied the UN human rights apparatus in the 1960s. Despite this congruence, the antiwar movement rarely appealed to the international human rights system either as a source of legitimacy or of redress for claims of injustice. When it came to killing, torture, political imprisonment, or war crimes in Vietnam, antiwar activists protested on the grounds of morality, sometimes with reference to the laws of war but almost never with reference to international human rights.[4]

The Vietnam War created a rupture that made possible, intellectually and emotionally, a new organizing principle for U.S. foreign relations that became thinkable only after the war was over. What is striking about the emergence of the new brand of liberal human rights thinking in the 1970s is precisely the timing: even under the impetus of the Democratic Party's New Politics, a fixation on rights of all kinds, and a search for a new morality in international relations, the language of international human rights did not find fertile ground for growth in the liberal imagination until after the war had ended. As long as the war went on, it branded the United States a major source of oppression and violence in the world, making it impossible to propose that the country champion a crusade against those evils elsewhere.

A demonstration against the Vietnam War in New York City. Rev. Martin Luther King, Jr., is at center; child-rearing expert Dr. Benjamin Spock is on the left; a child holds a sign protesting the use of napalm. Morality suffused opposition to the war. (AFP/Getty)

The absence of human rights talk from the debate over the war arguably was a precondition for its eventual postwar rise. Each side in the debate had claimed for its arsenal the standard lexicon of American foreign policy values: freedom, democracy, honor, peace. To backers the war was being fought for these moral values; to detractors these values required ending the war. Evidence streaming out of Vietnam—about the destructiveness of the air war and the repressiveness of the South Vietnamese government in particular—continually undermined official efforts to associate the war with traditional rallying cries. The offsetting moral claims devalued these abstractions. Public cynicism stripped them of their moral force.[5] When human rights emerged in the foreign policy vocabulary of the early 1970s, its apparent novelty in that context imparted an authenticity and purity that the old standards could no longer muster.

Before the Vietnam War, America's moral imperative abroad was the worldwide struggle against communism. Americans believed that the requirements of security and morality coincided: containing communism was both a strategic and a moral necessity. In the second half of the 1960s, however, the liberal Cold War consensus unraveled. By 1971 the majority of Americans had come to believe that their nation had made a grave mistake in trying to contain communism in South Vietnam, and many began to question the strategy itself, seeing the fight against communism as an effort that had distorted the nation's priorities and subverted its values. The country seemed overcommitted, overinvolved, overstretched. The efficacy of intervention, even in such innocuous forms as foreign aid, seemed more and more dubious. In the face of what appeared to be overwhelming evidence of failure, opinion leaders of all stripes went back to the drawing board to rethink America's approach to the world. The promotion of international human rights was one answer to the question of what should replace anticommunism as the driving force of U.S. foreign policy—but it would require the end of the Vietnam War and the personal endorsement of a new president to make it the most appealing one.

If the war spurred intellectual reassessments of America's Cold War strategy, its emotional repercussions were even more consequential. As ubiquitous descriptions of it affirm, the war was a national trauma, and it had profound and lasting effects on American self-perception. Writing in 1970, radical historian Eugene Genovese lamented the "spiritual crisis" caused by the Vietnam War and spiraling racial tensions, which caused "our celebrated sense of national virtue and omnipotence to crumble." In the past, Americans had believed their country was invincible and all problems were soluble. Now the country was experiencing "a massive breakdown, manifested in every section, class and stratum, in faith in its ideals, institutions and prospects."[6] American foreign policy appeared to be in a shambles.

The combustible mix of doubt, anxiety, shame, anger, and frustration produced by Vietnam would shape foreign relations for years after the end of the war. Nixon sought a new framework for prosecuting the Cold War, ushering in a restructuring of U.S. foreign policy in the form of détente with the Soviet Union and a rapprochement with China. Liberals disillusioned by the war in Vietnam welcomed these changes, which seemed to lessen the prospect of future conflicts and nuclear war, but Nixon continued to wage war in Vietnam for four years, he framed his foreign policy in the language of amoral Realpolitik, and he approached Third World issues within a traditional Cold War framework. Emotionally, his policy offered the battered national ego no prospect of redemption or moral comfort.

The 1972 presidential campaign, waged in the year before the successful conclusion of a peace accord, pitted Nixon against a Democratic Party in the grip of a shifting political sensibility. The so-called New Democrats embraced a New Politics underpinned by a "new morality." Minorities, youth, women, and highly educated elites supplanted the party's traditional blue-collar power brokers. The New Politics aimed at protecting the environment, achieving greater equality at home, making government less corrupt and more open, and rejecting militarism. The Democratic contenders for the nomination talked about change, a better future, and cleaner government. The sensibility of the electorate was captured in what people remembered about the opening campaign speech of Edmund Muskie (who would serve as secretary of state in Carter's final year): his emotional appeal to reclaim an America "we love and believe in and want to fight and die for," an America that had slipped away.[7]

The liberal, social-justice concerns of the new "politics of conscience" would seem to have offered fertile ground for international human rights talk. The 1972 Democratic Party platform, which was very much a centrist product of the New Politics, referred to rights extensively. The key debates in its drafting came over the rights-related issues of busing and abortion. As finally hammered out, the platform had planks on the rights of children, veterans, the mentally retarded, the elderly, consumers, and poor people. It even acknowledged "the right to be different." The war aside, its priorities were overwhelmingly internal, as reflected in its opening statement on foreign policy: "The measure of our nation's rank in the world must be our success in achieving a just and peaceful society at home."[8]

Its foreign policy section criticized racist regimes in South Africa and Southern Rhodesia, advocated cutting off military aid to repressive undemocratic governments in NATO allies Greece and Portugal, and called for lobbying the Soviet Union to loosen restrictions on Jewish emigration. All of these were among the issues soon subsumed under the broader label of international human rights. In the party platform, they remained distinct, particular problems, without unifying features or overarching solutions. The overall ethos of the document, moreover, was of noninterference in foreign affairs. The thrust was that other people should be left to decide their own fate under fair conditions. It said some global problems required international action, highlighting population control, pollution, health, communication, and technology, without mentioning what would soon be the top liberal human rights causes of torture and political imprisonment. Its only use of the term human rights came in reference to the "constitutional and human rights" of criminals.[9]

The Democratic platform offered a striking contrast to its Republican counterpart's unequivocal endorsement of international human rights and the UN's Universal Declaration. The Republican manifesto declared that "our country, which from its beginnings has proclaimed that all men are endowed with certain rights, cannot be indifferent to the denial of human rights anywhere in the world." It went on to deplore "oppression and persecution" and to strongly endorse self-determination, the right of emigration, and a commitment to the UDHR, particularly as directed against the Soviet Union.[10]

While the country was mired in Vietnam, human rights as a liberal foreign policy paradigm was, in a sense, an intellectual impossibility. It was unthinkable in the circumstances of the war. Above all, a profound fatigue with and abhorrence of the very idea of intervention precluded the development of any new, systematic effort to inject American power or values abroad. McGovern's campaign slogan, "Come Home, America," expressed the sense that the country's urgent need was to look inward rather than outward. As did the nation's youth, by huge margins, the candidate believed that the country should set its own house in order before policing the rest of the world.[11] He said over and over again that the country needed to pay more attention to problems at home and less to those abroad.[12] Reiterating the "come home" theme, he told Americans in his nomination acceptance speech that "the greatest contribution America can now make to our fellow mortals is to heal our own great but very deeply troubled land."[13] He said the same thing in private. "After thirty years of obsession with foreign policy," he told a friend, "probably the greatest contribution we can make to the world and to ourselves is to put our own house in order."[14]

Liberals could not raise the banner of international human rights while their country was mired in a brutal war whose strategy was premised on violations of human rights. While bombs and napalm and Agent Orange were falling, the war created an insurmountable obstacle to a new approach to foreign affairs. As the powerful Senate leader and critic of the war J. William Fulbright told a group of Methodists seeking his support for ratification of the UN human rights covenants in 1966, "to talk about human rights when we are killing men by the thousands in Vietnam is hypocritical."[15] Much of the world believed the United States was denying self-determination to South Vietnam, torturing and murdering its people, and destroying its land and culture. Only once the war was over would American liberals feel they could credibly moralize to the world.

Perhaps surprisingly to later observers surrounded by the language and suppositions of human rights, opponents of the Vietnam War rarely cited the concept. Most opponents of the war believed it to be immoral, but they couched their moral concerns in personal, philosophical, or religious terms, rather than using rights talk or appeals to international law.[16] Aside from the far left, who believed that the American military was engaging in an imperialist mission to suppress the just revolutionary cause of the North Vietnamese, most critics condemned the war for not serving America's best interests. Although opposition to the war was extraordinarily variegated, one of the most common themes was a sense that the brutality of the war was disproportionate to the gains sought. The most powerful military in the world appeared to be raining destruction on a small peasant country, inflicting immoral if not illegal levels of suffering on the Vietnamese for gains that could not be justified. For opponents, the massive bombing campaigns along with practices such as the retaliatory burning of villages, high levels of civilian casualties, indiscriminate use of napalm and chemical defoliants, forced relocations, free-fire zones, and torture made the war fundamentally immoral. They sometimes cited international laws of war to make a case for the illegality of the war, but most often the moral issues felt so obvious that juridical justifications seemed superfluous.[17] That the United States was fighting to prop up a brutal dictatorship that suppressed dissent, held large numbers of political prisoners, and practiced torture was another reason to label the war immoral. A 1972 statement by the National Council of Churches, representing liberal mainstream Protestantism, summed up the moral case: the United States was abusing its power and weapons, devaluing the lives, lands, and property of non-Americans, ignoring international laws and agreements, pursuing a racist agenda, and supporting a corrupt and oppressive dictatorship that denied its people self-determination. It concluded: "Imposing our will on distant lands and poor and non-white peoples, we have participated in their destruction while thwarting their self-determination."[18]

Conceptions of American self-interest naturally played an important role in fueling antiwar sentiment. For many opponents of the war, the benefits to American security of defending South Vietnam did not merit the high costs in blood and dollars.[19] To many it seemed that the energies and tax dollars diverted to war in Indochina would be better spent addressing problems at home. By the late 1960s, with tens of thousands of Americans killed, tens of billions of dollars diverted from domestic needs, and no end to the war in sight, few Americans could easily justify the resources that continued to be poured into the conflict. Vietnam Veterans against the War member David Shoup declared that all of Southeast Asia was not "worth the life or limb of a single American."[20]

Opponents raised a wide range of additional objections. College students liable to face the draft argued that burdens of fighting were inequitably distributed. Civil rights leaders pointed out that racism, manifested in the operation of the draft and in deployment decisions, consigned African Americans and other minorities to a disproportionate share of the fighting and dying. To many Americans it was a deep source of frustration and anger that such a war was being fought unconstitutionally, without a clear congressional mandate and outside democratic processes. The frustration and rage provoked by feelings of impotence and of having been deceived and manipulated by an imperial presidency would linger long after the war, shaping the trajectory of politics in the 1970s.

The rhetoric of human rights was largely absent from the antiwar discussion because the term itself was still so closely tied to domestic civil rights issues; *international* human rights were not on the radar screen of most Americans in the 1960s. A 1966 report of a private-public committee on international cooperation, for example, included an extensive discussion of the links between human rights and peace, but referred only to America's civil rights problems, without even a single oblique mention of the Vietnam War.[21] When a group advocating ratification of UN human rights covenants canvassed key senators in 1967, only the maverick and long-standing critic of the war Ernest Gruening made the point that the conflict involved "blatant violations of human rights."[22] For the radical left, talk of human rights merely distracted attention from the real culprit: imperialism. To the extent that the student left was even aware of the norms and treaties of the UN's universal human rights system, it regarded them as ineffectual fakery or mere instruments of the status quo. Moderate antiwar activists, who aimed to influence the political establishment and the broader public, would have had little reason to frame arguments around a UN human rights system that was barely known and seemed to have little appeal. Opponents of the war sometimes cited the laws of war—the Hague and Geneva conventions and the Nuremberg principles—but these standards singled out civilians and victims of war for consideration, rather than encompassing a vision of universal human rights. In contrast to the 1990s, when the language and laws of international human rights were the central grounds on which Western observers denounced abuses and brutality in the Yugoslav wars, human rights simply did not have traction in the Vietnam War.

\*    \*    \*

The impact of the antiwar movement on American politics was shaped by the clash of two forces. On the one hand, most Americans eventually came to see the war as immoral, viewing the intervention in Vietnam or the conduct of the war, or both, as contravening both American and universal moral—and, to a lesser extent, legal—standards. On the other hand, they were reluctant to see it as a sign of more general moral failings. They came to disapprove of the war but were reluctant to assign blame and especially to assume any blame themselves. The spectacle of students condemning the country's institutions inspired disgust among many Americans, who linked antiwar sentiment with the counterculture's sowing of disorder and disrespect. For many in the center of the political spectrum, the country's moral failings seemed to reside with youth who lacked decency and respect for the country's traditions. Prowar counterdemonstrators raised "Love it or leave it" banners; conservative politicians and administration officials tarred opponents of the war as communist agents. Both sides of the debate were deeply concerned with national honor, an emotionally laden concept around which anxiety about the country's character and behavior coalesced.

Questions of international human rights were raised only by the groups initiated into the language and rituals of human rights in the 1960s: international lawyers and a few church groups. In 1966 the International League for the Rights of Man (ILRM), an organization whose mission was to promote the UDHR, declared that human rights were being "continuously violated at a considerable scale."[23] Two years later, the league published a statement titled "Human Rights in the Vietnam War," signed by prominent intellectuals and international lawyers from around the world. In its cover letter appealing for support, the league assured prospective signatories that all sides in the conflict were violating international law and that the statement took no stand on political or ideological issues but merely called attention to "the effects on the human beings caught in its midst."[24] The statement deplored "the extensive failure of the combatants in the Vietnam war to observe the established codes of conduct in warfare and armed conflict and the established norms of human rights." Refusing to take a position on the legality of the war, the league declared that "the departure on a massive scale from observance of the Geneva and Hague Conventions relative to the conduct of the war and from the intent of the Universal Declaration of Human Rights has precipitated a descent into cruelty of great dimension." The statement detailed violations of the Geneva Conventions including torture, killing of prisoners, indiscriminate bombing of civilian areas, forcible population transfers, mass destruction of crops and property, and use of weapons that cause disproportionate destruction, such as napalm.[25]

The press took little note of such statements. In a tiny article on the league statement, the *New York Times* summed it up as "cruelty in Vietnam is laid to both sides." Responding to league complaints, Secretary of State Dean Rusk insisted that U.S. forces were adhering to the Geneva Conventions and suggested that "instances of brutality" are inevitable in war, while assuring the league that safeguards to prevent such "instances" were in place.[26]

In this context, evidence about the brutality, atrocities, and war crimes committed during the war outraged some Americans, causing a deep sense of shame, yet failed to register significant effects on mainstream opinion. In 1966 British philosopher Bertrand Russell staged war crimes hearings in Stockholm, charging the United States with "aggression, civilian bombardment, the use of experimental weapons, the torture and mutilation of prisoners, and genocide involving mass burial, concentration camps and saturation bombing of unparalleled intensity." But Russell's rhetoric was too overheated and too far to the left to have much impact in the United States. Even in left-leaning Sweden, the public viewed the proceedings as one-sided, anti-American, and overwrought; in the United States, the tribunal was virtually ignored.[27]

The issue of war crimes did not gain significant public attention until the end of 1969, when freelance journalist Seymour Hersh broke a story about a massacre in a hamlet designated My Lai 4 in the village of Son My, in the South Vietnamese province of Quang Ngai. Hersh revealed that on March 16, 1968, a company of the American Division had systematically slaughtered an estimated five hundred South Vietnamese villagers, almost all of them women, children, and the elderly. Many were beaten, raped, or tortured before being murdered. The massacre came to light only through the persistent efforts of Ronald Ridenhour, a veteran who had heard of the killing and waged a letter-writing campaign that eventually spurred action by the Pentagon and Congress.[28] Hersh recalled later that the difficulties of getting the story published were "rather staggering" and that the story "got out . . . at first largely through Europe." It was only after CBS broadcast an interview with one of the participants, Paul Meadlo, who matter-of-factly confirmed the details, that the story became a sensation. The idea that American soldiers had gone to the village with the intention of killing anyone on sight was "a pretty heavy issue for us to cope with," Hersh said.[29]

Photographs of the massacre, taken by Army photographer Ron Haeberle on his personal camera and published in *Life*, shocked even Secretary of Defense Melvin Laird. In a private conversation with Henry Kissinger when the story broke, Laird demonstrated the combination of defensiveness and rationalization that would characterize much of the public response. He told Kissinger, "You can understand a little bit of this," because one of the men in the company had been killed in a skirmish just a day before, "but you shouldn't kill that many." Even speaking in private, Laird insisted that the orders in Vietnam were such that "only someone who had lost his sanity could carry out such an act."[30]

Reaction to My Lai followed the fault lines of opinion about the war itself. Liberal critics of the war were quick to conclude that the massacre was a logical corollary of the flawed military tactics and premises that undergirded the entire conduct of the war: mass bombing, reprisals against villages, forced removals. They typically concluded that all Americans bore a measure of responsibility not only for My Lai but for failing to stop the war.[31] Conservatives were more cautious, more likely to contextualize My Lai in a much longer history of wartime atrocities, and inclined to insist that the atrocities of the North Vietnamese mattered more. The conservative *National Review* called the reaction from much of the liberal left "dark and sick."[32] Like Laird, most Americans viewed the mass killing as an aberration, and some felt the report was entirely fabricated.[33] Others believed the media should not have publicized the massacre.[34] *Time* observed that for many Americans the notion that laws existed during combat was "absurd."[35]

Evidence that My Lai was not an aberration but part of a pattern of atrocity soon materialized. Two groups of Vietnam veterans tried to convince the public that atrocities were widespread and resulted from official policy. In Washington, D.C., in December 1970, thirty veterans testified at "war crimes hearings" organized by the Citizens Commission of Inquiry, founded by lawyer Todd Ensign and antiwar organizer Jeremy Rifkin. They reported incidents of torture, the intentional killing of unarmed civilians, and retaliatory napalm attacks that destroyed villages. A military intelligence officer said he had witnessed the daily use of electrical torture on people often found in the end to be innocent civilians. Two months later, in early 1971, Vietnam Veterans Against the War held the Winter Soldier Investigation in Detroit. Over three days, more than a hundred veterans testified to having seen or participated in atrocities.[36]

Few Americans cared. The national media provided sporadic coverage of the first hearings but virtually ignored the Winter Soldier event, partly for the prosaic reason that it was held in Detroit.[37] As one participant recalled, the terse report in the *New York Times* essentially shrugged off the hearings, saying, in effect, "This stuff happens in all wars."[38] CBS was the only network to mention the hearings. The Nixon administration worked hard to undermine the credibility of the Winter Soldier witnesses, whose testimony seemed suspect because of their principled refusal to name perpetrators. (They wanted instead to focus attention on the leadership at the highest levels that made crimes possible.) It did not help that a key organizer, Mark Lane, had just published a book of interviews with veterans alleging war crimes that had been sharply criticized by reviewers as inaccurate, embellished, and "a hodgepodge of hearsay."[39] Although McGovern invited the group to send a veteran to testify before the Senate Foreign Relations Committee (the one chosen would be Obama's future secretary of state, John Kerry), most Americans who heard of the charges were reluctant to believe them.[40]

Other groups also issued reports and held hearings to raise awareness about the conduct of the war, but met with similar indifference. These included a January 1968 report by Clergy and Laymen Concerned about Vietnam and a 1970 conference on war crimes convened by Oakland Congressman Ron Dellums.[41] For those willing to believe, there were plentiful accounts of mistreatment of prisoners, torture, mass bombing, the use of napalm and chemical defoliants, forced transfers of civilians, and other violations of the Geneva Conventions. In early 1971 former Vietnam correspondent Neil Sheehan surveyed thirty-three books on the conduct of the war and concluded that the evidence justified a national inquiry into war crimes.[42] Yet most Americans averted their eyes.

The Phoenix program became notorious in some circles as an assassination program, but mainstream public opinion again grasped at the plethora of excuses that rationalized atrocity. "Asian" practices and values and the difficulties of counterinsurgent warfare were cited to counter evidence of the war's brutality. Phoenix, funded by the U.S. government as a joint effort between the CIA, the U.S. military, and South Vietnamese counterparts, targeted the National Liberation Front's shadow government in South Vietnam. In earlier years, American efforts to root out this shadow government, variously labeled "pacification," "counter-terror," and "counterinsurgency," had often resorted to assassination. The Phoenix program was developed to bring greater order and precision to these efforts, in theory using intelligence to find and arrest National Liberation Front political cadres rather than simply killing them. In practice, tens of thousands of innocent South Vietnamese were swept up into inhumane and indefinite detention or killed outright. Although various congressional committees investigated Phoenix and other issues in the conduct of the war, even antiwar members of Congress were disposed to accept official assurances about good intentions, difficult conditions, and unfortunate accidents. Most Americans, too, accepted the government's assurances that the Phoenix program brought order to a chaotic wartime situation, that the large numbers of deaths could be explained by the fact that many suspects were killed in firefights during attempted arrests, and that the American influence moderated and restrained abuses by the South Vietnamese. The liberal Massachusetts congressman and Catholic priest Robert Drinan was one of the few to chastise William Colby, who directed Phoenix before he became head of the CIA, saying that the Phoenix program had brought "shame to the American people" and was "the most despicable part of the war which most Americans feel was the greatest mistake the United States ever made."[43]

Charges of war crimes and the routinization of atrocity were not hard to refute. The Nixon administration went to a great deal of trouble to undermine the credibility of witnesses, but the veracity of their reports was already tainted by the irrefutable existence of a powerful political agenda. Critics of the conduct of the war wanted to end the war, and even some Americans sympathetic to the cause assumed that lies and exaggerations were part and parcel of the antiwar movement's tactics. Moreover, just as Americans during World War II found it hard to credit the numerous reports pointing to Hitler's genocide, Vietnam-era Americans were subject to the same psychological biases that make it hard for people to accept information that undermines cherished beliefs. Until the Army's post–My Lai Peers investigation proved otherwise, Laird could not believe mass murder of civilians was a common occurrence in Vietnam. Military and political leaders, of course, had reason to avoid confronting the full consequences of their decisions, but similar dynamics affected ordinary Americans.

As a result of these factors, most Americans accepted the official line: that there had been few serious incidents, that they were the products of a few aberrant individuals and/or were largely justified by the nature of the war, and that criticism of the military undermined the war effort. In a phone conversation after the only conviction to result from My Lai, of Lieutenant William Calley, Nixon and Kissinger joked about the public reaction. There had been a public "spasm" over the massacre, Nixon said, but it had not played out the way the "liberals" had hoped. Kissinger commented that the doves had expected "a feeling of revulsion against the deed [but] in fact, the deed itself didn't bother anybody." Nixon agreed: "Matter of fact the people said sure [Calley] was [guilty] but by god why not? [Laughter]."[44] Nearly two-thirds of Americans polled agreed that such incidents were "bound to happen in a war."[45] Across the country rallies in support of Calley followed the verdict.[46] General William Peers, head of the extensive investigation into the massacre, lamented that Calley became "practically a hero."[47] Surveying hundreds of letters about the Calley verdict, historian Bernd Greiner concludes that Americans may have come to see the war as immoral but did so without questioning their belief in a special American mission. They continued to link national prestige to their personal sense of self-worth and were therefore reluctant to condemn institutions like the military.[48] Many Americans could not accept the verdict, another historian notes, "because it seemed to them like a condemnation of all the young men they had sent to fight in Vietnam and ultimately of themselves for sending them there."[49]

Yet for the liberals who later took up the cause of human rights, My Lai and atrocities like it were profound cause for shame and soul-searching. As columnist Russell Baker put it, My Lai struck a blow "against one of our fondest illusions, the American fighting man as G.I. Joe," the soldier of the "good war" who handed out chocolate bars to poor kids and was met with garlands by liberated townspeople. Now, Baker said, "we are challenged to see him as a guy whose answer to a pleading mother hugging her child is a burst of automatic rifle fire."[50] After news of My Lai broke, theologian and opponent of the war Reinhold Neibuhr declared, "This is a moment of truth when we realize that we are not a virtuous nation."[51]

The fallout from the debate about American conduct of the war was clear. A minority of Americans, mostly on the antiwar left, accepted the charges and came to believe that the war was being fought in ways that were racist, brutal, and criminal. They felt revulsion and guilt. But most Americans were swayed by official propaganda, which achieved great success in casting accusations of war crimes as unreliable, mendacious, and even treasonous. The small number of cases that could not be denied were minimized, portrayed as anomalies committed by "a few bad apples" and, at the same time, understandable overreactions in a difficult, harrowing guerrilla war against an unseen enemy.[52]

Above all, by 1970 the public was tired of war and wanted to change the channel. The predominant attitude toward antiwar activists who bombed defense labs, burned draft cards, and staged demonstrations calling for war crimes investigations was hostility tempered with fatigue.[53] In the first half of 1971, opinion polls showed that only 15 percent wanted to continue the war, almost 60 percent characterized U.S. involvement as "immoral," and over 70 percent agreed that the war was a "mistake" and favored withdrawal.[54] But what most people wanted was for the war to go away. They were tired of upheaval and contention and blame.

David Hawk was typical of the kind of antiwar activist who later moved into human rights work. Having participated in civil rights campaigns in

Mississippi and elsewhere in the mid-1960s, he moved into the antiwar movement after graduating from college and starting his divinity studies at Union Theological Seminary. (His résumé touches on virtually every progressive cause of the sixties: from press aide to Daniel Ellsberg to promoter of rock concerts for Peace, Inc.)[55] He was drawn to the moderate strand of activism espoused by antiwar organizer Allard Lowenstein, and when Lowenstein created the Campus Coordinating Committee in 1968 to attract nonradical students, Hawk opened an office at Union Theological.[56] One of the group's first moves was to draft a letter from a thousand seminarians calling on Secretary of Defense Robert McNamara to permit conscientious objection to particular wars, rather than to war in general, as a way of helping otherwise "law-abiding young Americans."[57] The *Washington Post* described Hawk as one of the moderates who came from "the conventional leadership sector of the universities."[58] He saw electoral politics as an avenue for change, working for antiwar presidential candidate Eugene McCarthy in 1968, and he was one of the student leaders who met with Kissinger and Nixon's aide John Ehrlichman in 1969.[59]

By 1969 growing anger and frustration pushed some antiwar activists to turn to more militant tactics and even violent confrontation. Their aim was to stop the "war machine" by burning draft cards, blockading draft offices, destroying government property, sending bomb threats, and in a small number of cases exploding real bombs. Moderates like Hawk remained committed to capturing mainstream public sympathy and influencing government policy through tactics such as nonviolent marches and vigils. In 1969 Hawk played a leading role in staging one of the antiwar movement's most successful demonstrations, the Moratorium. The brainchild of Boston businessman and antiwar activist Jerome Grossman, who proposed to stage a national protest so massive the White House could not ignore it, the Moratorium was intended, as Grossman put it, "to mobilize the broadest combination of antiwar citizens in a legal and traditional protest action."[60] Hawk and his fellow organizers tried to reach millions of Americans who were disaffected but still believed in the legitimacy of the political process. Their success is reflected in the breadth of the endorsements they gathered from members of Congress, labor and business leaders, academics, and many others. Arthur J. Goldberg, former U.S. representative to the UN and former Supreme Court justice, United Auto Workers leader Walter Reuther, former diplomat Averell Harriman, and Congressman Morris Udall were among the endorsers.[61]

The Moratorium was a great success. On Wednesday, October 15, 1969, millions of Americans took part, simply pausing in their daily routines to hold vigils or meetings in town squares or campuses. They showed films, listened to speeches, read the names of Americans and Vietnamese killed in the war, or held candles. One activist recalled, "It was a very, very mainstream approach. . . . It allowed people to express their opposition to the war in a way that was comfortable. It could be wearing an armband, it could be honking your horn, it could be leaving your lights on." People of all political persuasions could join in.[62] One historian called it "the largest protest demonstration in American history, with a size and diversity that not even the participants could comprehend."[63]

Hawk's activities brought him into contact with antiwar congressmen who would later initiate the liberal human rights insurgency. In 1968, when Lowenstein set up a group to work to get Johnson off the November ticket, Minnesota Congressman Don Fraser gave it names of people who might be sympathetic, and California Congressman Don Edwards openly identified with the movement. In 1969 Fraser supported the Moratorium and with three other congressmen, including Lowenstein, set up the Vietnam Coordinating Committee as a strategy center to plan and push for peace legislation. The sentiments of the committee's statement lauding the Moratorium's success were indicative of middle-of-the-road inclinations that Hawk, Fraser, and others who would join the human rights movement embraced: "We were pleased that the expression of concern over Vietnam . . . was eloquent, peaceful and dignified."[64]

Although Hawk's opposition to the war was morally based, he never thought of it in terms of human rights. His introduction to human rights came after the war, when he went to England to study international relations at Oxford University; it was there that he first heard about the work of Amnesty International.[65] When he returned to the United States in 1974, the connections he had made in the antiwar movement helped land him a job as executive director of Amnesty's U.S. section. For moderate liberals like Hawk, the war fostered a new interest in morality in foreign policy, a sense of empathy with victims of violence and oppression abroad, and training in political organizing. The war laid a foundation for later human rights organizing, and it was central to the mind-set of the liberal human rights movement, but the path from opposition to the war into human rights was not predetermined. That much is clear from the McGovern campaign.

Observers today still look back on the Nixon-McGovern contest of 1972 and see the hinge on which the next half-century of American politics turned. Because of the staggering proportions of his loss, McGovern inaugurated years of questioning about the future of liberalism and the soul of the Democratic Party.[66] His presidential effort was a breeding ground for the New Politics that would later foster a human rights movement, yet in some ways his campaign was a case of the dog that didn't bark. His embrace of morality, his calls to repentance over the Vietnam War, and his sensitivity to the lives of people in distant countries suggested a frame of mind that would be receptive to the language of international human rights. A month before the election McGovern confided to a British journalist that he "lacked a slogan but would like to find one that implies that this nation must have a new morality."[67] Late in the campaign, after struggling to articulate a general foreign policy doctrine, McGovern issued a call for a "new internationalism" that combined peace, democracy, a greatly expanded economic aid program disbursed through multilateral agencies, and ending military aid to anticommunist dictators and racist regimes.[68] Although it included components consonant with human rights, McGovern's foreign policy agenda crucially lacked not only the concept of universal human rights promotion but also its outward-looking ethos. He denied that he was an isolationist but spoke of retrenchment and a more modest, cooperative approach to the world, devoid of "delusions of superiority." Nixon was said to spend 80 percent of his time on foreign affairs; McGovern promised to spend 80 percent on domestic affairs. Deeply skeptical of any exercise of American power, he said the problems of Third World countries were "primarily theirs" alone and the United States had little ability to influence outcomes.[69] Calling the Soviet threat exaggerated, he advocated huge cuts in defense spending (a reduction of about a third), withdrawal of 170,000 troops from Europe, and a unilateral freeze on nuclear weapons development.[70]

Before 1975 McGovern did not speak in terms of human rights. He did not advocate a morally crusading foreign policy and did not justify his policy prescriptions on the basis of international norms. In 1972, for example, when voting for economic sanctions on the racist government of Rhodesia, he explained his vote not in human rights terms but as a demonstration of his commitment to the cause of African Americans.[71] He was an early supporter of efforts to link Soviet trade to emigration for Soviet Jews, but he framed the cause most often in terms of justice, not rights.[72] He announced that as president he would immediately terminate aid to the Greek junta, but he spoke of democracy, not human rights.[73] His running mate said that a McGovern administration would "stop intervening" and join "the side of life and justice" by ending military aid to Greece, South Africa, and Brazil.[74] When his campaign ads declared that a vote for McGovern was a vote for human rights—along with peace, jobs, fairness in taxation, better crime control, and decency in government—they were referring to civil rights at home.[75]

The liberals who took up the cause of international human rights just a few years later came out of the McGovern camp, and his campaign is a key fork in the genealogy of the human rights movement. His candidacy aroused hopes not only at home but abroad, where overseas critics of the Vietnam War believed McGovern would repudiate the long-standing pattern of U.S. support for repressive right-wing dictatorships. Melina Mercouri, an opponent of the Greek junta that had aroused international outrage by seizing power from a democratic government in 1967, wrote a note to McGovern in 1972: "You must know that whoever talked to me [in Athens] kept repeating your name—McGovern, McGovern—whispered, but with such hope and admiration. Yes, indeed, you are their hope."[76] Similar sentiments were voiced by Dutch novelist and radical Hans Koning, who wrote that the brutes of the world, from Johannesburg to Saigon to the torturers in Argentina, were watching the election nervously.[77]

But 1972 was too early even for a deeply moralistic, liberal presidential candidate to embrace the discourse of human rights. The war was still going on, and public ownership of the term was already being staked out by conservatives for whom it meant a continuation of the Cold War. Nevertheless, McGovern's 1972 presidential campaign is crucial to understanding the emotional terrain on which the liberal human rights program would emerge. In essence, thwarted "McGovernites" would be the ones who grasped the mantle of human rights after their defeat, but they would do so in a way that avoided the mistakes of the 1972 campaign. They would find content for McGovern's vague grasping for "a new morality," but only after exorcising guilt from what they tried to sell to the public. It was a crucial elision, one that meant that human rights would be largely about forgetting the brutality of the war rather than reckoning with it.

Balding, with a professorial air, McGovern was convinced of his own righteousness. Despite a star-studded entourage that included Shirley MacLaine and Warren Beatty, he was handicapped by a lack of television appeal, a plodding speaking style, and (it was said) the frozen smile of a man holding fast to false teeth.[78] A World War II pilot who had intended to follow his father into the Methodist ministry before deciding instead to earn a doctorate in history, McGovern was shaped by his deeply religious upbringing, which included daily Bible readings and strict injunctions to work toward a just social order.[79] As South Dakota's junior senator, he became one of the earliest critics of the war, speaking out against Kennedy's deepening commitment when he first arrived in Washington in 1963. He voted for the Tonkin Gulf Resolution in 1964, but when Johnson began massive air strikes against North Vietnam in early 1965, McGovern and his Idaho colleague Frank Church called for a negotiated settlement.

McGovern was an outsider, not a candidate of the party establishment, and his drive for the nomination succeeded due to a novel grassroots campaign made possible by new party convention rules. (Here, too, the antiwar and human rights movements link, for Donald Fraser played a central role in the party reform process before spearheading congressional involvement in human rights.) Before 1972, delegates to the conventions that selected presidential candidates were party insiders. In some states delegates were chosen by governors; in others there were no fixed rules; in many states party bosses picked delegates behind closed doors. Choosing a presidential nominee was a game played by union leaders and city machine bosses in smoke-filled rooms. In 1968 New Democrats successfully demanded change after the convention endorsed establishment nominee Hubert Humphrey, who refused to repudiate the war. First McGovern and then Fraser, who had long been concerned with party reform, headed the body charged with developing new selection rules.

The outcome was a much more open and democratic process. What one scholar has termed the "quiet revolution" made the 1972 Democratic Party Convention a vastly different affair from any that had come before. Fifty percent more delegates than in the past were chosen by primary voters; 80 percent of the delegates had never before attended a convention, and new quotas radically reconfigured the gender, ethnic, and racial makeup of the delegates. Reflecting the resentment of the labor unions, whose power was now marginalized, AFL-CIO leader George Meany characterized the delegates as "hippies, women liberationists, gays, kooks, and draft dodgers."[80] Circumventing the Democratic establishment to draw on the energies of activist antiwar Democrats and advocates of the New Politics, including feminists and environmentalists, McGovern won the nomination against Humphrey, the establishment favorite, and moderate candidate Edmund Muskie.

The McGovern campaign was a great success in grassroots mobilization of Democrats on the left. It was also an unmitigated electoral failure. By October the question was not whether Nixon would win, but whether Nixon would win all fifty states. In the end he carried forty-nine states, including the home states of both McGovern and his running mate, Sargent Shriver, translating into 521 Electoral College votes versus McGovern's 17. The popular vote was a lopsided 61.7 percent to 37.5 percent. Two-thirds of white men voted for Nixon, as did 70 percent of southerners. Nixon even won a majority of the blue-collar and union vote.[81] At the same time, Democrats carried both houses of Congress, making the lopsided presidential tally look like a verdict on McGovern himself. It was one of the most crushing defeats in American history.

The reasons for McGovern's success and failure are largely the same. Nixon swept to victory by positioning himself as the candidate of "law and order" in the face of widespread fear and unease over domestic unrest and rising crime rates. Having originally promised to end the war, he had instead prolonged it for four years, but he had blunted his failure to extricate the country from the war by lowering U.S. troop levels and conducting peace negotiations. McGovern, on the other hand, was profoundly weakened by perceptions of his mishandling of his first running mate's mental health problems. During the selection process, vice-presidential candidate Senator Thomas Eagleton hid that he had been treated with electroshock therapy, and when McGovern's staff found out—after McGovern had said he would back his running mate "1000% percent"—Eagleton insisted on public disclosure of only part of the truth. As a result McGovern's dumping of his running mate generated public sympathy for Eagleton and became the prime charge in an indictment of McGovern's inconsistency and incompetence. Capturing growing skepticism about the Democratic nominee's competence, columnist Art Buchwald commented that if Nixon looked like a dodgy used-car salesman, McGovern looked like one of his customers. Instead of appearing as a strong liberal, he looked like a weak radical.[82] Republicans skillfully characterized him as "the candidate of the three A's: acid, abortion, and amnesty" (for his alleged plans to liberalize drug laws, legalize abortion, and grant amnesty to draft dodgers), and critics branded his supporters as "a small group of radicals and extremists" who would "abandon prisoners of war and friends in Saigon . . . [and] cripple our Army, Navy and Air Force," leaving the country "begging, crawling to the negotiation table."[83]

Such charges were a product of McGovern's promise to end the war virtually without condition. He pledged to stop the fighting when he took office and to withdraw American troops within three months. To Nixon's promise of "peace with honor," McGovern offered failure with dignity. The war was his "magnificent obsession," and it was his stand on "the stupidest, cruelest war in all history" that brought him the nomination.[84] On this issue, McGovern's campaign resonated deeply with the feelings of Democratic activists on the left. Like them, McGovern was profoundly anguished by the war. In a speech late in the campaign, he said, "For almost a decade, my heart has ached over the fighting and the dying in Vietnam. I cannot remember a day when I did not think of this tragedy."[85]

McGovern's campaign was infused with calls to morality. He felt himself engaged in "a fight for the soul of America," as one of his speechwriters recalled.[86] His speeches, especially on the war, could reasonably be called jeremiads: calls for a once-blessed people to account for their fall into sin and to return to the path of redemption.[87] The American promise had diminished, McGovern said in announcing his candidacy in 1971. "We must undertake a reexamination of our ideas, institutions, and the actual conditions of our lives."[88] "I want America to come home from the alien world of power politics, militarism, deception, racism, and special privilege to the blunt truth that 'all men are created equal. . . .'"[89] He told Americans that "we have strayed" and called on them to better themselves, to search their consciences, and to place their trust in his morality: "Our deepest problems are within us—not as an entire people, but as individual persons," he chastised. "We must look into our souls to find a way out of the crisis of our society."[90] Although he promised to pursue reconciliation rather than official investigations of war crimes, he was explicit about crimes and atrocities American soldiers had committed. He called the war "a moral and political disaster—a terrible cancer eating away at the soul of the nation."[91] He used harsh, uncompromising language that was alien to mainstream American politics, even going so far as to condemn the massive bombing that underpinned Nixon's war strategy as "the most barbaric action that any country has committed since Hitler's effort to exterminate Jews in Germany."[92] During one speech in mid-October, a campus audience listened in "stunned silence and tears" as the candidate played a tape of a Vietnam veteran describing atrocities. McGovern's portrait of the war was grisly and guilt-ridden.[93]

In giving voice to the anguish of a liberal antiwar minority, McGovern alienated the center and ensured his own defeat. Critics were not merely irritated at what they saw as his preachiness and sanctimony; they were outraged. Some leading Democrats, including Governor Jimmy Carter of Georgia, refused to endorse the party's choice on the grounds that his views were "completely unacceptable to the majority of the voters." In October, as the scale of McGovern's impending loss was becoming clear, the *Washington Post*'s William Greider observed that "McGovern has been insisting with increasing fervor that the United States must confront its own character as it is reflected in the war," delivering a moral message

that "is repugnant to a great many American voters who not only disagree with it, but are outraged that a major party presidential candidate
should even be saying such things." Georgia Senator Herman Talmadge
said that McGovern "gave the impression he was mad at the country. . . .
People aren't going to support a candidate like that. This is a great
country. It makes mistakes, but by God if you get up there and preach
day and night against America, you're not going to be elected." Jackson
campaign aide Ben Wattenberg said McGovern's charges that the country
was "immoral and genocidal," culminating in a comparison of the
Vietnam War to the Nazi slaughter of the Jews, were "catastrophic."
McGovern saw it differently—he thought he was showing his love of the
country—but he acknowledged later, "My very anguish may have pushed
voters in the other direction." As Garry Wills wrote, "McGovern was
hysterically feared because he was an accuser."[94]

It was not, as columnist David Broder suggested, that McGovern lost
because his positions were too moralistic. The problem was the tone of
his moralism, his stridency, and his call for Americans to accept part of
the blame for the war. His criticism of the war was a criticism of the
country. During his September 1970 speech on the floor of Congress in
support of the Hatfield-McGovern amendment to end the war, his colleagues froze in silence and anger when he fingered them for blame:
"Every senator in this Chamber is partly responsible for sending fifty
thousand young Americans to an early grave. This Chamber reeks of
blood."[95] In his presidential campaign, he included the whole country in
the circle of responsibility. "We" were in Vietnam to prevent the
Vietnamese from choosing their own government, he told *Playboy* in
August 1971, and "toward that insane end, we have nearly destroyed
their nation with our guns and our bombs. My Lai is just a tiny pimple
on the surface of a raging boil. The whole war is a massacre of innocent
people and we all share in the guilt of it." The policy of mass bombing
was a "deliberate national policy" to devastate Vietnam. "In that sense,
we're involved as a free people in decisions that are murdering innocent
individuals. So I think everyone from the President on down is as guilty
as Lieutenant Calley."[96]

The problem, as McGovern admitted later, was that most Americans
did not want to feel guilty. "It was said that I made people feel guilt when

A 1972 cartoon portrays George McGovern and running mate Sargent Shriver as priests failing to fill their church. Americans rejected McGovern's hectoring, self-righteous rhetoric, especially his message of guilt about the Vietnam War, and his slogan "Come Home, America" was criticized as isolationist. (Doug Marlette, *Charlotte Observer*)

I indicted the sins of the nation and called the sinners home," he wrote in his autobiography. He closed every speech with the hope that the American people would change, improve, and hearken to the "better angels of our nature."[97] Reflecting bitterly on his defeat in later years, he said he should have placed more emphasis on "appeals to self-interest" and less on lofty ideals. He warned of the dangers in drawing an issue too sharply in moral terms. "It might even repel large numbers of people who don't want to be disturbed in their lethargy and apathy and who prefer not to feel conscience-stricken about what the nation is doing."[98]

The politicians and activists who sparked the liberal stand of the human rights movement in the mid-1970s almost without exception had been

McGovern supporters. They had been moved by McGovern's appeals; they had felt guilty about the war; and they craved a new moral foundation for the country. McGovern's staggering defeat taught them that guilt was not the way to sell a policy. Selling the American people on their own virtue was the way to create support for policy.

Patrick Anderson described the emotional trajectory of many liberals when he summarized his political journey in the 1960s and 1970s. He saw himself as "a fairly typical New Deal liberal" when he began his career as a writer on Robert Kennedy's staff in 1962. "The world was simple then. We were the good guys," he recalled. But then came Kennedy's assassination and the Vietnam War and Nixon. He joined the antiwar movement and in 1972 was a delegate for McGovern, putting in long hours knocking on doors, making phone calls. He and his wife were crushed when McGovern lost. "I vowed," Anderson wrote, "that next time around, if I had anything to do with it, it would be those sons of bitches on the other side whose wives would be crying." By 1976, he said, "Like a lot of survivors of the McGovern campaign, I was looking for a winner," and when he was hired by a little-known governor of Georgia running for the presidency, he put all his "anger and frustration and lingering idealism" into the speeches he wrote.[99]

In 1976 Jimmy Carter would run a campaign for the presidency that was very similar to McGovern's. It, too, was an antiestablishment, overtly moralistic campaign. But this campaign did not call Americans to account for mistakes and misdeeds. Jimmy Carter told voters that he hoped to make the American government as good and kind and decent as the American people already were. Americans, Carter said, did not need to feel guilty. The country's problems were not their fault, and nothing was wrong that could not be fixed with a simple change of president. What kind of foreign policy was as good and kind and decent as the American people? In Carter's hands, the answer became international human rights promotion.

## CHAPTER 4

# The Liberal Critique of
# Right-Wing Dictatorships

A S THEIR DISCOMFORT with the Vietnam War grew, liberals could not help but become queasy about their country's support for an array of authoritarian regimes similar to the one in Saigon. Anticommunist but repressive, poor but seemingly impervious to the uplifting effects of aid, South Vietnam was not what a public relations firm would have chosen as a model Third World country for which a costly war should be fought. If the United States could be drawn into fighting a war on behalf of such an ally, how many other places might produce similar quagmires? Aiding anticommunist allies looked like a slippery slope that led first to sending economic assistance, then military aid, and then American GIs.

The desirability and efficacy of American support for Third World development, around which so much liberal hope had revolved in the early 1960s, had fewer and fewer defenders as the 1970s approached. Around the world, the short wave of democratization that followed the Second World War was receding. Newly independent African states adopted authoritarian governments; Latin American countries experienced a series of military coups, including Chile and Uruguay where there was a long history of democracy; Taiwan, South Korea, Indonesia, and the Philippines slipped under increasingly authoritarian rule; even in India, Indira Gandhi suspended democratic practices and declared emergency rule; and Greece and Turkey underwent periods of military rule.[1] In the face of democracy's receding prospects in the 1960s, liberals shifted gears, scaling back their earlier, ambitious dreams of uplift and social and political reform through modernization and development, and grasping instead at modest goals such as reducing the use of state-sponsored torture.

The Greek junta that seized power in 1967 triggered the most important of the early liberal campaigns that would develop the language of human rights as part of a broader rethinking of U.S. foreign policy. Coming at a time when questions about the Vietnam War were mounting, the Greek coup, and the Johnson and Nixon administrations' support of the military dictatorship, helped transform liberal doubts about Vietnam into a wider critique of America's Cold War strategy. The Greek case was not a solitary catalyst but the most important of several issues, including torture in Brazil and racism in Africa, that liberals gradually began to see as linked. At first responding on an ad hoc, case-by-case basis, they began to build coalitions and to develop tactics that would underpin the human rights campaigns of the middle and late 1970s. Until the early 1970s, Greece as a political issue in the United States was dwarfed by the Vietnam War, and it did not involve a full-fledged embrace of human rights rhetoric—rather, human rights appeals were part of a broader repertoire of moral and political arguments. The attraction to human rights was still tentative. But the forces that came together over Greece—liberal congressmen like Donald Fraser and Amnesty International's fledgling U.S. section, among others—would be the ones to take center stage once the war was over, and they would draw on the ideas and tactics worked out in the late 1960s.

Donald Fraser was the national politician most closely and consistently associated with the liberal international human rights agenda before Jimmy Carter made it central to U.S. foreign policy. More than anyone else, Fraser is responsible for creating a framework that linked disparate global problems under the heading of human rights. By the late 1960s deeply unhappy with U.S. ties to repressive regimes abroad, Fraser began to push for a reorientation of foreign policy away from reflexive support of anticommunist dictatorships. His early involvement in the Greek case focused his attention on two of the key issues that came to dominate the liberal human rights agenda in the 1970s: political imprisonment and torture.

Although dozens—probably hundreds—of accounts name Fraser as the driving force behind Congress's liberal human rights drive in the early 1970s, the routine invocation of his name has never been paired with an investigation of his motives, personality, or background.[2] He is the wallflower of the human rights movement: glanced at and then ignored. He was equally neglected in the 1970s, despite playing a lead role in the McGovern-Fraser Commission that rewrote the Democratic Party convention rules, with far-reaching consequences. In 1975 journalist Richard Reeves called Fraser one of "the most impressive [figures] in American public life," someone political reporters would anoint as a presidential candidate if the choice were up to them—but even Reeves could not remember which state he represented.[3] Overshadowed in his native Minnesota by two political giants, Hubert Humphrey and Walter Mondale, Fraser never became a truly national figure. He lacked charisma, had little flair for press relations, and spoke in a monotone. In a political arena that rewarded self-promotion, his shyness and modesty were liabilities that overshadowed his ambition and hard work. When human rights became "hot," more powerful figures seized the limelight.

The story of how Fraser came to human rights is the story of a quintessential liberal of moderate bent whose aspirations to do good started large and then, chastened, grew smaller. He came of age and ran for office when liberalism was the country's hegemonic ideology; in his choice of causes and tactics, he hewed to liberalism's aims and proclivities. By the time he left Congress after a failing bid for the Senate in 1978, he had accumulated one of the legislature's most liberal voting records.[4] Before slipping off the high rungs, he had worked his way steadily up the political ladder: he served in the navy during the Second World War; became a lawyer; in the late 1940s helped his political mentor Hubert Humphrey found the Democratic-Farmer-Labor Party; in the 1950s served in the state legislature; and in 1963 started the first of eight terms in Congress, representing a highly liberal Minneapolis district that would later elect the first Muslim to Congress. He spoke out against McCarthyism in the

1950s and in the 1960s enthusiastically supported civil rights and women's rights. For decades he worked with ADA, the liberal policy-slash-advocacy group founded in 1947 as the institutional embodiment of "Vital Center" liberalism. Fraser would serve as ADA's national chairman from 1974 to 1976.[5] He joined other groups that brought together like-minded liberals, including the Democratic Study Group, Members of Congress for World Peace through Law, and the Anglo-American Parliamentary Conference on Africa. Commenting on Fraser's leading role in the party convention reforms of the early 1970s, an unsympathetic political scientist called him "a winsome, romantic, little Quixote [who] dogtrots concerned and happy through life behind a briefcase almost as big as he is, and fervently argues that he can create the Kingdom of God on earth through the Democratic party with the aid of complex rules."[6]

His reformist impulse manifested itself most prominently in foreign affairs, a topic of long-standing interest to Fraser. He sought and obtained a seat on the House Committee on Foreign Affairs when he arrived in Congress. He was a frequent traveler, attending conferences or participating in study tours in twenty-two countries from 1965 to 1975, crisscrossing Europe, Asia, and Latin America and visiting the USSR, Israel, and Tunisia.[7] He had a strong interest in Third World issues and in parliamentary exchanges, particularly with Canada and Western Europe. His internationalist outlook made him unusually sensitive to foreign opinion, and he was greatly pained by the global condemnation heaped on the United States for its conduct of the Vietnam War. His interest in foreign affairs was not reciprocated by his constituents, who paid little attention to his foreign policy work and sometimes complained that he was more concerned with the problems of foreigners than with his own district.[8] It was an area he pursued without regard for the usual political payoffs: votes and campaign contributions.[9]

Like almost everyone else in Congress, he had initially supported the Vietnam War because he believed President Johnson's claim that what was at stake was the freedom of a small country. He voted in favor of the Gulf of Tonkin Resolution in 1964, which gave Johnson authority to take whatever steps he thought necessary in Southeast Asia. For the next several years, even as he grew increasingly distressed by the scale of American bombing, Fraser continued to believe that the country was taking the moral path in seeking "to preserve the independence" of South Vietnam.[10] In 1965 he said that U.S. policy in Vietnam, aimed at maintaining South Vietnamese freedom, was morally justified: "I know of no objective which should be more acceptable on moral grounds." He was anguished at the criticism U.S. intervention was already generating. "It is baffling to feel we are right and yet find that our efforts are not only unavailing but that we are sharply attacked by others on moral grounds." Yet already he expressed doubts. He acknowledged that the Eisenhower administration's move to prevent elections due to be held under the Geneva Accords constituted a violation of self-determination. He worried about the inconsistency of fighting communist oppression while ignoring oppression when it came from right-wing governments. America's Cold War strategy fixated on saving people of other nations from falling to communism, he wrote in 1965, but there was no reason to believe that communist systems were more evil or more harmful to their citizens than the "totalitarian regimes of the right" with which the United States so often allied. "Ruthlessness and denial of personal and political rights" were features of "totalitarian" regimes of both right and left. "In fact the Communist system, no matter how abhorrent its means, is oriented to the improvement of the lot of its people, a trait noticeably absent from the rightist regimes."[11]

A 1966 note penned to Johnson tellingly illuminates how liberals in the mid-1960s could connect war in Vietnam with the cause of racial justice abroad. The president, Fraser suggested, could win liberal support for the war in Vietnam by supporting Great Britain's position in the crisis over Southern Rhodesia, as the former colonial power tried to undermine a whites-only government that had declared independence. Johnson need only explain that the principle at stake in Vietnam and Rhodesia was the same, Fraser explained: supporting "the right of people to self-determination without oppression."[12] His view of the war in Vietnam as a struggle to support South Vietnamese self-determination would soon shift dramatically.

Liberal morality was the touchstone of his approach to foreign policy. When he looked around the world, he saw people who needed a helping hand, not pieces on a geostrategic chessboard. Grand strategy held little interest for him. Starting with his role as a junior member of the House

Foreign Affairs Committee in the 1960s, he consistently espoused positions calling for greater concern with morality in approaching international problems. He condemned racism and favored self-determination, economic development, and political freedoms.[13] As early as 1964, he expressed skepticism about giving aid to authoritarian governments, suggested that greater attention ought to be paid to "moral standards" in U.S. foreign policy, and proposed the formation of a UN peacekeeping force that could prevent military coups.[14] When the issue of trade with communist countries came up in the mid-1960s, Fraser took a position that prefigured the one Scoop Jackson would so effectively adopt in 1972, advocating the use of trade relationships as leverage for promoting greater freedom in the Soviet bloc. Moral interests had to play a role in trade decisions, he said: when a government "fails to conform to ordinary standards of decency upon which a world civilization must finally rest," American trade policy should be designed to affect that government's conduct.[15] He told the public that morality in foreign affairs sprang from the imperative of international order, but also from "our personal conscience, our convictions about the golden rule, about personal worth and human dignity, about truth and honor."[16]

Like other liberal internationalists, Fraser believed in the importance of working through the United Nations and cooperating with international organizations even when it diminished national sovereignty. In the mid-1960s he extolled the creation of a world community and called for the United States to work "toward a world of peaceful change under a system of order based on consent in which cooperation is an international way of life." Cooperation under the rubric of international organizations was essential to create "the kind of safe and open world we want to live in [and] the kinds of rights and opportunities we want to see secured to every human being." Nations were interlinked by new technologies in ways that made the idea of "total independence" a "costly and archaic anomaly." In utopian language he declared that "the growth of cultural uniformity throughout the world, the development of education, and the consequent recognition that men of all races are basically alike have made the maintenance of national boundaries appear increasingly irrational."[17]

As Fraser turned toward human rights, tentatively in the late 1960s and then fully in the 1970s, he did so under the impetus of earlier failed efforts to enact much more ambitious civil and political reforms in developing countries. Political development was his core cause in the mid-1960s. Though it lacked the backing of international law and the universalism of human rights, political development in some ways represented a more broad-based effort to create rights-bearing citizens in developing countries than his later efforts to free them from headline-generating depredations of state power like torture. Supported by Massachusetts Republican Bradford Morse, in 1966 Fraser modified the structure of the foreign aid program so that it would foster not only economic growth but also political development. The measure, which became Title IX of the basic text of the Foreign Assistance Act, made local political participation an explicit aim of the U.S. aid program. What Fraser and Morse proposed was "a basic reorientation in our thinking . . . to put social and political evolution as the first concern of our foreign assistance program with economic aid playing the supporting role rather than the other way around." Title IX mandated that the U.S. Agency for International Development (AID) assure "maximum participation in the task of economic development on the part of the people of the developing countries, through the encouragement of democratic private and local government institutions."[18]

Until then, the aid program had been based on security concerns: the idea was to contain the spread of communism by assisting friendly governments with economic and military aid. As modernization theory gained hold in the 1960s, democratization came into the picture, but only as an assumed by-product of economic development. Fraser's measure drew on the ideas of social scientists who suggested that economic growth did not necessarily produce positive political developments and could even reinforce repression by strengthening existing economic and political inequalities.[19] As political scientist Samuel Huntington put it, creating a new agency for political development could produce "a new-style CIA, more skilled in building governments than subverting them."[20]

Early disillusionment with the Vietnam War thus produced, for Fraser, a preference for activist promotion of political liberty. The political development of Title IX would prevent future Vietnams: political development was "the final answer to the terrible tragedy of Vietnam," and its promotion would reduce deaths, war, and disorder across the board.[21] It was, moreover, a program with global appeal. "The rights of majority rule and the protection of the rights of the individual have universal appeal," he declared.[22] To critics who said U.S. political and social concepts could not be transplanted to other countries, Fraser emphasized commonalities among peoples, cultures, and governments and the utility of sharing experience and expertise in a spirit of mutuality.[23]

As Fraser explained it in 1966, a core goal of U.S. foreign policy ought to be to assist developing nations toward democracy and the kind of government that "embraces the fundamental values centering around the dignity and worth of the individual."[24] He described political development as a means of getting "new nations to stand on their own feet as stable and responsible members of the international community," a process that would not happen on its own or through economic aid programs alone. Instead, he proposed, "We should systematically try to trigger, to stimulate, and to guide the growth of fundamental social structures and behaviors." He saw parallels between this exercise—which he saw as modeled on "bottom-up" programs like the Peace Corps, community development projects, and educational aid—and the struggles of farmers, organized labor, and African Americans in the United States. He thought foreign sensitivity to the specter of interference in internal affairs could be soothed by American circumspection and moderation.[25] After succeeding with the amendment, Fraser continued to lobby other members of Congress, State Department and Agency for International Development officials, and major philanthropic foundations such as the Ford Foundation for support of political development initiatives.[26]

Fraser's measure was supplemented the following year with text added to the preamble of the act, offered by Iowa Democrat John Culver, that called on the president to take into account "the degree to which the recipient country is making progress toward respect for the rule of law, freedom of expression and of the press, and recognition of the importance of individual freedom, initiative, and private enterprise."[27] Although they were not framed in rights terms, both Title IX and Culver's amendment were precedents for the human rights measures that would be attached to foreign aid legislation in the mid-1970s. In a similar move, in 1968 Wisconsin Democrat Henry Reuss proposed amendments to the Export-Import Bank Extension Act and the Foreign Military Sales Act urging the president to deny credits and military sales that "would have the effect of arming military dictators who are denying social progress to their own people."[28] Two years later, Republican Senator John Williams, an antigovernment, free-market advocate, successfully proposed that the wording be changed to refer to dictators who were "denying the growth of fundamental rights or social progress."[29] In this case the insertion of rights-based language was a conservative move to shift the discussion from economic and social goals to political and civil liberties. Although these arms sales resolutions are sometimes cited as precursors to the human rights legislation of the 1970s, what is notable about these measures is how little discussion and action they provoked at the time.

The outcome of Fraser's first major venture to spread liberty was the creation of a special division within AID, numerous conferences, research projects, and papers, and a great deal of talk. The impact of Title IX in the form of programs explicitly designed to promote democracy was nil, thanks largely to AID's construal of the measure as aiming at fostering participation more than democratic institutions. Criticized in some quarters as simpleminded, naïve, and dangerous, Title IX was based on little evidence that its objectives were feasible, suitable for other societies, or likely to have the intended effects. Like the human rights initiatives of the mid-1970s, Title IX was an ambiguous congressional mandate imposed with little consultation on a reluctant administering agency, without new funds to implement it, and in contradiction to an ingrained predisposition to avoid meddling in the politics of aid-recipient countries. It was also ill timed, for the rising tide of dictatorship in those years left few footholds for democratic institutions. By the late 1960s, aid priorities deemphasized economic growth in favor of meeting basic human needs for food, shelter, and medicine. By the mid-1970s, Title IX had faded into irrelevance.[30]

Despite his faith in Americans' ability to foster new political cultures in foreign countries—a delusion common to most liberals in the 1960s—Fraser was also cognizant of risks and difficulties. Is the United States obligated to support the democratic process in another country even when its voters might elect a communist government? he asked in a speech in 1964. "I wish I knew," Fraser told his audience. Backtracking on his reluctance to aid authoritarian governments, he admitted that such aid might slowly lead to greater levels of freedom. "Whether or not all of this is true I cannot tell you," he said, "but it dismays me to see the apparent conflict between our professed moral principles and our expediency. . . . There should be some better way of reconciling our international policies with accepted moral principles, for regardless of the ethical or religious foundation for our principles, we all like to believe that in the long term they work to the best advantage of man."[31] When a House committee held hearings on South Africa in 1966, Fraser reflected on more general dilemmas: "As members of the human race we have to have a basic regard for individual dignity and freedom whether our concern stems from the Soviet Union, South Africa, or wherever it is, and . . . the sole question that remains to be answered is how do you go about expressing our concern in a way that doesn't draw you in over your head, and which is compatible with your capabilities, and doesn't lead to worse evils than you try to correct."[32] In 1967, he told his fellow members of Congress that it was obtuse to talk with confidence about the capacity to intervene in foreign societies. "We know very little about nation-building," he said, and "operate on simplistic, almost pious assumptions which have failed repeatedly. There is as much risk—yes, even greater risk—in overestimating our capacity to be helpful in this respect rather than underestimating it."[33]

Fraser's belief in an American mission to promote democracy and his interest in foreign aid, rather than his doubts about the efficacy of U.S. action, would shape his reaction to the suppression of democracy in Greece. In addition to stimulating new ways of thinking about democratization and about the costs to America of supporting repression abroad, the Greek case would nudge Fraser toward a new paradigm for U.S. foreign relations, one centered on human rights.

In April 1967 a group of Greek colonels seized power in the name of anticommunism, ending Greece's brief and unstable experiment in democratic government. Whether the new junta headed by George Papadopoulos was more brutal and repressive than the police states that had ruled Greece for most of the postwar years is open to question, but the timing of the event and the peculiarly rebarbative actions of the regime (which attempted, for example, to ban Sophocles, long hair on men, Russian caviar, and modern music) ensured that Western Europeans took special umbrage at the barbarity in their backyard.[34] The new regime instituted martial law, prohibited strikes and political demonstrations, and severely curtailed civil liberties, empowering the police to arrest people for making statements "likely to arouse anxiety among citizens or lessen their sense of security and order."[35] Small-scale, ineffectual resistance, including bombings, provided the junta with an excuse for ongoing repression. Imprisoning or forcing into exile thousands of leftist, centrist, and monarchist Greeks, including union leaders, journalists, and intellectuals, the colonels inadvertently created a potent locus of opposition abroad. Until the junta brought itself down in 1974 with an ill-advised attempt to "reunite" with Cyprus, the exiles proved effective critics, forming myriad organizations and mobilizing Western opinion against the junta.[36]

Opponents of the junta inside and outside Greece, especially in Western Europe, began to use the language of human rights and international human rights treaties to mobilize public attention. When the Scandinavian countries brought a case against Greece before the European Commission on Human Rights in late 1967, it marked the first time that countries party to the European Human Rights Convention lodged a case against another government when no clear national interest was at stake. After a years-long series of hearings in Strasbourg and elsewhere, the commission ruled that democracy had been suppressed without justification and that torture was officially sanctioned. Under threat of expulsion from the Council of Europe, Greece withdrew in December 1969.[37]

Americans were too consumed by the drama of Vietnam for Greece to become a major issue, but even so, the junta's suppression of democracy and brutal treatment of dissent provoked liberals into mounting a new kind of political campaign that began to bring together the building blocks of a new foreign policy agenda. Antijunta opinion in the United

States was fueled by what appeared to be official indifference to the suppression of democracy. The Johnson and Nixon administrations adopted a position one official characterized as, "Do business with the Junta but do it with some show of reluctance." Viewing Greece as an important NATO ally and eager to maintain valued Mediterranean bases and overflight rights, neither Johnson nor Nixon exerted genuine pressure on the Greek junta to moderate repression or to return to democracy. Under pressure from liberals, the Johnson administration cut off the supply of heavy weapons to Greece immediately after the coup, but the suspension was first evaded and then ended.[38] American liberals found official attitudes infuriating. They argued that U.S. support for the colonels offered legitimacy to the regime and identified the United States with the dictatorship, and they were proven right when U.S. backing contributed to a rise in anti-Americanism after Greece's return to democracy in 1974.[39]

Public opposition to the Greek junta in the United States came from a committed group of liberals in Congress, organized labor leaders, and academics. They typically had personal ties to Greek opposition figures like the well-connected Andreas Papandreou, a Harvard-trained economist and cabinet member in the government the junta overthrew. Papandreou had many friends in the United States, where he had taught at four universities in the 1940s and 1950s, and his arrest triggered a wave of activism on his behalf from former colleagues such as John Kenneth Galbraith. Some Greek American academics spoke out against the junta, along with the indefatigable exiled journalist Elias Demetracopoulos, who acted as a one-man lobby in Washington, but the great majority of the Greek American community was either supportive of the junta or indifferent.[40]

The liberals who became the leading antijunta voices were determined opponents of the Vietnam War. One of the key figures in Washington was Don Edwards, a longtime civil rights proponent and Democratic congressman representing a district in the southern San Francisco Bay Area. Edwards saw in Greece a shameful U.S. policy very much like the war in Vietnam. In a 1967 speech Edwards said the Vietnam War was "only a symptom of a sick and misguided view of our role in the world," and what was needed was "a new direction" or "there [would] be other Vietnams."[41] In 1970 he charged the United States with genocide in

Indochina.[42] Fraser, New York Democrat Benjamin Rosenthal, and Arizona Democrat Morris Udall, all early opponents of the Greek junta, were also by this time congressional opponents of the war.

Personal links among antiwar Democrats brought them together in antijunta activities. Edwards's leading role in the Greek campaign was spearheaded by his aide LuVerne Conway, a lawyer who had long-standing connections to Greece. Her husband was AFL-CIO official and ADA executive director Jack Conway. Victor Reuther, the international director of the United Auto Workers, was, with his wife, personal friends of Paul Lyons, the executive director of Amnesty International's U.S. office (AI USA).[43] Jack Conway, along with Fraser and Edwards, founded the U.S. Committee for Democracy in Greece in October 1967. Lyons would become its executive director for a time, concurrently with his directorship of AI USA. The Greek actor and singer Melina Mercouri, who was performing in New York City when the coup took place, became one of the most vocal opponents of the regime abroad, eventually taking up residence in Paris and denouncing the junta in speeches, interviews, recordings, marches, concerts, and hunger strikes. She had close ties to several members of Congress, including Fraser and Edwards.[44] Beautiful, charming, and famous, the actress was a welcome figurehead for these male liberals. Famous for her starring role in the hit film *Never on Sunday*, directed by her husband, Jules Dassin, she was a frequent visitor to Washington, working the Georgetown cocktail circuit, granting interviews, and never failing to attract publicity.[45] One local newspaper article about a tony cocktail party organized by the committee noted that Mercouri, wearing a "golden brown, fox-trimmed Pierre Cardin shift" and "batt[ing] her amber eyes," used "aplomb and grace" to lobby lawmakers, including Senate Foreign Relations Committee Chairman J. W. Fulbright.[46]

The committee's tactics resembled those of the human rights organizations that would crisscross Washington a decade later: it gathered information, worked to attract publicity, spotlighted the celebrities who backed its cause, and lobbied Congress, policy makers, and pundits.[47] The committee was not the only antijunta force in Washington, but it wielded influence far out of proportion to its small membership, with a significant voice in the media and in Congress.[48] Two journalists wrote that it had "access and class . . . and a friendly press."[49] It placed numerous articles in the *Congressional Record*, briefed the media, pressured the State Department, and issued joint statements by members of Congress condemning the junta's human rights violations and calling for cutoffs in aid to Greece. It hosted visiting Greek exiles who spoke out against the regime, including Papandreou, Constantine Mitsotakis, George Rallis, Eleni Vlachou, Lady Amalia Fleming, and others.[50] It issued a newsletter—to a mailing list of 70,000 in 1968—that generated enough revenue from small donations to cover its costs, and sent out fund-raising appeals to about 10,000 names.[51] Its own mailing list comprised about 6,500 names in 1971, and it traded mailing lists with likeminded organizations such as the ACLU.[52] Edwards and Fraser would each later serve as chairman of the committee. Other prominent members included liberal establishment names, most with backgrounds in civil rights, antiwar, and labor issues, including Victor Reuther, old New Dealers such as Francis Biddle, journalist and former socialist Maurice Goldbloom, John Kenneth Galbraith, Michael Straight, and A. Philip Randolph. Senators Joseph Clark and Claiborne Pell offered nominal support to the group.[53]

The importance of opposition to the Greek junta for the origins of a human rights movement in the United States is underscored by the tight links between the U.S. Committee for Democracy in Greece and Amnesty International's fledgling U.S. section, which were born almost simultaneously. Ten years before it became the best-known human rights organization in the United States, Amnesty was almost entirely unknown to Americans. It had started in Britain in 1961 when British lawyer Peter Benenson penned an appeal on behalf of what he called prisoners of conscience: people jailed by their governments for no reason other than their political or religious beliefs. The moment coincided with a brief thaw in the Cold War, Benenson later recalled: "Without it I don't think we'd have got anywhere."[54] Headquartered in London, the organization grew rapidly, sprouting national sections in Western Europe, and by 1967 adding the prevention of torture to its original mandate to help political prisoners. The organization's appeal was due partly to its ability to generate interest in individual prisoners, many of whom were mistreated. It was based on a simple idea: that ordinary people could create so much noise—flooding offending governments with polite letters—that officials would decide to release prisoners rather than suffer the shame of global condemnation. Its appeal also hinged on its success in casting its program in minimalist, apolitical terms that promised a new universalism in place of old Cold War dichotomies.[55] Surveying the organization's first decade, Martin Ennals, Amnesty's secretary general, wrote: "Amnesty International is based on the belief that ordinary people care about the human rights of other ordinary people and that human rights and responsibilities are not limited to national boundaries."[56] When the Greek colonels seized power, the international body was weathering an internal crisis over the clandestine acceptance of British government funding and Benenson's resignation.[57] The struggling organization's handling of events in Greece proved critical for its future development, at first testing but ultimately enhancing its credibility, garnering a bonanza of media attention, and substantially increasing membership and name recognition.[58]

In the United States Amnesty faced a long, uphill struggle to gain a significant foothold. It would be nearly a decade and a half after Amnesty's founding until it attained a solid organizational presence and a substantial membership across the Atlantic. (Indeed Amnesty's first presence in the United States was not in the form of an American AI group but a British AI delegation making a report on civil rights in the South in the summer of 1964.)[59] Until the mid-1970s, the competition for Americans' humanitarian impulses was simply too keen. The intense preoccupations with civil rights and the war in Vietnam left little space for other concerns to take root. In 1967 the director of Amnesty's fledgling American office described organizing "a human rights movement in the United States" as akin to "trying to go up the down staircase."[60] The group was saddled, too, with a name that for most Americans immediately conjured up the deeply polarizing issue of amnesty for Vietnam War draft resisters. In the early 1970s the AI USA staff feared its mail was being sabotaged by postal workers who misconstrued the amnesty in its title.[61]

Despite its loud claims to be apolitical, AI USA was a child of the liberal left. The first U.S. office of Amnesty was the brainchild of ACLU founder Roger Baldwin and the leftist intellectual Michael Straight. The son of New York millionaires, Straight was educated in Britain and fell in with the infamous Cambridge spy ring in the 1930s, becoming a member of the Communist Party and a Soviet agent. In the 1940s, back in New York, he assumed the editorship of the magazine his parents had founded and his mother still financed, the progressive-left *New Republic*. When he took interest in Amnesty, a decade after stepping down from the editorship to write novels, the organization had virtually no presence in the United States. A few hundred Americans had participated in a "postcards for prisoners" program after *Reader's Digest* reprinted a 1965 article on Amnesty from Britain's *Saturday Review*—an article that was very nearly the only publicity Amnesty received in the United States in the five years after its founding—but there were only two adoption groups. One was in Missoula, Montana; the other, which would form the core of Amnesty's American operations for many years, was in Manhattan's Riverside Heights, founded in 1965 by Ivan Morris, a professor of Japanese literature at Columbia University. It was not until Straight stepped in that a formal American section was established.[62]

At the end of 1965, Straight, Baldwin, Frances Grant (Baldwin's longtime colleague at the ILRM), and a handful of others decided to incorporate an Amnesty section in the United States. The group incorporated in January 1966 in the state of New York, later gaining federal tax-exempt status as a charitable organization. It was roughly the twenty-fifth national affiliate of the London organization, which had a total international membership of about ten thousand. In April of that year, Peter Benenson visited the United States on a lecture tour, and a few dozen committed people began trying to build up the organization, which was run at first out of a corner in the New York office of the ILRM. It soon had a handful of adoption groups and about a hundred members, yet its director would note a year later that no "formal relations" had been established with the London Secretariat.[63]

Amnesty's American backers in the 1960s were almost without exception liberal Democrats who had been prominent in international campaigns for the UN, disarmament, civil liberties and civil rights, and peace. Publicity was sent to the *Nation, Ramparts*, the *Progressive*, and the *New Leader*. Solicitations and newsletters went to mailing lists shared by the ACLU, the ADA, the *New Republic*, and the American Veterans Committee, a group Straight had headed. In Washington its meetings were often held at the headquarters of the United Auto Workers, which also maintained AI USA's core mailing list of three thousand names. The mostly New York–based board consisted of prominent liberal activists. Treasurer Nelson Bengston served on the board of the ILRM, the American Committee on Africa, the Committee for World Development and World Disarmament, and the League for Industrial Democracy. Lewis Carliner had worked with Victor Reuther at the United Auto Workers. Nathan Perlmutter was an official of the American Jewish Committee. Three relatives of Peter Benenson, William, Charles, and Mark, were also board members. The most active of the Benensons, Mark, was an attorney of libertarian bent active in Reform Democratic politics. Along with Biddle and Reuther, honorary members of the board included Francis Rivers, president of the NAACP's Legal Defense Fund.[64]

If a mostly New York liberal elite found time for Amnesty among their other philanthropic activities, the same was not true of other Americans. On a grassroots level, Amnesty struggled to find adherents. AI USA's first secretary recalled that "young people who opposed the war and the draft were not interested when they learned they could not use Amnesty for their own purposes, and older people were so angry at the protestors that they didn't want to get involved." She recalled that most of the early members had friends or relatives imprisoned abroad or some other personal connection to political imprisonment.[65] Early efforts to foster new adoption groups failed.

AI USA's day-to-day activities in the late 1960s were managed by Paul Lyons. One of the first to volunteer for Straight's new group, Lyons was a thirty-year-old law school dropout with a B.S. in foreign service from Georgetown University, working as an export control agent at the Department of Commerce. He described himself as "creatively resentful of authority." His involvement in AI USA was largely serendipitous: he had no particular experience with political prisoners or political or grassroots organizing, but was dissatisfied with his Commerce job and wanted a position with more autonomy. Intrigued by an announcement of an AI meeting, he decided the group's international flavor suited his educational background and talked himself into a job.[66]

It was a tiny operation on a shoestring budget. With money from his grandfather's philanthropic foundation, Straight hired Lyons as executive director and his wife Maryanne Lyons as part-time secretary on a joint annual salary of $15,000.[67] The couple worked out of the basement of their home in Chevy Chase, Maryland, and were so appreciative of Straight's generosity that they named their firstborn son Michael in his honor.[68] Despite the new director's enthusiasm and energy—he and his wife claimed to work from eight o'clock in the morning until eleven at night seven days a week—Lyons never succeeded in establishing a solid financial base for the organization.[69] He spent much of his time on direct-mail campaigns, setting up his own database of prisoners, and seeking publicity, choosing to downplay Amnesty's core mission of cultivating grassroots groups on the grounds that it did not suit American temperaments.[70] His use of direct mail was innovative—the technique was not harnessed with frequency by liberal groups until later in the 1970s—but it was so expensive relative to returns that it resulted in financial disaster.[71] The high expenses devoted to fundraising were also problematic for maintaining the group's tax-exempt charity status.[72] Appeals for funding from foundations such as the Twentieth Century Fund and the Ford Foundation failed; international human rights promotion was too novel to meet the funding priorities of such groups. Lyons's sometimes eccentric, attention-seeking proclivities were illustrated in one letter to board members and sponsors, which attached a dollar bill "to buy enough time for you to read the enclosures. It's also a way to get your attention, if you are normal."[73] He would eventually be forced out after his maverick style incurred the wrath of the London Secretariat. His sense of humor did not help: in 1968 he forged on secretariat letterhead a satirical dossier for a prisoner named Gunga al-Surfit and got the story in the newspapers. The prisoner, described as having twenty-seven children and a wife who weighed four hundred pounds, had supposedly been arrested for putting an aphrodisiac in the tea of a government official's wife. The London office did not appreciate the prank.[74]

Although some early Amnesty participants later recalled that they had thought of themselves as prisoner advocates rather than human rights activists, Lyons almost from the beginning saw Amnesty as a human rights movement.[75] Explaining the group's purpose to potential funders, he repeatedly wrote of human rights and described Amnesty's purpose as "the tangible advancement of human rights through seeking the release and comfort of people everywhere regarded by the association as 'prisoners of conscience.'" Amnesty members, he wrote, "are generally sympathetic to all serious efforts in favor of human rights," but what made Amnesty unique was that it focused on individual victims and involved its members directly in helping them.[76] The newsletters he published included a coupon for readers to clip out and send in, which read "I would like to support Amnesty's struggle for human rights through the release and comfort of prisoners of conscience."[77] In late 1967, he described his vision as building "a strong private voice for human rights." He went on to say that "although we are certainly not doing a job that is likely to attract the kind of attention that the civil rights or Vietnam (anti thereto) movements do, I become more convinced all the time that there is a crying need for expanded activity among American private citizens in the area of human rights around the world, on an ACLU-type basis. . . . There simply is no organization other than Amnesty doing this on a serious, continuing basis in Washington."[78]

Amnesty's global spread was a product of proliferating transnational links of all kinds, but the U.S. branch's relationship with the parent organization also illustrates the limits of transnationalism. Until the early 1970s, AI USA's links to London were tenuous, irregular, and often adversarial, and its organizers saw their mission as adapting a foreign mandate to American conditions. In 1968 AI USA issued its own report on Greece, rather than using one published by the London Secretariat. The American press, Lyons explained, is "more demanding than the European press," and "a London report is not an AI USA report." To a critic he wrote, "What the English or others do is their business, what we do is ours."[79] Amnesty's international affiliates were supposed to function primarily through adoption groups, with each group taking up the cause of prisoners assigned to it and supporting the research work of the London office through annual dues. Lyons took a different approach. He dismissed small-scale fund-raising and letter-writing as "amateurish"— like "old ladies tea parties"—and said it was absurd to expect Americans to take to a system in which they are given no say as to which prisoners they helped. It was not, Lyons repeatedly said, "the American way."[80]

Instead he focused on producing a newsletter and on direct-mail efforts, which by mid-1969 had sunk the organization into a $36,578 deficit.[81] Lyons's approach caused friction with London headquarters, partly because the International Secretariat was dependent on funding that came from groups. Although the American section promised a special supplemental levy due to its unique organizational structure, it quickly fell into arrears, exacerbating the London Secretariat's own financial difficulties. By 1970, AI's head, Martin Ennals, had helped force Lyons out, and the AI USA office moved to New York.[82]

In the late 1960s AI USA's work on Greece was virtually indistinguishable from that of the U.S. Committee for Democracy in Greece. Lyons served for a time as executive director of the committee at the same time as he was working for AI USA, while the U.S. Committee paid a portion of the salaries for Lyons and his wife.[83] Biddle and Reuther, honorary members of AI USA's board, also had honorary titles on the U.S. Committee. As Lyons explained to the AI USA board, "It goes without saying that AI USA is very much a part of this [antijunta] movement as far as the political imprisonments and related violations of human rights are concerned. Concurrent with the growing importance of the Greek case are our own efforts. . . . The two may fit together very well. As Michael Straight saw . . . the elimination of civil liberties in Greece was, and is, on such a large and grotesque scale that an organization such as Amnesty has no real choice but to help the public interest in the situation grow." In order to help Amnesty grow, he promised to bring an Amnesty presence to every major antijunta event in the United States.[84] In addition to participating in events such as vigils and marches in New York, Lyons, wearing his AI USA hat, organized a number of his own activities. In September 1967, for example, he staged a demonstration in a central Washington park with a cardboard mock-up of a prison cell, representing political imprisonment in general.[85] But the publicity Amnesty got in 1967 and 1968 was almost exclusively related to its activities related to Greece.[86]

Appeals to human rights appeared as part of the antijunta campaigns from the beginning, but initially concerns were less often framed in terms of international law than more general moral or democratic values. As indicated by the names of antijunta organizations that sprang up around

A 1967 Amnesty International demonstration, including a mock prison cell, at a monument to Ukrainian poet Taras Shevchenko in Washington, D.C. The organization was tiny and little known in the United States until the 1970s. (*Washington Post*/Getty)

the country, what mobilized people into action was the imposition of dictatorship: Stephen Rousseas's New York–based American Committee for Democracy and Freedom in Greece; the Union of Greeks and Americans for Democracy in Greece; the American Committee for Responsible Democratic Government in Greece; Southern Californians for Democracy in Greece; the Illinois Committee for Freedom and Democracy in Greece; the California Committee for Democracy in Greece; and many others.[87] Such groups endlessly characterized Greece as the cradle of democracy, rarely noting that the country's most recent experiment with democratic government had lasted only a few years.

References to democratic liberties, individual civil rights, and freedom were common, and American opponents of the junta were animated above all by outrage that a NATO ally—a European member of the "free world"—had abolished democratic government and constitutional rule.[88]

Yet references to human rights, the Universal Declaration, and international law appeared with enough frequency to constitute an important theme. As early as September 1967, AI USA's newsletter, *Amnesty Action*, featured a statement by Edwards on "the cause of human rights in Greece." In his capacity as executive director of the U.S. Committee, Lyons wrote a letter to the *New York Times* in 1967 criticizing the junta's "performance in the area of basic human rights." In November 1967, nineteen congressmen signed a joint letter to Secretary of State Dean Rusk asking that the government take a stand on "the denial of human rights in Greece today" lest silence lead to "national shame." The New York–based American Committee for Democracy and Freedom in Greece sent out an appeal centered on the UDHR, noting that the UN was about to celebrate the anniversary of its adoption. The Greek junta had "refused to acknowledge the natural human rights of mankind," it stated, proceeding to list the rights that were being violated in Greece. On the anniversary of the UDHR, the group held a "March in Mourning for the death of human rights and freedom in Greece," walking silently with lighted torches from the New York Public Library to the UN. "We appeal to every American to demonstrate his solidarity to the Universal Declaration of Human Rights." Fraser similarly rued the fact that the UN's International Year of Human Rights in 1968 had turned out to be one of denial of such rights in Greece. A 1969 U.S. Committee statement called on the UN and other bodies to enforce human rights in Greece.[89]

By 1969 the hearings and rulings of the Council of Europe and its European Commission of Human Rights pushed U.S. organizations increasingly to frame Greek repression in human rights terms, a shift in outlook that was also reflected in media coverage. The National Council of Churches, for example, passed a late 1969 resolution on Greece expressing concern over "denial of many human rights and fundamental freedoms," including lack of elections, denial of citizenship rights, torture, and lack of religious freedom. In an article detailing the testimony of three torture victims, *Newsweek* referred to charges that the junta had trampled on "political and human rights."[90]

Yet even as they began to frame their concerns in universalistic language, junta opponents were slow to tie the Greek case to global issues. In 1968 Roger Baldwin chided Fraser and Reuther at the U.S. Committee for not mentioning the pernicious influence of anticommunism in U.S. support for Greece. "I would not think your work effective unless you can get support for the general position of repudiating dictatorships whose only merit for the United States is their anti-Communism," Baldwin wrote. "We've suffered this foreign policy so long in so many countries we should point up its price in terms of the evidence you cite, in strengthening reaction and in weakening American prestige as a champion of democracy and a 'free world.' "[91] During congressional hearings in 1971, Fraser discussed balancing the inevitability of living with "right-wing governments" against the need to "have some respect for the basic values which we regard as at the heart of American society and its institutions," but his core argument rested on Greek "totalitarianism" as a threat to NATO security.[92] In other words, despite some moves toward creating general principles to justify stopping the flow of arms and aid to dictators, liberals did not make universalistic, rights-based claims the lynchpin of their case. Greece was treated as unique, a country that by virtue of its NATO membership and importance to European security required the imposition of special standards.

When, after years of failed attempts, the House voted in 1971 to ban military aid to Greece, the U.S. Committee celebrated it as "the first time since World War II that either House of Congress has taken action against a right-wing tyranny."[93] The committee's influence on the vote is one reason the authors of a 1977 study of lobby groups judged it a successful force in Congress.[94] Nixon promptly took advantage of a loophole in the aid ban for a waiver on national security grounds, but the vote was an important precedent for later congressional human rights efforts, signaling the end of an era when friendly governments could count on U.S. support without regard to their records at home.[95]

The antijunta efforts were important partly as a seedbed for explicitly human rights based appeals, but their greatest significance lay in what they revealed about public responsiveness to the abuses that would become the headliners in the 1970s—above all, political imprisonment and torture—and in developing a program of action that centered on public shaming and cutoffs of aid. Torture was a key focus of antijunta appeals in Europe and in the United States, and it is in large part Greek torture (along with torture in Brazil) that showed how powerfully torture aroused public outrage, giving it momentum that would propel it into the cause célèbre of human rights in the 1970s.[96] It became a prominent issue not because it was new—torture had been widely used by postwar Greek governments—but rather because Western eyes suddenly found it a compelling issue.

Torture proved a powerfully emotive subject. The U.S. Committee raised the issue of torture early, writing in the opening paragraph of a May 1968 fund-raising letter that many opponents of the Greek junta "have been subjected to sadistic torture," and its publications often gave prominent attention to torture.[97] A draft of one early appeal—later toned down—described the junta's torture as "unspeakable in its bestiality, unprintable in its detail." The appeal, titled "An Appeal to Conscience—Yours," exhorted: "To witness a crime in silence is a crime in itself."[98]

The public readily identified with the young, sympathetic, and often well-educated and English-speaking victims of brutality who brought their stories to the media. An eight-minute-long prime-time NBC news segment in 1969, covering the European Commission's findings on torture in Greece, included interviews with three victims who described falanga, psychological torture, and pressure clamping the head. That same year Christopher Wren published a breathless piece in *Look* entitled "Government by Torture," calling the stories of Greek torture "so grotesque as to seem unreal" until he talked to victims and heard their accounts at first hand. The piece featured a sidebar with the question, "Why should we hand over American taxpayers' money to a government that rules by torture?" When Greece withdrew from the Council of Europe in December 1969, NBC ran a three-minute-long interview with Pericles Korovessis, then living in London, who recounted in halting English his experience with falanga and electric shock. Also trading on torture testimony's shock value, the *New York Times* printed a lengthy excerpt from the European Commission's 1970 findings on torture in Greece, opening with the testimony of a pregnant woman who had been

A 1973 conference on torture in New York City sponsored by Amnesty International's U.S. section, as part of Amnesty's new Campaign against Torture. Pictured here are participants Margaret Papandreou, wife of former Greek prime minister and political prisoner Andreas Papandreou, former U.S. attorney general and antiwar activist Ramsey Clark, and Soviet dissident Alexander Volpin. (Amnesty International)

beaten until she miscarried. Media coverage in turn had clear effects on Congress: many members of Congress who eventually came to support efforts to cut aid to Greece cited torture in their reasoning.[99]

Brazil provided the other major case that magnified concerns about torture in the late 1960s and early 1970s. After Brazil's military dictatorship clamped down on domestic terrorism in 1968, it, too, became a focus of international condemnation, with torture taking center stage. The Médici regime scaled back civil liberties and launched a counterterrorism program undergirded by official use of torture.[100] Internal resistance groups, including church groups, academics, and lawyers, linked with exile networks and sympathizers abroad to generate publicity and public pressure for reforms.[101] U.S. newspapers sharply increased their reporting on torture in Brazil in 1970, with reports in major outlets touching on torture in Brazil on average about one a month.[102]

Accounts of torture in Brazil almost invariably included specifics—names of victims, their ages and personal backgrounds, dates, places, and sometimes the names of torturers. Critics of torture focused on victims who were easy to sympathize with: students, young women, priests, nuns. Ralph della Cava's early effort to publicize torture in Brazil, for example, begins with the case of Sister Maurina Borges da Silveia, a Roman Catholic nun arrested and tortured with electric shock in 1969. The average age of victims was twenty-two, according to a European report, and affluent, middle-class university students and even high school students were "the chief victims."[103] Reports often highlighted the torture of dual-nationality victims and foreign victims.[104] One activist noted, "Torture in Brazil is the only democratic institution, because anyone is liable to become its victim."[105] The distance between victims and readers was thus narrowed: victims were very much like the readers themselves, or (perhaps an even more powerful identifier) like the readers' sons and daughters.

Such stories almost never provided any context in which to understand why victims had been arrested or acknowledged the possibility that victims might have been associated with terrorist groups; their innocence was taken as a given. By stripping the victims of their context, and speaking of victims purely as innocents, such stories made it easy for readers to feel as though they, too, could be victimized. In charging the Brazilian regime with using torture not just to extract information but also to silence dissent, critics of torture implicitly acknowledged the possibility that torture's reprehensibility was not absolute but depended on what purpose it was used for.[106]

As was the case with Greece, opponents of the Brazilian regime emphasized U.S. complicity in permitting abuses to occur. A 1970 *Post* editorial warned that "the United States is in danger of getting itself caught up on the side of the oppressors." The sense of complicity went beyond specific claims that U.S. taxpayers were financing torture through the millions of dollars in AID funds spent on the Office of Public Safety program to train and supply Brazil's police. Complaints that Americans were training their Brazilian counterparts in the use of coercive interrogation techniques began in 1969 and ran through the 1970s. But even without that very direct connection to torture (never proven), the U.S. government's "strong support of Brazil at every level," as two conservative columnists put it in an editorial called "Brazilian Blood on Our Hands," was enough to give Americans reason to feel responsible for "keep[ing] in unchecked power the most repressive regime in the Western Hemisphere."[107]

Accounts of torture produced strong emotional effects. In September 1970, the *Post*'s Jack Anderson wrote a column about Senator Frank Church's plan to hold hearings on U.S. aid to Brazil and on the regime's use of torture. The widely reprinted column claimed that "even women and priests have been horribly, inhumanly abused," and detailed the case of Gisela Maria Concenza Avenlar, a twenty-five-year-old social worker who was sexually tortured and whose infant was threatened with torture.[108] Dozens of Americans wrote to Church to say that Anderson's column had sickened, shocked, disturbed, appalled, horrified, and alarmed them. "I cannot express to you, in any words, the anger and sorrow I feel," one woman wrote. "Please, please do something to help end this horror."[109] Several respondents reported feeling ill. A Maryland woman who had read the column with "horror" wrote, "[It] literally nearly made me ill!" "What can be done?" they asked in various forms.[110] Some compared Brazilian brutality to Nazi atrocities.[111] Others connected torture in Brazil to torture in Greece. A number of letters suggest the influence of disillusionment with the Vietnam War. "It is difficult to carry on from day to day without carrying the burden of so many things that our country is doing," wrote a New Jersey woman.[112] A Californian pleaded, "Why are we always on the wrong side?"[113]

By the beginning of the 1970s, liberals were beginning to find new modes of action to address U.S. support for undemocratic and repressive governments around the world. The mantra of the new decade was global interdependence, as televisions, satellites, and communications advances made Americans feel less insulated from what happened elsewhere. Massacres and humanitarian crises in places such as Biafra, Burundi, and Bangladesh; racist regimes in southern Africa; state-sponsored torture by U.S. allies in Greece and Brazil; and a swelling number of dictatorships around the world seemed, in the minds of liberals, to be problems Americans could not afford to ignore, particularly when American influence seemed partly to blame. Rising Holocaust sensibility in the 1960s fixed in the public mind the equation of silence with complicity, and liberal guilt about the Vietnam War fostered a desire not to continue lining up on the "wrong side." But until U.S. involvement in the war ended, Americans found the type of human rights activism peddled by Amnesty International to be almost totally irrelevant, and no one as yet had thought to offer human rights as a panacea for America's foreign policy dilemmas.

## CHAPTER 5

# The Anticommunist
# Embrace of Human Rights

T o WRITE OF Senator Henry M. Jackson is to conjure up the Cold War. Anticommunism was his defining cause, and the affable Washington senator, known by his childhood nickname Scoop, played his most important role in spurring the country to greater vigilance about the Soviet threat. But his legacy outlasted that conflict, reverberating in American politics into the twenty-first century, for Scoop was the grandfather of neoconservatism. A pundit might even postulate, half-seriously, that the Iraq War began in Jackson's office.[1] In the early 1970s his office was staffed by young men who would roam the corridors of the White House and the Pentagon thirty years later, providing the intellectual undergirding for President George W. Bush's war on terror and the invasion of Iraq. Among them were Richard Perle, who found working for Jackson "love at first sight" and later headed Bush's Defense Policy Board, and Douglas Feith, who served in Bush's Defense Department. Elliott Abrams, a special assistant in Bush's National Security Council (and before that Reagan's human rights officer in the State Department), worked on Jackson's 1976 presidential campaign, and Paul Wolfowitz, Deputy Secretary of Defense under Donald Rumsfeld, collaborated with Perle in Jackson's office when working for the Arms Control and Disarmament Agency in the mid-1970s.[2] These were men who began their political careers as Jackson Democrats—"Scoop's Troops," they called themselves. Their belief in a strong military to protect the United States and to advance human rights and democracy was forged in "the bunker" in the Senate Office Building where they labored with Jackson, trying, in their view, to set the country right after Vietnam.

Jackson and his sympathizers took up the cause of human rights promotion in the 1970s for reasons strikingly at odds with those that animated liberals. Liberals aimed to abandon what they saw as an outmoded fixation on anticommunism, and their interest in human rights was driven by a desire to distance their country from responsibility for abuses. Though concerned about Soviet repression, they felt that it was most important to battle repression where there was an element of American culpability—an approach fueled by feelings of shame about the Vietnam War. The neoconservative turn to human rights, in contrast, was driven by a fervent rejection of shame and guilt. Its prime movers were viscerally opposed to McGovern and McGovern-style criticisms of American failings. For them, the self-doubt provoked by the Vietnam War threatened to weaken America's resolve in what remained a life-or-death struggle against communism. It was to resurrect the American will to wage this all-important fight that they took up the language of universal human rights, which they appear to have borrowed from American Jewish groups and a Soviet dissident movement that gained global fame around 1970.

Human rights were ripe for new meaning by the end of the 1960s, as the civil rights movement receded as a mainstream political priority. But by the time liberals seized on the concept as a foreign policy paradigm, conservative forces who backed the stop-McGovern drive had beaten them to it. Headed by Jackson, unrepentant Cold Warriors took the rhetoric of human rights newly popularized internationally by Soviet dissidents and fashioned a straightforwardly anticommunist policy around the universalist language. It was a stunning shift in the rhetoric of conservative anticommunism, which in the 1950s and 1960s had been overtly hostile to the UN and, Bricker-style, had seen UN human rights instruments as a dangerous threat to American values. Before Jackson, anticommunism had been framed around American values, with freedom as the headliner. What was markedly new about Jackson's framing of the issues was the rhetoric of universal rights rather than of liberty and the invocation of international norms and UN standards as moral sanction for American goals.

Jackson's human rights campaign was initially limited to pressuring the Kremlin to increase Jewish emigration. His humanitarian efforts had political implications: he wanted to undermine détente, which in his view was dangerously weakening U.S. security through unwarranted concessions to the Soviets. Jackson is sometimes dismissed as peripheral to the history of human rights because his aim was too "narrow" to constitute a "general" human rights vision.[3] The titan of the Soviet dissidents, Aleksandr Solzhenitsyn, thought emigration rights a "petty" issue and "minor detail" that could be solved by a general broadening of freedoms in the USSR.[4] Yet selectivity and political motives are necessary features of any human rights campaign, and at root Jackson was doing precisely what liberals would soon take up with equal enthusiasm: using universalist claims to focus attention on some rights for some people.

The conservative strand of international human rights promotion drew inspiration from the dissidents who began to organize in the Soviet Union in the late 1960s by using the language of human rights. Physicist Andrei Sakharov and writer Aleksandr Solzhenitsyn were the best known in the West: they were celebrated as moral and intellectual titans, their publications widely translated, their statements publicized and discussed. Their courageous, principled protest sent out ripples well beyond the USSR that altered the intellectual and political climate of the 1970s. Because the dissidents carried enormous moral authority in the West, their use of the language of human rights and their appeals to the Universal Declaration played a key role in resurrecting and shaping a global human rights discourse in the 1970s. Beginning in the late 1960s, dissidents consciously adopted the label of a movement for human rights *(prava cheloveka)*. Jackson's embrace of the terminology of universal human rights seems to have flowed from the language of Soviet dissidents, as well as of American Jewish groups that had long used appeals to UN human rights documents as a means of universalizing their own concerns.[5]

Dissidents challenged the premises of détente. The new strategy embraced by Nixon and Brezhnev moved the superpowers toward a more cooperative, less confrontational relationship, based on the assumption that a state's external behavior was all that should matter in the formulation of foreign policy and that interference in internal matters should be avoided. The Nixon administration treated the Soviet Union as a normal rival in international affairs, not as an ideological opponent beyond the pale of diplomacy. Dissidents, in contrast, argued that global security and internal affairs, in the form of respect for human rights, could not be separated. Solzhenitsyn encapsulated this sensibility in the Nobel lecture he published in 1972, in a phrase often quoted by Jackson. "There are no internal affairs left on our crowded Earth!" the famous chronicler of the Gulag declared. "Mankind's sole salvation lies in everyone making everything his business, in the people of the East being vitally concerned with what is thought in the West, the people of the West being vitally concerned with what goes on in the East." He called the UDHR the UN's "best document in twenty-five years" but assailed the body for cowardice in failing to make its observance obligatory.[6]

The Brezhnev-era dissident movement originated in the years after Stalin's death in 1953, when Soviet Premier Nikita Khrushchev set in motion a de-Stalinization and cultural thaw that allowed an extraordinary intellectual ferment, including public discussion of some of Stalin's crimes. In 1964 Khrushchev's successor, Leonid Brezhnev, put the brakes on de-Stalinization, signaling the end of the thaw with the arrest and trial of writers Andrei Sinyavsky and Yuli Daniel for publishing "anti-Soviet" stories abroad. Demanding that the trial be open to the public, over a hundred intellectuals gathered in Moscow's Pushkin Square in December 1965 in a demonstration that marked the birth of a Soviet civil rights movement.[7]

Civil rights activists in the United States had adopted civil disobedience—defiance of laws—as a primary tactic in the struggle to secure domestic human rights. The distinctiveness of the Soviet movement lay in its embrace of civil *obedience:* the demand that the government adhere to its own laws.[8] *Politiki* tended to favor overturning the system, but the most influential strain of thinking in the Soviet human rights movement was represented by the self-styled *pravozashchitniki*,

Soviet dissident Alexander Solzhenitsyn with Senator Henry M. Jackson during a visit to the Senate in July 1975. Jackson drew on the language of Soviet dissidents in linking human rights to U.S. trade policy. (University of Washington Libraries, Special Collections UW27848z)

the rights-defenders: those who tried to persuade the Soviet government to respect its own laws and the international agreements it had signed. Thus, the signs that the Pushkin Square demonstrators carried in 1965 called for an open trial and respect for the Soviet constitution, and the petitions that dissidents sent to the Soviet regime routinely referred to the Soviet constitution and Soviet laws.[9]

Within a few years dissidents were mixing appeals to domestic civil rights with invocations of international human rights.[10] Formed in 1970 by Sakharov, A. N. Tverdokhlebov, and Valerii Chalidze, the Moscow Committee for Human Rights dedicated itself to writing and publishing scholarly analyses of international human rights law, as well as of the Soviet legal code.[11] Accepting his Nobel Prize in December 1970, Solzhenitsyn stressed the "symbolic meaning" of the fact that the award ceremony fell on International Human Rights Day, marking the date of the signing of the Universal Declaration.[12] From its beginning in 1968, taking advantage of the fact that it was the UN's International Human Rights Year, each issue of the major samizdat periodical began by reprinting the UDHR's Article 19 on freedom of opinion and expression, using the international document to legitimize its propagation of information. Although it became known by its subtitle, *The Chronicle of Current Events*, its original title was *Human Rights Year in the Soviet Union*.[13] Its editors described their goal as chronicling "the suppression of human rights and the movement for them" in the USSR.[14] Imprisoned dissident Anatolii Marchenko compared the Soviet case to repression elsewhere, writing: "I should like my testimony on Soviet camps and prisons to become known to humanists and progressive people of other countries—those who raise their voice in defense of political prisoners in Greece and Portugal, in the South African Republic and in Spain."[15]

Activists appealed not only to Soviet authorities but to the United Nations and to the rights embodied in its human rights covenants. From 1969 to 1970, the Initiative Group for the Defense of Human Rights sent the UN dozens of letters about Soviet violations of the UDHR.[16] In 1969 the group asked UN Secretary General U Thant to "intervene against human rights violations in our country and also to take steps to present this issue before the United Nations Human Rights Commission." (The UN still resolutely avoided criticism of individual members, and Thant promptly instructed UN offices to refuse future petitions.)[17] When appeals to the UN received no response, the audience was broadened to include the World Health Organization, the International Congress of Psychiatrists, the papacy, and Western media, in the hope that external pressure from world opinion would impel the Soviet regime toward reform.[18]

Pressure was also mounting from Soviet Jews. As was true elsewhere, Jews in the Soviet Union experienced a rise in Holocaust consciousness and an attendant interest in Jewish identity in the 1960s. The Israeli victory in the 1967 Six-Day War evoked pride, a newly militant mood, and rising interest in Zionism and emigration to Israel. The Soviet regime, which imposed strict controls on travel and emigration for all of its citizens, viewed growing demands for Jewish emigration as a threat to Soviet legitimacy. The Soviet ambassador to the United States, Anatoly Dobrynin, later explained that Soviet leaders viewed any demand to leave "as a reproof to our socialist paradise. That anyone should have the temerity to want to leave it was taken as a rank insult!" Dobrynin exaggerated only a little when he said that qualifying to emigrate was nearly as difficult as being accepted for cosmonaut training.[19]

The Soviet regime greatly increased the numbers allowed to emigrate in the hopes of removing internal discontent and improving the Soviet image abroad, but it also engaged in a burst of anti-Zionism, condemning Israel to shore up its Arab allies in the wake of the 1967 War. To longstanding anti-Semitic discrimination in employment and higher education, the Soviet regime added virulently anti-Zionist propaganda and a wave of arrests, imprisonment, and harassment of Jews who sought to emigrate or to preserve their cultural identity.[20] Those Jews who were undeterred found that applying to emigrate typically resulted in refusal followed by harassment, loss of employment and educational opportunities, and sometimes arrest. They joined the growing ranks of the so-called *refuseniks*. To press their case in the court of public opinion, *refuseniks*, like other dissidents, invoked international human rights norms, including the right to emigration outlined in the UDHR and in UN human rights instruments such as the International Convention on the Elimination of All Forms of Racial Discrimination, which the Soviet Union had ratified in 1969.[21]

The Western media found the struggles of dissidents, including *refuseniks*, irresistible sources of human drama, and their stories received voluminous coverage. The courage of the dissidents was undeniable: they were willing to suffer harassment, arrest, exile, and imprisonment, including in brutal psychiatric facilities, for expressing their beliefs. Sakharov and Solzhenitsyn became household names in the West, routinely identified in the Western press as "human rights advocates." The media's intensive coverage of the struggles of dissidents, including Soviet Jews, helped internationalize American understandings of human rights, uprooting the term from the domestic context of American civil rights and shifting it to the international sphere.[22]

For American Jews, the cause of Soviet Jewry was deeply emotional. Remorseful that the generation before them had done so little to stop the slaughter of Jews by the Nazis, American Jews were determined not to remain silent when Russian Jews—the last great center of East European

Jewry—asked for help. The American Jewish press throughout the 1960s denounced Soviet discrimination in education, restrictions on cultural and religious life, and emigration barriers. Calls to act increased in the 1970s.[23]

At the end of 1970, Soviet Jewry suddenly became a global cause célèbre, when the leaders of a group of Jewish *refuseniks* who had attempted to emigrate by hijacking a plane were sentenced to death in Leningrad. The harsh sentences provoked global protests and a flood of publicity about the repression faced by Soviet Jews. U.S. government pressure on the Soviet Union to alleviate discrimination against Jews, including in the realm of emigration, dated back at least to the 1950s, and Nixon himself had raised the issue of Jewish emigration with Soviet leaders when he had been vice president.[24] In the 1970s, as the Jewish community began to flex its political muscles, such lobbying vastly increased. Under congressional pressure spearheaded by New York Congressman Ed Koch, the Nixon administration agreed in 1971 to lift entry quotas for Soviet Jews in the event greater numbers were ever permitted to leave.[25]

Many American Jewish groups had long situated their efforts to create better conditions for Jews within a larger struggle against discrimination in general. The mainstream American Jewish Committee, for example, worked on the principle that "Jews can be effectively protected only as particulars within" a program of "universal human rights and welfare."[26] It founded the Jacob Blaustein Institute for the Advancement of Human Rights in 1971, whose first head, Sidney Liskofsky, had played a role in nongovernmental organization efforts to incorporate human rights into the UN Charter in 1948.[27] Jewish groups had taken an early interest in the Convention against Genocide. The driving force behind the Ad Hoc Committee on the Human Rights and Genocide Treaties, which was primarily interested in seeing the passage of the Genocide Convention, was the Jewish Labor Committee. One sign that such efforts were beginning to bear fruit was the Nixon administration's push to get the Genocide Treaty through Congress after twenty-two years of inaction. In December 1970 the Senate Foreign Relations Committee for the first time voted to put the treaty before Congress, a decision repeated in 1971 and 1973, though the full Congress declined to take action.[28]

American Jewish groups often framed their concerns about Soviet Jews in the language of universal human rights and lobbied on those grounds at the UN.[29] Because Soviet treatment of Jews was one of the charges U.S. officials used to flog the Soviet Union at the UN and its human rights bodies, there was a relatively long history of situating repression of Jews within the UN human rights framework. In 1965, for example, the U.S. representative to the UN human rights commission, Morris Abram, suggested that the UN Subcommission for the Prevention of Discrimination and the Protection of Minorities investigate charges of Soviet anti-Semitism. Applauding Abram's suggestion, New York Senator Jacob Javits called Soviet anti-Jewish measures "contrary to the laws of man, the U.N. Charter, and to international morality."[30] Javits, the son of a Jewish Ukrainian immigrant, would become a major supporter of international human rights. Nixon's UN Human Rights Commission representative, lawyer Rita Hauser (who also served on the Committee to Re-elect the President), voiced official American concern over impediments to emigration.[31] At a congressional hearing on Soviet repression of religion, second-term congressman Donald Rumsfeld commented that "those who believe that the protection of human rights and fundamental freedoms is basic to the cause of peace" should take action against religious discrimination in the Soviet Union.[32]

American Jewish organizations campaigning for Soviet Jews were also following the practice of *refuseniks* themselves in invoking Soviet obligations under the UDHR. The increasing flow of Jewish tourists to the USSR and the extension of contacts through phone calls and samizdat ensured that Jewish groups in the United States were familiar with the writings and positions of Soviet dissidents, and there was increasing coordination between the two groups.[33] The support of civil rights leaders, including Martin Luther King, Jr., Bayard Rustin, Roy Wilkins, and A. Philip Randolph, further suggested to the American public that the issue had a broad relevance beyond the concerns of a single group.[34] In a 1966 speech on Soviet Jews, King said, "The denial of human rights anywhere is a threat to the affirmation of human rights everywhere."[35]

The practice of situating American concerns for Soviet Jews in the framework of international human rights thus had substantial roots. From the 1966 Declaration of Rights issued by the American Jewish

Conference for Soviet Jewry, which invoked the UDHR, to the "Human rights for Soviet Jewry" signs at a 1967 protest in New York, American Jewish groups made human rights a theme of activism on behalf of Soviet Jews.[36] In late 1971, explaining the newest incarnation of the Freedom Bus—this one dedicated to publicizing the cause of Soviet Jews—the chairman of the American Jewish Student Network suggested that the goal was the "basic human right to emigrate" for Soviet Jews.[37] Such activism helped make the UN's human rights system more familiar to legislators and the broader public. On the UDHR's anniversary in 1968, 357 members of Congress signed an appeal by the Conference on Soviet Jewry for the Soviet Union to remedy its breaches of the declaration.[38] Senators Jacob Javits and Abraham Ribicoff wrote to Nixon in 1969, "The problem of Soviet Jewry is a problem which must concern moral leaders everywhere and all of us who believe in human dignity and fundamental human rights."[39] Editorializing in the *New York Times* in January 1971, Morris Abram condemned Soviet emigration policies for violating the UDHR.[40]

Yet appeals to international law were not ubiquitous, and the justifications for free emigration did not always refer to human rights.[41] The hearings held in May 1971 by New York Congressman Benjamin Rosenthal suggest the important but still somewhat uncertain place UN human rights norms had gained among proponents of Soviet Jewish emigration. Opening the day of testimony on the subject of the "Denial of Human Rights to Jews in the Soviet Union," Rosenthal said that Soviet conduct violated "the basic principles of humanity" and the UDHR. He and others framed issues of morality in the specific language of UN human rights.[42] Yet although the UDHR was cited by several witnesses, legislators were clearly unfamiliar with it. New York Congressman Jonathan Bingham asked Ed Koch, appearing as a witness to discuss his recent travels in the Soviet Union, whether Soviet officials had criticized the United States for not signing the UDHR. Koch, apparently unaware that the United States had voted to ratify the declaration but the Soviet Union had not, and that as a declaration no country had "signed" it, blithely responded that the Soviets had not raised the issue. He explained that he had urged the secretary of state to submit the "treaty" to the Senate for ratification so that the United States could "bring charges" against the Soviet Union under its provisions. Bingham then expressed doubts about "some things in that treaty that we would find very difficult to agree with."[43] They were likely confusing the UDHR with the newer Convention on the Elimination of All Forms of Racial Discrimination, which the Soviet Union but not the United States had ratified.

Despite the congressional hearings and a brief flurry of media interest around the Leningrad hijacking trials, the plight of Soviet Jews remained on the margins of American politics, an issue taken up primarily by those actively involved in Jewish causes or the politics of large Jewish population centers. At the end of 1972, however, Jackson would put Soviet Jews squarely on the national agenda, and in so doing would make human rights a prominent motif in American foreign policy.

Senator Jackson was foremost among the conservative Democrats who, aiming to rekindle Cold War priorities, grasped the language of international human rights and in doing so aligned the concept with conservative priorities in the first years of the 1970s. He had represented Washington State in Congress since 1940, building a record on labor, civil rights, and environmental conservation that pegged him as a New Deal/Fair Deal liberal. His religious upbringing as the son of Norwegian Lutheran immigrants taught him what he called the Nordic code of "rugged individualism and a social conscience."[44] When the demands of social conscience came into conflict with security interests, the latter won: thus, during the Second World War Jackson had been a strident advocate of the internment of Japanese Americans.[45] He repeatedly said he was a true liberal, but in 1973–1974 he voted with the Conservative Coalition nearly 40 percent of the time, compared to Ted Kennedy's 4 percent. Nixon was so favorably disposed to Jackson that in 1968 the incoming president, hoping to bolster his legitimacy after winning only 43 percent of the vote in a three-way race, offered the senator the job of secretary of state or defense.[46] Jackson refused, probably determining that the Senate was a better launchpad for future presidential bids. When the Senator did run, dismally, for the Democratic presidential nomination in 1972, Nixon's reelection campaign judged Jackson its biggest threat because he was strong on foreign and defense issues, had a perfect record on labor issues, and was good enough on civil rights to satisfy African American groups without being so outspoken that he would antagonize whites.[47]

An unapologetic Cold Warrior, Jackson was the Senate's most outspoken advocate of a strong defense, and defense was the issue he rode to national fame.[48] His enthusiasm for military spending was sometimes explained by his nickname, "the Senator from Boeing," but his militarism ran far deeper than mere constituency service. By the late 1960s many liberals had begun to feel that American behavior in the world had too often been unwise, threatening, and even immoral. For Jackson, the role of bad guy belonged unequivocally to the Soviet Union.[49] He believed that standing up to the Soviets was the central imperative of his age. Befitting someone often called "the Last Cold Warrior," Jackson demanded nuclear superiority rather than mere parity with the Soviets, even in an era in which both sides had arsenals that could destroy the world.[50] "I believe that the men in the Kremlin wake up every morning and calculate whether they can do us in today," he told his staff. "The key to our survival is always to make sure that their answer to the question is no."[51]

Like many Cold Warriors, he prided himself on his toughness. In sharp contrast to McGovern's empathetic, emotionally open displays, Jackson's persona was hard and unemotional. "I don't want to be mush," he told a journalist. "I don't like mushy people." Talking to two biographers, Jackson recalled that he had been physically sickened when he saw a matador kill a bull in Mexico. When the conversation moved on to Vietnam and the death and mutilation Jackson had seen during his visits to Southeast Asia's battle zones, the biographers asked whether these scenes, too, had sickened him. Jackson said they had not. Pressed to explain why he found a bull's death sickening but not the deaths in Vietnam, Jackson replied, "Because killing the bull was not necessary."[52]

When it came to the Vietnam War, Jackson and his supporters were on the opposite side of the barricades from liberal Democrats like Fraser, backing the war with unremitting devotion nearly to the end. Writing much later, an aide put it this way: "Scoop saw the human rights implications of the Vietnam War," namely, that failure to win would "undermine the forces of law and civilization in the most fundamental way."[53] In 1965

Jackson thought Johnson's escalation of the war too tame and called instead for invading North Vietnam and mining Haiphong Harbor. The Nixon administration judged him a supporter of its policies in Southeast Asia and tallied that in 1969 Jackson had supported the president on 100 percent of foreign policy votes.[54]

The war split the Democratic Party in two, with fateful consequences for human rights. The rift opened in 1968, when antiwar candidates Eugene McCarthy and Robert F. Kennedy challenged establishment choice Hubert Humphrey for the party's nomination. The challengers failed in 1968, but succeeded in 1972, when the party nominee turned out to be someone its conservative faction regarded with horror. Jackson's prowar stance had already induced some antiwar Democrats to campaign against him in his home state. Jackson's 1972 presidential bid drove the knife in deeper, as he donned the mantle of leader of the anti-McGovern forces. A Republican senator had coined the wounding caricature of McGovern as the candidate of "amnesty, acid, and abortion," but it was Jackson who popularized the remark during his own campaign speeches. Antiwar liberals denounced him as a warmongerer and spoke of a walkout if he were nominated.[55]

After McGovern's massive defeat—proof, in Jackson's eyes, that the party had veered too far to the left—"Scoop's Troops" worked to retake control of the party through the Coalition for a Democratic Majority (CDM), a conservative group chaired by Jackson and Humphrey and including future neoconservatives Ben Wattenberg, Norman Podhoretz, and Jeane Kirkpatrick.[56] These Old Guard Democrats resented the left-wing turn toward more liberal social policies at home, but what drew their ire most of all was what they saw as the craven and misguided foreign policy stance of the New Politics. They despised the content and style of McGovern's opposition to the Vietnam War and saw as weak and dangerously wrongheaded his broader critique of Cold War militarism.[57] Disliking Nixon's realist accommodation with communist powers just as much as McGovern's dovish approach, they were convinced the country had had it right in the 1950s when it identified the Soviet Union and its allies as the overriding threats to the United States and to global peace and security. The Coalition's members were convinced that the vast center of the American electorate shared its views, but the group's

fortunes seemed to falter as Watergate reconfigured the political landscape. Bella Abzug famously quipped that the coalition was not a wing of
the party but "a feather."[58] Despite its small size, its morally based attacks
on détente would form one of the two key prongs of human rights activism
in the 1970s.

Above all, for Jackson and the coalition, the Vietnam War required no
apology. It was not immoral; on the contrary, it was an admirable expression of the nation's moral principles, as well as a strategic necessity, and
consonant with America's consistently beneficent role in the world. In
1965 Jackson outlined the basic position that he maintained throughout
the war: "The United States need apologize to no one for its policies in
the years since World War II. We have responded to the needs of the
poor and the hungry and the sick with a generosity unmatched in history. Good works are our preferred course of action, when the choice is
up to us. We covet no one's territory. We have committed no act of aggression. We have aided independent people whose crime, in communist eyes,
is that they dare defend themselves against aggression."[59] He repeated
these themes through the 1970s. "I'm proud of America," he said.[60]

The rejection of guilt was a major factor in shaping the post-Vietnam
foreign policy views of Jackson Democrats. "I don't buy the nonsense
some of the candidates are saying over and over again: 'This is a sick
country,'" Scoop said in one speech.[61] "This society is not a guilty,
imperialistic, and oppressive society. This is not a sick society," he said
in another. He condemned Democratic leaders who pandered to the
"intolerant extremists who have come to despise America and who would
destroy the Democratic Party if they took it over." He was incensed that
McGovern and "the New Left establishment" denounced "American
policy in Vietnam as 'barbaric' and 'immoral'—while not condemning
Hanoi's aggression."[62] Jackson would have concurred wholeheartedly
with Podhoretz's revulsion during the last years of the war, when "the
moral character of the United States was being indicted and besmirched"
by the large number of Americans who questioned the war.[63] What
Jackson and the CDMers saw as a liberal spirit of self-loathing spurred
their opposition, perhaps even more so than did disagreements over specific policy issues.[64]

\* \* \*

Before 1970 Jackson had not been outspoken either about international human rights or Israeli or Jewish issues. He had supported civil rights legislation and occasionally used the term human rights to refer to individual rights at home, but he seems to have had little familiarity with universal human rights before 1972.[65] In December 1971, for example, accepting the United-Italian American Labor Council's Four Freedoms Award, Jackson had much to say about defending freedom at home and abroad but never specifically mentioned human rights.[66] Nevertheless, his key foreign policy aide, Dorothy Fosdick, had served on the U.S. delegations to Dumbarton Oaks, the San Francisco Conference, and the UN from 1946 to 1948. She was, Joshua Muravchik later recalled, "deeply steeped in UN documents and the UN idiom."[67]

The precise reasons Jackson took up the cause of Soviet Jews when he did remain uncertain, but owe something both to personal values and to political calculation. Cultivation of American Jewish donors was a sensible measure for a politician with Jackson's presidential ambitions, and his close allies in the labor movement opposed increasing trade with the Soviets. The press-release version of the origins of Jackson's obsession with Soviet Jewry is that it began with a congressional visit to the Buchenwald death camp days after its liberation in 1945 and Jackson's resulting sense of regret that the United States had failed to prevent the Holocaust.[68] Although his legislative activities on behalf of Israel were not notable before the 1960s, he was an early supporter of Israel, and over his decades in the Senate developed a cherished and romantic attachment to the Jewish state.[69] Jackson was surely also influenced by his brash and intellectually formidable aide, future neocon Richard Perle, a Jew deeply devoted to anti-Soviet causes. Jackson evidently found personal satisfaction and emotional sustenance in pursuing Jewish causes. In 1976 reporter Richard Reeves described Jackson's Jewish connection as "a personal joy": he "is turned on by Jews." Usually an indifferent, droning public speaker with a "sleepily nasal voice"—the joke was that when he gave a fireside chat, the fire fell asleep—he came to life when he donned a yarmulke for Jewish groups. Reeves observed that "he acts differently in front of Jewish audiences—a little excited, more animated, his voice rising, arms waving, arms clasped over his head like a fighter, grinning, bouncing."[70]

Jackson's opposition to Nixon's pursuit of accommodation with the Soviet Union materialized in earnest when the president returned from his first Moscow summit in May 1972. Jackson railed against the Strategic Arms Limitation Treaty (SALT I) for allegedly ceding U.S. nuclear superiority and objected to the Anti-Ballistic Missile Treaty's restrictions on a program he considered vital for defense against a nuclear first strike. With détente enjoying broad bipartisan support, especially among the liberal Democrats who dominated Congress, Jackson was able only to extract small concessions on arms control.[71] When it came to tackling the Soviet Jewish issue, he would have far greater success.

At the Nixon-Brezhnev summit, the Soviets had eagerly pressed for a trade agreement. In mid-October, Kissinger returned from Moscow with one in hand. It called for the Soviets to pay $722 million in World War II Lend-Lease debts, while the administration pledged to secure most favored nation (MFN) trading status from Congress. Ever since the Soviets had been denied MFN status in 1951, they had seethed at the cutoff as an act of discrimination—despite its selective-sounding moniker, MFN status was enjoyed by every U.S. trading partner—that needed to be removed for "normalization" of relations to occur.[72]

MFN required congressional approval, which might have been readily forthcoming if not for the confluence of several events. In a scandal that became known as the "great grain robbery," it became public in late 1972 that the Soviets had quietly purchased nearly the entire U.S. surplus grain reserve at low prices, with the encouragement of an administration eager to cater to farm interests but unaware of the scale of Soviet purchases. The public was outraged when grain prices for American consumers shot up. Even Kissinger admitted, "The Soviets beat us at our own game."[73] The grain affair diminished American enthusiasm for the commercial side of détente, making passage of MFN more difficult.

An even more troublesome wrench was thrown into the works in August 1972, when the Soviet regime introduced an "exit tax" on emigrants. Justified as a means to force those leaving the country to repay the costs of the higher education the state had provided for free, it was a prohibitive penalty aimed at stoking anti-Semitism and stemming the outflow of emigrants. (Apparently it was adopted by a hardliner, Mikhail Suslov, who was left in charge while most of the rest of the politburo was on vacation.)[74] Its introduction soon after the Nixon-Brezhnev summit raised suspicions that Nixon had tacitly acquiesced in the measure.[75] Public opinion in the United States was outraged. Twenty-one Nobel laureates signed a letter condemning the "massive violation of human rights."[76] Several senators, including Humphrey and McGovern, urged the president to negotiate the removal of the exit tax.[77] In a speech on August 30, Javits, a moderate Republican, publicly proposed linking trade privileges to Jewish emigration. Already deeply committed to the cause of Soviet Jews, American Jews saw the new restriction as a crucial test of their commitment to defend Eastern European Jews threatened with repression.[78] One analysis suggested that among American Jews, Soviet Jews overshadowed aid to Israel as the prime concern in the lead-up to the November 1972 election.[79]

In the midst of the outrage provoked by the exit tax, Jackson launched a campaign for Soviet Jews. Over the two years it dragged on, it would position the senator as a major actor in Soviet-American relations, grab countless headlines, and give international protection of human rights a newly prominent place in national politics. In 1974 a Jewish supporter called Jackson's campaign "the single most focused, forceful and conspicuous congressional effort since World War II to shape American foreign policy in the image of human rights." Contrary to some characterizations, Jackson's move was not "a visceral reaction" to the shock of the exit tax, since even before the tax's introduction he had been preparing to target restrictions on emigration of Jews in the first appropriate legislation.[80] The idea originated with Perle, who probably came to it through his connections to Jewish organizations.[81] Such linkage had been broached in 1971 by the Union of Council for Soviet Jews, which had lobbied Congress to tie any agreement with the Soviet Union to free emigration for Soviet Jews, and a June 1972 international conference in Uppsala on the right of emigration had brought together scholars and representatives from nongovernmental organizations on the premise that the right to leave was "essential for the effective enjoyment of other human rights."[82] The 1972 Republican Party platform, adopted that summer, had strongly endorsed international human rights and the

UDHR, while referencing only one specific violation of human rights: denial of emigration to Soviet Jews.[83] On September 27, 1972, Jackson drew together all these threads, announcing that he was offering an amendment to link trade concessions to the freedom to emigrate without prohibitive exit taxes. It stipulated that in order for a country to gain MFN status, the president would have to submit a report on the country's adherence to standards of free emigration.

Throughout the long battle over the amendment, Jackson's rhetoric drew on the language of universal human rights, in part as a pragmatic strategy to draw in political support from across the political spectrum.[84] He titled his measure "East-West Trade and Fundamental Human Rights" and spoke of it as serving "the cause of human rights and individual liberty." It began with the words "to assure the continued dedication of the United States to fundamental human rights. . . ."[85] In the press release announcing the amendment, he made the astonishing claim that the exit tax was "the most dramatic violation of basic human rights" in the Soviet Union, presumably eclipsing even political imprisonment, forced labor, and incarceration of dissenters in psychiatric prisons.[86] Announcing in April 1973 that the amendment would now be attached to the Trade Reform Bill (and directed at all nonmarket economies), Jackson began by saying it represented "the deep commitment of the American people to the fundamental human rights affirmed more than 25 years ago by the United Nations. America then played a leading role in the drafting and the adoption of the Universal Declaration of Human Rights," in which the right of free emigration was "central."[87] He cited the UDHR's Article 13 as the main source of inspiration for the legislation. When it passed the House in September 1973, Jackson called the vote "a most welcome affirmation of the commitment of this country to the cause of human rights." When he was finally able to claim victory in October 1974, the senator boasted, "We have reached what I think is an historic understanding in the area of human rights."[88]

In a September 1973 *New York Times* editorial, Jackson called for "human détente." First drawing parallels between the Soviet Union and Nazi Germany, he argued that the lesson of both was that "a regime that denies the rights of man can never be reconciled to membership in the community of nations." Genuine détente could not occur without increasing individual liberty in communist states. Peace was at stake, Jackson claimed. The most "fundamental" of all human rights, "first among equals," was expressed in the UDHR's Article 13: the right to free emigration. It was the most fundamental, he explained, because whatever other civil liberties might be denied, they could all be restored by emigration "to the free countries of the West." The United States must not make concessions in the name of détente without attaching conditions to "promote human rights in the Soviet Union." Reprising these themes in a speech in October, he declared that he believed in the UDHR and that it was time to begin to implement it. "A true peace, an enduring peace, can only be built on a moral consensus. What better place to begin building this consensus than on the principles embodied in the Universal Declaration of Human Rights, among which the right to choose the country one lives in—the right to emigrate freely—is perhaps the most basic."[89]

Appeals to human rights, initially not ubiquitous among supporters of the amendment, soon became more prominent. In September 1972 Javits had argued that "the Charter of the Human Rights of the United Nations [sic] to which the Soviet Union is a party" gave the United States an interest in Soviet internal affairs such as Jewish emigration.[90] Hubert Humphrey called the exit tax a "violation of human rights" and cited the UDHR's provision on emigration rights.[91] Yet Senator Abraham Ribicoff, a Democrat from Connecticut and one of Jackson's key cosponsors, initially made his case in purely moral terms, decrying the "outrageous," "barbaric," and "heinous" behavior of the Soviets, their violations of "norms of civilized behavior," and the preponderance of "amorality in international relations," without ever mentioning human rights or international law.[92]

By 1973 references to the UDHR had become a standard part of the repertoire of arguments in favor of the amendment. Liberals like Robert Drinan, a Jesuit priest elected to the House from Massachusetts and a strong supporter of the Soviet Jewish cause, cited "basic human rights and freedoms" and the UDHR in public appeals.[93] In June 1973, when Jackson attacked détente in a high-profile speech, the press highlighted Jackson's use of human rights claims. The *New York Times* quoted Jackson's demands that détente not be "a formula between governments for capitulation on the issue of human rights" and that trade concessions be made only with conditions "to promote human rights in the Soviet Union."[94]

Jackson's amendment had merely been a warning shot in 1972, when it had been introduced without a realistic vehicle or timeline for passage. Although the Soviets dropped the exit tax in early 1973 and raised emigration levels to unprecedented heights in the hope of placating Congress, Jackson was not mollified. By spring 1973, his reintroduced amendment had an astonishing 75 cosponsors in the Senate and 272 in the House.[95] Backers ranged across the political spectrum, from liberal Democrats such as Kennedy and McGovern to conservative Republicans such as Barry Goldwater and John Tower. Buttressed by heavy lobbying from Jewish groups and organized labor, the amendment seemed unstoppable. Members of Congress from districts with sizable Jewish constituencies or those who were staunch anticommunists were the first to fall behind the measure. New Soviet repression directed against Sakharov and Solzhenitsyn in late 1973 and early 1974 helped bring in other organizations, including Americans for Democratic Action, the Federation for American Scientists, the American Psychiatric Association, and various church groups.[96] Congressional liberals often felt caught in a bind, supporting the amendment even while harboring deep misgivings about its potential effects on détente.[97]

Throughout 1973 and 1974, Jackson engaged in a diplomatic dance, with Kissinger forced to act as a reluctant intermediary between the Senator and the Soviets in an effort to salvage a deal acceptable to both sides. Incensed at what he saw as unwarranted congressional interference that undermined the national interest, Kissinger warned that the Jackson-Vanik amendment would produce a "tragedy" by derailing détente. Private diplomacy was more effective than public pressure, the secretary of state argued, claiming that he had already quietly wrung significant concessions from the Soviets. He growled privately about the hypocrisy of activism on behalf of Soviet Jews when more serious humanitarian issues were ignored. Though atrocities in Bangladesh had provoked Congress into barring aid to Pakistan earlier in the year, Kissinger told a columnist after Jackson first introduced his amendment in 1972, "I don't see, for example, that anyone is putting in amendments for the B[i]haris and Bangladesh[is] who we know have been slaughtered," referring to mass killings in the newly formed Bangladesh that were sparking charges of genocide.[98] At his confirmation hearings, Kissinger denounced the amendment as an attempt to "transform the domestic structure" of the Soviet Union that could lead to the U.S. being "massively involved in every country in the world." (In response to such charges, Perle effectively renounced any interest in pressing other human rights issues in the Soviet Union, saying, "We don't want to go into the Soviet Union and tell them how to treat the people that remain—we just want people to be allowed to come out.")[99]

The esteemed Soviet expert George Kennan agreed with Kissinger's position, calling the fawning Western press coverage of Sakharov and Solzhenitsyn "a hysteria." Kennan said many of "the most important other Russian intellectuals have turned against them," and went on to claim that they had "provoked" many of the repressive measures they were now complaining about. Restating Kissinger's own position, he said it was wrong "for a great government such as ours to try to adjust its foreign policy in order to work internal changes in another country. . . . We can't sacrifice the whole relationship for these people."[100]

As the House prepared to vote on the amendment in September 1973, Sakharov threw his support publicly behind it. Despite suffering increased harassment from Soviet authorities, the renowned physicist wrote a forceful open letter to Congress, urging that body to "realize its historical responsibility before mankind" and warning that "capitulation" would be "highly perilous." He described the amendment's provisions as "minimal" and as "a defense of international law" necessary to ground détente in "democratic principles." The letter, which appeared as a full-page advertisement in the *Washington Post* a few days later, powerfully linked Jackson's cause to the dissident struggle for human rights.[101] Jackson, too, continued to link the specific issue of Soviet Jewish emigration to larger themes of human rights. Talking to reporters, Jackson explained that he was not trying to influence domestic policy in the Soviet Union but merely trying "to guarantee human freedom" by asking the Soviet Union to follow "the Universal Doctrine [sic] of Human Rights adopted by the United Nations." People around the world should protest as a means of forcing the Soviet government to respect the civil rights of individuals, he said.[102]

Despite Jackson's use of human rights language in the case of Soviet Jews, when it came to other cases, the senator reverted to more traditional concepts of liberty and democracy. Jackson's use of human rights terminology did not extend beyond the Soviet Union. In supporting congressional efforts to cut off military aid to the dictatorship in Greece in the years 1971–1973, for example, Jackson cited more general notions of freedom. In June 1973 he explained that he opposed aid to the military dictatorship because it was not fulfilling its NATO commitment to "the principles of democracy, individual liberty and the rule of law" and instead had "abrogated the liberties of [its] citizens" and resorted to "brutality" to maintain its rule. He advocated steps to nudge Greece back toward "individual liberty and democratic procedures." Yet his core concern was not the welfare of Greek citizens but Greece's contribution to NATO and the effects of the junta's role on the erosion of the Greek military's fighting capacity—particularly in the wake of an incident in which a Greek destroyer had sought to defect.[103] Human rights, for Jackson, meant the liberties abrogated by the Soviet Union and its allies, not the abuses committed by anticommunist governments.

The Jackson-Vanik amendment remained a troublesome issue throughout the 1970s—and indeed for nearly four decades until its repeal in 2012. During negotiations in 1973 and 1974, Jackson insisted on wringing from the Soviets a commitment to a specific number of emigrants. He then outraged the Kremlin by publicly flaunting Soviet concessions, and Brezhnev, bristling at the appearance that American Jews were dictating Soviet policy, dropped the trade agreement entirely. The effectiveness of the amendment, passed in modified form at the end of 1974, is debatable. Before it passed, the Soviets made significant concessions and raised emigration levels, but after its passage a Soviet backlash stemmed the outflow of Soviet Jews for years. Not until the Soviets were looking for support for SALT II in 1979 did emigration levels rise again to the heights they had reached in 1973.[104]

The liberal Democrats who had vigorously opposed Jackson on the Vietnam War joined in support of Jackson-Vanik. They sympathized with Soviet dissidents. Fraser, for example, always kept one eye on violations of rights in the Soviet Union. Yet the cause of human rights in the Soviet Union pulled liberals in two directions, for they also strongly supported improved U.S.-Soviet ties, reduced tensions, and the broad aims of détente. They knew that at the most basic level, their aims diverged from those of hardliners like Jackson who sought to derail détente.

Jackson's anti-Soviet human rights campaign was similar in many key respects to the ones liberals would wage against right-wing dictatorships. Both used the annual foreign aid appropriations bill as a core target of amendments. (Before attaching his amendment to the trade bill, Jackson had first attached it to the foreign assistance act.) Both often drew on the Holocaust-derived lesson that silence meant complicity. Introducing his amendment, for example, Jackson likened the exit tax to conditions under Nazi Germany, "when Himmler sold exit permits for Jews. . . . We are aware of the Holocaust. We see the parallel. And that is why we must do whatever we can to prevent a repetition of that horrible catastrophe." Both groups argued that trade and aid should not be used merely for strategic purposes but entailed an American responsibility to ensure some basic moral standards in recipient countries. If it were not enough that American principles were at stake, Jackson said, the American financial stake in MFN status also justified intervention. Participation in American credit and investment programs must be reserved, Jackson concluded, for "those countries who accord their citizens the fundamental human right to emigrate."[105] Both groups argued that international law and growing interdependence brought internal affairs into the legitimate purview of the world community. Jackson, for example, quoted Solzhenitsyn's Nobel lecture appeal to make "internal" affairs everyone's business. Both were clearly motivated by a feeling that the executive branch was wielding too much unfettered power in foreign affairs. And both groups portrayed their stance as a return to American tradition.

Ultimately, however, the aims of the two groups were incompatible, involving as they did irreconcilable visions of the nature of the world and American foreign policy priorities. They diverged crucially on the question of guilt, and it was McGovern's rhetoric of guilt, perhaps as much as any other single factor, that drove Jackson to the corner of the party, where he and like-minded Democrats nursed the sense of grievance that fed neoconservatism. For a brief moment in 1976, it would seem that human rights offered a way to bring both wings of the Democratic Party back together. But the apparently unifying rubric concealed the fact that as long as the Soviet Union existed, liberal and neoconservative visions of human rights were fundamentally at odds.

## CHAPTER 6

# A New Calculus Emerges

I N 1973 THE American war in Vietnam finally came to an end. At midday on January 23, National Security Adviser Henry Kissinger and his North Vietnamese negotiating partner, Le Duc Tho, emerged from the Hotel Majestic in Paris with glowing smiles. They had concluded a years-long series of negotiations by initialing a peace accord, and hours later a jubilant President Nixon announced that U.S. involvement in the fighting was over. The nation greeted the long hoped-for news with an overwhelming sense of relief. It was "the end of a nightmare," the *New York Times* exuded, "the lifting of a staggering burden from the nation's resources, energies and conscience." The editors expressed the views of many when they hailed the agreement as "a diplomatic triumph," even while conceding that it probably would not bring genuine peace to South Vietnam and that its terms probably could have been achieved years earlier.[1]

The fighting and killing were over, at least for Americans, but the passions and the debates that the war had aroused would be redirected rather than quenched. While the war continued it had acted as a container, bottling up energies within certain parameters. With the war over, emotions spilled into new areas, casting old questions in fresh light and creating novel possibilities for action. Slowly, as a process of accumulation rather than epiphany, human rights became one of those possibilities.

The year the war ended was a liminal moment for human rights. The Jackson wing of the Democratic Party, along with liberal allies in both parties, had just months earlier harnessed the language of universal human rights to the cause of Soviet Jews. The publicity devoted to Jackson's efforts was alone responsible for a significant shift in the ways human rights were understood in the United States, marking the onset of a shift away from domestic concerns and toward a preoccupation with international problems. The conservative conception of human rights remained predominant in 1973, as illustrated in the September confirmation hearings of Henry Kissinger for the post of secretary of state.[2] Although Kissinger's neglect of human rights would soon become a monotonic refrain in a liberal chorus of criticism, in 1973 liberals condemned Kissinger not for ignoring human rights but for bypassing and deceiving Congress and the public. The few critics who faulted him on human rights issues were primarily concerned with Soviet Jews. Yet by midyear, as part of a convulsive effort in Congress to shed U.S. involvement in Indochina once and for all, liberals on Capitol Hill also reached for human rights as a legitimizing rubric for their causes, above all torture and political imprisonment. They began to write human rights legislation and hold general hearings on human rights. Jackson, having been the first to attach human rights to a foreign policy issue of national importance, continued to play a key role in defining its meaning for the American public, but a competing liberal vision of human rights promotion slowly gained ground.

In September 1973, just a few weeks after Don Fraser's obscure subcommittee began holding hearings on the protection of human rights at the UN and in U.S. foreign policy, the Minnesota congressman testified to the Senate Foreign Relations Committee as it considered Kissinger's confirmation. Strangely, despite presiding at the same time over hearings on precisely that topic, human rights seemed not to be on Fraser's mind as he commented on the nominee's qualifications. Offering "grave reservations" rather than outright opposition, Fraser cited "the democratic conduct of foreign relations" as the key area in which Kissinger needed to improve. The bombing of Cambodia, incursions into Laos, the unofficially acknowledged "tilt" toward Pakistan in the Indo-Pakistani War of 1971, and Kissinger's role in wiretapping his own staff showed a pattern of "official deception and contempt for congressional authority," Fraser said. In his usual tempered tone, he lamented that Congress had to rely on the press to find out what the government was doing in foreign affairs. He criticized Kissinger's neglect of Japan and overemphasis on relations with the Soviet Union and China. He mentioned "a growing number of world problems, such as environmental decay, disarmament, and the law of sea" that required multilateral diplomacy, and found time to ridicule the administration's "childish" failure to send an ambassador to Sweden in retaliation for Swedish criticism of the bombing of North Vietnam. But aside from an opening reference to "ethical and constitutional principles in *executing* foreign policy" (emphasis added), he said not a word about human rights as a general principle.[3]

At first glance, this omission appears inexplicable. Fraser was that very week holding hearings that would make him the most vocal proponent of human rights in the House. Over the next few years, he would repeatedly decry Kissinger's seeming indifference toward human rights violations by U.S. allies. If liberals would so soon be apoplectic about Kissinger's disdain for morality in foreign policy, why did this human rights enthusiast fail to critique Kissinger's human rights record at this important juncture?

The simple answer is that it was all about timing. Kissinger's human rights record became an issue only *after* the rise of human rights. Liberal opposition to Kissinger through 1973 centered on how the Vietnam War had been prosecuted, above all on the secret extension of the war into Cambodia. (This had been Nixon's policy, but Kissinger was rightly seen as having encouraged and abetted it.) The Vietnam War was not seen in human rights terms, and much liberal antagonism toward the Nixon administration's conduct of the war was framed in terms of its undermining of democratic processes, including failures to consult Congress and to inform the public.

In late 1973, moreover, Kissinger was still enjoying one of the most extraordinary honeymoons the American press has ever bestowed on an

American official. Kissinger's standing rose as Watergate brought much of the rest of the administration down. To paraphrase one commentator, he became a giant among pygmies and crooks.[4] By early 1974, in the wake of his Middle East shuttle diplomacy, the press was fêting the secretary of state—he was confirmed without difficulty—as "Super K" and "the world's indispensable man."[5] When Fraser testified, Kissinger was best known for a policy of détente that liberals applauded, and many of the alleged crimes that would form the basis for denunciations of Kissinger as a war criminal remained in the future, including sanctioning the 1975 Indonesian invasion of East Timor, fueling Angola's civil war in 1975–1976, and coddling Argentina's brutal military dictatorship in 1976. Just a few days before Fraser's testimony, General Augusto Pinochet Ugarte swept to power in a military coup in Chile, but it would be months before suggestions of U.S. involvement in undermining Chile's democratically elected government washed up at Kissinger's feet and still longer before the Ford administration's tight embrace of Pinochet became a scandal. Above all, what Fraser's prepared statement highlights is the extent to which the developing confrontation with Kissinger over human rights was as much about the role of Congress in foreign affairs as it was about the appropriate direction of American foreign policy.

The testimony of others who spoke against Kissinger's nomination reflected the peripheral status of human rights as a foreign policy issue in the year the Vietnam War ended. To the extent the concept had traction, it was in its anticommunist version. The language of human rights was not invoked by most of the witnesses who testified against the nomination, and it was used centrally by none. Kissinger's enemies on the far right opposed the nomination on the grounds that he was too accommodating to communist powers. Opponents on the left raised Kissinger's complicity in the brutalities of the Vietnam War, but grounded their opposition on his practice of deceit and exclusion of Congress, and on the diminution of U.S. prestige his policies produced. Some speakers cited specific issues that would later be grouped under the rubric of human rights, such as trade with Rhodesia, Soviet treatment of Jews, and South Vietnamese political prisoners, depending on their group's particular aims and interests, but these were construed as individual failures to promote America's best interests, not as lapses linked to over-arching human rights principles.

Bronson Clark, representing the American Friends Service Committee, summarized Kissinger's record as "a foreign and military policy with a shocking history of war and deceit." He criticized the administration's prosecution of the Vietnam War for uprooting and bombing civilians, torturing and murdering prisoners, and violating the Hague and Geneva Conventions and the principles established at the postwar Nuremberg trials. He noted that under the Phoenix program the CIA had been responsible for imprisoning twenty-nine thousand South Vietnamese and killing twenty thousand, lamented that the program was continuing even after the U.S. withdrawal, and cited the notorious tiger cages and the thousands of political opponents held in South Vietnamese jails. Yet his summation laid the blame on problems in the domestic arena. He called for an American foreign policy of which "we shall be proud, proud before each other, our children and the world family," one developed by open debate in public and in Congress, without lies, without undermining civil liberties with wiretaps and surveillance, rather than policy developed "in secrecy and by illegal and unconstitutional means."[6] Even while accusing the Nixon administration of crimes under international law, in Clark's presentation, as in Fraser's, the core issue was the exercise of power at home.

Only on the fringes did critics see morality in foreign policy as a central issue. Representing the Lawyers Committee on American Policy Toward Vietnam, a group formed in opposition to the war in 1965, Joseph Crown raised similar complaints about the prosecution of the war and about the administration's continued indifference to the "human rights" of tens of thousands of political prisoners in South Vietnam. The United States "cries out for moral leadership," Clark said, urging a return to "morality and honesty and decency in our foreign policy."[7] Ernest Gruening, who had opposed the war in the Senate from its inception, spoke movingly of the human costs of the war and called for a foreign policy that reflected "a new decency, a new humanity, a new honesty, a new respect for the Constitution, and regard for the opinion of mankind."[8]

When senators questioned the nominee, concerns about Kissinger's wiretapping of his staff and his secretive methods predominated, with human rights raised as an afterthought. In the context of recent reports of increased repression against Solzhenitsyn, Sakharov, and other dissidents, and just after Jackson had published his ringing call for "human detente," human rights was above all linked to the question of relations with the Soviet Union.[9] When the topic was raised, Kissinger's responses consistently presented an unvarnished Realpolitik perspective that exaggerated the risks of becoming "massively involved" in the internal affairs of foreign countries. Reducing the dangers of nuclear war was the greatest moral goal, he insisted.[10] When Republican Carl Curtis, noting Soviet repression of dissidents such as Andrei Sakharov and Aleksandr Solzhenitysn, asked how Kissinger would ensure that détente was not used to further the suppression of liberties, for example, Kissinger answered in terms of U.S. security interests.[11]

Javits, a liberal Republican and Jackson ally, made the most explicit and extensive comments about human rights. He brought up Sakharov's support of the Jackson amendment and expressed concern about the USSR's failure to respect "fundamental human rights" embodied in the "fundamental tenets of the United States," the European Conference on Security and Cooperation, and the "Declaration of Human Rights." Kissinger replied that though he felt "emotionally connected to Sakharov," it would be foolish to base "our entire foreign policy" on the issue of free emigration. Strikingly, Javits then linked communist violations with right-wing repression. Citing Rhodesia, Spain, Greece, Portugal, Angola, Mozambique, and South Africa, he asked, "Can you now synthesize . . . some basic principle by which American policy ought to be guided in respect of human rights [alongside security interests]?" With an insouciance that seems shocking in retrospect, Kissinger responded by suggesting that only something as "repugnant to human morality" as Nazi extermination camps should lead to a reduction in the level of cooperation the United States extended to a country. Again and again, he cited the imperative of reducing the risk of nuclear war as the highest aim of U.S. foreign policy.[12] (In a private conversation with Nixon earlier that year, Kissinger told his boss that even Soviet gas chambers would not infringe on American interests.)[13]

Although Senator Edward Kennedy had occasionally denounced human rights abuses in Latin America, his written questions to the nominee flowed from his subcommittee's mandate over refugees and humanitarian issues such as disaster relief and were not substantially concerned with human rights. He posed a single question about the topic, simply requesting Kissinger's opinion as to whether U.S. foreign policy ought to take into account issues such as Soviet repression of dissidents and religious groups, mistreatment of political prisoners in Greece, Brazil, and South Vietnam, and massacres in Burundi. Kissinger's reply again emphasized noninterference and "liv[ing] with" all but the most "offensive" violations. "I believe it is dangerous for us to make the domestic policy of countries around the world a direct objective of American foreign policy," he said, underlining the basic position he would continue to hold for the rest of his tenure.[14]

Human rights were not yet a core element of liberal objections to Kissinger's foreign policy, but the end of the Vietnam War opened the door for action on what a significant number of congressional liberals had come see as an urgent problem: aid to right-wing dictatorships. This in turn was an issue that was first framed in an American idiom of self-government and democratic liberties and only later couched in reference to international human rights standards. In 1973 Congress passed the first of what would become a string of legislative initiatives tying foreign aid to human rights considerations: Section 32 of the 1973 Foreign Assistance Act, a watered-down version of an amendment offered by Senator James Abourezk. Studies of human rights often cite Abourezk's measure as a key starting point in the development of a congressional human rights insurgency, but almost none acknowledge that it targeted South Vietnam, and none have probed its origins.[15] The story is an important one if we are to understand why some legislators seized on the language of human rights at this time and why majorities in Congress voted to pass so much of the legislation liberals put forward. Abourezk's measure, as well as subsequent legislation that built directly on its precedent, succeeded because the end of combat activities in Vietnam opened the way for members of Congress to vent long-brewing anger at the

South Dakotan Senator James Abourezk, who set in motion liberal human rights legislation in Congress, watching a South Dakota basketball team in Havana with George McGovern in 1978. (AP)

conduct and content of U.S. foreign policy. The birth of U.S. human rights diplomacy in a cauldron of anger, frustration, guilt, and longing to *be done with Vietnam* would indelibly shape—and sharply limit—the liberal strand of human rights promotion at least through the end of the Cold War.

Five months after the Paris Peace Accords were signed, Abourezk spoke to the Senate Foreign Relations Committee about the Nixon administration's proposed aid package to South Vietnam. Still in his first term, the South Dakota Democrat had already made a name for himself as an outspoken maverick with, as one commentator put it, "a marvelous unwashed style and a howitzer laugh that he uses constantly to shoot down Senatorial pomposities."[16] He was known as one of the most liberal members of the Senate at a time when liberals were at the apex of their power on Capitol Hill. "Worse than McGovern" was the assessment of one of Nixon's advisers.[17] Like McGovern, he thought the Cold War was over and that U.S. foreign policy should move beyond obsessive anticommunism. His interest in human rights issues seems to have been sparked when activist Brady Tyson visited his office with a Brazilian who recounted tales of torture.[18] He viewed it as an outrage that U.S. economic and military assistance continued to flow to South Vietnam's repressive dictatorship. He was convinced that such aid raised the specter of the "horrible nightmare" of renewed war and renewed involvement of American troops—and flew in the face of liberal demands to stop propping up Thieu's unpopular government.[19]

In the Senate hearing room, Abourezk waved before his colleagues a 1970 *Life* magazine picture of a monk imprisoned in South Vietnam. The caption, Abourezk told the committee, read: "I am a Buddhist monk and I spoke for peace in 1966. I am here for no reason except wanting peace. I have been beaten. I have been shackled. But I still speak out for peace."[20] The unnamed monk had been encountered by the 1970 congressional delegation that had uncovered the infamous tiger cages on Con Son Island: the shallow, overcrowded underground pits where prisoners were held, shackled to the ground, with so little room for movement that their legs often atrophied and they lost the ability to walk.[21] Earlier that year the evening news programs had shown former tiger-cage prisoners moving themselves slowly along the ground by their arms, their legs entirely immobilized.[22] "It is not really proper to call them men any more," *Time* magazine commented. " 'Shapes' is a better word—grotesque sculptures of scarred flesh and gnarled limbs . . . [forced] into a permanent pretzel-like crouch. They move like crabs, skittering across the floor on buttocks and palms."[23]

The monk, whom Abourezk described as one of tens of thousands of political prisoners held by Saigon, had died in January, just weeks before the peace accords were signed. Americans, Abourezk declaimed, were "to a very great extent" responsible. "We have been deeply involved in the creation of the entire [police and prison] system, and we are still paying the bills." The United States had helped build the prisons where political prisoners were held, had funded interrogation centers where prisoners were tortured, and had propped up the repressive regime behind them. The Paris Accords required "the end of American participation in Vietnamese internal political affairs," he declared, and it was time to stop helping Thieu "squash" his political opposition.[24]

The amendment that would become Section 32 recommended cutting off military and economic assistance to any country that practiced "the internment or imprisonment of that country's citizens for political purposes," and in arguing for it, Abourezk tentatively began to draw connections in human rights terms. "As we help South Vietnam return to a period of stability and peace," he said, the United States must stop funding a South Vietnamese police system in which "thousands of innocent Vietnamese citizens . . . are still being imprisoned and tortured as political prisoners under programs which we helped initiate and continue to maintain in that country." He drew a parallel between South Vietnam's repressive policies and those in Rhodesia, Pakistan, and the communist bloc, where "we point to the cruelty of such policies as contrary to the basic rights of man and condemn the torture of these prisoners as gravely inhumane." American support of repression in South Vietnam had to stop, he said.[25] In a lengthy address to Congress in October pressing for a stronger version of his amendment, he said American support for repression in South Vietnam, Brazil, Greece, and Indonesia had detracted from "basic human rights" and "clings like a filthy stench on the American people," who "share in the guilt and horror."[26] It was McGovernite guilt, with the addition of human rights.

The measure may have come directly from the antiwar movement (its precise origins are unclear); certainly, the antiwar movement backed it strongly. With the withdrawal of American ground troops, the antiwar movement lost its raison d'être—almost. The energies that had been harnessed to the urgent goal of ending the war diffused into an array of causes ranging from environmentalism to corporate responsibility. But a significant remnant continued to fight for a complete end to U.S. assistance to Thieu. Some were pro–National Liberation Front radicals who wanted a North Vietnamese victory; others were simply appalled by Thieu's repression and wanted to leave the Vietnamese to sort out their own future. Ending aid to Thieu was a key priority. The old divisions flowed seamlessly into the postwar period, as the American Conservative Union, Young Americans for Freedom, and the Young Republicans tried to rally support for continued economic and military aid to Thieu, while the NCC and Jane Fonda and Tom Hayden lobbied Congress to cut funding.[27]

Bringing public attention to prison conditions and political prisoners under Thieu's regime was a focal point of the strategy. As one activist recalled, the issue had obvious emotional resonance: "We recognized that this would be a tender issue for American political liberals, to lift up the cause of people who are *just like us*—religious people, humanists, artists—liberals. They were being imprisoned for doing the things that we do—for signing petitions, going to rallies, for associating with other people. For having children who do things. And they are held upside down and water is forced up their nostrils, they are held in tiger cages."[28] Allegations that a U.S. firm had built new tiger cages after the 1970 scandal caused further outrage. Throughout the summer of 1974, a range of peace organizations worked together to stage tiger cage vigils on Capitol Hill and in major cities across the country, building cardboard replicas of tiger cages and handing out leaflets claiming the Thieu regime held two hundred thousand political prisoners.[29] Allegations of torture and other forms of mistreatment were central to the indictment of Thieu's regime. Amnesty International's 1973 *Report on Torture*, for example, included a section on what it claimed were one hundred thousand civilians imprisoned by Saigon. "In revolting detail," liberal columnist Anthony Lewis commented in the *New York Times*, the report detailed "what is done to human beings" in South Vietnamese prisons: "the use of electricity, beating, water; the crippling and death that result."[30]

The peace agreement required Saigon to release civilian political prisoners, something it refused to do. (It refused to acknowledge that it *had* civilian political prisoners.) It was thus possible for antiwar activists to frame the question of prisoners as one of upholding the peace agreement and as an issue fundamental to securing genuine peace. But in all other ways, the issue was not new. Though the tiger cages had received a burst of publicity when uncovered in 1970, reports of them had been around since the early 1960s. The widespread use of torture, the harsh conditions of imprisonment, the frequent arrests of suspected subversives on the basis of unreliable denunciations, their indefinite detention without trial, and Thieu's intolerance of dissent were all widely known and publicly aired, for example in discussions of the Phoenix program in the early 1970s.

Why these issues became so prominent in Congress in 1973 thus deserves explanation, for it could at any time earlier have reduced aid to South Vietnamese prisons or pressed for the release of political prisoners. The traction these issues gained after the peace accords reflected fatigue with the whole "Vietnam mess" and frustration at having been shut out of foreign policy making for so long. Congress was in a mood to "do something, anything," and more specifically to get out of Vietnam for good, and the dark underside of Thieu's regime, most graphically exposed in the torture and mistreatment of prisoners, offered a means to both goals.

Political prisoners were not, of course, the only congressional concern in Indochina. The Abourezk amendment came as part of a broader congressional assault on the executive's power to subsidize Thieu and continue limited combat operations in Indochina. Continued bombing in Cambodia provoked Congress into a series of headline-making votes that resulted in a compromise setting an August 15 deadline for the cessation of Cambodian operations. Later that year, overriding Nixon's veto, Congress tried to reclaim its constitutional prerogative to declare war by passing the War Powers Act. In the foreign aid bill, Congress set a ceiling on military assistance to South Vietnam and Laos, slashing $285 million off the figure the administration had requested. In 1974, as fighting in the region escalated, Congress cut both economic and military aid levels far below the administration's request, added further restrictions, and put specific country-by-country ceilings in place. In 1975, in the final months of the war, Congress refused Ford's urgent pleas for additional military aid that, the president said, was the only way to save Saigon from communism. After Saigon fell in April, funding debates shifted to refugee and humanitarian assistance.[31] Throughout the period 1973–1975, even as most of the rest of the country turned weary eyes away from the region, Indochina remained a key arena for the tug-of-war between Congress and the executive.

Abourezk's proposal also drew on more general congressional frustration with the foreign aid program. By the early 1970s foreign aid was on shaky ground: liberals criticized it for buttressing oppressive regimes without helping their poorest citizens while conservatives condemned it as a giveaway, and both sides cited American economic woes as cause for rethinking the multibillion-dollar program.[32] Twice in the early 1970s, in unprecedented moves, the Senate had defeated foreign aid authorization bills. One reason liberal human rights initiatives were successfully attached to foreign aid bills in the mid-1970s is that archconservatives like Jesse Helms and Strom Thurmond were willing to support any measure that might have the effect of lowering aid expenditures.[33] Moreover, because it was one of the few bills that required annual authorization (and hence was sure to come around every year), foreign aid had become a lightning rod for all sorts of initiatives, with so many amendments attached to each one that the bills were likened to Christmas trees festooned with paper decorations.[34] Changes in 1973 to restructure foreign aid away from large-scale capital projects such as dams and toward meeting "basic needs" though technical assistance, food transfers, population planning, health care, education for the poor, and industrial goods, which had been pushed by Fraser and others for years, were only partly successful in regenerating support for foreign aid.[35]

Anger at the Nixon administration's repeated deceptions of Congress— a theme in most discussions in Congress in these years—fueled Abourezk's concern with South Vietnamese prisoners. Citing numerous ways that the administration's aid proposal hid police and prison aid under more neutral categories—the Department of Navy, for example, had authorized an American construction firm to spend $400,000 on new isolation cells on Con Son Island from funds generated through the "food for peace" program—Abourezk declared, "The basic point I would like to make is that we in Congress have been the victims of a monumental pile of contradictions, denials, and obfuscations regarding the public safety program in Vietnam—and no doubt public safety programs elsewhere."[36] It was as a follow-up to a comment about Nixon's habit of secrecy that the senator told the press, "Maybe the American people don't have to know about troop movements or the location of nuclear weapons, but by God they sure as hell can decide whether they want to support torture or not."[37]

Along with another Abourezk measure banning aid for foreign police training, the South Dakotan's proposal to ban aid to countries with political prisoners made it through the foreign aid authorization process without attracting much attention, either in Congress or in the media.[38] It certainly was not hailed at the time—as it has been since—as the first general human rights legislation to pass Congress. The Senate Foreign Relations Committee incorporated the measure into the foreign aid bill partly in recognition of the wide resonance the issue of Saigon's political prisoners had generated. A flurry of articles and editorials appeared, like the hard-hitting *New York Times* editorial by activist Fred Branfman that reminded readers of the Phoenix program's assassinations and U.S. responsibility for building prisons in South Vietnam and "suppl[ying] the generators used for torture by electric shock."[39] Prominent members of Congress, such as Senator Kennedy, spoke out forcefully against funding Saigon's police system; in September, hearings in a House sub-committee specifically on Saigon's treatment of political prisoners gave further airing to the charges of brutality and torture.[40]

No one in Congress was willing to defend political imprisonment. As Amnesty International had already demonstrated, it served as a kind of lowest common denominator: people of all political persuasions could oppose it as a minimal aim. Yet Section 32 was also so weak as to be patently toothless. It was worded as a "sense of the Congress" statement rather than as a binding legal requirement, and its lack of a definition of "political prisoner" left the door open to semantic stonewalling. Both Saigon and the U.S. embassy maintained with straight faces that according to their definition the regime held no political prisoners. Abourezk had undertaken his fight in the naïve faith that it would work— that "it would frighten those governments into stopping torture and imprisonment. I am sure," he said, "they are not going to give up this sizable fortune from the U.S. taxpayers in order to keep torturing their people." His optimism notwithstanding, Section 32's effects on funding to South Vietnam were nil.[41] Its effects in fueling a congressional insurgency on human rights would be considerably greater.


For Don Fraser, Section 32 was a beacon. He had long sought to limit U.S. aid to repressive dictatorships, a project that until that point had proven fruitless and demoralizing. Abourezk's amendment showed that such measures could now succeed. In 1974 Fraser would build explicitly on Abourezk's measure in drafting and securing passage of an amendment that broadened Abourezk's focus on political prisoners to encompass human rights considerations more generally. This 1974 measure, partly a product of the opening provided by Abourezk, was also an outgrowth of Fraser's decision in 1973 to undertake a more general examination of the UN human rights system, which would lead him to develop a greater interest in the UN human rights framework than anyone in Congress had yet taken.

The Fraser subcommittee hearings of late 1973 are often regarded as the moment when a movement for international human rights in the United States began to take off. The hearings would provide the blueprint for much of the congressional human rights efforts of the next few years, and in many ways provided the basic template for the Carter administration's foreign policy. They were the first to pull together diverse international problems under the heading of international protection of human rights, and the resulting report was largely responsible for key organizational changes in the State Department, which in turn made human rights diplomacy a constituent element of U.S. foreign policy. It is thus worth examining in some detail how and why these hearings came to be.

Fraser's realization of the potential of human rights was part happenstance, made possible by broader changes in Congress and the particular conditions of his committee assignments. It was also, of course, a product of his personal interests and proclivities, which had manifested themselves in 1966 in his Title IX mandate for political development through community building. The experience of the Vietnam War shifted his thinking away from such ambitious, hands-on efforts to reshape foreign societies, toward the more modest goal of moral dissociation from repressive regimes, even if such dissociation did not change those regimes.

The early 1970s were a time of fundamental restructuring of the power relations in Congress, a restructuring that would create the conditions that enabled the human rights revolution. The House Foreign Relations Committee in these years was headed by the docile Pennsylvania Democrat Thomas "Doc" Morgan, who had little interest in challenging executive dominance of foreign policy and saw his committee's primary role as shepherding the annual foreign aid bill through the House.[42] Had he maintained his traditional prerogatives as committee chairman, human rights would have made little headway.

Instead, however, congressional reforms implemented in the early 1970s offered upstarts like Fraser scope for a greatly expanded role. In 1971 liberal Democrats pushed through new rules requiring that each member head no more than one subcommittee. The reform process also vastly increased staff sizes in congressional offices, for the first time allowing Congress a significant degree of independence in gathering information and formulating foreign policy. Whereas before foreign policy legislation had been worked out quietly in negotiations between key committee chairmen and the executive branch, the reforms gave greater powers to subcommittees, to which legislation was now required to flow; by weakening the power of committees, they created an explosion of amendments offered from the floor. They also opened the process to greater media scrutiny, for example, by requiring hearings to be open to the public. The result was that each member of Congress could now gain enough staff and influence to "establish his own domain of power and prestige"—to the point where some government officials began to complain that there were 435 secretaries of state on Capitol Hill.[43] The biggest impact of these changes was felt in the House Foreign Affairs Committee, which brought in three new subcommittee chairmen, all liberal activists dedicated to raising the kind of issues that the placid committee had avoided in the past. New York Democrat Benjamin Rosenthal's stewardship of the Europe subcommittee, for example, was directly responsible for the House's startling 1971 vote to cut off military aid to the Greek junta, and Rosenthal would become closely associated with Fraser's international human rights efforts.[44]

Fraser ascended to the chairmanship of the Foreign Affairs Committee's Subcommittee on International Organizations and Movements and, buoyed by the new conditions in Congress, would build it into a highly influential platform.[45] When he took over, it was an obscure subcommittee with jurisdiction over issues guaranteed to attract little, if any, public attention. In the previous decade, the subcommittee had held soporific hearings on issues such as the Red Cross, ocean resources, commemorating the UN's twenty-fifth anniversary, and encouraging private participation in international activities.[46] The UN was the "international organization" that the subcommittee saw as its prime interest. Like most of his colleagues on Capitol Hill, Fraser was a lawyer, and his long-standing interest in international law as the basis for world order drew him to a subcommittee whose main jurisdiction was UN affairs, but it could hardly have seemed a promising vehicle for an ambitious politician.[47] Yet within a few years, its hearings would be filled with headline-generating topics like torture and mass murder and its activities would routinely intrude on U.S. relations with key allies.

Fraser stumbled onto the formula for headlines and influence almost inadvertently. Ever the energetic and hardworking investigator, he quickly doubled the number of hearings held, but his initial agenda remained in keeping with the subcommittee's mandate to cover international organizations, especially the UN.[48] In his first two years, he stuck primarily to issues relating to the UN, looking at the Law of the Sea, the UN Environment Program, and a World Food Resolution, but giving particular attention to the efficacy of UN sanctions in the case of southern Rhodesia.[49] Although the United States had initially joined the UN boycott of the white supremacist regime in the former British colony, American conservatives argued that Rhodesian chrome—the only significant U.S. import from Rhodesia—was too strategically significant to be part of a boycott. Played up as a Cold War issue by the right, who claimed UN sanctions were leading the United States into dangerous dependence on chrome from communist countries, Congress effectively rescinded U.S. participation in sanctions in 1971. Although Fraser tried for years to restore sanctions, it was not until 1976 that the United States again came into compliance with its international treaty obligations.[50]

Not until two years into his tenure did Fraser consider human rights as a general topic for his subcommittee. Looking toward future priorities in 1973, staffer Robert Boettcher provided his boss with a list of a dozen possible subcommittee activities that centered on the UN, including such rousing topics as UN finances, UN environmental protection, UN peacekeeping, cooperation with the Senate on UN affairs, and visits to the UN. Near-last on Boettcher's list was "International Civil Liberties." It was, Boettcher suggested to Fraser, "a topic in which you have expressed a continuing interest," and he proposed holding hearings to look at "international institutions for guaranteeing civil liberties" as well as specific cases such as Greece, Spain, and the USSR.[51] Fraser's long-standing interest in political development in the Third World, his interest in torture and denial of civil liberties in Greece, and his new role as monitor of the UN thus coalesced to push him in a novel direction. His subcommittee had provided an entrée into the world of the UN, and his prior interests ensured that this new mandate would bring the UN's human rights structures squarely into view. He may also have been influenced by a 1972 *Christian Science Monitor* article by AI USA's Mark Benenson, which proposed many of the reforms Fraser's hearings would champion.[52] Fraser soon decided to make human rights at the UN one of his subcommittee's priorities.

A new staffer would also prove important in shaping the tone and direction of the subcommittee's new interest. Looking for help to prepare for the human rights hearings, Fraser hired John Salzberg, a young human rights expert at the UN with a Ph.D. in political science. He had written his dissertation at New York University on the UN's Subcommission on the Prevention of Discrimination and Protection of Minorities.[53] His dissertation adviser, Thomas Hovet, was the ACLU's representative to the UN, and when Hovet moved to Oregon, Salzberg succeeded him in that (purely voluntary) position. When Fraser hired him, he was working for the American Association of the International Commission of Jurists, pushing for ratification of the Genocide Convention.[54] The young Quaker came to Fraser's attention when he sent Fraser a copy of a letter to the editor he had penned about "gross violation of human rights" in East Pakistan during the Indo-Pakistani War, a topic Salzberg knew Fraser had spoken about publicly. Salzberg's letter had called for improving the UN's capacity to investigate serious human rights violations—precisely the point of Fraser's eventual hearings.[55] Salzberg's experience with the UN system provided his primary qualification for the job, and it was through Salzberg's deep knowledge of the UN human rights system that Fraser developed his own familiarity with it.

In announcing the hearings, Fraser flagged what he saw as the most pressing human rights issues. "We will examine the UN and U.S. responses to human massacres, to torture and political oppression, to racial discrimination."[56] Though the hearings took up human rights in the Soviet Union, most of the countries chosen were the focus of liberal concerns: racial discrimination in southern Africa, torture and suppression of civil liberties in Greece, Brazil, and Northern Ireland, and genocidal killings in Nigeria's Biafra region and in Burundi. Unlike Jackson, who was most exercised about the denial of freedoms found under communism, Fraser believed the problems that mattered most for U.S. foreign policy were those that it had the greatest capacity to influence: abuses committed by allies.[57] The prioritizing of certain abuses above others was explicit: torture, apartheid, and mass killings were most deserving of international attention and action. Fraser explained that human rights provided a new way of measuring behavior that could "replace" the Cold War's ideological framework by establishing "a rather standard set of ideas in terms of how they treat their own people" to be applied to regimes on both the right and the left.[58]

The hearings provided an education for many, not least Fraser himself. He later recalled that his knowledge of the UN human rights system was "very modest" before the hearings began and that chairing them "helped clarify my views."[59] Fraser's early question to his first witness, International Commission of Jurists head Niall MacDermot, reflected his still tentative command of the concept that he was raising to prominence. What were human rights, the chairman asked, and how were they different from civil and political rights? MacDermot explained that the UDHR was the basic statement of what was meant by "human rights," though he noted that his own group worked primarily for the civil and political rights codified in the declaration.[60]

Though sometimes mischaracterized as hearings on human rights in U.S. foreign policy, the hearings were about protection of human rights at the UN and, secondarily, about how the United States could both strengthen the UN human rights system and give greater weight to human rights in its own policy-making. Thus the title of the hearings was "International Protection of Human Rights," not protection of international human rights, and the subtitle was "The Work of International Organizations and the Role of U.S. Foreign Policy."[61] The hearings were very much in keeping with the subcommittee's general orientation toward the UN, and U.S. foreign policy was included in part because it would have been hypocritical to critique UN human rights activities without acknowledging the role of the United States.[62] As Fraser was well aware, for example, the United States was then violating UN Security Council sanctions imposed because of racism in Rhodesia.

The hearings were a major endeavor. Conducted over fifteen days and drawing on forty-five witnesses, the testimony ran to over five hundred pages, supplemented in the published version with nearly five hundred pages of appendices. A large portion of the latter consisted of the endless resolutions the UN had been producing for decades, but much of it was a testament to rising activity by nongovernmental organizations: reports and articles by Amnesty International, the American Committee on Africa, the U.S. Catholic Conference, the National Council of Churches, and the International Commission of Jurists. Nongovernmental organization representatives, academics, international lawyers, and other representatives of what would soon constitute a "human rights lobby" considerably outnumbered the various State Department and other government officials Salzberg brought in to "balance" the numerous critics of UN and U.S. human rights policies.[63]

Despite touching on sensitive subjects, the hearings were ignored by the press. Much of the time Fraser was the only person in the room.[64] Several members of the subcommittee evinced markedly little enthusiasm for the subject. Florida Democrat Dante Fascell, for example, doubted that the United States ought to apply its own definition of morality to the rest of the world.[65] Two others would make an unusual dissent from the resulting report. It was primarily insiders to the UN system who took interest in Fraser's initial activities. The Washington area chapter of the United Nations Association, for example, declared Fraser a "distinguished contributor to human rights" for hearings that had "revitalized" the UDHR.[66] For participants, it was, as Fraser called it, a "consciousness-raising process." As Joseph Eldridge, the future head of the Washington Office on Latin America, later recalled, the hearings "got debate started. Don Fraser and John Salzberg helped me understand how U.S. policy could give articulation to international standards. . . . I really learned the limits of indignation and how to put it in a language that Washington can digest."[67]

Indicative of the still marginal status of human rights, even as Fraser was beginning to tout it as a "more sophisticated" framework for a post–Cold War foreign policy, it was some time before he realized he had hit a vein that could be mined indefinitely. It had been Fraser's intention to move on to other topics after the initial hearings, and he did. At the end of 1974, Fraser embarked on a major new project on the "great global issues" of food and energy shortages, disarmament, environmental protection, population growth, and economic development.[68] In 1974 and 1975 his subcommittee hearings were dominated by international issues other than human rights: export of nuclear technology, Middle East peacekeeping, the Law of the Sea, global food issues, and general UN issues. Salzberg, who had initially been expected to stay for about six months, continued on, organizing a few human rights hearings in 1974 on Chile, Africa, the UN, and the UN Commission on Human Rights, and then in 1975 on South Korea, Brazil, Haiti, and the Philippines. It was not until 1976, however, that Fraser turned to human rights as his top focus, holding on average more than one set of hearings per month, often jointly with regionally focused subcommittees.[69]

As Boettcher put it, human rights "far exceeded original expectations."[70] Fraser soon found himself identified as the human rights person in Congress. In early 1974 he was appointed congressional adviser to the UN Commission on Human Rights, as a result of which he spent four months in residence in New York in late 1975, and with Amnesty's Martin Ennals he helped start a splinter AI group called Association of Parliamentarians for Human Rights, positions from which his interest and expertise grew.[71] (Coincidentally, his tenure at the UN overlapped with that of Pat Moynihan, who used his UN post to broadcast a different, neoconservative vision of human rights.) The growth of his connections to and interest in the field of international human rights coincided with rising media attention to issues that were increasingly framed under that rubric. But it is worth emphasizing that Fraser's identification with human rights grew relatively slowly, and ambition probably played a role alongside personal conviction. Despite his constituency's general lack of interest in foreign affairs, identification with a high-profile issue like human rights might have seemed like a canny move for someone with senatorial ambitions.

Yet the subcommittee did not follow through on its original goal of making the UN more effective; instead Fraser shifted his attention to

U.S. relations with individual countries. As Boettcher described, it was in this area that action "seemed more likely to have a decisive effect than would the United States position on resolutions and procedures in the United Nations." Fraser's claim to jurisdiction over core elements of U.S. foreign policy, in a subcommittee devoted to international organizations, came to rest tangentially on the UN's role in defining global human rights standards.[72] (Later the subcommittee would be renamed to include human rights.)

That a small effort ballooned into such an astoundingly large one is due in part to Salzberg's skills, to Fraser's growing interest in and realization of the scope of "human rights" as a rubric for understanding the world's problems, and to a dynamic of confrontation with the executive branch.[73] Had Kissinger's State Department made a modest effort even to appear to accede to congressional initiatives on human rights, congressional interest would have sputtered out of its own accord. Instead, Kissinger took a deliberately hostile, unyielding approach, flouting Congress's wishes and, in a Watergate-fueled climate, provoking a serious congressional backlash.

Abourezk and Fraser set off a wider movement in support of congressional human rights legislation that would slowly but surely revise the State Department's conduct of foreign policy. Yet despite their tangible effects on the conduct of diplomacy, liberal congressional human rights initiatives had little resonance in public consciousness. Human rights-based legislation received minimal media attention and remained almost totally unknown outside the Beltway.

The watershed event that would grab headlines and bring liberal human rights concerns—political imprisonment and torture above all—into mainstream public consciousness was the coup in Chile. On September 11, 1973, military forces led by General Augusto Pinochet overthrew a democratically elected socialist president, Salvador Allende Gossens, in a coup accompanied by a wave of violence. Allende had awakened an extraordinary wave of sympathy around the world because he seemed to offer a third way for poor countries to move toward greater social justice and prosperity, a peaceful route to economic development dependent on neither superpower. As with Greece in 1967, reports emphasized the overthrow of democracy in a country with a history of democratic rule—and possible U.S. complicity in the coup, reports of which would eventually lead to congressional investigations. (Incontrovertible evidence that the Nixon administration had undermined Allende for years would soon be available, but the question of whether it abetted the coup itself remains open.) The military dictatorship that replaced Allende proceeded to abrogate constitutional protections, proclaim martial law, and arrest and kill political opponents in the thousands, to the horror and outrage of many observers around the world. The American press reported mass arrests and executions, and a sensationalistic piece in *Newsweek* titled "Slaughterhouse in Santiago" described a "reign of terror." Correspondent John Barnes wrote of seeing mass graves and more than a hundred bodies in a morgue, most shot at close range; the article included photographs of corpses, including one of a middle-aged amputee lying in the street.[74]

At the end of October, the Subcommittee on Inter-American Affairs, chaired by Dante Fascell, tallied the flood of correspondence it had received on Chile as it prepared to hold hearings. Of the 2,695 letters, telegrams, and petitions that had come in, only two were supportive of the junta. The rest, the majority coming from California, supported the holding of hearings, expressed "concern with human rights," and/or called for cutoffs in aid.[75] One of Fascell's constituents complained of "the savage terror now rampaging" in Chile, "*very upsetting* reports of physical torture," and European news reports that U.S. Public Safety officers or School of the Americas instructors had provided training in torture techniques. The writer warned that if Fascell remained silent in the face of such outrages, he would be as complicit as a bystander to the crimes of the Nazis.[76]

Suddenly the media and politicians were abuzz with calls to do something about repression in Chile, and "human rights" was the phrase on the tip of everyone's tongue. Speakers elbowed each other to get on the floor of Congress to express concern about U.S. support for the new regime and to call for the United States to protect human rights.[77] The *Post* headlined an editorial "Human Rights in Chile."[78] Proliferating congressional resolutions referred to human rights and pointed to UN human rights instruments as the standards to uphold. Congressman Edward Roybal's proposed resolution of October 2, for example, called on the United States to put "violations by Chile of human rights and basic freedoms, which violations contravene the United Nations Universal Declaration of Human Rights," before the UN Commission on Human Rights.[79]

Kennedy's role in framing the Chile issue as one of human rights was critical. His foreign policy adviser, Mark Schneider, was a former Peace Corps worker in Latin America who wanted to see human rights become a key component in U.S. foreign policy. (He would go on to become assistant secretary of state for Human Rights and Humanitarian Affairs under Carter.) Immediately after the Chilean coup, he urged Kennedy to use his subcommittee on refugees to hold hearings on Chile. A week after the coup, Kennedy and Fraser proposed a resolution demanding that political prisoners in Chile be treated in accordance with "international legal standards and conventions on human rights."[80] As Fraser's office explained, the change of government in Chile was a matter that should not be subject to foreign intervention, but "the protection of human rights is a legitimate interest of all persons throughout the world who believe in maintaining standards of due process under humanitarian laws."[81] On October 2, Kennedy offered an amendment to the Foreign Assistance Act calling for a cutoff of aid to Chile until its government protected "human rights." A watered-down version of the amendment made it into the act, calling on the president to urge Chile to respect human rights.[82]

In the House and Senate, hearings drew attention to the human rights effects of the coup. Kennedy's refugee subcommittee held hearings in October; Fascell's subcommittee held hearings in November; in December Fascell and Fraser teamed up for another set of hearings. The American embassy in Santiago had responded unhelpfully to the disappearance and killing of two Americans, Frank Teruggi and Charles Horman. The murder of the two Americans and the apparent indifference of U.S. officials spurred media interest in Chile, and it did not help the Nixon administration that Javits, already a voice for human rights, was a friend of Horman's father.[83]

Why was outrage over Chile couched in the language of international human rights? Fraser offered a clue when he supported a ban on aid to Pinochet's regime by linking Chile to the Jackson amendment, also then being debated in the House. Speaking of arbitrary arrests without charges, he said, "This treatment of Chilean citizens is in violation of the guarantees of international rights. It was violations of human rights which formed the foundation we accepted earlier today"—when the House had voted for the Jackson-Vanik amendment because the Soviet Union was violating its human rights obligations under international agreements. "There is much to be said for the United States speaking out about violations of human rights," Fraser continued, "but for our position to be credible, we need to do it, whether it is occurring in the Soviet Union aimed primarily at Soviet Jewish citizens, or in Chile involving Chilean citizens who are in prison."[84] Fraser's familiarity with human rights predated the Jackson amendment, but it is important that he was not significantly attracted to the concept as a general framework for foreign policy until after Jackson's success with it. Many other members of Congress had become familiarized with international human rights through Jackson's oratory. Now it was the turn of liberals to harness human rights for use against right-wing dictatorships.

A month after the coup in Chile, the Nobel Committee awarded its Peace Prize to Kissinger and Tho for ending the war in Vietnam. Séan MacBride, a founding member of Amnesty International and until recently head of the International Commission of Jurists, had lobbied the committee to award the 1973 prize to Amnesty. When the prize went to Kissinger and Tho instead, MacBride was outraged, as were many others. A South Vietnamese spokesman likened awarding Tho a peace prize to granting a chastity prize to a pimp. A former Harvard colleague said Kissinger ought to be given a "booby prize." In the Nobel Committee's home country, the ruling Labor Party voted to condemn the award after a mere five-minute debate, and there was dissent even within the normally tight-lipped committee.[85]

Kissinger's confirmation hearings and the Nobel Committee's award a month later reflect the peripheral status of international human rights in the global imagination. Kissinger may have been a controversial choice for a Nobel Peace Prize, but the controversy revolved over the peace accords, what they augured for the future of Vietnam, and what they had cost—not over his stance on morality in foreign policy, and still less on human rights as a subset of that concern. International human rights advocate Moses Moskowitz, whose 1973 book *International Concern with Human Rights* was mostly a lament that there was so little, put it well. Human rights advocacy had not "[lit] a flame of high purpose among the mass of people anywhere" nor "seize[d] the minds of men," he observed.[86]

By the end of 1973, a new wind was blowing. First Jackson had tied the language of universal human rights to a high-profile foreign policy issue. It would soon occur to liberals that the rubric Jackson was using to such great effect could be given the same high profile in their own causes. *New York Times* columnist Tom Wicker wrote in September 1973 that Americans supported the Jackson amendment because MFN trading status was in effect a subsidy, and they did not want their tax dollars subsidizing Soviet repression. That logic, he wrote, also applied to the military aid the United States sent to authoritarian regimes in Greece, South Vietnam, and the Philippines with the express purpose of helping their governments stay in power. "Can the United States logically, sensibly or ethically demand a standard of conduct by the Soviet Union that it does not demand of its own allies and client states?" Wicker asked, singling out the use of taxpayer funds to build tiger cages in South Vietnam and to support torturers elsewhere. If Congress were willing to stop sending money to allies to be used for repressive purposes, he said, "it would stand on firmer ground in its attitude toward Soviet repression."[87] Similar arguments were made in other cases.[88] By the end of the year, Congress had tried to put a stop to indirect U.S. financing of tiger cages and South Vietnamese political imprisonment and torture, and in picking up the cause of Chilean human rights, the targeting of right-wing dictatorships would quickly gain speed. The Nobel Peace Prizes immediately after 1973 reflected the rising prominence of human rights: MacBride himself won in 1974 for his years of work in the human rights field; Sakharov won in 1975; Amnesty received the award two years later. The human rights idea was on the upswing.

## CHAPTER 7

# Insurgency on Capitol Hill

I F ONE WERE to bestow a citation on the person most responsible for advancing the cause of international human rights in the mid-1970s, the list of nominees ought to begin with Henry Kissinger. He did not intend to advance human rights. He tried very hard to make human rights a nonissue in U.S. foreign policy. But intentions and outcomes rarely align in history, and despite his best efforts, Kissinger played a pivotal role in moving human rights from the sidelines to the center of American diplomacy.

At his confirmation hearings in late 1973, Kissinger had been given a pass on morality in foreign policy. He had been grilled on the legality of his wiretaps, the constitutionality of his circumventing of Congress, and the consequences of secrecy. The effects of his policies on peoples abroad, Indochina excepted, were largely ignored. But what waxes must wane, and Kissinger's towering reputation began its inevitable decline by 1975. Liberals were energized by the coup in Chile and its bloody aftermath; conservatives, by the publication of Solzhenitsyn's *The Gulag Archipelago*, which first appeared in a U.S. edition in 1974, and the author's expulsion from the Soviet Union. Both Jackson Democrats and liberals were now pressing in human rights directions. When their initiatives met with Kissinger's resolute opposition, they redoubled their efforts. Kissinger's refusal to bend turned a trickle into a torrent.

Drawing strength from the support and moral authority of dissidents like Solzhenitsyn and Sakharov, the Jackson-Vanik amendment, delayed in 1973, passed in 1974. For many Americans Solzhenitsyn and other resisters within the communist bloc remained the face of human rights. Drawn into American debates over détente, Solzhenitsyn became a vocal critic, arguing that if rapprochement were used as an excuse to overlook "acts of cruelty and even brutality," it would encourage more persecution.[1] By aligning himself on such a prominent issue with the much-fêted human rights movement in the Soviet Union, Jackson made himself America's leading advocate of international human rights. By speaking out against Jackson-Vanik and negotiating with the Kremlin on Soviet Jewish emigration only at the point of a congressional gun, Kissinger in turn became the country's leading opponent of international human rights.

Lacking Jackson's national visibility, but growing in strength, were the proponents of a liberal vision that took aim at right-wing authoritarianism: Donald Fraser, Edward Kennedy, Tom Harkin, and others in Congress. Their motives in pursuing human rights after the Vietnam War seemed to them to be simple and straightforward. They had opposed the war. They found it reprehensible that the United States had fought, and fought so brutally, to keep a repressive government in power. Most were convinced that the United States was guilty of war crimes or moral violations, but after the war they tended to avoid McGovern-style references to American guilt. Instead they spoke more obliquely of indirect responsibility. They disavowed the intention to reform or to restructure other governments, proposing instead simply to avoid strengthening the repressive apparatus in brutal dictatorships. It was a modest and relatively uncontroversial position: why should the United States equip police states that tortured thousands of their own citizens? Yet the approach had obvious limitations. It defined American responsibility in narrow terms and suggested that alleviating American responsibility for gross injustice was relatively easy: cut off aid to dictators who torture. The legislative flurry was also a kind of revenge for having been shut out of decision-making about Indochina for so many years. Its proponents were, quite simply, angry. And their measures rode to success on the strength of widespread anger and frustration on Capitol Hill about the state of executive-legislative relations.

Their small initial steps toward extending Jackson's universalist appeals to right-wing dictatorships might easily have been both temporary and barely noticed had it not been for Kissinger's counterproductive intransigence. Despite facing Democratic majorities in both houses, Kissinger went out of his way to pick a fight in 1974 and 1975. He believed human rights initiatives would hurt relations with allies, but what most spurred his opposition was resentment at congressional intrusions into foreign policy. He saw it as a matter of principle. Rather than deflecting the legislature's energies with token reductions in aid to the most offensive dictators or cosmetic changes in rhetoric, under his leadership the State Department increased aid requests to some of the countries that most offended liberal sentiment and openly flouted each new piece of legislation.

In the context of congressional assertiveness already spurred to high heat by Vietnam and the unfolding of the Watergate scandal, Kissinger's obstructionism stirred a hornet's nest. It inflamed liberal ire and triggered more activist legislation than Congress would have passed had the legislature's initial moves been met not with flagrant noncompliance but even with noncompliance couched in more subtle or respectful terms. As Robert Drinan, one of the liberals pushing for human rights legislation in Congress, later told an interviewer, human rights took off because "we in Congress were very, very annoyed at the administration." Abourezk said that "dislike of Kissinger" helped him get votes for his human rights legislation.[2] In the escalating battle, liberals tapped general congressional resentment to pass a series of human rights measures that changed the face of American diplomacy.

The history of human rights has often been written as a story of linear progress and intentional political action. The growing power of liberal human rights in Congress suggests a different narrative, one of ad hoc, reactive efforts in which the human rights idea was an almost accidental tool picked up to fight other battles. A key battle was over regaining a voice for the legislature in foreign policy; others were about restructuring foreign aid and reducing military spending and arms sales. Filling internal psychological needs was another important aim, for liberals spoke repeatedly of human rights as a way for Americans to regain confidence in their country's foreign policy. The new agenda was an outlet for moral indignation and a program for virtue without cost. Least of all was it a method to effect change in the rest of the world. The liberals who worked for human rights were well-meaning, decent people who wanted a better America and a better world. But as often as not they admitted that they had no evidence that their methods would lessen repression abroad, and they openly acknowledged that the domestic functions of human rights promotion mattered most.

It started with a whimper, not a bang, and grew by fits and starts, in unpredictable fashion. In March 1974 Fraser's subcommittee issued a little-noticed report on the hearings it had held at the end of the previous year. It declared that simple self-interest made it "morally imperative and practically necessary" to accord human rights more importance in shaping foreign policy. Such a stance would enhance U.S. moral leadership in the world, the report argued, and it would strengthen America's own security. Just as Nazi "violations of individual freedoms" had triggered the Second World War, the report suggested, similar violations in other countries could trigger new conflicts, and growing interdependence heightened the risk that such conflicts could threaten U.S. security.[3] Without ignoring human rights violations in communist countries, the report focused on prime liberal concerns: torture and political imprisonment in right-wing dictatorships. A Fraser staffer commented that the countries the subcommittee had in mind "include[d] Greece, Brazil, Chile, Spain and Portugal"—all of them U.S. allies.[4]

If international human rights seemed like the obvious choice for a post–Vietnam War foreign policy, it was lost on the press. The report's issuance was perfunctorily noted in the major papers, which that day devoted about three times the space to a different congressional subcommittee's discussion of grain reserves.[5] Reaction was favorable, but fleeting. The *Boston Globe* breathlessly declared Fraser's report "the first of its kind" since the country adopted the UDHR. An approving editorial in the *St. Louis Post-Dispatch* proposed that financial assistance to "brutal totalitarian" governments should end. Reports in the *New York Times* and the *Washington Post* foregrounded the subcommittee's emphasis on torture and right-wing allies.[6]

If it had no discernible effects on public opinion, the subcommittee's report did spur changes in the way the State Department operated. At first insignificant, they might have remained minor institutional reforms had not the gradual proliferation of congressional demands squeezed more and more tangible outcomes out of them. During his 1973 hearings, Fraser had professed to be appalled that the State Department had but one person who worked full-time on human rights issues, an officer whose major tasks involved technical matters at the United Nations. The Office of Legal Affairs also had an officer whose mandate included human rights issues. For the rest of the diplomatic corps, human rights were irrelevant.[7] Fraser's efforts forced the State Department to give human rights a home, creating an institutional framework that in itself helped legitimize human rights as an element to be considered in shaping foreign policy. By 1975 a central bureau dealing with human rights and refugees had been established, but its importance in general human rights terms is too often overstated. Initially most of its staff time and resources were devoted to dealing with refugee crises caused by war in Indochina. Senator Kennedy's long-standing push for the creation of such a body had focused on its potential humanitarian impact, especially on refugee issues, and in the mid-1970s the new bureau was less a human rights advocate than a humanitarian relief office.[8]

It may well be that the refugee functions of the new bureau were what persuaded Kissinger to accede to Congress's wishes in establishing it. To be sure, the decision was largely a matter of preemptive action to avoid a probable congressional mandate.[9] It would be virtually his only concession to the new mood in Congress, and he ensured that the office would stir up as little trouble as possible. The bureau had only a coordinating and not an operational role, and a career diplomat with a traditional mind-set and little creativity was plucked from assignment in Micronesia to head it. Its tiny staff was swamped with refugee issues. Each of the State Department's regional bureaus had a newly designated human rights officer, but most allotted human rights at best 10 percent of their time and spent it gathering information for reports. Only in the Latin

American bureau was the human rights officer a specialist in that field, and even then retired diplomat George Lister was rehired only on a half-time basis.[10]

As another diplomat later put it, the new bureau head, James Wilson, had been "handed a dead cat."[11] With a weak mandate and virtually no authority—"I really couldn't do anything to anybody except talk to them," Wilson's deputy recalled—Wilson could do little more than push paper.[12] His own view was that human rights were a "laudable" goal but that "quiet diplomacy" was preferable to public criticism of foreign governments. To that end he remained steadfastly mute, shunning the media and making only one public appearance.[13] He had neither the will nor the staff to do anything more than cope with the paperwork generated by congressional human rights mandates.

Thanks to unrelated developments, this timid start would soon be amplified. In August 1974, after eighteen months of revelations of deception and "dirty deeds" in the Watergate scandal culminating in the release of secret White House tapes, President Nixon resigned in disgrace. The affair deposed more than a president; it also produced a revolution that seemed, briefly, to have radically recalibrated the distribution of power. To say that it was a victory for the legislature at the expense of the executive branch would be too simple, for among the losers were the senior leaders of Congress—the party and committee leaders who were now too closely identified with accommodation and advancement of presidential initiatives. With the exception of Senator Edward Kennedy, who would have been the leading Democratic contender for the presidency in 1972 and 1976 had he not been saddled with the taint of Chappaquiddick, Capitol Hill's liberal human rights advocates were lesser-known rank-and-file members. In both houses, the senior leadership—national figures like J. William Fulbright and Hubert Humphrey—were indifferent or hostile to initiatives at odds with their own long-standing foreign policy priorities. The proposals of the upstarts seemed to them impractical, impossible to enforce, or likely to backfire by leading to further repression in authoritarian countries.[14] To the extent human rights targeted the Soviet Union, they worried it would undermine détente.

Fulbright, who was voted out of office in 1974, was convinced of the need for greater international community and new standards in international relations. The Democrats' most famous critic of the Vietnam War, he spoke of the need for a "new idealism" and "a moral purpose or frame of reference."[15] Yet he prided himself on his realism, saw human rights diplomacy as misguided interventionism, and sneered at "the crusades of high-minded men bent on the regeneration of the human race."[16] For many years he used his position as chairman of the Senate Foreign Relations Committee to delay consideration of the moldering human rights conventions that had been awaiting ratification since the 1950s, citing Bricker-style concerns about undermining the Constitution and granting excessive power to the executive branch.[17] Humphrey, a liberal icon whose famous line about "human rights" in a 1948 speech had energized the civil rights movement, was too closely tied to the Vietnam War to feel susceptible to liberal guilt about it. He adhered to a Manichean view of the Cold War and served as honorary cochairman of the Coalition for a Democratic Majority. He began the 1970s not as a critic of aid to repressive dictatorships but as a critic of aid in general. "We loan money to Rio de Janeiro at lower rates of interest and longer term than we'll loan it to St. Petersburg or Tampa," he said in 1972. "As a matter of fact, we're much more generous with the rest of the world than with our own people. . . . We've helped the rest of the world for 25 years and I hope nobody will think I'm selfish when I say that for the next 10 years we might want to help ourselves."[18] Until 1975 he was a resolute foe of human rights legislation, abandoning his hostility only after such initiatives had proven unstoppable.[19]

A loose group dubbed "the new internationalists" set much of the agenda in the new political environment fostered by the congressional reforms of the early 1970s, when deference to the seniority system and the power of congressional committees and their chairmen gave way to a do-it-yourself attitude, producing what a pair of commentators called a kind of "post-revolutionary anarchic euphoria."[20] They were liberal advocates of economic cooperation, cultural exchange, support for democracy, a less militarized foreign policy, and human rights. With limited power to shape foreign policy, this group used the tools at their disposal: targeting spending measures, holding hearings, and trying to generate publicity.[21]

What they took to be the lessons of the Vietnam War framed the way liberal internationalists in Congress approached problems of global justice. Large-scale proactive efforts along the lines of the developmentalism favored in the 1960s now seemed futile and hubristic, and smaller-scale efforts to alleviate immediate humanitarian crises became the preferred method. Doubting American power to do good, they set their sights on a lesser target: not abetting evil. Liberal internationalists wanted to distance American power from foreign repression. If the United States provided military or economic assistance to regimes that violated human rights, they believed, the country became partly responsible for those abuses. Sometimes such connections were drawn in direct terms, as with accusations that U.S. training or equipment was used by regimes that tortured. More often connections were drawn implicitly, on the grounds that U.S. aid helped repressive dictatorships remain in power and hence contributed to or even increased repression. As Fraser put it, "Military aid to a regime which practices torture was simply wrong on its face, [because] it enhanced the power of that government to remain in control and repress its own citizens."[22] Such formulations provided ammunition to critics who charged the human rights liberals with working to overthrow governments, but it is more accurate to say that they simply did not want to stand in the way of reformist impulses in countries under authoritarian rule. Liberals hoped that cutting aid would stimulate reforms and reduce repression, but Fraser and others admitted that they had little evidence that targeting aid would work as planned. Tangible effects were not, however, the key measure of success. The crucial task was to restore a commitment to American values by dissociating from regimes that tortured and murdered political opponents.

Fraser had a long-standing interest in democratization, and since his success with Title IX had been attempting to restrict aid to military dictatorships, without success.[23] In 1969 one such amendment made it past the Foreign Affairs Committee before being voted down. It stated that military aid "should not be provided to any government which opposes the free and peaceful development of democratic institutions or which denies fundamental freedoms to the people of that country" or has come to power unconstitutionally. His press release singled out Greece as one of its targets.[24] An earlier draft had referred to "fundamental political and civil rights" and had required that each military aid recipient be "evolving toward greater freedom for its people in the exercise of those rights."[25] As did Title IX, these efforts demonstrated a concern with political liberties, sometimes expressed in terms of rights, but at other times framed under the concept of "fundamental freedoms"—a UN phrase that was frequently paired with "human rights" in the 1940s but would fade in American usage in the 1970s.

Abourezk's political prisoner amendment offered Fraser an opportunity to take up the cause again in 1974. In Kissinger's State Department it was a given that a provision like Section 32, with its toothless, morally inflected advice to cut aid to countries with political prisoners, would provoke no action other than obstruction and eye-rolling. This attitude would be an enormous help to Fraser as he sought to push further legislation. With Congress in a newly assertive mood, revelations of the executive branch's disregard for Abourezk's measure were the equivalent of waving a red flag in front of a bull: regardless of their feelings about political prisoners, most members of Congress were not in a mood to be snubbed. In hearings on the 1974 foreign aid bill in June, the State Department representative acknowledged that it had ignored Section 32. Asked what steps had been taken to implement the provision, Deputy Secretary of State Robert Ingersoll said, "I know of none." Fraser queried, "You know of none?" Ingersoll repeated that he did not. "In other words," Fraser countered testily, the provision has had "no consequence." It was too difficult to define "political prisoner," Ingersoll haplessly tried to explain, and in any case quiet diplomacy was more effective than cutting aid. The department later backpedaled, telling Fraser that it had asked posts in aid-recipient countries to collect information on abuses, but the damage had been done.[26]

Abourezk immediately took aim at the executive branch's failure of implementation, adopting a noticeably new language of human rights to do so. Arguing against those who maintained that human rights provisions constituted interference in the internal affairs of other countries, Abourezk noted that the administration was quick to criticize unfriendly countries on human rights grounds, so why not allies, too? Moreover, if the State Department was concerned about whether people in aid-receiving countries were getting enough food to eat, then it "should be as

Congressman Donald Fraser and former Secretary of State Henry Kissinger at
one of Fraser's subcommittee hearings in 1978. Their friendly demeanor here
belies what was often an adversarial relationship when it came to international
human rights. (AP)

equally concerned about whether they are being tortured or not—or
more fundamentally, whether their most basic human rights are being
insured."[27]

Speaking to the Senate Foreign Relations Committee in July, Abourezk
cited growing concern about "rampant violations of human rights" that
was uniting "a large and ever-growing number of Americans" across the
ideological spectrum. Almost everywhere in the world, Abourezk
lamented, "gross and malicious violations of human rights" persist.
"Mass imprisonment, torture, and summary executions" are common in
America's "closest friends." Twenty-seven aid recipients held political
prisoners. The South Dakotan argued that when governments violated
human rights, it became the responsibility of the international community to take action. The measures he proposed included requiring that
the executive branch report on implementation of Section 32 and cutting
off military aid to countries that did not allow respected groups such as

the Red Cross or Amnesty International to investigate prison conditions. The latter was clearly aimed at Chile, which was then refusing international inspections.[28] J. Bryan Hehir of the U.S. Catholic Conference applauded Abourezk's proposals as "minimally necessary safeguards."[29]

As Fraser also took up the cause of strengthening Section 32, he profoundly scaled back his ambitious 1960s interests in democratization and spreading civil liberties. Essentially, he now simply took aim at torture. Having considered an amendment merely requiring that the president report on implementation of Section 32, he chose instead to broaden the provision into a more generalized human rights provision directed at security assistance. An initial draft's language echoed the Abourezk amendment's language about political prisoners, but the final version deleted any reference to prisoners, shifting the focus instead to torture. The early draft called for cutting aid to any government that "engages in a consistent pattern of gross and reliably attested violations of human rights," language drawn directly from recently enacted UN guidelines about handling human rights complaints. It was intended to ground the provision in a reading of international law according to which gross violations could not be regarded as merely domestic issues, so intervention to alleviate them did not violate state sovereignty.[30] The final version, expressed in nonbinding "sense-of-the-Congress" language, stated that "except in extraordinary circumstances, the President shall substantially reduce or terminate security assistance to any government which engages in a consistent pattern of gross violations of internationally recognized human rights."[31] It included a general statement that security aid should be deployed to "promote and advance human rights and avoid identification of the United States . . . with governments [that denied human rights and fundamental freedoms]." It also included a loophole allowing the president to justify aid on security grounds even in cases of gross violations.[32]

Because the State Department had evaded Section 32 by fudging the definition of "political prisoner," Fraser offered explicit examples of what might constitute gross violations. His intention, he said, was to focus on what he described as "those most fundamental of all human rights, the right to the integrity of one's person" and the right not to be subjected to torture or inhuman or degrading treatment. In language that drew on the UDHR's Articles 3, 5, and 9, the amendment singled out torture, prolonged detention without trial, "or other flagrant denials of the right to life, liberty, and the security of the person" as likely to constitute gross violations.[33] If the concept of "gross violations" came from the UN, the focus on imprisonment and torture was surely strongly influenced both by Fraser's earlier experience with the Greek junta, as well as Amnesty International's priorities and those of the rump antiwar movement, which had singled out those abuses in South Vietnam in its campaign to cut aid to Thieu's regime.

On close inspection, Fraser's amendment was less the generalized human rights provision it has often been labeled, and rather more a liberal counterpart to Jackson-Vanik: focused on a narrow right (not to be tortured) and aimed not universally but at a specific class of countries (those receiving security assistance). In floor debate, Iowa Republican H. R. Gross, a fervent opponent of all foreign aid, proposed revising the amendment to allow aid to flow only to countries that respected human rights. Objecting that such a goal was much too broad, Fraser said that many countries violate freedom of the press, freedom of association, and other rights, but "every nation on Earth agrees" that the "more fundamental rights dealing with torture and cruel and inhuman treatment" should be upheld.[34]

Why did Fraser settle on cutting security aid as the way to advance human rights? In part he was limited by what Congress could do, and its financial control over aid was an easy lever to grab. Yet in the 1960s, with Title IX, he had tried to redirect how aid was spent to make it more effective in building democratic institutions. He was instrumental in shifting foreign aid toward "basic needs" in 1973, but now he was in effect throwing up his hands, practically disavowing the power of targeted aid to reshape other societies. The new liberal priorities, stemming from a more skeptical view of American power, were to reduce the flow of arms and to redirect military spending to domestic needs. Fraser returned to his political development ideas in 1977 with a small provision inserted in the foreign aid bill for $750,000 to be spent on research, workshops, legal services, and other activities to promote civil and political rights abroad, but it was a drop in a bucket overflowing with punitive measures focused on integrity-of-the-person abuses.[35]

California Democrat Alan Cranston, offering a similar amendment in the Senate, agreed with Fraser's approach. There would always be authoritarian governments, Cranston conceded, and the aim was not to try to change their governments; the point was simply that "we don't have to pay for other peoples' dictatorships." The Cranston measure was identical to Fraser's except that it removed the sense-of-the-Congress limitation to give it "teeth," as Cranston put it. It stated that no country would qualify for military assistance unless the president certified to the Congress that it had not recently engaged in "a pattern of gross violations of human rights." Humphrey, the Senate Foreign Relations Committee's foreign aid bill shepherd, asked Cranston to withdraw his proposal in exchange for the assurance that the committee would hold hearings on military aid to repressive governments early in the following year, and Cranston agreed.[36] Javits, too, drafted and then dropped an expansion of the Abourezk amendment.[37]

Fraser's measure was an important innovation in the integration of human rights considerations into foreign policy. With the exception of a watered-down attempt to cut off aid to Greece in 1971, which the White House easily circumvented, prior efforts to prohibit assistance to repressive governments had failed. Before Section 32, such efforts had been ad hoc, aimed at specific countries. In 1972, for example, California Senator John Tunney offered an amendment to cut off aid to Brazil until it stopped torturing political prisoners, but it was overwhelmingly defeated.[38] The Fraser amendment was nevertheless a small step: it was a recommendation rather than a requirement, it was effectively limited to torture, and it was aimed at recipients of U.S. security aid, not gross violators of human rights in general. Over time, though, its effects would be wide-ranging. Soon strengthened under the impact of congressional frustration with the State Department's failures of implementation, the gist of 502B remains on the books even today.[39] Fraser set out a template that at least for the rest of the decade constituted the core of U.S. human rights efforts: reductions (or, more often, the threat of reductions) in security aid for gross violations such as torture, coupled with the requirement that the State Department issue reports critiquing foreign countries' human rights records.

\* \* \*

Kissinger viewed Fraser, Kennedy, and other human rights proponents as minor but irritating thorns in his side. When the Indian foreign minister complained to him in 1976 about Fraser's subcommittee hearings on India, Kissinger responded, "As I have said publicly, I am in total disagreement with Fraser. He would make us the world's policeman." Kissinger further observed, "There are certain human rights which are important"—but these presumably did not include protections from torture and political imprisonment.[40] When Kissinger took human rights issues into account, he did so only reluctantly or as a means to a different end. In a revealing phrase, he distinguished between "those that care and those that *do.*"[41] Determined to augment U.S. support for authoritarian anticommunist regimes as part of his quest for global stability, Kissinger was equally allergic to ambitious schemes to promote democracy and to modest efforts to moderate internal repression by allies. He dismissed human rights concerns as "easy slogans," "empty posturing," "sentimental nonsense," and "malarkey."[42] As Nixon declared, in a phrase penned by Kissinger's staff, "We deal with governments as they are."[43]

Even after he moderated his public stance in response to growing public discontent with his amoralism, Kissinger's policy remained unchanged. After a 1976 speech in Santiago endorsing human rights, for example, he immediately gave word to his staff not to take the message too seriously, and he personally assured Pinochet that the speech was solely a tactical response to criticism from Congress.[44] He sometimes asked violators for token concessions and public relations gestures, but when his subordinates seemed to show genuine concern for human rights, Kissinger derided them as "bleeding hearts," "theologians," and "people who have a vocation for the ministry" who had gone into diplomacy only because they could not find enough churches.[45] In a July 1976 tirade, for example, he railed against a démarche to the newly installed and highly repressive Argentina junta about its human rights record, demanding to know "in what way is it compatible with my policy" and suggesting that the person responsible be transferred.[46] He repeatedly demanded from Congress the flexibility to use quiet diplomacy on human rights issues, but his quiet diplomacy was better characterized as inaudible, and at key moments he endorsed or gave the green light to major abuses.[47] "The quicker you succeed the better," he told the Argentine junta about its mass killings, disappearances, and torture. "We won't cause you unnecessary difficulties."[48]

In 1973 and 1974 Kissinger had been forced to bend to Jackson's will in pressing the Soviets to improve their record on Jewish emigration. His response to the liberal human rights initiatives that Congress began passing in those years was to man the battle stations. Jackson had the votes to stir up trouble in the priority area of Soviet-American relations; Kissinger had had little choice but to compromise. Liberals, however, targeted regions such as Latin America where Kissinger felt the stakes were smaller and he could stand firm.

His advisers implored him to develop a proactive stance on human rights. The Policy Planning Staff described human rights violations abroad as "an increasingly urgent problem" because they harmed the country's image and undermined Americans' confidence in their own benevolence. It offered suggestions for developing a positive approach to human rights promotion.[49] Kissinger ignored them.[50] He told his staff that what was at stake was a matter of principle. Congress was improperly intruding into day-to-day operational decisions and doing so in ways that undermined the national interest.[51] He said that Fraser and his colleagues were interested only in "grandstand plays" and "public humiliation of other countries" about issues that had no place in foreign relations. The State Department could not become "a reform school for allies," he declared. "They want us to be anti-Philippine, anti-Korean, anti-Chilean—pro what? Castro? I don't know what they us to be pro. Nor do they explain how other countries can in any way deal with us."[52]

His advisers repeatedly proposed some degree of cooperation with Congress, if for no other reason than that human rights advocates were likely to pass even more restrictions if the department was seen as obstructionist. As Assistant Secretary for Latin America William Rogers told him at the end of 1974, "There are an awful lot of Democrats on the Hill this coming session who want to go to the mat on the issue of human rights and want to make a fight about it," and they were eager to "stick it" to the department because they "didn't think we were sincere." Rogers wanted to head off the impending confrontation by making an effort at least to appear concerned.[53]

In the atmosphere of the mid-1970s, Kissinger's intransigence was fatal for congressional cooperation. It was not that most members of Congress were eager to remove the executive's traditional flexibility in the implementation of foreign aid. But as staffer Pat Holt recalled, there was a "credibility gap" of "cosmic proportions," and "the prevailing mood [in Congress] with respect to almost anything out of the White House was one of cynicism." When Kissinger went to the Senate Foreign Relations committee after Section 502B was proposed, he gave an "impassioned plea not to tie his hands, that progress in human rights was best promoted through 'quiet diplomacy.'" Most of the committee agreed, at least in the abstract. The trouble, Holt said, "was that nobody believed there had been any 'quiet diplomacy.'"[54]

As revelations of White House dirty deeds mounted, Holt recalled, "the attitude of the whole damn Congress changed."[55] Congress became less and less compliant as the White House was engulfed in scandal. Soon after Nixon's resignation, the elections of November 1974 brought in a class of restive "Watergate babies." As the State Department flouted congressional sentiment and increased military aid to brutal and repressive regimes in Indonesia, Iran, the Congo, and elsewhere, critics in Congress grew increasingly irate.

Crucial to heating up the confrontation was Kissinger's stance on aid to Chile in 1974. The media kept up a steady drumbeat of publicity about abuses under the new regime, which had declared a "state of siege," imposed martial law, and ruled by emergency decree. The junta censored the media and held book burnings across the country. It banned trade unions and political parties and swept up thousands of political opponents into arbitrary detention, using torture as a routine tool of interrogation and intimidation. A steady flow of émigrés, investigative reports, and painstakingly documented testimony ensured that the Western press had access to plentiful firsthand accounts of horrors. Corpses floating down rivers, university students arrested and killed, gruesome mutilation and torture of popular singers and artists with leftist political leanings, and other tales transfixed a significant portion of the American public in the years after 1973. Drawing on the report of an Amnesty International investigation, AI USA board member Rose Styron published a gruesome account of Chilean torture in the *New York*

*Review of Books.* Folk singer Victor Jara had had his fingers broken and cut off before he was shot and killed; pregnant female prisoners were subjected to electric torture that produced fetal brain lesions and abortions; children had been tortured to death in front of their parents. Excerpts from a firsthand account of torture rounded out the litany of horrors: "They tied me to a table. . . . They passed cables over my naked body. They wet me and began to apply currents to all parts of my body and the interrogator did not ask me, he assured me, 'You did this thing.' I denied the monstrosities and the blows began to my abdomen, ribs, chest, testicles, etc. I don't know for how long they massacred me, but with the blows in my chest, my throat and bronchial tubes filled up and it was drowning me. I was dying."[56]

Such stories fed liberal outrage over the administration's moral and financial support of Pinochet's regime. As a steady stream of congressional hearings touched on issues relating to Chile, the State Department's staunch defense of the junta and its claims that the United States had not been involved in Allende's overthrow sparked congressional acrimony. In July, Kennedy, like Abourezk, followed up on Section 32 implementation, asking a State Department official testifying before his refugees subcommittee whether Chile held any political prisoners. The official, Harry Shlaudeman, replied that the Chilean junta said it did not. Kennedy ridiculed the department's reliance on Chilean assurances rather than its own findings and demanded to know, "Can we find out if anything we do up here in Congress makes any difference at all?"[57] The effort Kennedy had spearheaded to cut aid to Chile had failed at the end of 1973, but instead of heeding warnings about congressional sentiment, Kissinger dramatically increased the level of aid to Chile requested in the new foreign aid bill. Thanks to his perceived arrogance, this time around the cuts passed.[58]

Feuding between Kissinger and Congress took on a new level of animus in September 1974, when Seymour Hersh, the famed investigative reporter at the *New York Times*, published a series of articles that were deeply damaging to the administration. The first showed that the CIA's extensive covert involvement in Chile before the 1973 coup directly contradicted previous State Department assurances to Congress that there had been no intervention of any kind. The next described Kissinger himself as the mastermind behind the effort to destabilize Allende's government.[59] The third revealed that Kissinger was actively preventing his staff from implementing congressional human rights instructions. The U.S. Ambassador to Chile, David Popper, who was a strong advocate of U.S. support for Pinochet's regime, had brought up human rights in discussions with Chilean officials about military aid—essentially fulfilling Congress's weak request to press the regime on human rights. When Kissinger learned that Popper had raised the topic, he angrily admonished the ambassador to "cut out the political science lectures," prompting the department to issue a formal reprimand. Popper and his staff in Santiago were "amazed" and offended, and some officials in State's Bureau of Inter-American Affairs were so irate that they leaked the incident to Kissinger's most devoted enemy in the press.[60]

Hersh's account of the Popper affair caused a minor flap in Congress. It appeared just two days after Fraser submitted a letter to Kissinger signed by 104 members of Congress urging greater attention to human rights in the distribution of foreign aid, especially military assistance. "It may not be realistic to expect strict observance of political, civil and other human rights by [governments indifferent to human rights] while their political systems are still evolving," the letter noted, but that did not mean that the United States could not insist on adherence to minimum norms such as freedom from torture. "We cannot, in good conscience, associate ourselves with policies which lack active concern about the fate of people living under oppressive governments," Fraser's letter continued. "While it may be beyond our power to alleviate the plight of those people, we can refuse to be identified with their oppressors."[61] The timing of the rebuke to Popper, though unrelated to the Fraser-sponsored letter, seemed like a calculated insult. "Kissinger's scolding of Popper is a damn outrage," Fraser's staff wrote in an internal memo, and "flies in the face" of Congress's stated positions on human rights.[62] Fraser, in only slightly more temperate language, told the press he found Kissinger's action "outrageous—incredible," and questioned whether Kissinger should remain in office. He demanded a meeting with Kissinger and told the other 103 signatories of the letter that Kissinger was "in direct opposition" to them.[63]

Kissinger remained unyielding. Assistant Secretary Rogers argued that compromising with Congress was necessary to retain the department's freedom of action. Congress, he told Kissinger, had cut off aid to Chile because "they didn't think we were sincere on the human rights issue." "There is a more fundamental problem," Kissinger responded. "It is a problem of the whole foreign policy that is being pulled apart, pulling it apart thread by thread, under one pretext or another." If the department were to go to Congress and ask for a reinstatement of aid on the basis that the Chilean government had released two thousand prisoners, he said, Congress would merely demand the release of five thousand. If the department gave way on the issue of human rights violations in Chile, South Korea would be next, and no U.S. ally would be immune. "There isn't going to be any end to it," Kissinger insisted. Conceding the principle that human rights had a legitimate role in determining policy would merely ensure—rather than deter—further legislative meddling. "We have to make a stand now."[64]

Meanwhile public distaste for U.S. aid to dictators continued to grow. America's Catholic bishops adopted a resolution urging the U.S. government to use its power "in the service of human rights" and cited "the link between our economic assistance" and regimes that torture or hold political prisoners.[65] The National Council of Churches passed a resolution in late 1974 urging the suspension of military and economic aid to countries that flagrantly abused human rights.[66] Liberal newspaper columnists such as Jack Anderson and Anthony Lewis, as well as television producers looking for a compelling story, pressed the connections between taxpayers' dollars and repression abroad. In early 1974 NBC's *Tomorrow* show featured a discussion of torture in Brazil. One upset viewer wrote in afterward: "We give Brazil $67 million a year to torture those poor citizens," observing that the United States had done the same thing with Greece and South Vietnam. "I'll be damned if I will allow my tax dollars to torture and kill other people."[67] Reflecting an increasingly widespread view, one concerned citizen wrote to her senator to complain that "we have been sending American tax money to dictatorships that have used it for nothing but bloodshed, more torture and even greater degrees of repression of individual freedom and rights."[68]

Legislative efforts picked up speed as liberals pushed through country-specific aid measures, reducing or cutting off aid to South Korea, Chile, and Uruguay in the years 1974–1976.[69] More general human rights legislation followed as well. The following year, the Harkin-McGovern-Abourezk amendment, formally known as Section 116 of the 1975 International Development and Food Assistance Act, added economic assistance to the aid programs now tied to human rights standards, keeping the same focus on integrity-of-the-person abuses such as torture and requiring the executive branch to provide annual human rights reports. It included an exception for aid that directly benefitted needy people.[70]

Earlier congressional initiatives had developed largely independently of lobbying from human rights groups. The Harkin amendment seems to have been the first that was directly the result of nongovernmental organization lobbying. Joseph Eldridge of the Washington Office on Latin America, a Methodist-backed group formed in 1974, and Ed Snyder of the American Friends Service Committee, an organization long dedicated to reducing military spending, drafted the bill and then shopped it to potential sponsors. They went first to Fraser, who declined, correctly anticipating that it would be exploited by conservatives opposed to any form of foreign aid. Harkin, a newly elected congressman who had been a staffer on the congressional group that had discovered the tiger cages of Con Son Island, took up the cause, with McGovern and Abourezk coming on board later as cosponsors.[71]

Like other human rights measures, this one depended for its passage on a strange alliance of liberal human rights advocates and conservatives hostile to foreign aid. When it came before the House Committee on International Relations, as the body was now known (*"foreign"* affairs" had been deemed politically incorrect), it seemed Democrats Dante Fascell and Clement Zablocki might shut the amendment down, but Wayne Hays, an enemy of foreign aid in general, became annoyed at their equivocations. The provision was hardly too much to ask of the foreign aid bureaucracy, Hays said, because on any given day, "20 percent of them [are] asleep, 20 percent reading newspapers, 20 percent out for coffee, 20 percent in the various men's or ladies' rooms, and another 20 percent are taking a vacation." The "well-intentioned" amendment might "do some good," he said, and Congress "ought to put their feet to the fire and give them a chance to try it." His conservative colleague John Ashbrook agreed. Aid should be cut off entirely, but until then, he said, "we should at least cut off aid to repressive regimes." In this fashion the amendment passed the House; in the Senate, Humphrey reluctantly accepted the amendment to prevent the entire aid package from being sunk.[72]

The next stage in the confrontation developed over the reports on the human rights records of aid recipients that the State Department had been required to compile as a result of Section 502B. As it came time to present the reports to Congress, Policy Planning head Winston Lord pleaded with Kissinger to reconsider his stance on aid. "We face an extremely important moment both in our relations with Congress and on the substance of [the human rights issue]. I believe both require your urgent attention," Lord wrote. Agreeing that security assistance was a poor tool for influencing the behavior of foreign governments and suggesting only the most minimal effort to placate Congress, he nevertheless argued that a blanket refusal to modify aid levels on human rights grounds was unwise. "We are faced with a law about whose intent its supporters are very clear," he told Kissinger. "If we ignore the spirit of this law we may well pay a substantial price."[73]

Lord's staff suggested that the 502B report could follow the spirit and the letter of the law by singling out Chile for proposed reductions. Such a move, they argued, would take the initiative away from Congress, which was likely to reduce aid to Chile again. The costs of such a move would be small, but the benefits would include a more favorable attitude in Congress. It might even reduce human rights abuses by making aid recipients more cautious about engaging in human rights abuses likely to provoke Congress. The Policy Planning Staff suggested that three other countries under the spotlight for poor human rights records—South Korea, the Philippines, and Indonesia—could be cited as problems, avoiding the label "gross violators" but at least attempting to set the parameters of discussion, rather than allowing Congress to do so. Staffers presciently warned, "We are in for grave difficulties," including a tougher 502B law, "if we are seen as flaunting [the law]."[74]

The secretary of state ruled against these recommendations: neither cuts to aid nor criticism of the worst violators would be on the table. Nor, indeed, would private criticism.[75] Fraser, Javits, and Cranston had been expecting for months that Congress would be given individual country reports summarizing human rights conditions in each country receiving assistance.[76] Anticipating the reports' eventual release, the department engaged in strenuous internal debates over how frank to be. Not surprisingly, in the end the reports were extremely circumspect. The three-page South Korea report, for example, went through a process of stripping down details until it became what is best described as a whitewash. Instead of a richly detailed account of repression in South Korea, a "bloody fight" ended with a bland and evasive document that referred vaguely to "significantly restrictive measures" in place under Park Chung-hee's dictatorship.[77] But Kissinger withheld from Congress even the watered-down country reports.

Salzberg had been showing around a draft of a stronger 502B "as a kind of warning of what could happen" if the reports produced by the current 502B were not frank enough, but Kissinger failed to take heed.[78] When Maw sent the secretary of state eight draft country reports, Kissinger refused to provide any of them to Congress. He told aides that it was pointless to single out U.S. allies for criticism when almost every country in the world committed abuses. He ordered instead that an evasive, general report be prepared. Delivered to Congress in November, the report did not discuss specific violations of human rights in individual countries, nor did it attempt to determine which countries engaged in repeated gross violations of human rights. Following Kissinger's line, it merely stated that human rights violations were common around the world. "Human rights abuses follow no pattern" and occur in countries receiving U.S. security assistance and in those that do not. Belying the department's initial assessment that some violators were more egregious than others, the report concluded that "in view of the widespread nature of human rights violations in the world, we have found no adequately objective way to make distinctions of degree between nations." Neither human rights nor U.S. security would be served by "the public obloquy and impaired relations" that would follow the making of "inherently subjective" decisions about levels of abuses. Defending the decision not to name violators, Maw told Congress that "it was difficult and perhaps wrong for any country to accuse another of 'gross violations' of human rights."[79]

As many State Department officials had feared, congressional liberals reacted strongly to the failure to provide individual country reports. As Wilson recalled, Fraser and others who had been told repeatedly that individual reports would shortly be forthcoming "went through the roof" when they received instead the department's equivocating document.[80] "I found the report to be primarily a defense of the State Department's apparent intention not to comply with the law," Fraser told the press. Cranston railed that "it amounts to a cover-up."[81] Humphrey, jumping on the human rights bandwagon, called the report unresponsive and "about as bland as swallowing a bucket of sawdust."[82] The report was immediately leaked to the *New York Times*, which played the refusal to provide individual reports as front-page news. The *Washington Post* filed a Freedom of Information Act request for the reports, which the State Department denied.[83]

Fraser, Cranston, and Humphrey immediately decided to introduce tougher amendments that would give Congress a role in determining which countries engaged in "gross violations" and make cutoffs in aid mandatory unless justifications were provided.[84] Delayed by Ford's veto of the bill, a significantly strengthened version of Section 502B came into effect in June 1976 as part of the 1976 International Security Assistance and Arms Export Control Act.[85] Still focused on military aid, the new version prohibited assistance to governments engaged in gross violations unless certain extraordinary circumstances could be demonstrated. It mandated a "full and complete report" on every country slated to receive security assistance. Congress could request a report on a specific country at any time, and if a requested report was not delivered within thirty days, aid would automatically be terminated.[86] Congress also strengthened the Human Rights Bureau, making the coordinator a presidential appointment subject to Senate confirmation.[87]

As congressional legislation accumulated, the State Department slowly shifted its behavior and its mind-set, even despite Kissinger's recalcitrance. A significant outcome of the congressional human rights insurgency was new precedents, procedures, and modes of thought in American diplomacy. Embassies gathered information on human rights practices, diplomats prepared required reports for Congress, ambassadors embarrassed their foreign counterparts with lectures about abuses, and White House officials scrambled to avoid aid cutoffs to allies.[88] Some officials in the State Department began to factor human rights considerations into policy-making.[89] Human rights reports were prepared, delivered to Congress, and made public. Within ten years of the first cursory and "bland as . . . sawdust" exercise, State's country reports, by then an annual publication of over a thousand pages that covered not only recipients of military aid but all members of the United Nations, would be widely known and respected.[90]

Limited by the tools at their disposal and moved by festering resentments about the Vietnam War, congressional liberals created a reactive, punitive, and unilateral approach that would set the human rights agenda long after the Ford administration. The template Congress constructed in the mid-1970s comprised the use of hearings to shape public opinion and signal concern about human rights abuses; a focus on sensationalistic abuses, torture above all; cuts in aid to friendly but strategically expendable governments; and mandates to the State Department to collect and to disseminate information on abuses and to liaise with human rights organizations. The results were inevitably ad hoc and inconsistent, with some countries and some abuses drawing attention and sanctions while others were largely ignored. Human rights activists who came from countries with large populations of exiles, who joined networks with U.S. academics, churches, and nongovernmental organizations, and who delivered complaints about repression in moderate, depoliticized language, were more likely to have their voices heard.[91] In some cases congressional pressure contributed to modest alleviation of abuses, and in other cases it produced nothing but soured relations.[92] The opportunity to develop a more coherent, proactive, and incentive-based approach to human rights, which had support within the State Department, was squandered by Kissinger.

Human rights diplomacy required answers to difficult questions about which rights would be pursued, for whom, and at what cost. Which is more urgent: acting against electric-shock torture of suspected terrorists, preventing children from dying of malnutrition, or promoting freedom of the press? Would quiet diplomacy, multilateral initiatives, public condemnation, symbolic gestures, or sanctions be most effective? The answers Congress gave in the first half of the 1970s—essentially, torture and sanctions—in some respects avoided the truly difficult questions. It was often easy enough to cut aid to friendly regimes that engaged in widespread torture, but many of the worst violators did not receive U.S.

aid and were immune to such blandishments. Instead of convincing the American public to pay an economic price for the promotion of rights, the congressional initiatives fostered the illusion that the restoration of American virtue could be achieved by spending less money.[93] Many observers in Europe and the Third World wanted to see a vast increase in U.S. economic aid to developing countries, not campaigns that gave opponents of aid a reason to condemn it.[94]

Despite signs that international human rights promotion was gaining adherents, at the end of 1975—and, as we will see, well into 1976—it was not firmly implanted in the vernacular of American politics as a foreign policy concern. As one 1975 State Department report put it, human rights was "no longer a bleeding heart issue presided [over] by fairies in Geneva."[95] But academic analysts still at times overlooked it entirely, writing articles on the future of foreign policy or the role of Congress in foreign affairs without even a nod to the central issues associated with human rights.[96] There was, moreover, a strong sense in which liberal congressional efforts were focused not on truly fundamental human rights issues but rather on concerns that more properly fell under the heading of humanitarianism. Like disaster relief, stopping a recent turn to torture by particular regimes had the feel of an emergency action to avoid short-term suffering of passive victims, rather than an effort to build more just and democratic societies. Fraser's 1970s human rights goals, pitched around preventing outbreaks of torture and political imprisonment, arguably had more in common with humanitarian relief than with the ambitious schemes to create rights-bearing citizens that had been implicit in his political development ideas of the 1960s.

Yet the liberal human rights initiatives were not a retreat from engagement with the world but a way of reinvigorating American global involvement. As Harkin put it, part of the appeal of human rights was that they served as "a legitimizing factor for U.S. policy in general [that] can provide a needed sense of purpose and unity for Americans."[97] Jackson and the neoconservatives wanted human rights to rekindle American will for a renewed Cold War struggle. Liberals wanted to move beyond the Cold War, but they, too, saw human rights as way to regenerate the American spirit.

**CHAPTER 8**

# The Human Rights Lobby

H ow can i help?" was a common refrain in Americans' responses to the all-too-frequent reports of torture, starvation, and repression appearing in their morning newspapers and on their evening television news programs. Although the decade is sometimes described as an era of greater self-absorption than the protest-heavy 1960s, activism remained widespread, if less dramatic. It was more diffuse, less radical, more practical. Environmentalism, women's rights, gay rights, and consumer advocacy were among the major causes that drew in the fragmenting energies once harnessed to the civil rights and antiwar movements. The rising power of the Christian right was evident in campaigns for school prayer and against abortion, pornography, new sexual mores, and homosexuality. By mid-decade international human rights was one pole toward which significant numbers of Americans gravitated, making it for the first time a mass movement that drew in tens of thousands of participants. New forms of mobilizing meant that participation was easier than ever. With the rise of direct-mail campaigns, Americans wondering "How can I help?" were likely to find the answer in their mail, in the form of targeted appeals to donate, write letters, sign petitions, or attend events.

The new human rights movement in the United States was but one manifestation of a global phenomenon powered by transnational flows of people, information, and money. In Chile, for example, where human rights abuses became the decade's cause célèbre, domestic human rights groups gathered and funneled out of the country the information about abuses that international actors used to mount campaigns against the junta. The Vicariate of Solidarity, a Catholic Church group, was a crucial conduit, collecting and disseminating credible reports of torture, arrests, and extrajudicial murder. International groups in turn provided visibility, funding, and moral support to Chilean groups.[1] Long-distance travel became less expensive and more common, facilitating efforts by exiles, missionaries, journalists, and academics to form transnational networks, found organizations, and take stories of abuses to the UN, the media, human rights groups, and professional associations.

Like the antiwar movement from which so much of it evolved, the human rights movement in the United States was highly diverse. It encompassed a range of aims and organizations that spanned the political spectrum and that sometimes took starkly incompatible views of which provisions of the Universal Declaration of Human Rights mattered most. For groups on the right, such as the Estonian National Council and other "Captive Nations" groups that had used human rights language throughout the Cold War, the key target remained the USSR. Freedom House, a decades-old group devoted to the cause of freedom, began to talk in human rights terms in the Carter years, and Helsinki Watch, precursor to Human Rights Watch, was founded in 1978 to monitor Soviet-bloc adherence to the human rights and human contacts provisions of the 1975 Helsinki Accords. The tiny Coalition for a Democratic Majority, significant only in retrospect, devoted enough energy to the cause of Soviet dissidents in the late 1970s to be considered the neoconservative pole of the decade's human rights impetus.[2]

The radical left came to human rights more grudgingly. The solidarity groups that proliferated in these years, often founded by expats or former antiwar radicals, typically Marxist or communist and focused on a single country or region, were interested in the root causes of imperialism and oppression. They tended to regard human rights talk as a distraction that turned revolutionary "heroes" and "martyrs" fighting for righteous causes into "victims" of government brutality, distinguished not by their politics but by the kind of official violence inflicted on them.[3] Their adoption of the language and aims of human rights was often tactical rather than programmatic.

Radicals and liberals nevertheless found considerable common ground, as the list of members of the Human Rights Working Group suggests. Formed at the beginning of 1976 by Clergy and Laity Concerned's Jacqui Chagnon, a longtime organizer in the civil rights and antiwar movements, the Working Group was allied to the Coalition for a New Foreign and Military Policy, a new group formed as a merger of the Coalition to Stop Funding the War and the Coalition on National Priorities and Military Policy. The Working Group included representatives from twenty or thirty organizations, including the Center for International Policy, the Washington Office on Latin America, the Friends Committee, Americans for Democratic Action, Clergy and Laity Concerned, the Council on Hemispheric Affairs (which counted Fraser and Abourezk as members), the National Council of Churches, the Transnational Institute, the U.S. Catholic Conference, and the Women's International League for Peace and Freedom. It also included more specialized groups: the Argentine Commission for Human Rights, the Chile Committee for Human Rights, the Chile Legislative Center, Friends of the Filipino People, Movement for a Free Philippines, Nonintervention in Chile, the North American Coalition for Human Rights in Korea, the Panama Committee for Human Rights, Taiwanese Rights and Culture Association, the Indonesian human rights group TAPOL, the Uruguay Information Project, and the Washington Office on Africa.[4] As human rights became an issue that affected almost everyone, groups with much wider mandates, such as the United Presbyterian Church and the National Association of Social Workers, also joined.

The Coalition for a New Foreign and Military Policy itself was so avowedly leftist that about half the members of the loosely affiliated Working Group abstained from joining, but the Working Group, too, had clear left-liberal priorities.[5] It worked for the ratification of UN human rights covenants and pressured U.S.-allied dictatorships, but did not mention human rights violations by the Soviet Union and avoided discussing the Jackson-Vanik amendment.[6] Cochair of the Working Group and ADA legislative representative Bruce Cameron recalled later that "one of my lines used to be that I find 80 percent of Soviet foreign policy acceptable and basically on the side that I was on. . . . The core group [in the human rights movement] clearly thought of the world divided between the evil U.S., the questionable Soviet Union, and the good Third World people. . . ."[7]

Although right-wing conceptions of human rights remained visible in public discourse, by the second half of the 1970s, and especially after Carter came to office, liberal definitions came to the fore. International human rights promotion became a cause most closely associated with the liberal mainstream. Sitting squarely on top of the organizational heap, and epitomizing the movement's political center of gravity, was Amnesty International's American branch. Tiny and virtually unknown in 1970, it expanded over the course of the decade to become the single largest and best-known human rights organization in the country. By the end of the 1970s it was the face of mainstream liberal human rights activism—not yet the universally recognized name it would become by the end of the 1980s, but well known and well respected. The politics and culture of human rights in the United States were indelibly shaped by Amnesty's ethos and methods.

Amnesty's aims proved ideally suited to the Zeitgeist of the seventies. The idealistic zeal of the 1960s, with its grand, technocratic, or revolutionary schemes of social transformation and the soaring rhetoric of Kennedy's "pay any price, bear any burden" inaugural, gave way to a chastened sense of limits in the 1970s—limits to the world's resources, to America's own economic might, and to humanity's capacity for fundamental change. Instead of trying to remedy oppression and injustice by targeting their sources, Amnesty held up a much simpler goal: freeing or alleviating conditions of confinement for people jailed for their speech or beliefs.[8] Its American branch lobbied for aid cutoffs to regimes that tortured and jailed opponents in large numbers. Its advocacy thus dovetailed with the message coming from congressional liberals: that alleviating American responsibility for injustice and oppression abroad could be accomplished with simple, small-scale acts rather than costly, fundamental changes.

The daily routine of George Lister, the human rights officer in the Latin American Bureau at the State Department, exemplified the new climate for human rights in post-Watergate Washington. His major purpose at

Foggy Bottom was to liaise with what he called "the movement." Already retired when he was rehired for the new post in 1974, he embraced human rights as a second career. As one of his colleagues put it, his heart was "genuinely" in his human rights work.[9] He lauded human rights as "the authentic world revolution, democratic, peaceful and very effective."[10] He began his days by reading the newspapers, then spent working hours attending meetings and hearings and reading and writing memos. In his spare time he attended human rights–related events, making a circuit of the proliferating concerts, symposia, vigils, rallies, and receptions. Activists were initially puzzled by the presence of the man in the suit among the "hardcore leftists," but suspicion soon gave way to camarade-rie.[11] He became friends with many activists, including Tom Quigley of the U.S. Catholic Conference, Joe Eldridge of the Washington Office on Latin America, and Bill Wipfler of the National Council of Churches, with whom he kept in close contact. He told "the movement" how to work with government officials, sometimes instructing them on polite manners, and explained "the movement's" point of view to government officials.[12]

Lister urged human rights groups to spend less time on demonstra-tions and more time on lobbying. It was through Congress that they would have the greatest effect, he told them, and they took heed. He facilitated the flow of information: as one official recalled, Lister was "always Xeroxing things." He arranged for activists and dissidents to meet with State Department officials and members of Congress.[13] Lister's efforts, of course, could not satisfy all parties. His State Department col-leagues often saw him as an irritant or, worse, ignored him, and the human rights community was frequently disappointed in the State Department's responsiveness. But his post was a sign of the new trend: human rights groups had entrée to the halls of power, and their voices sometimes mattered, even if they were heeded far less often than they would have wished.

The end of the Vietnam War was a precondition for the rise of a human rights movement in the United States. Not only did internal conflict over the war leave little room for other major initiatives, but until the war was over, Americans could not credibly lecture to others. It is no surprise, then, that international human rights began to seem appealing only in the Ford administration, as liberal internationalists sought ways to move beyond the war and to reclaim American virtue while abjuring McGovern-style guilt. (The radical left, of course, continued to denounce the United States as guilty of imperialism and other crimes.) Most of the mass movement was nonpartisan on its face, yet entwined with liberalism in its wellsprings, its most heartfelt causes, and its composition. It meshed with many Americans' desire to do good—and to feel good again. In the face of stories about horrific abuse, often committed by regimes supported by the United States, it offered a program that suggested that it was possible to help suffering individuals with small, easy steps.

Sensing a sea change at the beginning of 1976, Amnesty USA's executive director, David Hawk, predicted that "awareness and concern for human rights" would "open up" and "probably peak" within the next two years.[14] He pointed to congressional legislation, the UN's recent AI-sponsored Declaration against Torture, and a dramatic rise in media attention as signs of an "extraordinary growth in consciousness about and concern for human rights."[15] At the end of the year, just after Democratic presidential candidate Jimmy Carter had raised the national profile of human rights promotion, *Washington Post* reporter David Ottaway wrote a long, flattering piece on Amnesty International, which he called "the human rights lobby." "Our time has come," an Amnesty staffer told Ottaway: "The interest in Amnesty has just absolutely boomed." Until recently a "fringe 'special interest' of imperceptible influence," Ottaway wrote, Amnesty had blossomed into a highly effective lobby, providing receptive legislators with a deluge of reports and targets for action.[16]

The earliest congressional human rights moves had been largely independent of the influence of nongovernmental organizations. Jackson's framing of the cause of Soviet Jewish emigration was influenced by American Jewish organizations—as well as Soviet dissidents—and he pursued it in part through continuing collaboration with Jewish organizations, but these groups provided coloring for a political project already conceived. For their part, congressional liberals, Fraser especially, traded ideas with European colleagues, were influenced by human rights

developments in European forums, and drew on information and expertise from Amnesty and other groups, but they created their own agenda.
Fraser's activities gave a huge boost to nongovernmental organizations,
not the other way around.[17] His early 502B legislation and subsequent
efforts to strengthen it provided a focal point for a rising tide of nongovernmental organization lobbying on human rights.

Amnesty's American branch pursued two main forms of human rights
action. In the first, Americans joined local adoption groups, where they
wrote polite letters to foreign governments to try to secure freedom or
better conditions for "prisoners of conscience." When "urgent action"
requests came through, they sent telegrams to foreign governments to try
to stop or limit immediate abuses such as torture. Groups also showed
educational films, picketed, or staged modest protest actions. It was a
small-scale, ostensibly apolitical, minimalist approach: not about saving
the world, it was about helping individuals. The second major approach
had overtly political goals. After it was set up in 1976, Amnesty USA's
Washington office became a hub of human rights lobbying, helping to
shape U.S. government priorities by channeling information to members
of Congress, the State Department, and opinion leaders, testifying at
congressional hearings, cultivating media attention, and backing aid cutoffs to major human rights violators.

The middle years of the decade were transformative for Amnesty's
U.S. section. In the words of one organizer, Amnesty started "selling like
motherhood."[18] In 1970 it had few members and a nearly invisible presence on the national stage. Politicians sometimes cited its published
research, it had been mentioned in a smattering of reports in the mainstream media, and its mailings reached thousands of people, but not
until 1977 would it have measurable name recognition among the general
public. Until 1973, it was severely handicapped by Americans' preoccupation with the Vietnam War, which left little energy for other causes. As
noted earlier, Amnesty's name was also a major stumbling block, conjuring up the highly contentious issue of amnesty for draft resisters. The
mere mention of amnesty incited angry opposition from much of the
American public.[19]

Trying to explain to London headquarters why the United States section was so small, its head explained in 1970 that because the country

was in the midst of "internal paroxysms," Americans in search of causes found them readily enough close to home. Students and draft resisters jailed in their own towns seemed a more urgent concern than strange prisoners in distant countries.[20] The end of the war, coinciding with a compelling AI special Campaign Against Torture, created the conditions for Amnesty's cause to begin to win over a significant following in the United States: over the course of 1973, the number of members and adoption groups quadrupled, foundation grants and individual contributions doubled, and the office staff expanded from one to five full-time positions.[21] By AI USA's count, in that year the organization was mentioned in almost a hundred articles, about evenly divided between small local or campus newspapers and major national newspapers and magazines such as the *New York Times* and *Ms.* magazine. NBC's *Today Show* featured AI USA twice.[22] Name recognition remained low, however, and membership numbers were small both in absolute terms and relative to Western European sections. A group touring the country found that outside small handfuls of academics and activists in the New York–Washington corridor and the San Francisco Bay Area, the organization was almost entirely unknown.[23]

Amnesty was an international organization, but its American section exhibited a high degree of independence. Its organizers saw their task as adapting a British idea to American conditions. Paul Lyons had taken up the reins at a time when the London headquarters was in turmoil in the wake of a scandal over British government funding that led to the ouster of founder Peter Benenson. Taking advantage of the temporary uncertainty, Lyons had established an Amnesty section that differed fundamentally from the model London had promoted elsewhere—a "buccaneer" outfit in the eyes of Amnesty's leadership. Instead of forming adoption groups, most American AI "members" were in effect simply small donors. A handful of adoption groups worked according to Amnesty guidelines, writing letters on behalf of prisoners assigned to them, but the American section's main work was conducted through direct lobbying of embassies and UN missions and through letter-writing appeals conducted through its newsletter. Lyons had even set up his own prisoner research service, accumulating 1,200 dossiers, rather than relying on London's case sheets.[24] After an expensive mailing campaign in 1969 had failed to generate sufficient returns, plunging the organization into serious debt, the board decided to transfer its head office from Washington, D.C., to New York, and Lyons, who had so antagonized London headquarters that it issued him a no-confidence vote, was forced out. Chairman of the Board Mark Benenson, a lawyer of libertarian bent and lifetime member of the National Rifle Association, took charge.[25] He took the unusual step of writing to supporters with a plea for emergency funds to rescue the organization from financial "crisis."[26]

When Amelia "Amy" Augustus arrived as the new executive director in early 1971, soon after completing a doctorate in education at Columbia University, the rented offices on West 72nd Street were in a chaotic state. The files had been damaged in a fire, and Benenson had had to shovel them out from under ashes and charred ceiling beams. Some of the office equipment had been stolen when it had been left in the hallway to dry. Relations with the London Secretariat were tense, and the board was so divided it was hardly meeting.[27] As the newly launched *Ms.* magazine put it in a 1973 profile, "The organization had hit rock bottom."[28] Earlier links between AI and opposition to the Greek junta were still apparent, for Augustus, a Greek American, was hired in part on the basis of her antijunta lobbying in the late 1960s. It was in that connection that she had met journalist and former socialist Maurice Goldbloom, one of the links between Amnesty and the U.S. Committee for Democracy in Greece, who brought the AI USA executive directorship to her attention.[29]

When Augustus started there, she later recalled, international human rights activism was a "backwater" that received little press coverage, and the term itself was rarely used outside the halls of the UN. She worked long hours to change that situation. Energetic and enterprising, Augustus brought Amnesty's finances into the black and fostered the growth of adoption groups. But she butted heads with a fiercely independent West Coast office and with powerful board member Ivan Morris, who would take over as chairman in 1974. (Morris would also have difficulties with Augustus's successor.) Morris was irked by turf disputes with London, especially Augustus's agreement to represent the International Secretariat at the UN while AI USA was paying her salary. When it was revealed that she had surreptitiously taped a conversation with the head of the

West Coast office, Ginetta Sagan, the board summarily fired her.[30] Partly on the recommendation of SANE Executive Director Sanford Gottlieb, former student antiwar leader David Hawk was hired to replace her.[31] Arriving in 1974, Hawk—like most AI staff, young, passionate, and hardworking—would find that he had stepped on a steam engine.

That year Amnesty garnered increasing media attention, almost all of it favorable. Liberal columnist Anthony Lewis called AI "the highly-respected group that favors no ideology except humanity."[32] In May 1974, shortly after Amnesty had pushed through an antitorture resolution in the UN, Colman McCarthy penned a laudatory profile in the *Washington Post*. The organization's letter-writing and publicity-seeking methods might seem "trifling," McCarthy wrote, but its record of releases was impressive: 842 prisoners released in 1972 alone. The author went on to discuss the Fraser subcommittee report on human rights and Abourezk's efforts to stop funding to foreign police forces that used torture, linking a variety of issues under the rubric of human rights. Praising the article on the Senate floor, Abourezk declared that "it is the duty of this country to foster in the policy of friendly governments a deep and continuing concern for the fundamental human rights of every human being."[33]

By 1976 Amnesty's American branch had clearly placed itself on the map. AI's membership figures are difficult to evaluate, because adoption groups sometimes folded as quickly as they formed, and the numbers in each group also fluctuated. Aside from the test of whether a group submitted its annual dues, it was often hard to know if was active. In the United States, moreover, where Amnesty sympathizers were most often one-time donors or subscribers to the newsletter rather than adoption group members, numbers were even fuzzier.[34] Data handling was imprecise, and duplicate or even triplicate mailings were common, suggesting that in some cases donors were being counted more than once. AI USA figures showing that membership jumped from three thousand to fifty thousand between mid-1975 and late 1976 should thus be treated with caution. Even so, the numbers point to a stunning turnaround in the group's fortunes. If in adoption groups it continued to lag far behind the major European sections, in financial and political power it was leaping to the head of the class. As of May 1976, the U.S. section had offices in

David Hawk, executive director of Amnesty International's U.S. branch, in his Broadway office shortly after Amnesty won the Nobel Peace Prize in October 1977. *(New York Times)*

New York and San Francisco with a salaried staff of nine, supplemented with extensive volunteer labor. Its direct-mail fund-raising letters were sent to three million people, and income from donations approached a quarter million dollars. The *Amnesty Action* newsletter, appearing nearly monthly, had a mailing list of twenty-thousand, while the Western regional office published its own thick, photograph-filled quarterly journal called *Matchbox*.[35] Under the competent leadership of Rick Wright, hired as a half-time staffer, it opened an office in Washington, D.C. The chronic shortages of cash that had plagued it for years came to an end.[36]

Although Amnesty billed itself as a worldwide human rights organization, it was fundamentally different from the first generation of nongovernmental organizations focused specifically on human rights, exemplified by the International Commission of Jurists and the International League for the Rights of Man. The commission, based in Geneva and the best-known human rights nongovernmental organization internationally, was a small group of judges and jurists whose work aimed at strengthening the rule of law and human rights. Commenting on AI's formation, former commission head Norman Marsh acknowledged that "there was room for a body concerned simply with intervention, protest, relief, as distinguished from a body like the ICJ," with its slow, patient, long-term focus on changing underlying legal cultures. To some, Marsh noted with a hint of envy, a more appealing mode of action was "sending telegrams at the last minute to save people from the gallows."[37]

The only U.S.-based organization exclusively devoted to international human rights was the International League for the Rights of Man, formed in 1942 at the instigation of ACLU founder Roger Baldwin in an effort to reconstitute the French interwar Federation Internationale des Droits de l'Homme. Like Amnesty, it engaged in fact-finding and information-gathering, and it tried to publicize information on abuses in a variety of ways, from press releases to published reports to testimony before congressional committees. But the league took the entire Universal Declaration as its mandate (and spent much effort in its early decades on decolonization issues), whereas Amnesty limited its causes to political prisoners and torture. The league, moreover, was an elite, professional, predominantly male group, consisting mostly of lawyers, with no aspirations to generate grassroots membership or to mobilize broad-based public opinion. Akin to a social group generated from an old boys' network, it preferred "discreet and indirect political action." Even after many years of frustratingly meager results, it never gave up on the empty rituals of UN lobbying.[38]

Amnesty, in contrast, was mass-based and dependent on publicity to advance its cause. Like many other nongovernmental organizations, it had consultative status at the UN's Economic and Social Council and worked hard to strengthen international legal standards, drafting and then spearheading the 1975 adoption of the UN Declaration on Torture. But AI USA's leaders mostly disdained UN work. Mark Benenson, writing in 1970, was sharply condescending:

> For Amnesty the UN is really a sideshow, a lot of talk mostly, and the basic work of prisoner assistance isn't done there and can't be. Unless one is careful, unlimited time can be wasted fluffing about the corridors, gossiping at parties, and making courtesy calls. Everyone there spends lots of effort massaging the other fellow's ego and few of them realize what a monument to Parkinsonism the UN is. Less is done in more time by high IQs about human rights there, especially at committee meetings, than anywhere else on this planet. . . . It is too easy for an NGO to become UNified and to fall into the easy ways of the new international bureaucrats of human rights, who spend most of their time talking to each other.[39]

Amnesty's primary target for generating action was global public opinion, and it chose from the beginning to harness its fortunes to media attention. As an organization it would prove especially adept at mobilizing the energies and talents of women (the ones who, in its founder's patronizing view, had failed to fulfill their maternal instincts).[40] The league's approach was legalistic; Amnesty's was emotional, emphasizing empathy more than legality as the wellspring of action. When the Greek dictatorship garnered headlines for its abuses, the league compiled a 175-page complaint, heavy with detailed evidence of torture, arbitrary arrest and detention, and suppression of free speech and press, and submitted it to the UN. The UN's Subcommission on Prevention of Discrimination and Protection of Minorities considered the complaint but predictably did nothing, and the media ignored the entire effort.[41] In comparison

Amnesty gained extensive recognition and respect from its headline-garnering public reports on torture in Greece and its special campaign against torture in 1973 and 1974, which included mass actions like gathering a million signatures on a petition to ban torture.[42]

Those who joined believing that the purity of Amnesty's mission would override personal politics, however, were quickly disillusioned. Amnesty attracted able, energetic, and dedicated volunteers and paid employees, but was also a haven for people with, as one member put it, "power problems." Some were anarchists who philosophically refused to abide by organizational principles; some were ambitious, self-directed people who disliked following directions. The outcome was dissension at all levels: within national headquarters, between national headquarters and regional offices, and within regional offices.[43]

Relations between the U.S. section and London headquarters were often tense, characterized by mutual suspicion and misunderstanding. The Americans at first argued that they should be free to choose which prisoner cases to pursue, how to pursue them, how to raise and spend funds, and how to structure their organization. London, in their view, took the attitude that "Father knows best" and "we are the boss," and often appeared more interested in stamping out dissent than in fostering vigorous national sections.[44] In the early 1970s there were clashes over funding, as both London and New York sought grants from U.S.-based philanthropic bodies such as the Ford Foundation.[45] AI USA took up arms when the secretariat opened a tax-exempt charitable corporation called Amnesty International Development in order to solicit funds in the United States. Benenson threatened to prevent the incorporation if it happened in New York, so London moved it to Pennsylvania. It was apparently never used, and London eventually ruled out foundation money altogether, but the damage to relations was significant.[46] Many in the American section were enraged by a sharply critical London report on Israeli human rights violations.[47] Until the second half of the 1970s, AI USA participated very little in shaping the direction of AI as a whole, and face-to-face meetings were infrequent. Only when American board member Andrew Blane became a member of the International Executive Committee in 1975 was a regular conduit for influence established.[48]

The issue that caused the most heated confrontations stemmed from London's suspicions about its American affiliate's relationship to the

U.S. government. In London's view, it was fine to work with Congress, but the State Department was to be avoided. It was a view shared by some others in the movement, who also worried that AI USA was being co-opted by the U.S. government.[49] By 1976, as one American put it, "the U.S. section [was] at least emerging as a force of its own in A.I.," particularly because of its influence in Congress, but it resented the way the secretariat treated it as a bunch of "amateurs." American Tom Jones angrily accused the Londoners of translating a "mistrust of the U.S. Government Yankee Imperialist War-mongering Capitalists" into mistrust of AI USA—despite the fact that "many of us have spent a good number of years in open opposition to U.S. policies in Vietnam, South Africa, Latin America, you name it." American staffers took offense at London's insinuations that they pursued contacts with ambassadors, generals, and Cabinet secretaries because they were in awe of powerful men and suggested that London was in the grip of "paranoia" for fearing that "somehow Kissinger is going to use A.I. without doing anything to help us."[50] Tensions subsided only gradually.

Amnesty resolutely portrayed itself as nonpartisan—indeed as beyond politics. AI USA sometimes took nonpartisanship to the point of cultural relativism, as when Amy Augustus was quoted as saying, "All systems, all governments are tainted. Anyone who fights in a war for any of them has to be crazy."[51] Despite its apolitical mantra, its most prominent activities and the majority of its leaders and grassroots members were on the left of the political spectrum. In 1974 an advertisement for Amnesty publications listed thirty that dealt with specific countries, of which only two were communist countries. More than half covered right-wing dictatorships in Latin America, and the rest were on other U.S. allies.[52] The U.S. branch advertised in liberal news outlets such as the *New Republic* and the *New York Review of Books* (whose editor, Whitney Ellsworth, was on the board).[53] The direct-mail lists that brought in the biggest responses to AI USA solicitations came from liberal-minded religious groups and charities (Clergy and Laity Concerned, World Mercy Fund); environmental groups (Environmental Action, Natural Resources Defense Council); liberal political groups (ADA, National Coalition to Ban Handguns, Planned Parenthood, Ramsey Clark '74, Udall '76, lists called "recent donors to liberal candidates" and "contributors to peace and progressive organizations"); civil rights and civil liberties groups (Southern Poverty Law Center, the ACLU); liberal journals (the *New Republic,* the *Nation,* the *Progressive,* the *New York Review of Books*); and peace and antinuclear organizations (Fund for Peace, Union of Concerned Scientists, *Bulletin of Atomic Scientists*).[54] The list reads like a who's who of 1970s liberal causes.

The presence of conservative commentator William F. Buckley, Jr., on Amnesty USA's board (and later on its National Advisory Council) was a modest effort to feign political balance. Until resigning in 1977 over Amnesty's campaign against capital punishment, the well-known journalist was, as a colleague put it, "a solitary conservative on the masthead surrounded by dozens of liberals."[55] The most prominent conservative associated with AI maintained an arm's-length relationship, sympathetic to the group's stated aims but never quite comfortable with its tactics. Lyons was always eager to be provocative, and it had been his idea to ask the famed conservative editor of the *National Review* to join the board after Buckley publicly criticized Amnesty's reporting on torture in Greece as "undocumented." In a column on his decision to join, Buckley "defensively" explained that "by and large Amnesty is concerned with the kind of thing decent people ought to be concerned about, mainly the imperative to help others who are in trouble. In Amnesty's case, political trouble."[56] Extending the invitation to Buckley, Lyons acknowledged that AI USA was situated on the left of the political spectrum. "We would like to have at least one or two people in our hierarchy who would not take everything emanating from the liberal establishment, to the periphery of which I suppose we are attached, as Olympic pronouncements," Lyons wrote. "We proclaim we are apolitical, let it be a little more so."[57] Though Buckley published occasional articles featuring the cases of political prisoners and twice covered Amnesty on his television program, *Firing Line,* he never attended Amnesty meetings and in 1971 resigned from the board, accusing the organization of antinomianism and decrying AI's adoption of American draft resisters as prisoners of conscience. He was persuaded to stay on the larger advisory council as "a lurker among the liberals," as Benenson put it, but his role after 1971 was mostly nominal.[58]

The relatively conservative Democratic foreign policy expert and Columbia University professor Zbigniew Brzezinski, liberal Republican

Senator Jacob Javits, and Nixon's UN Human Rights Commission representative Rita Hauser were as far right as the rest of the masthead went. As Amnesty's profile grew, conservative publications repeatedly branded it as leftist, marshaling evidence that it concentrated on abuses in right-wing dictatorships and sometimes displayed a lenient attitude toward dictatorships on the left. Measuring the tone of reporting and column inches spent criticizing particular countries, they charged that Amnesty downplayed and even sometimes excused communist brutalities.[59] Responding to one such critique, AI USA board member Andrew Blane explained that Amnesty neither supported nor opposed political groups and governments; it only opposed specific acts by governments or groups.[60] It was a position that was unacceptable to many on the right, who saw it as a kind of moral relativism that failed to take into account the essential facts of the communist world's pervasive repression and threat to world peace.

The charge that Amnesty's reporting devoted the most space to more open societies was fundamentally correct, and the appearance of political bias troubled some AI USA members. In 1973 they proposed a resolution to the secretariat expressing concern over a lack of evenhandedness. It noted that AI had devoted major attention to abuses in Chile but virtually none to Cuba; had detailed allegations of torture by Israel while virtually ignoring torture in Arab countries; and had sent missions to South Vietnam but not to North Vietnam. The organization appeared to have two sets of standards, it said: one for open and another for closed societies. The resolution noted that AI's 1973 *Report on Torture* had spent over four times as much space on South Vietnam as it had on Cuba.[61] To address such concerns, AI's International Council set up a Committee on Impartiality in 1974. Amnesty devoted notable attention to Soviet dissidents, and after first demurring had agreed to the establishment of an AI office in Moscow. It sponsored the publication of a translated version of the major samizdat outlet, the *Chronicle of Current Events*. But internal documents noted that only 15 percent of AI's work dealt with communist countries, while just over half targeted the Third World. Internal critics singled out its lack of attention to China, North Korea, and North Vietnam.[62] Largely for the pragmatic reason that information remained far easier to obtain in more open societies, the disproportionate attention to abuses in those countries—typically allied with the United States—continued.

The extraordinary role that AI USA's West Coast branch played in its development suggests how much left-liberal politics worked as an engine of growth for grassroots human rights organizing. The San Francisco Bay Area had been the epicenter of the counterculture and antiwar movements of the sixties, and its leftist atmosphere, its appeal as a magnet for Asian and Latin American émigrés, and its money would make it important also for the human rights movement of the seventies. Tellingly, if San Francisco and Berkeley had been the hot spots in the sixties, the smaller and quieter human rights movement had its geographic center in the suburbs to the south, in small towns like Atherton and Woodside. Amnesty USA's rapid expansion was powered in large part by its West Coast branch, which by 1974 claimed more than half the country's members.[63] The New York branch was dominated by academics and professionals, especially the long-standing members of the highly successful Riverside adoption group, people like Ivan Morris, a professor of Japanese literature at Columbia University, Arthur Danto, a professor of philosophy at Columbia, and Barbara Sproul, a professor of comparative religion at Hunter College, along with what one staffer called "rich New Yorkers"—men like Whitney Ellsworth and Michael Straight.[64] The Californians, in contrast, were younger, hipper products of the sixties counterculture. Men predominated in New York; in California women ran the show. The West Coast branch had more women in more prominent positions, and its booming success was due to the efforts of its all-female leadership: former political prisoner Ginetta Sagan and famed folk singer Joan Baez, with crucial financial backing and contacts provided by philanthropist Sally Lilienthal.[65]

Sagan might have stepped out of the pages of Betty Friedan's 1963 blockbuster *The Feminine Mystique:* a college-educated suburban housewife and mother, in search of greater meaning in her life. An Italian émigré, she was herself a former political prisoner who had suffered imprisonment and torture for her resistance work against Mussolini's regime during the war. Living in Washington, D.C., after moving to the United States, she joined Paul Lyons's fledgling organization, spurred by hearing "horrible, horrible stories of torture" from friends and acquaintances in Greece.[66] When her husband moved the family to northern California in 1968, she founded the first AI group on the West Coast, which began meeting in her living room.[67] Passionate and energetic, colleagues likened her to a hummingbird or "a force of nature."[68] She spent days and weeks on the road traveling around the western states talking about Amnesty and soliciting new members. "I think she has probably organized more people than anyone else in the human rights movement globally," said her Amnesty colleague David Hinckley in 1995. "She really is the one who got Amnesty International off the ground in this country."[69] Even when she talked about torture, her message was compellingly optimistic, grounded in a faith in American goodness that echoed the kind of language Jimmy Carter would use. "I believe very firmly that there exists a basic, innate decency in the American people," she wrote. "Once they become aware of the atrocities committed against human beings all over Latin America, the Soviet Union, and in 60 other nations in this world . . . they will want to do something."[70]

The prominent involvement of left-wing icon Joan Baez reinforced the West Coast branch's identification as an organization of the left. What would be a long-lived partnership between Sagan and the famous folk singer began with a serendipitous house call. Working the neighborhoods around her hometown of Atherton, Sagan simply walked up to Baez's house, holding a big bunch of documents with "grisly pictures of tortured prisoners," and told her about Amnesty.[71] Baez leapt on board with characteristic enthusiasm. Her politics and her celebrity associations with sixties heroes such as Martin Luther King, Jr., and Bob Dylan endeared her to those on the left; her principled tax evasion and 1972 visit to North Vietnam made her an enemy to many on the right. Raised by parents who converted to Quakerism, she embraced pacifism and social justice as an adult. Looking for an outlet for ill-defined political energies in the midsixties, she had founded the Institute for the Study of Nonviolence, which drew dozens of acolytes to a quintessentially sixties curriculum that included yoga, meditation, and free-form group discussions.[72] When Sagan approached her, "the barefoot Madonna" had tired of the institute, and her antiwar work was winding down. Amnesty seemed perfectly to fill her needs. Her antiwar friends "burned out" when the war ended, she recalled, but she started to read Amnesty torture reports that "literally" made her sick. A spark was lit.[73] In contrast to her other political causes like disarmament, which were never-ending quests, she felt that Amnesty "produced tangible results." The coup in Chile and the "monstrous" repression that followed was a key catalyst, she later wrote, convincing her to take "a year out of [her] life" to get Amnesty set up on the West Coast.[74]

Like the former civil rights advocate and folk singer Theodore Bikel, who worked for Amnesty on the East Coast, Baez was precursor and precedent for the much larger-scale involvement of celebrities, especially celebrity musicians, in Amnesty activities in the 1980s, when U2, Sting, and other major bands performed across the United States and the world to raise awareness of human rights. At her own initiative, Baez began holding benefit concerts across the western United States, donating the proceeds to Amnesty. When the concert ended, an AI staffer would hold a meeting to explain AI's work, often drawing more than a hundred people.[75] In 1974 the singer recorded a Spanish-language album, *Gracias a la Vida*, dedicated to all the people of Chile, especially the victims.[76] She joined AI USA's board, performed in Paris at Amnesty's 1973 antitorture conference, and became a rallying figure for AI and its U.S. section. Like Mercouri—with whom she did a benefit concert on behalf of Greek political prisoners—Baez's fame fed public and media interest in her cause.[77]

Baez and Sagan fostered an explosion in West Coast adoption groups, but their office was also deeply involved in fund-raising, publicity, and press relations. Like the New York headquarters, which had much better luck with direct mail in the 1970s than it had in the 1960s, the West Coast unit used direct-mail campaigns to great success. An early effort in 1974 organized by Frank Mankiewicz netted $3,000 just within the first two weeks.[78] That year the San Francisco office reported that with donated help they had produced fifty copies of radio spots and fifty copies of television spots and could hardly keep up with the demand from stations wanting to play them.[79] The rival Los Angeles–area office was almost as innovative. By 1976, for example, the Southern California district had

Folk singer Joan Baez, here being interviewed on television, spent a year building up Amnesty International's U.S. West Coast branch, giving fundraising concerts, handing out leaflets, and soliciting wealthy donors. (Getty)

eleven adoption groups, eleven action groups, two professional support groups (for clergy and academics), a speakers' bureau, a journalists' group (which worked for imprisoned journalists), and press and fundraising committees. The academic group consisted of regional experts who participated in press conferences to corroborate charges or provided advice about working effectively in particular countries. The Southern California groups brought in enough money to pay a full-time organizer.[80]

The California branch was successful because it concentrated on causes dear to the political left. Writing in the *National Review*, George Nash attributed much of AI USA's distinct leftward tilt to the "young,

superliberal activists from California" who constituted half the membership.[81] Sagan objected to the characterization—she was herself a conservative, she wrote—but she acknowledged that despite her efforts AI was
attractive primarily to liberals.[82] "It seems as though the liberals are
always ready to take a public stand and speak out for human rights, but
not the conservatives," she lamented.[83] One of Sagan's early financial
coups was a $25,000 matching grant from Max Palevsky—McGovern's
former finance chairman.[84]

Typical of the West Coast organization's efforts was one of the many
speaking tours that were becoming a staple of human rights activism.
Getting victims in front of audiences to talk about their experiences fostered empathy between Americans and the individuals who were now
the focus of humanitarian sentiment. Financed by Sagan and Sally
Lilienthal and with the cosponsorship of the American Friends Service
Committee and Clergy and Laity Concerned, the San Francisco office
arranged a three-week, cross-country speaking tour for Jean-Pierre
Debris and André Menras, French teachers who had been imprisoned in
South Vietnam for two and half years for staging a pro–National Libera-
ion Front demonstration. After their release the Frenchmen had published an account of the brutal treatment meted out to prisoners under
Thieu's regime, pointing to American complicity in the injustice and
brutality of the regime.[85] After 1975 Sagan and Baez became outspoken
critics of the Vietnamese communists and their brutal reeducation
camps, for which they incurred the ire of many National Liberation Front
sympathizers on the American left, but the West Coast AI USA's emphasis
remained on abuses in right-wing dictatorships, especially in Latin
America. Much of its popularity was due to its close association with
activism on behalf of Chile after 1973.

The enterprising efforts of the West Coast activists were not always
appreciated back east. Tensions erupted periodically between the New
York headquarters of the national section and the West Coast leaders,
who had incorporated independently instead of as an arm of the New
York unit. Distance and lack of oversight and coordination led the San
Francisco section in particular to chart its own course, sometimes at
odds with national directives.[86] Hawk was hired in large part to bridge

the continental divide. As a former antiwar activist with contacts across the country, he was one of the few candidates acceptable to both coasts. Healing the rift and bringing organizational coherence to AI's disparate units would take him a couple of years.

Amnesty's image as a grassroots organization masked a more complicated reality. In theory, national sections comprised adoption groups, each of which was assigned cases by the international research office in London. To foster impartiality, groups were governed by the "rule of three," advocating for a set of three prisoners, one from the West, one from a communist country, and one from the Third World. They were enjoined from acting on behalf of prisoners in their own countries. Dedicated individuals held group meetings, perhaps monthly, writing letters to governments to request the release of "their" prisoners and holding bake sales and other small-scale fund-raisers to send relief to prisoners or their families and to fund the dues each group had to pay to the central organization.

In the mid-1970s AI USA moved closer to this model than it had under Lyons and Benenson, who had scorned it as impractical under American conditions, but adoption groups remained secondary to its overall mission. The vast bulk of its income came not from group dues but from direct-mail solicitation, from which one-off donations or "membership dues" of ten or later fifteen dollars a year streamed in. This income in turn allowed Amnesty's U.S. section to hire more staff, which then engaged in publicity to raise awareness about human rights and about Amnesty itself, in lobbying and pressing individual cases in Washington, and in information-gathering.[87] AI USA was acutely conscious of the politics of image. In 1974 its board member Norman Schorr, head of a New York public relations firm, oversaw a new publicity committee to monitor and coordinate television and radio appearances, press releases, and advertising.[88] In 1977 it added a press office, "incalculably" increasing media coverage.[89]

AI USA's direct-mail solicitations struck a chord with many recipients in part because they so closely dovetailed with the prevailing political Zeitgeist. Burying 1960s visions of revolutionary social transformations,

Amnesty instead created a micropolitics of "individuals working for individuals."[90] Amnesty branded this approach apolitical, but it had politics at its very core. It was a politics based on alleviation of the plight of victims, with victimhood defined and certified by the West. Advocacy of violence disqualified a prisoner from Amnesty's definition of prisoner of conscience, and adoptees were chosen by Amnesty's research office without consulting the prisoner or the prisoner's family. The voices of victims were present in Amnesty campaigns, but in most cases only to describe their bodily violations, rather than their society's problems or their political visions. Apart from some of the communist-bloc dissidents, the prisoners Amnesty adopted were almost entirely unknowns, meaning that instead of offering up heroes like Sakharov whose resistance could be celebrated and whose courage provided inspiration, Amnesty's efforts tended to evoke simple pity for Third World victims. Courageous activists in the countries where repression was occurring often assisted Amnesty and even made its work possible, but in important ways the narrative Amnesty conveyed was one of Western do-gooders rescuing helpless Third World victims.

Though Amnesty International's achievements are impossible to measure precisely, the organization undoubtedly helped thousands of prisoners, giving them hope, reducing the terms of their imprisonment, and providing relief to their families. Amnesty could point to many letters of gratitude from freed adopted prisoners. On a grander scale its efforts inspired the world to hold governments accountable for some of the most horrifying state-sponsored abuse of individuals. But its efforts inevitably involved political trade-offs. Amnesty treated political problems as moral ones, thereby eliding the deeper political changes that social justice often required. Focusing on "mere" protection of individuals from "fundamental wrongs" did not move above politics or create an antipolitics but instead worked to push politics, as a project of collective empowerment, to the sidelines. Amnesty's critics saw well-intentioned arrogance and a form of Western cultural imperialism.[91] Its mode of action tried to create ties between Western members and foreign victims, and adoption groups sometimes directly corresponded with prisoners or their families, but in others ways it created distance, for helping victims of anomalous evil acts tended to push out of view deeper structures of economic and political interdependence in which the helpers themselves might be implicated. The West German section of Amnesty in these years was much enamored of the idea of "coresponsibility" for repression, but the concept did not have much resonance in the U.S. section.[92] The rule that groups could not work on their own countries reinforced the conceptual shift that congressional legislation had initiated, turning human rights from domestic politics into foreign policy.

AI USA's fund-raising and publicity efforts had the effect of echoing the message of the liberal human rights initiatives that were coming out of Congress: torture and political imprisonment were the worst abuses, problems were elsewhere, Americans were moral. A sense of responsibility surely spurred the appeal of liberal human rights initiatives, particularly since they so often targeted countries in which the United States appeared to have had a role in abetting repression. Yet implicitly part of the message was that the country's responsibility for injustice abroad was indirect and easily alleviated.

In Amnesty's operational code, prisoners of conscience were fundamentally the same everywhere. The international organization built its reputation on the provision of information: detailed prisoner case sheets and reports filled with firsthand testimony about mistreatment. The reliability of this information, gradually established by the early 1970s, gave the organization credibility. But in other respects the details were beside the point. The political causes prisoners waged and the political and social contexts in which they lived were elided as irrelevant. The decontextualized approach the West Coast office honed so successfully is apparent in direct-mail letters that highlighted the stories of particular individuals, sometimes composites rather than real people, most often of prisoners who had been subjected to brutal torture, treating prisoners generically. "Your brother died as well as could be expected," began a fund-raising appeal generated by the West Coast office, which told the reader that his or her "brother" had died under torture and for believing in freedom of conscience—"the fundamental freedom." Would the reader, the appeal asked, acknowledge his or her kinship with this "brother" in the "family of man"?[93] Another letter took a similar approach:

Dear Reader:

You are walking toward your favorite store, thinking about a wedding gift you plan to buy. An unmarked car pulls up. Two men leap out, drag you into the back seat, plunge a hypodermic needle into your arm.

When you come to, you find yourself lying half-naked in a pool of dirty water on the floor of a windowless cell. Your captors keep beating you with truncheons, kicking you, pushing you up against the walls. Then they attack you sexually, mocking you and hinting that other members of your family are undergoing the same horror.

You don't know *why* you've been imprisoned. You don't know *what* your torturers hope to make you say. You don't know *where* to turn. You've joined the nightmare world of the political prisoner.[94]

Contrary to what the letter suggested, many dissidents would have known precisely why they were being imprisoned. Revolutionaries would have known that their torturers wanted the names of fellow conspirators. But much Amnesty literature suggested that those arrested were entirely innocent—not only of any crime that could justify torture, but of any political activity at all.

Such appeals derived much of their success from Amnesty's narrow mandate and a concomitant sense that small actions could have tangible effects. Amnesty specifically abjured studying or trying to remedy the root causes of abuses. As one publication put it, "Amnesty's mission is to help people and not to reform governments."[95] Success, framed in these narrow terms, seemed relatively easy to achieve: it could be measured, confirmed, celebrated. Americans could write a letter, sign a petition, or send a check for ten dollars, and—Amnesty told them—that small action would help someone somewhere, probably someone being tortured or brutally mistreated merely for expressing their opinion.

Fund-raising letters promised readers that they could feel good. "Sometimes you will succeed," one of Sagan's appeals began. "Through your efforts, a fellow human will be spared from the firing squad, or will be released from torture, or will be set free and returned to his loved ones. . . . You cannot imagine, until it happens, the emotions you will experience when you can say to yourself, 'Because of me, he lives.' And this *will* happen. I can promise you that."[96] It was true that Amnesty

# The gang that got Fernando
# Flores out of a Chilean jail

This Amesty International group in San Francisco was assigned the case of Fernando Flores, a former Chilean Cabinet Minister who was imprisoned by the Chilean military government following the 1973 coup. They spent three years writing letters, making phone calls, drawing public attention to Flores' condition and raising money to help his family. Finally Fernando Flores was freed.

If you would like to work in a group or as an individual in letter writing and publicity campaigns to free those imprisoned for their beliefs and to stop torture throughout the world, join Amnesty International, 2112 Broadway, New York, New York 10023. And become part of a movement that last year got 1600 prisoners of conscience out of jail.

An early 1980 Amnesty International USA poster suggesting that a San Francisco group secured the release of a Chilean prisoner. Amnesty International flowered in the United States because it seemed to promise tangible results. (Amnesty International) donors might feel anguished to read about torture, Sagan admitted, but they could also "experience the supreme joy of learning about case after case where prisoners have been set free . . . thanks to *their* help." She exhorted, "I assure you—it's a beautiful feeling. I invite you to experience it."[97]

Amnesty USA's publications assured readers that action would be effective. Its cause was not a noble one doomed to failure but a noble one guaranteed results. Although Amnesty could rarely document a clear connection between its efforts and the release of prisoners—few governments were willing to admit that they were susceptible to such pressure—AI USA often boldly claimed credit for every adopted prisoner eventually released. "We have freed over 10,000 men and women. . . . Amnesty International does get results." Amnesty was unique, its organizers claimed, in that it gave members "a chance to take direct, effective action to assist other human beings"—even "to alter the course of history." Change one life for the better, Sagan assured prospective members, and they would "change the world."[98] "You should also know that no matter where these people are imprisoned—even in the deepest pit of the most remote chamber of horrors—there is a way you can help them regain their freedom," Sagan told them. "And by you—I mean *you*." Amnesty donors sometimes wept, sometimes rejoiced, she wrote, but they could always take heart in being "part of the most unrelenting force ever to set itself against the bastions of tyranny and inhumanity." "I hope you will help us liberate a 'brother' or 'sister' from a torturer's cell by giving as much as you can," Sagan implored. "If you can afford $15, make a sacrifice and give $25. . . . Please remember, many good people are counting on *you*. You are their hope."[99] Responsibility came not from any preexisting condition but existed only if the reader failed to take action once asked to do so.

AI USA, and especially its Washington office, was the most prominent member of a rapidly multiplying population of left-leaning nongovernmental organizations that created the first American mass movement on behalf of international human rights. Observers were already beginning to identify this constellation as a major political force—or more derisively, "the human rights industry." These groups often coordinated their activities among themselves, trading tips and personnel. This was especially true for Latin America, for it was the abuses of the new military dictatorships in the Southern Cone that generated the most concerted Western outrage. Latin America was at the vortex of the swirling networks of activists, émigrés, academics, and missionaries that achieved remarkable success in bringing abuses to worldwide attention.

These groups, including AI USA, worked hard to change American diplomacy. In contrast to peace and church groups earlier, which Congress and government officials had tended to see as naïve and outside the mainstream, human rights groups by the mid-1970s were perceived as legitimate participants in policy-making. Their staffs worked closely with sympathetic members of Congress. They undertook local letter-writing and petition-gathering campaigns to pressure less sympathetic members of Congress before key votes. By the late 1970s members of Congress found the voice of the human rights lobby impossible to ignore. An unsympathetic Senate committee staffer described the situation as "Human rights is now big politics."[100] The attitude of Congress increasingly forced the executive branch to pay heed as well. In 1976, for example, Congress made the extent to which countries permitted investigations by groups like AI part of the process of assessing whether countries were eligible for aid by international financial institutions. Even before then, AI USA board member Rose Styron had convinced Treasury Secretary William Simon to represent Amnesty's interests during his travels, and he presented Amnesty-prepared lists of prisoners to governments in Eastern Europe, Saudi Arabia, and Argentina. In May 1976 he took a well-publicized "mission of liberation" to Chile asking for prisoner releases and expressing general concerns about human rights.[101] As a result of congressionally mandated human rights reforms in the diplomatic machinery, State Department officials took calls from representatives of groups like Amnesty, met them for lunch, read their reports, and crafted their own public statements partly with the reactions of these groups in mind. The new strategies marked a sharp change from earlier periods, when groups like the International League for the Rights of Man had poured their time and effort into fruitless lobbying of UN bodies and an occasional ineffectual letter of protest to the State Department.[102]

Fraser's office had long-standing close connections with Amnesty, no doubt in part a product of aide John Salzberg's previous work for the International Commission of Jurists. It was AI's testimony to Fraser's hearings that led a staffer to boast in late 1974 that "our clout on the Hill is not to be believed," and Fraser had pushed for Amnesty's U.S. branch to open an office in Washington.[103] Amnesty's head, Martin Ennals, had been the first witness in Fraser's first human rights hearings, and the two men remained in close contact. When the U.S. ambassador to Saigon, Graham Martin, irritated by Amnesty's reports of high numbers of political prisoners in South Vietnam, wrote to Ennals accusing the organization of purveying propaganda, Ennals passed the letter to Fraser, who wrote a sharply worded letter to Kissinger demanding the evidence.[104] In 1975 the London office described the Fraser subcommittee hearings as "the main fora for publicizing AI information in Washington," noting, "Where possible, we should discuss with Donald Fraser or John Salzberg the countries on which publicized testimony could be most influential and the witnesses who should be invited to appear."[105]

Fraser's Section 502B opened up new opportunities for human rights organizations. It provided new channels of access to the State Department and new justifications for information requests. Indeed, there were complaints among some in Amnesty's new Washington office about the demands of responding to 502B-related information from Congress, the State Department, and other human rights nongovernmental organizations. Although some AI officials worried about "taking sides" and about violating the organization's tax-exempt status through legislative activity, others saw 502B as a "vital tool for AI to use." AI, working with alongside groups such as the ADA and the Institute for International Policy, provided information to the State Department, prepared dossiers for congressmen to use in reviewing State's country reports, and informally coordinated congressional activity on 502B.[106]

Navigating among independence, impartiality, and influence was a source of continuing tension and debate within AI USA, with the quest for influence often taking front seat. The office it opened in Washington in 1976 was intended to participate in the political debates that Fraser had set off. It maintained links with academics and networks of academics, church groups, and union-affiliated activists such as the international units of the AFL-CIO.[107] It also devoted much energy to publicity-gathering activities: holding symposia on human rights, benefit concerts, and endless fund-raising.[108] Much of its time was taken up with feeding the growing thirst for information about human rights coming from the media, other nongovernmental organizations, and government. When David Goren of the American Jewish Congress was preparing to meet with the new Chilean ambassador, for example, he asked AI USA for a briefing. When Amnesty staff learned that the House Inter-American Affairs Subcommittee was planning a trip to Argentina and Chile, they briefed several subcommittee aides and sent materials to others.[109]

In testifying before congressional committees, feeding stories to the media, raising particular cases with the State Department, and choosing where to spotlight attention, Amnesty was central to shaping the political agenda. When Amnesty began its first country-specific campaign against Uruguay, for example, the Washington office organized a typical small demonstration. The author of an academic study on Uruguay spoke about human rights abuses to a crowd of about fifty in Lafeyette Park, after which the group marched to Virginia Avenue carrying placards and distributing leaflets, while marchers posing as Uruguayan police pretended to arrest, handcuff, and hood mock dissidents. The affair was capped by an all-night vigil.[110] Far more important than such efforts to influence public opinion, however, was direct pressure on Congress. In late 1976 a group of nongovernmental organizations (the National Council of Churches, the United Auto Workers, the Friends Committee, and others) wrote a letter urging Congress to back a move by Ed Koch to prohibit military aid to Uruguay. Amnesty could not sign directly, but its Washington office provided a purpose-made two-page summary of information about abuses in Uruguay to attach to the appeal. "Uruguayans face a future filled with fear, repression and torture," it began, and ended with a thinly veiled call to support Koch's amendment: "The alarming deterioration of human rights in Uruguay requires a reassessment by each nation of its relationship to the present regime."[111] The brief, detailed account by Amnesty helped the legislation gather enough support to pass. Placing Uruguay on the agenda in the first place was also an Amnesty achievement: as an AI USA staffer later recalled, without Amnesty's information, "Koch would not have known Uruguay from the moon."[112]

AI USA was thus an essential part of the legislative effort around which so much human rights organizing in the 1970s revolved: cutting off military, and sometimes economic, aid to repressive American allies. Although enjoined by charitable tax law from directly lobbying the government and from AI rules prohibiting taking a position on foreign aid, the office worked closely with the State Department's new human rights officers and with sympathetic members of Congress, providing information, requesting action, and prodding them to ask questions. As one scholar concluded, the human rights lobby, AI above all, provided "virtually all of the data" on repression of human rights in Latin America. It was often "data" with a human face, as arranging for victims to visit with members of Congress became a powerful way to elicit support. One aide recalled a meeting at which the daughter of Mennonite missionaries described to a powerful member of Congress her rape by Argentine military officials. His boss's eyes "were ablaze," the aide recalled, "simply livid. I knew right then that there was no way those goose-stepping perverts were getting a cent out of us that year." A halt in military aid to Argentina succeeded in 1977.[113]

The coordination behind an ADA-led effort to press the State Department to release human rights country reports provides further illustration of the ways that AI USA engaged in covert lobbying to cut off security assistance to human rights violators. The AI USA–ADA partnership gave Amnesty's U.S. section a backdoor entry into lobbying work it was enjoined from doing openly, while the ADA gained access to research it did not have the capacity to obtain itself. In the words of AI Washington staffer Rick Sloan, the aim was "to build the factual foundation and the political coalitions necessary to ensure that 502B [would become] a viable tool for Congress to influence foreign policy." In August 1976 Sloan began meeting with Bruce Cameron of the ADA and the Human Rights Working Group, along with congressional aides to Steven Solarz, Alan Cranston, Donald Fraser, and Hubert Humphrey, to devise a program that would elicit the release of the State Department's country reports. Due to time constraints, the collaborators decided the most effective route would be to pressure Humphrey, head of the Senate Foreign Relations Committee, to request specific country reports. The group divided up the preparation of dossiers on the human rights records of countries of concern: Indonesia, the Philippines, South Korea, Haiti, Uruguay, and Argentina. These were to be sent to Humphrey for his use in buttressing his request to the State Department. Not without discord, the group agreed to throw in requests for reports on leftist dictatorships in Peru and Ethiopia in order to give the appearance of political balance. Cameron and Sloan worked together on the final wording of the letter to Humphrey. In early September, Humphrey duly forwarded to the State Department a request for reports on seventeen countries. To the group's disappointment, the State Department released the reports but insisted on keeping them classified, foiling the group's efforts to use them for publicity purposes.[114]

Amnesty's growing influence on the aid policies of the U.S. government (and on some European governments) led some members to call for the organization to develop a policy on aid, rather than insisting that its responsibility ended with the provision of information. Some members argued that political and economic problems were more important than the narrow legal issues that comprised Amnesty's mission, and that the problem of political imprisonment could not truly be tackled unless the larger structural problems that caused political imprisonment were addressed. "The economic, social and political context is not an abstract concern, but the problem itself," a 1976 regional report concluded.[115] At a 1978 conference on trade, aid, and human rights, Amnesty's leadership and outside experts discussed the history of development aid, links between economic structures and political repression, and the parameters of Amnesty's role in combating repression. Noting that the State Department's 1977 human rights country reports almost exclusively cited AI's information, former Amnesty researcher Roger Plant regretted that the reports therefore focused on the rights violations that fell within Amnesty's narrow mandate, rather than including economic and social rights. "Amnesty must find a better way of relating to" economic issues, Plant said. British member Dick Barbor-Might argued that it was not a question of whether Amnesty wanted to intervene in political decisions; it already was doing so. "We are not outside of what is happening," he said. "We are part of the reality in which we intervene." Chilean Carlos Fortin said that Amnesty would be called on more and more "to answer further questions about why repression happens. The answer that there are not sufficient men of good will in the world is not good enough; one has to move into muddier areas."

But key members of the International Executive Committee disagreed. Mumtaz Soysal explained that Amnesty should let others make the decisions; it "must retain its purist role and its clean conscience." The future head of AI, Thomas Hammarberg, concurred. "Our effectiveness depends on our narrow focus and we must get results," he told the seminar, and he took issue with the contention that providing policy-makers with information made Amnesty responsible for the decisions that resulted.[116] Hammarberg's views would prevail: until 2003, Amnesty remained committed to its narrow mandate.

The mass movement that coalesced under the slogan of international human rights in the 1970s was in some respects similar to the motley groups that had harnessed white activism in the 1960s, and there were substantial continuities in personnel. The human rights groups were white, middle class, and geographically concentrated on the coasts, with some representation in major cities and college towns in the Midwest. They took up a much quieter, less countercultural style of activism, one that—certainly in its liberal guise—tried not to seem politicized. Their members spoke the language of power and national interest. They advocated moderate programs. They ran sophisticated bureaucratic organizations with state-of-the-art communications and fund-raising efforts.[117]

Recalling the middle years of the 1970s, activist Jeri Laber wrote, "It was a heady, intoxicating time for all of us."[118] The prospect of making a difference was indeed "heady." For most, the price was small: a petition signed, a letter written, a check mailed. Yet, as Ginetta Sagan promised her audience with such great effect, results were virtually guaranteed— not for any particular victim, but for someone, somewhere. Surely this was a comforting salve for the consciences of liberal Americans who had so recently been horrified by accounts of American wrongdoing in Vietnam.

An early Amnesty document had described the organization's goal as a "sudden movement of the heart" to link men and women of goodwill across national boundaries.[119] The goal of the new activism, as one scholar has characterized it, was to "expand, enrich, and dignify" politics.[120] It provided new tools and a new language for activists around the world, and focused unprecedented global attention on horrifying abuse. It forged empathetic links between Americans and victims abroad. "Many of our active members become emotionally tied to the prisoners. We know them by name, know their families, occasionally even know the names of their torturers," a West Coast appeal said.[121]

Amnesty helped foster a new global consciousness and powerful fellow-feeling for distant suffering. But there were limits, for the links were necessarily shallow and rarely rested on deep understanding.[122] Except for members of solidarity groups, most Americans who took part in human rights campaigns in the 1970s knew very little about the politics and cultures of the societies they were trying to help. Human rights groups publicized the cases of individuals, but almost always stripped the cases of political context, such that consumers of the publicity campaigns emerged without a picture of why other societies were in turmoil. Victims of torture were depicted as innocents, even when they had engaged in revolutionary violence. Torture, the liberal human rights cause célèbre in the 1970s, was portrayed as a rising epidemic, a disease that spread from country to country and could be fought without regard to political conditions in any one place.[123] As horrific as torture was, human rights groups presented it as a problem with a solution. One need only shame torturers into stopping. In this framing, problems of brutality and inequality in the world were the products of specific deviant individuals who could be deterred by aid reductions, enactment of laws, or the staging of international tribunals. Evil was over there, not at home.

Increasingly Amnesty and others defined human rights in the American political scene. The strength of Amnesty and like-minded human rights organizations helped imprint human rights as a liberal concern, a version of human rights that worked for those who believed that the world had moved beyond the Cold War. But the meaning of human rights was still contested. While Amnesty observed Helsinki Final Act follow-ups with quiet circumspection, Americans more concerned with Soviet oppression founded what would become Amnesty's major rival: Human Rights Watch. Freedom House, another group that would later grow in importance as it positioned itself as a human rights body, emphasized to donors that it had no ties to Amnesty and privately criticized its rival for focusing on the effects rather than the causes of repression and for "emphasiz[ing] the most aberrational acts of violence by the government."[124] Meanwhile neoconservatives continued to promote their own conceptions of human rights, and the contest between left and right to define the scope and terms of a new moral agenda would play out with fateful consequences in the 1976 election year.

## CHAPTER 9

# A Moralist Campaigns for President

A S AMERICA'S BICENTENNIAL year opened—an anniversary cele-brating "a revolution made in the name of human rights"—many Americans felt that Washington politics had reached a historic low.[1] They had watched the Watergate scandal consume the nation's political life, a president resign in disgrace, and the war in Vietnam come to an ignoble end. Congressional investigating committees uncovered secret plots to assassinate foreign leaders and unsavory covert operations, including the manipulation of foreign elections—activities that made U.S. foreign policy appear violent, illegal, and antidemocratic. Though their election-year attention was dominated by serious economic problems at home, Americans yearned for a revitalization of morality.

Perhaps surprisingly, the widespread desire for more explicit moral purpose in framing America's role in the world did not translate into a ready embrace of international human rights promotion. Despite the attention human rights had gained in Congress, discussions of morality in the 1976 presidential contest rarely were cast in the language of human rights until it was almost over. In the Republican Party, a bitter struggle between the moderate wing headed by Ford and insurgent forces mustered by Ronald Reagan was waged in part over détente's apparent jettisoning of morality in foreign policy. The issue of human rights was but one in a broad arsenal of moral slogans bandied about in the Republican debate, and it never became a focal point for the party or the media. Even so, it was an identifiable theme in the GOP's effort to identify a moral thread to its foreign policy.

Acting as Ford's surrogate in the field of foreign policy, Kissinger made two major contributions to the 1976 campaign: keeping his head low to deflect attention from the newly toxic issue of détente, and using official speeches to declaim the administration's ostensible commitment to human rights. The secretary of state felt compelled to argue that his foreign policy took human rights into account, because he needed to counter the perception that détente ignored the moral dimensions of anticommunism. Reagan and his backers, echoing the kinds of concerns the Jackson Democrats had been raising, charged that the Helsinki Accords' alleged acquiescence to Soviet domination of Eastern Europe and the administration's neglect of the plight of Soviet dissidents proved that détente rested on a craven moral relativism.

The salience of human rights for the Democratic Party's presidential candidates was strikingly less obvious. Carter's embrace of the concept was both late and serendipitous, a product of lobbying from a key aide and the resonance the issue turned out to have among the public once it had been broached. His more liberal competitors for the Democratic nomination had almost nothing to say about human rights. Jackson was the only Democrat identified with international human rights, and until he was knocked out of the primaries, he ensured that international human rights had a conservative, anticommunist coloring. Carter tentatively picked up the issue after Jackson's exit left it politically available, but he did so without developing a clear conception of what it meant.

In the public mind, human rights still primarily conjured up the domestic sphere. Abortion, the Equal Rights Amendment, gay rights, and civil rights were vigorously contested issues, part of an ongoing rights revolution in which disadvantaged groups—women, homosexuals, and ethnic and racial minorities—used rights-based claims, including the language of human rights, to lobby for redress and advantage. An American who encountered a decontextualized reference to human rights in 1976 would likely have thought first of these prominent debates. Thus, for example, when the Republican Party formed a subcommittee on human rights and responsibilities for its national convention, its mandate dealt not with foreign affairs but with the headline-garnering issues of abortion and the Equal Rights Amendment, along with civil rights and gay rights.[2]

In 1976 bread-and-butter issues mattered far more than foreign policy. It was the first election year since the 1930s that saw no war or serious threat of conflict hanging over the country. In one poll less than 1 percent of voters cited foreign affairs as an issue of importance.[3] The issues that grabbed attention were inflation, unemployment, crime, abortion, and welfare. Despite the advantages of incumbency, Ford was vulnerable: the economy had been hit hard by the 1973 oil shock and had slipped into a period of stagflation. Most seriously, his pardon of Nixon for Watergate crimes, granted before the former president acknowledged any wrongdoing, had shocked the country and fatally undermined his reputation for honesty and incorruptibility.

In foreign policy Ford was handicapped by the perception that he had acquiesced in Soviet domination of Eastern Europe by signing the Helsinki Final Act of the Conference on Security and Co-operation in Europe. The product of a multilateral European conference proposed by the Soviet Union as a means of obtaining formal recognition of the territorial status quo in Eastern Europe, the Helsinki Accords were signed in 1975 by thirty-three European countries, along with the United States and Canada, and traded recognition of the status quo for Soviet concessions on human contacts and human rights. The American right immediately denounced the agreement as a sellout to the Soviets. William Safire labeled it a "Super Yalta"; the *Wall Street Journal*'s famous "Jerry, Don't Go" editorial implored the president not to sign it.[4] In one of history's unexpected twists, the Helsinki Accords turned out to provide opportunities for dissent in the Soviet bloc that helped undermine Soviet rule, but few signs of unanticipated dividends appeared while Ford was in office and the agreement remained a liability for him.

The crises of recent years had taken a heavy toll on the American psyche, and in addition to dealing with tangible domestic issues, the various presidential campaigns recognized and tried to address a generalized emotional longing to rise above the political muck that had engulfed the country. In the year before the presidential contest, Americans had been bombarded on television, on radio, and in newspapers with a seemingly endless parade of negative news: the fall of South Vietnam, a genocidal war in Cambodia, covert CIA activities, FBI spying, revelations about U.S. involvement in the Chilean coup, the trial of National Guardsmen in the Kent State shootings, embarrassing revelations from the Nixon White House tapes, and a series of corruption scandals. The result, one commentator remarked, was "a relentless negativism and feeling of betrayal, fueling a nation already feeling very sorry for itself."[5]

Two episodes in the year before the election campaign captured the national imagination in ways that hinted at the potential potency of human rights appeals for a public hungry for emotional succor. In mid-1975, Ford had set off a firestorm of criticism by refusing to receive Solzhenitsyn in the White House. The famous author, now living in exile in Switzerland, came to Washington at the invitation of George Meany, the staunchly anticommunist head of the AFL-CIO. Solzhenitsyn was at the height of his fame; the publication the year before of an American edition of *The Gulag Archipelago* had been a sensation, and although liberals were growing uneasy at signs of the dissident's Russian nationalism and criticisms of Western decadence, the American media hung on his every pronouncement. Jesse Helms was pushing a bill to grant the writer honorary U.S. citizenship. Jackson's embrace of Solzhenitsyn was particularly tight; the senator hailed the author as a moral hero and made frequent use of his fervent warnings about the perils of détente. In a move of astonishing political tone-deafness, Ford acceded to Kissinger's pleas to avoid offending the Soviets and refused both to attend the AFL-CIO banquet and to invite Solzhenitsyn to the White House, privately calling the writer a "goddamn horse's ass" who merely wanted to sell more books and drum up lecture dates.[6] The snub unleashed a barrage of editorial denunciations and public ire. Not a single letter to the White House supported Ford's decision. Jackson was among the loudest critics, accusing Kissinger and Ford of "cowering in fear."[7]

One of the few administration officials who attended the banquet was UN Ambassador Daniel Patrick Moynihan. The public flap over the

Solzhenitsyn affair was one sign of the potential power of a human rights politics in 1975; Moynihan's rise to acclaim was another. A Democrat of neoconservative bent and a darling of the CDM, Moynihan had crossed party lines to serve the Nixon administration first as a special advisor on urban affairs and then as ambassador to India. At the beginning of 1975 he wrote a much-noticed article in Norman Podhoretz's neoconservative journal *Commentary* that criticized the Third World's demands for a new international economic order and called forcefully for Western diplomats to stand up for democratic values. In essence, he responded to the developing world's clamorous calls for a redistribution of wealth by saying: no, have human rights instead.[8] The piece elicited the largest response of anything he had written—hundreds of approving letters, all of which, he told Donald Rumsfeld, point to one "unmistakable message": "People are tired of our being ashamed of ourselves." If we pressed our virtues in international forums, he predicted, the American spirit would rally.[9]

Appointed ambassador to the UN in mid-1975 on the strength of this critique, Moynihan decided to "make human rights the theme" of the General Assembly.[10] Now dominated by developing nations, the General Assembly had become a forum for endless denunciations of Western imperialism, racism, and exploitation. Angered by hearing such calumnies delivered by "our moral inferiors," Moynihan was determined to refute the idea that the United States was responsible for poverty and injustice abroad.[11] Writing of conversations with his friend Podhoretz, he pointed to the emotional underpinnings of his views when he recalled, "[We] had agreed that, come what may, we would not plead guilty."[12] "Every day, on every side, we are assailed" at the UN, he told the AFL-CIO, but "we repudiate the charge that we have exploited or plundered other countries." The United States was willing to act, not out of "guilt," but "out of a growing willingness in our culture to broaden the boundaries of fellow feeling" beyond national boundaries, and in particular to help individuals. When providing aid, he argued, the United States should insist that it benefitted individuals, not states, and that it promoted political and civil rights and the claims of the individual *against* the state.[13]

In an organization that, in his view, was dominated by an unruly Third World majority hostile to and disrespectful of democratic values, Moynihan launched an ideological offensive. He described his plans for dealing with Third World tyrants who dared to condemn others for human rights violations as "Shame them, hurt them, shout at them."[14] Pursuing his goals with a candor and pugnacity entirely out of step with the normally placid Western diplomacy at the UN, the flamboyant Irishman first drew attention for an intemperate condemnation of Ugandan tyrant Idi Amin as a "racist murderer." When the General Assembly passed an infamous resolution denouncing Zionism as a form of racism, Moynihan attacked it in inflammatory terms. "The damage we now do to the idea of human rights and the language of human rights could well be irreversible," he warned.[15] Indignant that Third World dictators with atrocious human rights records brazenly sponsored resolutions condemning others for lesser crimes, he proposed a worldwide amnesty of political prisoners. Drawing on data from Freedom House, he claimed that nearly half of the countries that had cosponsored resolutions against Chile and South Korea for political imprisonment themselves held political prisoners, and he called for a universal standard to replace the UN's selective morality.[16] If the substance of his initiatives seemed tame, the style and tone with which he pursued them outraged fellow diplomats and Kissinger in particular, who believed Moynihan's belligerence was unnecessarily provocative and damaging to Western efforts to win support in the developing world. After eight months, he was forced out.

The controversies he generated received extensive coverage in print and on television, including a spot on *Time* magazine's cover. Editorials and public mail ran heavily in favor of his approach, as Americans took satisfaction in his resolute stand in favor of American values. One opinion poll reported that 70 percent of respondents felt Moynihan should continue to speak out frankly.[17] Some observers suspected that he had been aiming at a domestic audience all along, and not long after his UN stint he ran for the Senate in New York, beating the left-wing incumbent Bella Abzug in the Democratic primary and going on to secure a victory in the general election, helped in part by Jackson's endorsement.[18]

Never one for modesty, Moynihan claimed after Carter's election that he and his UN team had been the ones who "changed the language of American foreign policy" by championing human rights.[19] But Moynihan's popularity as an advocate of human rights at this time should not be overstated. The deluge of publicity he received was about his muscular patriotism, not about human rights. "My personal hunch," Moynihan wrote to a State Department official after his resignation, "is that human rights is our secret weapon. Colonialism is over. . . . What is left on the rhetorical agenda of the United Nations, as it were, is human rights." But, he admitted, the idea was not catching on: "I really have had a bitch of a time getting others to follow me on the point."[20] As a human rights moment, Moynihan's stint at the UN was significant mostly for revealing that international human rights was not yet embedded in the national political vocabulary, but the public enthusiasm for Moynihan's broader moral offensive hinted that the concept might be useful for those who wanted to revive American pride.

In other, very different areas, the year brought further indications of a desire for a new, more moral approach to foreign relations and a growing attachment to human rights as a means to secure it. Professional organizations, spurred by a rise in international travel and international conferences, were drawn into human rights activism when members or colleagues abroad fell victim to government repression, or when conferences were staged in controversial locations such as Moscow. Reflecting the new interventionist consciousness, the National Academy of Sciences set up a human rights committee to work for detained or imprisoned scientists.[21] At the International Studies Association conference, scholars interested in human rights formed an "internet" on international human rights, with a newsletter to link activists and scholars.[22] Meanwhile the Ford Foundation, long committed to philanthropy that promoted "a world order of law and justice" and "greater allegiance to the basic principles of freedom and democracy," began to interpret that mandate in human rights terms. With 1976 appropriations for human rights activities totaling $1.5 million, the Ford Foundation signaled a major shift from funding for economic development to initiatives designed to address what one staffer called a "pandemic" of political imprisonment and civil and political rights abuses.[23]

The Ford administration heard echoes of these developments in the sentiments of ordinary Americans. In 1976, Kissinger's aides traveled to a half-dozen major cities to sound out Americans' feelings about foreign policy. In a series of town meetings, State Department officials met with local businessmen, labor leaders, academics, and ethnic groups and conducted telephone polls of local residents on key issues. In reporting their findings, officials consistently described "a deep-seated yearning" for greater morality in foreign policy. Commenting on their meetings in Minneapolis, the aides noted, "We heard the same desire expressed in all of the sessions—efforts to foster human rights throughout the world should be a more pronounced concern of American foreign policy." In Milwaukee, participants complained that arms sales to dictatorships and covert actions abroad had tarnished the country's self-image as a country that exercised "moral leadership in promoting human dignity and extending human rights." Many participants suggested that extending human rights in other countries was in America's long-term interest.[24]

Because Carter's name became so indelibly linked with human rights after 1976, it seems surprising that the issue had a higher profile in the contest for the Republican presidential nomination than it did among the Democratic contenders. As détente came under increasing attack for trading too many concessions for too few dividends, Kissinger became the political figure with the most to gain from appearing to align himself with international human rights promotion. As his reputation for cozying up to dictators of all political stripes increasingly made him a liability for Ford, Kissinger reversed his previous disdain for human rights—so much so that he gave more speeches on the topic in 1976 than any other major political figure, including Carter. Having ignored the phrase for his first four years in office, he mentioned it for the first time in 1973, when it came up primarily in relation to American prisoners of war in Vietnam. By 1976 he referred to human rights in 40 percent of his speeches. Having mentioned it positively a mere six times in 1975, in the election year he spoke of it favorably on forty-six separate occasions. It was testament to how deeply the concept had infiltrated U.S. diplomacy that a secretary of state who raged against it in private felt obliged to embrace it, within limits, in public—even if the public rhetoric was then disavowed in his conduct of foreign relations.[25]

Measured on the basis of public expressions of fealty, Kissinger was the nation's leading advocate of international human rights in 1976. After Reagan told the press that Solzhenitsyn would be welcome to dinner anytime at a Reagan White House, Kissinger let it be known that he had been wrong to advise Ford against meeting with Solzhenitsyn and told a journalist he had read *The Gulag Archipelago* in its entirety.[26] In February the secretary of state went to several Latin American countries and urged the defense of "basic human rights." In April he toured Africa, where he denounced South African apartheid on human rights grounds, and "reaffirm[ed] the unequivocal commitment of the United States to human rights" as embedded in the UN Charter and the UDHR. He pressured Rhodesia's white leadership into negotiations that, a few years later, produced majority rule. In a series of major addresses in Latin America in June, he called human rights "the very essence of a meaningful life." In September he called for human rights in South Africa and appealed to the UN General Assembly to create stronger procedures for dealing with "growing" human rights violations.[27]

Ford himself seems to have used the term infrequently, and it was not a theme of his campaign. He did, however, have a clearly enunciated position in support of human rights. According to one of his briefing books, his administration had "spoken out forcefully for human rights and support[ed] strengthening the international protection of human rights." Under this rubric what mattered most was "freedom for all men and women, the dignity and security of the individual, and the sanctity of law," but such goals should be pursued without "arrogance and self-righteousness" and with respect for historical and cultural differences among nations.[28]

Like Carter, Ford tried to link his leadership to the country's emotional well-being. His advisers, like Carter's, recognized that Americans sought uplift. Echoing a Sears jingle, Ford's campaign theme song was "Feeling Good about America." One of his television ads happily declared that "America is smiling again," and his campaign literature promised, "He's made us proud again."[29] But tied to Watergate by his

President Ford at a Vladivostok meeting with Soviet Premier Leonid Brezhnev in 1974, with Kissinger in the background, while Brezhnev tries on Ford's coat. In the eyes of many Americans, détente entailed an accommodation with communist adversaries that undermined the moral dimensions of American foreign policy. (Corbis)

controversial pardon of Nixon, Ford could not make his emotional appeals stick the way Carter's did.

Morality in foreign policy became a key point of contention when Ronald Reagan challenged Ford for the nomination. Like congressional liberals who had been spurred into action by opposition to Kissinger and his policies, Republicans on the right mobilized around antipathy to the secretary of state's conduct of foreign affairs. Reagan's critique of the administration's policies extended across a range of domestic issues, but it was his claim that détente ignored Soviet repression that drew the strongest public response. In Reagan's view détente was—in perhaps the single most widely used phrase of the election year—a "one-way street" that the Soviets had used to extract concessions, weaken U.S. security, and gain official acquiescence to their domination of Eastern Europe. So seriously did Ford take the threat from his right that he banished détente from his foreign policy lexicon.

The contest came to a head in the drafting of the party platform at the national convention, where Reagan's forces won a clear victory. Ford's staff drafted a lengthy outline for the foreign policy section of the party platform that included detailed discussions of strategic interests but only one reference to human rights, in the form of a requirement that the USSR abide by "the letter and spirit" of the UDHR and the Helsinki Final Act.[30] As part of a ploy by Reagan's supporters to pick off enough Ford delegates to claim the nomination, Jesse Helms and his chief aide wrote a plank on "Morality and Foreign Policy" that was a clear rebuke to Ford and Kissinger. The language drew on the symbols of Jackson-style human rights in an effort to reclaim the terrain of the "rights of man" for a renewed struggle against communism. Including an open swipe at détente and more veiled attacks on the pending Panama Canal Treaty and nuclear testing accords, the Reaganite plank advocated the pursuit of "liberty under law" and lasting peace "based upon our deep belief in the rights of man, the rule of law and guidance by the hand of God." The plank singled out "that great beacon of human courage and morality, Alexander Solzhenitsyn, for his compelling message that we must face the world with no illusions about the nature of tyranny," resurrecting the controversy over Ford's refusal to meet with the Nobel Prize winner.[31]

Ford's chief of staff, Dick Cheney, lamented that the Reagan plank "did everything but strip Henry [Kissinger] bare of every piece of clothing on his body." As Kissinger stormed and threatened to resign unless Ford's people fought it, one of them commented, "Well, Henry, if you're going to quit, do it now. We need the votes."[32] Ford's forces tried to delete the references to Solzhenitsyn and the morality plank's criticisms of the Helsinki Accords, but in the end accepted a watered-down version to avoid a floor flight at a potentially explosive moment in the convention.[33]

In the rest of the platform's lengthy discussion of foreign policy, human rights criticisms were reserved almost exclusively for communist countries. Conservatives ensured that the platform called for "basic human rights" in communist China. Liberal Republicans, spurred by recent media revelations that Kissinger had agreed to ignore human rights violations in South Korea in exchange for the dictatorship's supplying planes to South Vietnam in 1973, succeeded in inserting a call for the U.S. ally to extend "basic human rights." Conservatives broadened the provision to include North Korea. Despite widespread media attention to government torture and repression in the Southern Cone, the platform was entirely silent on human rights violations in Latin America except when it came to communist Cuba.[34] Liberal Massachusetts Congressman Silvio Conte proposed a general amendment supporting international human rights and another that recognized human rights violations in Chile, Argentina, and Uruguay, but was defeated on both counts by conservatives who wanted human rights criticisms reserved for communist countries, not U.S. allies.[35] It was a strong endorsement of human rights as part of a renewed Cold War. Ford won the nomination, but the conservative quest to redefine a Republican foreign policy in terms of a morally based anticommunism would win out in the longer term.

Human rights of a different valence were embraced in 1976 by a growing number of groups aligned with the Democratic Party. The liberal lobby Americans for Democratic Action proposed a resolution advocating an end to U.S. government "complicity in the suppression of human rights and the continuation of vast economic inequities around the world," referring to an "international human rights crisis" that identified the United States with continued injustice and oppression. Initially drafted only to criticize Asian and Latin American dictatorships on the right, the resolution was modified to include India, the Soviet Union, and Uganda.[36] In September, 102 incumbent members of the United States Congress— almost one-fifth of the legislature—issued a manifesto calling for all presidential candidates for public office to support prioritizing human rights in U.S. foreign policy.[37] Fraser and others in Congress joined with Amnesty International in drafting a statement other candidates could endorse, one that backed human rights considerations in foreign policy and singled out torture, political imprisonment, and restrictions on emigration as the core issues.[38] Fraser had pushed through an amendment upgrading the recently created position of coordinator for humanitarian affairs to the status of assistant secretary of state and requiring nominees to be confirmed by Congress.[39]

Despite an audible chorus of liberal human rights proponents in the background of the presidential race, in the first half of the year Jackson was the only Democratic candidate with what was seen as a human rights program. When Common Cause prepared a detailed analysis of six major candidates' foreign policy positions in April 1976, for example, the only one associated with human rights was Jackson.[40] In campaign speeches the Washington senator said protection of internationally recognized human rights should be a major element of foreign policy. He declared, "The United States stood by the importance of human rights when we negotiated the historic Universal Declaration of Human Rights in 1948," which he termed "a splendid pioneering document, which set forth a kind of Bill of Rights for the world."[41] Americans upheld human rights, he said, not only as ends in themselves but as means to peace and the spread of democratic values. He praised Moynihan, who frequently campaigned alongside him, for having spoken up for human rights at the UN, repeated many of Moynihan's criticisms of UN "hypocrisy," and suggested that he would make Moynihan his secretary of state.[42] Summarizing Jackson's foreign policy vision, Leslie Gelb wrote that the candidate proposed using America's vast power "to promote mutual arms control agreements and to advance the cause of human rights."[43] While Jackson remained in the race, his association with human rights as a foreign policy program ensured that it remained linked to a conservative Cold War vision.

On the face of it, Carter's more liberal Democratic opponents would have seemed like far more likely human rights candidates than the centrist candidate from Georgia. With the exception of Jackson, Carter, and Alabama segregationist George Wallace, the Democratic field was tilted to the left. Senator Birch Bayh, McGovern's former running mate Sargent Shriver (John F. Kennedy's brother-in-law), the "new Populist" former senator Fred Harris, and a late entry from California's Edmund "Jerry" Brown, Jr., were among the crowded field in the primaries. Generally regarded as the most credible liberal candidates were Arizona

Congressman Morris Udall and Senator Frank Church. Although both adopted some positions consonant with the liberal human rights program—opposition to military aid to repressive dictatorships, for example—neither the rubric of international human rights nor the violations most associated with liberal human rights priorities held much interest to them. The tenor of their campaigns, both of which emphasized retrenchment of the U.S. role abroad and reform at home, were incompatible with the righteous interventionism that underpinned liberal human rights initiatives.

Udall, who began as the most liberal candidate in the race, lacked foreign policy expertise; he had made his name in the very unsexy fields of congressional and postal reform. Yet he appeared to meet the prerequisites for an embrace of human rights. He was the candidate who could best claim to be McGovern's heir.[44] He had fought for civil rights legislation, spoken out against the Vietnam War, and pressed for investigation of war crimes.[45] A longtime member of the liberal group Members of Congress for Peace through Law, he had worked with Fraser on reforming governance in the House and had joined Fraser early on to work against the Greek junta.[46] He had voted for human rights legislation beginning with Abourezk's amendment on political prisoners in 1973.[47] Jessica Tuchman, who would go on to work in Carter's National Security Council with a brief that included human rights, was his issues coordinator. Human rights advocate Robert Drinan was among those who urged him to run.[48]

At the end of 1975, a newspaper in Udall's home state published an editorial calling for an embargo on aid to dictatorships engaging in "gross violation of human rights." A constituent clipped the editorial and sent it to the recently declared presidential candidate, with a scrawled note at the bottom: "Congressman Udall—Here's an issue for you!"[49] But Udall did not make human rights an issue. The concerns that dominated his foreign policy positions were climate change, natural resource scarcity, population control, arms control, and a reduced global role for the United States. He occasionally rued American support for dictatorships, and racist dictatorships in southern Africa in particular. But in discussing Latin America he said nothing about human rights violations; in talking about Soviet Jewish emigration, he said, "The United States should display more sensitivity in respecting the internal affairs of another nation."[50]

Udall's failure to take a proactive human rights stance reflected two of his core tenets. First, he was deeply reluctant to meddle in the affairs of other countries. What Vietnam had revealed was that the United States was "no longer a Gulliver among nations," he said, and it could no longer attempt "to impose its will" on others.[51] Second, he thought the United States could best exert a moral influence in the world by working to improve its own record. Like McGovern, he called the adage "physician, heal thyself" the best guide to "sound foreign policy." Diplomacy by example was a core theme of his campaign.[52]

As Udall's campaign faltered due to missteps, an inexperienced campaign staff, and public doubts about his Mormonism, Frank Church stepped into the race hoping to supersede him as the liberal standard-bearer. In 1975 the Idaho senator had made a national name for himself by holding hearings on CIA covert operations and assassinations. A staunch liberal with a long-standing interest in foreign relations, Church billed himself as the only foreign policy expert running for president in either party. An early critic of the Vietnam War, he became known for his sharp critiques of the excesses of Cold War anticommunism. In 1971 he held hearings on Brazil that gave attention to proliferating reports of torture. He supported the Jackson amendment on the grounds that détente could not condone the inhumane treatment of dissidents, and he spoke generally of the need to restore "our place of moral leadership in the world."[53] According to one observer, Church's investigations of the CIA were his only distinguishing characteristic in foreign policy, and there was "no sharp foreign policy guideline coming out of it, no direction coming out of it, no cleavage raised by him on which people [could] line up."[54] His views on foreign policy would seem to suggest that he would have been a supporter of human rights, but he did not take up the cause. Instead his stump speech on foreign policy spoke out against "the compulsive interventionism that has come to characterize American foreign policy in our time."[55]

Church's failure to see universal human rights as a useful unifying theme in foreign policy stemmed from his preference for restraint and modesty in framing the American role in the world. "If there is one thing we should have learned in this century, it is that the United States cannot mold the world to our liking," he declared. He repeatedly railed against global poverty and hunger, without describing them as human rights issues; having brought torture in Brazil to public attention in 1971, he had little to say about torture and political imprisonment in 1976, despite their new prominence in the liberal pantheon of human rights abuses.[56] He said U.S. foreign policy must again conform to Americans' historic "belief in freedom and popular government," but he believed the way to do that was to limit American involvement abroad and learn to live patiently with global ferment.[57]

Church had long taken a jaundiced view of foreign aid, withdrawing his support for the program in a widely discussed 1971 critique on the grounds that it was ineffective.[58] As a presidential candidate, he said Americans should not be indifferent to the "humanitarian needs" of the world's poor, but the country's economic assistance should be cut back, channeled through international institutions, and limited to easing the problems of population, hunger, and energy. Human rights advocates in Congress advocated reforming bilateral aid on human rights grounds; Church wanted to limit bilateral aid to those countries with major security significance, as in the Middle East. In addition to reducing aid levels, he wanted to deploy it strictly through international structures and only to the extent that other governments, such as the wealthy OPEC countries, contributed. The United States, he said, simply could no longer pretend to be the world's "policeman, banker and judge."[59]

In a campaign brochure touting his foreign policy credentials, Church included his positions in seven key domestic and foreign policy categories, but his entry under human rights focused entirely on his record on civil rights and women's issues at home.[60] Only in his speech at the Democratic National Convention in July, after he had decisively lost, did he pick up the language of the human rights advocates, describing a new Democratic administration's foreign policy as one that would be formulated in honesty and candor and would "underscore our abhorrence of the tools of tyranny, the repression of free speech, the detention of political prisoners, and the use of torture. With respect to those foreign governments which receive American aid, the United States should be open and unabashed in its exercise of diplomatic efforts to encourage the observance of human rights."[61] It was a ringing endorsement of liberal human rights goals—even more liberal than what the Democratic nominee would come to espouse that year.

Jimmy Carter's roots in the Democratic Party were closer to the Jackson faction than to the McGovern wing. In 1972 he publicly attacked McGovern and spoke of him privately with a loathing that seemed extreme even to fellow McGovern-haters.[62] Although Carter positioned himself to the center of Jackson's conservatism and relations between the two men later grew tense, his approach and values strongly resembled Jackson's. He had given a nominating speech for Jackson at the 1972 Democratic Convention that anointed McGovern, and his campaign staff had warned him that he seemed too "compatible and comfortable" with the Washington senator. With an eye toward running against Jackson in 1976, they advised Carter to stop praising a likely future rival.[63] Yet Carter had also opposed the Jackson-Vanik amendment, in 1975 calling it "ill-advised" interference in Soviet domestic affairs.[64]

On foreign policy Carter diverged from the liberal True Believers in the Democratic Party, above all on the issue of the war. He had not called for American withdrawal from Vietnam until 1971, and then did so on the grounds that "since we are not going to do what it takes to win, it is time to come home."[65] He did not express public concern over charges of brutality in the conduct of the war, and in 1971 when My Lai's Lieutenant Calley was convicted in a military court in Georgia not far from Carter's hometown, Carter issued a gubernatorial edict proclaiming "American Fighting Men's Day," a move widely seen as expressing support for Calley. In 1972 he urged Democratic governors not to make the war an issue in the presidential campaign.[66] He was one of the leaders of a stop-McGovern effort shortly before the 1972 nominating convention. In 1975, a week before the final fall of South Vietnam in April 1975, Carter sided with conservatives in arguing that the flow of military aid to Saigon should continue for at least another year.[67] Finally, and crucially, unlike McGovern in 1972, Carter had no inclination to make American guilt a campaign issue.

In a period of profound distaste for Washington politics, Carter's key asset was that he was an outsider with the appearance of honesty. He was

Carter waving to supporters during his 1976 presidential campaign. He stressed honesty and morality but made human rights important to his message only late in the campaign. (AP)

a former peanut farmer with limited political experience, all of it outside the Beltway: he had served in the Georgia state senate and spent four years in the governor's mansion. As journalist Richard Reeves described it, "He began many of his early speeches by saying that he would list his assets and liabilities, then said, well, his assets were all in his literature, so maybe he'd start with his liabilities. 'I'm not from Washington.' (There was laughter in the audience.) 'I'm not a member of Congress.' (More laughter.) 'I've never been part of the national government.' (There was often so much laughter that he couldn't continue.)"[68] Carter projected an image of believability, candor, honesty, and kindness that was astutely geared to respond to the nation's emotional malaise.

His turn to human rights, when it came, was facilitated by his religious beliefs and his interpretation of the civil rights movement. A born-again Southern Baptist, Carter was influenced by theologian Reinhold Niebuhr's Christian realism. The idea that the world could not be rid of injustice but that specific wrongs inflicted on individuals could be ameliorated fit readily with the emerging ideas of human rights promotion, which espoused not grand schemes to reform humanity but small-scale alleviation of suffering.[69] He had sat through the civil rights movement in the South largely as a bystander, and running for governor in 1970, he had appealed to the segregationist vote. Once in office, however, he had proclaimed the era of segregation over, and in later years he would repeatedly praise the effects of the civil rights movement. He described desegregation as "the best thing that ever happened in the South in my lifetime," liberating for both blacks and whites.[70] (Indeed the end of segregation and the rise of a New South made his career as a Southerner in national politics possible.) His later approach to pushing human rights reforms abroad would be influenced by his view that forcing change on the South from the outside—by federal courts and federal legislation—had given whites "secret gratitude" and "a sense of relief" in allowing them to confront their errors without losing face, "without admitting that we had always been wrong."[71]

Carter's personal background predisposed him to favor a preachy moralism in foreign policy, but it did not follow that his moralism had to be couched in the particular idiom of human rights.[72] Most of Carter's two years of whistle-stopping for the presidency passed without mention of international human rights. As was then newly fashionable, journalists flooded the market with postmortem analyses of the presidential race written and sent to publishers on the heels of the November election. Very few of them even mentioned human rights, let alone accorded it any prominence, so little did it register as a campaign issue.[73] Preparing the president's thick briefing book for the October foreign policy debate, Ford's staff also failed to notice human rights as a distinct theme. The briefers highlighted Carter's promises of openness in the making and conduct of foreign policy, greater respect for and consultation with allies, a tougher negotiating stance toward the Soviets, respect for the outcomes of democratic elections abroad, and fewer military interventions, along with his vague invocations of morality. Issues such as Rhodesian sanctions, aid to repressive allies, and Soviet Jewish emigration remained peripheral.[74]

With little experience or prior interest in the topic, Carter kept his pronouncements on foreign policy rare and vague. The candidate's foreign policy message was about America, not about the behavior of other nations.[75] He criticized the Ford and Kissinger style as too secretive and their approach to détente as not "tough" enough. It was a critique still firmly embedded in a Cold War framework. His speeches were vague: "I see an American foreign policy that is firm and consistent and generous, and that once again is a beacon for the hopes of the world."[76] He suggested that Nixon's and Ford's mistakes in foreign policy resulted from the exclusion of the American people in key decisions. In late 1975 he declared, "We've been excluded, we've been lied to, and we have lost the tremendous advantage of the idealism and the common sense and the basic honesty and character of American people which should accurately exemplify and be exemplified by our nation's own character as it relates to other countries." One of his key tenets was noninterference in the internal affairs of other countries. "I hope we've learned we ought to never again get involved in the internal affairs of other countries unless our security is involved," he said in February 1976. The lesson learned from conflicts like the Vietnam War, Carter said, was to stop "trying to tell other people what kind of government they ought to have or what kind of leader they should have."[77]

His lack of foreign policy experience meant he had had little exposure to international human rights issues. The phrase "human rights" does not appear in the chapter on foreign policy in his 1975 memoir, *Why Not the Best?*, which proposed a vague foundation of "ethics, honesty and morality" for U.S. foreign relations.[78] His sense of the meaning of the term "human rights" was rooted in its 1960s overlap with civil rights. In a June breakfast with reporters, for example, Carter used the term to mean domestic rights concerns.[79] Similarly, when a Southern newspaper editor endorsed him in April, he cited Carter's commitment to "full human rights for all citizens."[80] Accepting the nomination of the Democratic Party in July, Carter used the term when praising Johnson as the president who had done more than any other "to advance the cause of human rights," referring to LBJ's civil rights achievements.[81] It was arguably in reference to keeping America's own house in order that he spoke of human rights in announcing his candidacy in 1974. "This country," he said, "should set a standard within the community of nations of courage, compassion, integrity, and dedication to basic human rights and freedoms."[82]

Carter touched on international human rights at the very end of a speech in Tokyo in mid-1975, linking it with humanitarianism as a means to provide trustworthy, respectful, and enlightened leadership to the world, but it was not until the candidate gave his first foreign policy speech in June 1976 that he discussed the idea in any detail.[83] Drafted by advisers, apparently with little input from the candidate, its human rights references were inserted by speechwriter Patrick Anderson as a way to distance Carter from the policies of Nixon and Ford. The resulting "moderate, high-minded and unexceptional" speech was praised by the mainstream media. As the *CBS Evening News* reported it, Carter said the United States should stop playing the lonely game of power politics and promote basic global standards for human rights in places like South Africa. It remained Carter's only general foreign policy address of the campaign, because his staff felt he had nothing to gain by trying to top this success.[84]

At the Democratic Convention in July, it was Jackson Democrats who imprinted their views on the foreign policy planks of the party platform. Human rights had been given small recognition by the foreign policy study group headed by Averell Harriman that prepared papers on the principles that would guide the platform drafting.[85] When it came time to write the platform, Moynihan, Jeane Kirkpatrick of the Coalition for a Democratic Majority, and Jackson representative and CDM cofounder Ben Wattenberg took the lead. Criticizing the Ford administration's "sorry record of disregard for human rights," the platform affirmed "the fundamental American commitment to human rights across the globe." Although a pro-Solzhenitsyn reference was dropped early on, a key paragraph read like a recitation of the priorities Jackson, Moynihan, and the CDM had been touting: release of all political prisoners (as Moynihan had proposed in the UN); emigration rights; the right of workers to organize; and freedom of the press. It concluded: "A return to the politics of principle requires a reaffirmation of human freedom throughout the world."[86] It was Jackson and Moynihan and George Meany, one commentator observed—and no wonder, for the paragraph had been drafted by CDMers.[87] The coalition's newsletter gloated at the muscular language in the foreign policy sections—"tough bargaining," "the United States should be open and unashamed"—which it called "far different" from the "guilty America syndrome" that afflicted so much liberal thinking.[88]

It included, too, some recognition of liberal human rights priorities, enough that some observers hailed it as healing the foreign policy rift that had fractured the party since 1968. Sam Brown, a former student antiwar leader representing the McGovern wing of the party, wanted the platform to call for cutoffs in aid to regimes that did not respect human rights. Moynihan, speaking for the Jackson wing, argued that no credits should be extended to countries with unreasonable restrictions on emigration. "We'll be against the dictators you don't like the most," Moynihan told Brown, "if you'll be against the dictators we don't like the most."[89] When liberals proposed that American allies be censured, Moynihan and his allies insisted on criticizing communist regimes. New York liberal Bella Abzug had wanted simply to condemn South Korean violations, for example, but Moynihan insisted on inclusion of a reference to North Korean brutality.[90] In committee debates, Abzug and former U.S. Senator Joseph Clark denounced the platform as something that "could have been written in the Pentagon," but their objections were defeated.[91] Wattenberg concluded with relief that the party had overcome the stark differences of the past to rally around "the promotion of freedom."[92]

Where were the Carter forces in these debates? "Hard to say," one journalist noted. Moynihan described Carter's representatives as unfamiliar with the issues and undecided about them. A more charitable interpretation was that Carter was trying to avoid controversy and hoping to balance the two warring sides of the party. Providing further evidence that the nominee's commitment to this program remained tentative, his acceptance speech mentioned international human rights only peripherally. "Peace is not the mere absence of war," Carter said; "peace is action to stamp out terrorism. Peace is the unceasing effort to preserve human rights." Beyond a vague reference to a "dedication to democracy," the speech gave no indication of which human rights mattered most or how they were to be pursued.[93] Carter-Mondale campaign literature referred only vaguely to promoting "human rights abroad," and profiles of the candidate continued to be written without mentioning international human rights.[94]

* * *

Only in the final two months of the campaign did Carter fully embrace human rights, spurred by the clear resonance the issue had among the public. The Carter campaign was unusually attuned to polling data, thanks to the influence of Pat Caddell, a former McGovern pollster with a wunderkind reputation. Caddell was a new breed of political adviser, someone with a gift not only for collecting data but for interpreting its deeper cultural significance. Domestic affairs adviser Stu Eizenstat had been urging Carter to make human rights an issue, arguing that it was a "no-lose" proposition because it appealed to liberals who opposed right-wing dictatorships and to conservatives who saw it as anti-Soviet. Eizenstat, who had long been concerned about Soviet treatment of Jews, battled long and hard to make human rights a prominent part of the campaign. In Anderson's assessment, Carter "didn't share Stu's deep emotional concern" for Soviet Jews, "nor was it his instinct to identify with political prisoners around the world," but the candidate eventually came around to the issue because it resonated with his theme of restoring morality and, more pragmatically, because it would enhance his standing among Jewish voters.[95]

Eizenstat's push for human rights culminated in Carter's early September speech to a B'nai B'rith convention in Washington, D.C. Drafted by Carter adviser Richard Holbrooke, it was a strong endorsement of international human rights. "I share a total commitment to the preservation of human rights, individual liberty, and freedom of conscience," Carter declared in what the press dubbed "the human rights speech." The previous administration, Carter suggested, had been an aberration in ignoring the moral principles that made the country great and in temporarily embracing cynicism instead of the long tradition of acting abroad "in a moral, unselfish manner."[96]

The speech adroitly melded liberal and conservative priorities. It first singled out the Soviet Union, citing the cases of a dissident imprisoned for criticizing the regime and a Jewish engineer denied the right to emigrate to Israel. Carter promised that the fate of such people would be "very much on my mind as I negotiate with the Soviet Union." He went on to criticize political persecution and "brutal torture" in Chile, and governments such as South Korea's "which openly violate[d] human rights." The United States could not remake the world in its own image, he said, but it also could not look away when governments tortured their citizens, jailed them for dissent, or denied them the right to emigrate. "There can be many instances," he said, "when our power can make a crucial difference in the lives of thousands of men and women who have been the victims of oppression around the world."[97]

The speech was a key step in the evolution of Carter's efforts to define a new foreign policy. The precise history of the speech's drafting and the reasons for its emphasis on human rights remain unclear, but a comparison of Holbrooke's early draft and the final version suggests some key points about the origins and development of the Carter team's turn to this new idealism. In a line that was eventually cut, Holbrooke pointed to the internal emotional needs that human rights promotion was assumed to meet, explaining that morality in foreign policy was needed "to restore our self-respect and dignity domestically." Holbrooke's draft allotted roughly equal coverage to abuses by the Soviets and abuses by U.S. allies such as Chile and South Korea. Perhaps with the Jewish audience in mind, the final version spent considerably more time on Soviet repression. An insertion by Averell Harriman to the effect that efforts to redress hunger and poverty sometimes must supersede "less tangible freedoms and values" was eventually cut, prefiguring the Carter administration's ambivalent view of economic and social rights. In Holbrooke's draft, the rights that mattered were threefold: equality before the law and nondiscrimination; freedom from arbitrary arrest, imprisonment, and torture; and freedom of religion, expression, and association. Human freedom was not, he wrote, a matter of political systems, and attempts to restructure foreign political systems, even one-party dictatorships, must end. Most striking is the original draft's preoccupation with freedom. Variations on the word "freedom"—individual liberty, human freedom, human liberties—appear twice as often as do variants of "rights." Further revisions transformed what was a speech about liberty into a speech about human rights as the desired manifestation of liberty. Yet the vision of freedom Holbrooke offered specifically excluded what many Americans would have considered the essential, Wilsonian freedom—democracy—in favor of more minimalist individual protections against specific government abuses.[98]

When Carter and Ford did a series of televised debates in October, Carter again used human rights to harness public dissatisfaction with Kissinger's foreign policy. During the second of three debates, Carter reiterated his standard complaints that Congress and the public had been excluded from participation in and even knowledge of foreign policy. He said the Soviet Union had outmaneuvered the United States in détente. Trading on Republican dissension, Carter pointedly noted that the Republican platform itself criticized the Ford administration's foreign policy. Rather than betraying American principles by "supporting dictatorships [and] ignoring human rights," he said, the United States should reassume global leadership by designing a foreign policy that channeled the true character of the American people. When pressed to say whether he would risk an oil embargo to promote human rights in Iran or Saudi Arabia, the Democratic nominee skirted the question, but when Ford equivocated about human rights in Korea, Carter seized the opportunity to criticize Ford's support of the Chilean dictatorship. Using figures that had been cited in Congress, Carter claimed that 85 percent of all Food for Peace aid in 1975 had gone to the Pinochet regime. Having raised one of the causes dearest to liberals, Carter also made sure to offer something to conservatives on the human rights front, taking Ford to task for his infamous snub of Solzhenitsyn.[99]

The biggest fallout from this debate was Ford's shocking misstatement about Eastern Europe. In what ranks as one of the most serious presidential gaffes in history, Ford insisted that "there is no Soviet domination of Eastern Europe and there never will be under a Ford administration"— and when given the chance to clarify, dug himself deeper into the hole. Ford was garbling Kissinger's complex briefing books, trying to disarm criticism that the Helsinki Accords had signed away Eastern Europe to Soviet rule, but the gaffe seemed to validate caricatures of the president as dull-witted and not in charge of his own foreign policy.[100]

Capitalizing on Ford's flub in a speech at Notre Dame a few days later, Carter declared that human rights should be an overriding concern of U.S. foreign policy, framing it as a way of restoring American pride. "I know of no great nation in history that has more often conducted itself in a moral, unselfish, generous manner abroad," he said, but Nixon and Ford had strayed from this great tradition. America's leaders must let it be known that a country's human rights record would affect whether or not it was offered "friendship and support." Americans "want to be legitimately proud once again of the greatest nation on earth." Speaking out forcefully about torture was important, Carter said, because it would restore "the faith of our own people in our government." Coming in second place was the promise that it would also help alleviate torture. Once again he appealed to the fundamental goodness of the American people, whose yearnings to do good needed an outlet like human rights.[101] Such talk struck a chord because human rights seemed to recapture a sense of American pride and idealism.

Late in the campaign, Carter's skillful pollster Patrick Caddell identified human rights as an issue that united liberals and conservatives—"a very strong issue across the board."[102] Even so, Carter's human rights theme remained too marginal to sway many voters. His more general moralism, applied to domestic and foreign affairs, certainly did help him, enhancing his appeal as a candidate of healing and regeneration. Carter recognized, as one journalist put it, that "foreign policy is not only diplomacy; it's therapy."[103] Still, Carter's support was soft, and he won in a very tight contest. Carter won 51.05 percent of the popular vote to Ford's 48.95 percent, translating to 297 Electoral College votes to Ford's 241, while the Democratic majority in Congress increased by two seats. It was a razor-thin margin of victory, not an overwhelming mandate.

Until Carter's election it would have been possible for observers to see international human rights as a predominantly conservative cause. Conservatives such as Jackson had staked the strongest claim to it in the public mind. In 1976 Kissinger worked hard to claim it as a Republican project, and the Reagan wing's use of morality represented a convergence with the ideas Jackson and the CDM had been propounding. Liberal candidates such as Udall and Church could ignore human rights and refuse to take up a new moral crusade. The place of international human rights promotion in 1976 was thus very much up for grabs. Had Ford eked out a victory and replaced Kissinger with a new secretary of state, more attuned to the moral Zeitgeist and unburdened by years of open skepticism toward the concept, human rights could easily have become a Republican cause, embedded in reinvigorated pursuit of the Cold War.

It was in its anticommunist guise that Carter most strongly gravitated to human rights during the campaign. Once in office, though, he ensured that the idea would be newly branded a liberal dogma.

Carter's campaign morality echoed many themes McGovern had emphasized with such dramatic lack of success, but the Southerner's tone was crucially different. Dubbed a "wheeler-healer" by journalist Eric Sevareid, Carter promised national reconciliation.[104] He said Americans should not have to be "ashamed of what our government is as we deal with other nations around the world."[105] McGovern, in contrast, had included in the circle of blame the American people, charging that Americans, along with their government, needed to change. Carter's core message was that Americans were just fine. The problem was that the government had strayed from the wishes and the "decency and generosity and common sense" that Americans had.[106] As Carter put it, "Our nation should always derive its character directly from the people and let this be the strength and the image to be presented to the world—the character of the American people."[107]

Carter pitched the incorporation of human rights into foreign policy as a return to tradition. There had been, he said, "a forgetting about human rights."[108] That human rights seemed familiar to Americans was one reason it sold so well to the public. The Universal Declaration of Human Rights was hardly embedded in American consciousness, but standing for "rights" could be (and was) easily characterized as a return to long-standing tradition. But Carter's message of morality, while consonant with America's Wilsonian self-conception, need not have aligned with international human rights promotion. He spent two years campaigning as a moralist before he turned to human rights. It was an issue that had to be pressed by his advisers, and they did so, as politicos are apt to do, on pragmatic, vote-getting grounds. Had human rights not turned out to resonate with the public, Carter would never have made it a centerpiece of his foreign policy.

Human rights resonated because it satisfied the public's emotional craving to move beyond the moral taint of the war. Midway into his first year as president, Carter explained his administration's commitment to human rights: "We've been through some sordid and embarrassing years recently with Vietnam and Cambodia and Watergate and the CIA revelations, and I felt like it was time for our country to hold a beacon light of something pure and decent and right and proper that would rally our citizens to a cause."[109] In the new president's hands, human rights functioned to absolve sin. The Vietnam War grated on liberals for having been fought and on conservatives for having been lost. For both, human rights went far toward righting the damage the war had done at home and restoring the country's sense of virtue.

## CHAPTER 10

# "We Want to Be Proud Again"

Jimmy Carter's inauguration in January 1977 was an unusual spectacle. It was the first (and last) to feature a giant peanut balloon in the inaugural parade. It was the first (but not the last) in which the president walked rather than rode from the Capitol to the White House. In another vintage Carter move, the incoming president turned to Gerald Ford on the swearing-in stand, shook his hand, and said, "For myself and for our nation, I want to thank my predecessor for all he has done to heal our land."[1] The gesture was a brilliant piece of symbolism that conveyed Carter's earnest intent to close the chapter on a painful era in American history. His campaign had promised that he could move the country past the traumas of the Nixon era, which had tarnished Ford, too. The Georgia outsider had presented himself as someone who would make Americans feel better about themselves.[2] As a journalist astutely observed, "He had given the American people to believe that, if he became the President, it would be an act of cleansing for the American soul, a regeneration of its fouled spirit, the salvation it sought from the devils of its recent past."[3] The promotion of international human rights would become integral to this cleansing. Carter would indelibly link his name to the concept, and his administration's efforts to define and implement human rights policies would influence every subsequent president's engagement with the moral dimensions of foreign relations.

Carter, a latecomer to human rights who was in many ways an outsider to the passions that had given rise to both the liberal and neoconservative strands of rights promotion, succeeded in lifting the idea to unprecedented global prominence. In his first year he seldom seemed to raise a banquet toast, give a speech, or hold a news conference without touting human rights.[4] For all his administration's efforts to describe human rights as an imperfect tool, one of many considerations in policy-making, and a program whose success had to be measured in the long term, his evangelizing awakened hopes that he inevitably failed to fulfill. Above all Carter failed to heal the rift in the Democratic Party between those who saw the core task as reforming America's sphere of influence and those who saw the crucial battlefield as the life-or-death struggle against communism. Carter's failure to win over the latter helped drive neoconservatives out of the Democratic Party and into an evangelizing program of their own to promote human rights, eventually through force of arms. He also failed to please the liberal human rights wing, which now seemed to have the upper hand in defining the concept as its own, by too often sacrificing human rights on the altar of security interests. Public opinion polls consistently showed strong support for morality in foreign policy, but less enthusiasm when any specific case raised the prospect of tangible costs.[5]

Yet in its task of reviving the American spirit after the doldrums of Vietnam, Carter's human rights policy surely made a significant difference. In an America "thirsty for self-affirmation," as one commentator put it, the human rights issue was "a perfect prescription for making the country feel better about itself."[6] Human rights was "good propaganda" that "makes Americans feel good," a right-leaning Democratic policy analyst noted.[7] Reflecting on the achievements of Carter's human rights policy as Reagan was about to take office, a National Security Council staffer wrote that "many Americans were made to feel proud once again" because Carter had helped to "restore the American people's sense of moral worth" by allowing the country to "clear . . . its conscience."[8] Despite discontent over specifics, human rights went a long way toward restoring a sense of American virtue. Carter's presidency was widely judged a failure, and he lost a second term to Ronald Reagan, not because of the limitations of human rights promotion but because of double-digit inflation, rising unemployment, and a series of international setbacks that battered American confidence.[9] Of these, the most damaging was the hostage crisis that followed the Iranian Revolution in 1979. Carter's apparent helplessness fed feelings of humiliation and weakness that Reagan adroitly exploited. The charges of weakness and naïveté that stuck to the president also tarred the human rights policy that was so closely associated with him.

Carter had made competence and morality the centerpieces of his campaign, and these values had helped him win. How his vague prescriptions would translate into a foreign policy program, however, remained uncertain, as did the place of human rights in the administration's overall priorities. Observers who doubted that Carter had given any serious thought to what human rights meant were surely right.[10] Trying to predict the foreign policy priorities of the incoming administration days after the election, journalist and future Carter foreign policy appointee Leslie Gelb offered only a very tentative prediction that a new emphasis on human rights might be one element of Carter's policies.[11]

During the transition period, human rights moved only fitfully to a position of high priority. Carter's close friend and press secretary Jody Powell told a journalist that there was no particular point after election day at which a decision was made to make human rights a major theme. "The thing sort of evolved as opportunities presented themselves," Powell said in mid-1977, in part because it "seemed an outgrowth of our basic assumptions." He emphasized the "psychological effect" the policy seemed to fill for Americans who feared their country was in decline. "The country had been back on its heels for so long. We got the impression from two years of travelling around the country of a feeling worse than ennui, of a feeling that time was working against us." Americans had felt that for too long the country had been on the defensive, Powell said, and human rights offered a way "to claim the offensive."[12]

Despite a sense that human rights should be part of the agenda, its status—whether it would be one goal among many, on a par with, say, population control, or whether it would constitute a high-priority theme—was still undecided. In October Cyrus Vance, who would be tapped to be secretary of state, had sent Carter a long memo outlining a foreign policy agenda, which included sensitivity to North-South relations and global issues such as energy, population, environment, and nuclear nonproliferation. A staid member of the foreign policy establishment, Vance had stolidly centrist views. He listed continuing to speak about "the rights of free men" as a general consideration at the outset, but in the lengthy analysis that followed, human rights came up only as concerns in a few specific bilateral relationships (with the Soviet Union, South Korea, and southern Africa).[13] In December Vance gave Carter a draft of an inaugural speech that mentioned human rights only in passing. "We must not meddle in the affairs of other nations, unasked and unwanted," he wrote in his inaugural suggestions, but should instead seek "a new spirit of cooperative diplomacy" through international efforts to combat global problems, of which denial of human rights was but one.[14] Vance's own commitment to incorporating human rights into foreign policy considerations seems to have been genuine but limited, tempered both by his natural caution and an unwillingness to impede arms control efforts. His discussion of human rights in his memoirs was surprisingly cursory. His public statements projected ambivalence rather than enthusiasm, emphasizing the complexity of the issue, the need to balance it against other considerations on a case-by-case basis, and the constraints on achieving clear results.[15]

As the president's inaugural address was drafted, promotion of international human rights moved to a position of prominence in the foreign policy vision Carter wanted to convey. That it did so seems to owe much to Carter's choice for national security adviser, Zbigniew Brzezinski. Carter wrote much of the speech himself, but many of the themes Brzezinski suggested in a three-page memo on the inaugural made it into the final version. Brzezinski, though known as a staunch Cold Warrior, was also an advocate of accommodating the new global interdependence. The day after the election, he and his team had given the president-elect a lengthy memo on foreign policy priorities, which had nothing specific to say about human rights.[16] When it came time to present a foreign policy statement to the public, however, Carter's key foreign policy adviser highlighted human rights.

In his short memo on the inaugural, Brezinski's first general suggestions were about shaping a "truly humane" world and about respecting "minimum rights and minimum needs," because, he wrote, "for the first time we are approaching the reality of a mankind that is beginning to be governed by common norms." The crucial item in this global agenda was economic development, and the United States, Brzezinski argued, must do its part to fight hunger, poverty, disease, and illiteracy. But—and this was his third point—it was not merely a matter of improving the physical conditions of life but also of addressing spiritual needs. The new global spirit included "increased awareness world-wide of the illegitimacy of governmental violence, directed at individual human rights." The United States must welcome and promote this new awareness. In lines that Carter lightly rephrased in January, Brzezinski wrote, "Our fundamental sense of morality . . . dictates a clearcut preference for those societies and governments which share with us an abiding respect for individual rights and freedoms," such that Americans "cannot be indifferent to the fate of freedom elsewhere." It was not clear what Brzezinski meant by "preference," for he went on to say that the United States could not tell any other country how to behave in its internal affairs.[17]

The final version of Carter's otherwise unmemorable inaugural drew on Brzezinski's views to make a strong commitment to human rights. The declaration that "our commitment to human rights must be absolute," placed in an early draft in the foreign policy section, was moved to the domestic policy section, where it clearly was intended to refer to internal affairs.[18] This was "human rights" in their older guise as domestic civil rights. In the foreign policy section, promoting human rights abroad became a key theme, even if an ambitious declaration that "we must be the champions of human rights throughout the world, and the enemies of tyrany [sic] wherever it exists" was written out of the final draft. Echoing Brzezinski's words, the final speech proclaimed that a "new spirit" was ascendant around the world, and people everywhere were demanding "basic human rights." The United States must tap into this new spirit to help shape a "humane" world. "Because we are free we can never be indifferent to the fate of freedom elsewhere," Carter declared. "Our moral sense dictates a clear-cut preference for these societies which share with us an abiding respect for individual human rights." Though the speech linked human rights with the concept of freedom, indications in earlier drafts that human rights meant freedom from state violence and terrorism were dropped, leaving human rights undefined. Its endorsement of human rights promotion was qualified: it abjured "intimidation" and accented the importance of cultivating internal strength, saying that the most powerful way "to enhance freedom" elsewhere was to demonstrate the virtues of democracy at home.[19]

Underscoring the centrality of the new human rights emphasis as a program for Americans even more than for foreigners, Carter's unique "inaugural abroad"—an inaugural address intended for the rest of the world—seemed intended to proclaim a new era of American limits rather than an expansive commitment to rights promotion. In a short statement of modest tone and even more modest goals, Carter said that United States did not have all the answers and could not guarantee the "basic rights of all human beings" to be free from poverty, hunger, disease, and "political repression," though it would work with others to combat "these enemies of mankind." Promising to be sensitive and helpful but not domineering, Carter spoke of a cooperative effort to move the world "closer to the ideals of human freedom and liberty."[20]

Brzezinski's early role in cementing the prominence of human rights in Carter's foreign policy seems more important, and more enigmatic, than the common characterization of him as a hardline realist and anti-Soviet hawk allows. In addition to his role in the inaugural, he shaped Carter's 1977 Notre Dame address on foreign policy and human rights; as national security adviser he set up the Global Issues Cluster, which covered human rights. The son of a Polish diplomat, Brzezinski was a professor of political science at Columbia when he joined Carter's campaign as his chief foreign policy adviser and speechwriter. The two men had known each other since Brzezinski had invited Carter to join the Trilateral Commission, a group of businesspeople, academics, and lawyers formed by David Rockefeller (and headed by Brzezinski) to promote cooperation among the United States, Europe, and Japan. (According to conspiracy theorists, it also ran the world.) The professor and the governor hit it off, and Brzezinski provided much of Carter's foreign policy education. Once in office, Brzezinski developed an extraordinarily close relationship to the president, cemented by frequent one-on-one sessions, sometimes as often as five times a day. He seemed to know Carter's mind, and the president appreciated his adviser's ability to distill complicated ideas in meetings and his knack for writing easily digestible, one- or two-page memos with clear, catchy formulations.[21]

Brzezinski had argued for some time that the United States would best serve its own interests by aligning itself with Third World aspirations. In a 1970 book on what he called "the technetronic era," he described an interlinked world that called for a "rational humanism" based in part on an international consciousness and involvement in global rather than simply national problems.[22] Before taking office he had served on the mostly liberal National Advisory Board of Amnesty International's U.S. section, but he was also an active member of the board of the more center-right Freedom House—activities that point to an acquaintance with a range of ideas relating to international human rights.[23] He had signed the original Coalition for a Democratic Majority appeal in 1972 but had no subsequent links with the group, and his views about aligning U.S. policies with the developing world's aspirations were regarded as "Third Worldism" and pernicious "gobbledygook" by CDMers.[24] In his memoirs he explained that he had "long been convinced that the idea of basic human rights had a powerful appeal" in the mostly undemocratic, recently decolonized states, where demonstrating the "reality of our democratic system" could gain America friends. In a 1978 speech he proposed that "human rights is the genuine, historical inevitability of our times," "a central facet in America's relevance to this changing world," and "the wave of the present." It was, therefore, "just and right, morally correct, historically well grounded, and politically useful . . . for the US to carry high the standard of human rights, for we are then in the forefront of a powerful movement [with] world-wide appeal."[25] In short, Brzezinski's interest in human rights stemmed from his belief that power should be wielded in moral ways and from his sense of the strategic and political benefits, both at home and abroad, that aligning U.S. foreign policy with human rights could bring. In practice, however, his main interest would be using human rights as an ideological tool against the Soviets.

Even after announcing a ringing commitment to international human rights in his inaugural, Carter remained undecided as to where the issue fit in his foreign policy goals. Public approbation helped make the issue a priority. Aides had been pleasantly surprised by the issue's public appeal in September and October, and the day after the inauguration, Vance remarked on the interest he was seeing in human rights issues.[26] Once in office, the administration found that a few ad hoc human rights moves adopted in response to specific circumstances drew public interest, creating pressure for further human rights rhetoric and action. A foreign policy official told a journalist in mid-1977 that there had been no planning for human rights programs, but a few early steps drew "such enormous attention and acclaim—especially from the right." Human rights, another official explained, "acquired a dynamic of its own."[27] In his memoirs Carter recalled, "Judging from the news articles and direct communications from the American people to me during the first few months of my administration, human rights had become the central theme of our foreign policy in the minds of the press and public. It seemed that a spark had been ignited, and I had no inclination to douse the growing flames."[28]

It was politically shrewd to claim ownership of an issue that, as a principle, polled well with just about everyone. It helped the president with the right and the left, with Jews and Baptists, with critics and advocates of détente. It suited the president's own strong moral streak and his religious convictions. Sheer ignorance of its ramifications also was a factor in Carter's decision to take up the idea; as he admitted in his memoirs, he would be surprised to find out that promoting human rights would "cut clear across" relations with both communist countries and the developing world.[29] The key, however, was the concept's popularity, which in turn was a testament to its psychological value. Human rights promotion had such powerful appeal to Americans because it seemed to offer a way forward out of a period of crisis and self-doubt. Caddell told Carter that "the country faces the problem of understanding the events of the last fifteen years and being able to build off them." Americans were "psychologically damaged," Caddell wrote; "their sense of progress and purpose has been crippled," but they yearn to "go forward. . . . The only possible way out of this national trauma is a period of national progress that involves a reassumption of traditional idealism"—not in the overreaching style of the 1960s, but more somberly.[30]

Deciding what human rights promotion meant in practice, however, was far more complicated than anyone had anticipated. The difficulties the administration encountered in formulating a human rights agenda attest both to a lack of specific planning and to the sheer novelty of a human rights–based foreign policy. There were no precedents to draw on, no prior models from which to borrow. It took a full year for a presidential directive on human rights to be drafted and approved, and in the meantime there was little coordination as the administration struggled to articulate a vision and to implement it in ways that made sense to the public. The impression was one of incoherence and muddle. "Human rights is the most complicated foreign policy question before the government," an administration official remarked early in Carter's term. "No one knows what the policy is, yet it pervades everything we do."[31]

The administration's internal debates over human rights revolved in the first instance over which human rights mattered most. In order to develop a human rights policy, it had first to decide which human rights to promote. Arguments about whether food and housing (economic rights) or the rights to free speech and association (civil and political rights) were more fundamental were hashed out and then rehashed at Foggy Bottom and in the White House. The administration had proponents of economic and social rights, but in practice it devoted most of its efforts to the integrity-of-the-person abuses that had been popularized by Amnesty International and written into law by Fraser and other congressional liberals. Thus, in Vance's Law Day speech in April—the first major explication of U.S. human rights policy—the secretary of state pulled out a novel third group of rights in addition to the traditional categories of economic and social rights, on the one hand, and civil and political on the other. (An official on the State Department's Policy Planning Staff later suggested that economic and social rights were a late addition to the speech that might have emerged "more by accident than design.")[32] The third group, which included integrity-of-the-person violations such as torture and prolonged detention without charges, was implicitly the priority group. The rights in this third grouping were not themselves new; they had always been present in the civil and political category. But it was a significant and consequential innovation, surely copied from recent human rights legislation, to single them out as more fundamental than others. An end to violations of those rights, Vance said, might be "rapid"; whereas results in promoting other types of rights might be slower.[33] Explaining what remained a continuing prioritization for the administration, the National Security Council's Jessica Tuchman observed, "I think that the attempt was to draw a rather small category that we felt transcended political systems and were of universal human concern."[34] The tripartite categorization was formalized in the Presidential Directive on human rights that was produced, after lengthy delays, in early 1978.[35]

Beyond its implicit prioritization, Vance's cautious speech offered remarkably little insight into how the administration would promote human rights, unless it was to foreshadow how full of qualifications and hesitancies it would be. Carter's chief diplomat advocated a cautious, pragmatic, and flexible approach, in which every case was carefully evaluated to assess the causes, extent, and kinds of rights violations, the range of possible responses, and the weight of other interests. There was no "formula" that could be used, he warned.[36] In the end, the administration took an ad hoc approach in which the proclivities of the particular individuals involved in each case essentially determined policy. The administration continued to speak in many voices. That same month, Brzezinski put a different spin on human rights in a forty-three-page statement of strategic objectives, which suggested that the priority was using human rights against the Soviet Union, with initiatives aimed at other governments limited to adding human rights criteria to international loan programs.[37]

As the president approached his first major address on human rights, his advisers continued to disagree over the place of economic and social rights. Drafting the speech Carter was to give at Notre Dame in May 1977, speechwriter James Fallows inserted a reference to health care, jobs, and housing. His colleague Griffin Smith objected on the grounds that the president had made clear that his concern with human rights was about "torture, fair trials, emigration, and dissent," and the utility of the definition depended on its not being stretched to include too much. "I know the temptation is strong to define one's pet project as a human right so that the president will appear to be endorsing it," Smith wrote, "but let's keep human rights to mean human rights, and find another label for economic and social progress."[38] Smith was wrong: the president had spoken of economic rights as human rights, notably at the United Nations in March, but linking poverty, hunger, and disease to the rubric of human rights was never much more than a rhetorical device.[39]

The Notre Dame speech was one of Carter's major foreign policy addresses, and one of the most controversial. Speaking with the intensity of a prayer session, Carter acknowledged that human rights could never be the only factor in policy-making. Foreign policy could not be conducted "by rigid moral maxims," he said, countering critics who were taking him to task for soft-pedaling abuses in Iran, South Korea, and the Philippines. Yet, he continued, "America's commitment to human rights [is] a fundamental tenet of our foreign policy." Though others, including James Fallows and Carter himself, had contributed, the speech was drafted largely by Brzezinski, and clearly reflected the Trilateralist's preoccupation with changing centers of power and aligning American interests with rising aspirations in the Third World. Human rights are advancing around the world, Carter said, echoing Brzezinski's views, and the United States could not ignore the trend. "To lead it," he said, "will be to regain the moral stature that we once had."[40]

In a line that still makes conservatives shudder, the president horrified hawks by declaring that Americans were now free of "that inordinate fear of Communism which once led us to embrace any dictator who joined us in that fear." He spoke of the failed policies of the past, when the country had adopted "the flawed and erroneous principles and tactics of our adversaries, sometimes abandoning our own values for theirs," an approach of "intellectual and moral poverty" that culminated in the Vietnam War.[41] It was an extraordinary admission of American flaws. For a brief moment, Carter forgot the lesson of 1972: guilt did not sell.

Moynihan and his comrades saw it as a declaration of war against the right. "The tone, the formulations, the code words declared the complete ascendancy" of the McGovernite view of the legacy of Vietnam, he said, and the complete rejection of the views of the Jackson Democrats.[42] It was a bitter disappointment, for they had been heartened by the early anti-Soviet thrust of Carter's human rights initiatives. During the campaign Carter had seemed to lean toward conservative human rights priorities, including Jewish emigration and pressing the Soviets on upholding the Helsinki Accords, and one of his first moves in office was to respond to a congratulatory message from Andrei Sakharov. The first head of state to write directly to Sakharov, Carter assured the Nobel laureate that the United States would "continue our firm commitment to promote respect for human rights" and use its "good offices to seek the release of prisoners of conscience." The language was cautiously diplomatic, but the personal nature of the letter, its transmission through the American embassy in Moscow, and the ensuing publicity were provocative in the context of Soviet-American détente.

Soon after, setting a contrast with Ford's snub of Solzhenitsyn, Carter invited dissident Vladimir Bukovsky to the White House, using the occasion to announce that "our commitment to human rights is permanent."[43] The Soviets were irate. The Kremlin leaders regarded his human rights criticisms, Dobrynin later wrote, as "a direct challenge to their internal political authority and even as an attempt to change their regime."[44] Carter and his advisers were surprised; they thought the Soviets would be "sophisticated enough to understand" that human rights was a domestic maneuver to give the administration more flexibility on arms control.[45] Carter had disavowed "linkage" of human rights and arms control, hoping to speak out on behalf of dissidents without affecting the progress of SALT negotiations. The Kremlin's reaction indicated that human rights talk would exact too high a price. When Sakharov sent a second letter, Carter did not reply.[46] Within a few months the administration was furiously backtracking, taking a more conciliatory posture so as not to scuttle hopes for arms control.

The early moves had prompted the Coalition for a Democratic Majority wing of the party—Jackson, Moynihan, and others—to congratulate Carter three months into his tenure for his human rights stance and his arms control efforts. Noting that McGovern had recently criticized Carter's conservative foreign policy, the coalition countered that Carter was on "the right course." He had, the group said, taken "the first necessary step in leading our nation away from the secretive strategies of pessimism and back to the kind of affirmative foreign policy that suits a great democracy"—a foreign policy that emphasized the "defense and preservation of freedom in the world."[47]

The neocons, however, were worried by his appointments to foreign policy positions dealing with human rights. The coalition had been formed to move the Democratic Party back toward the center, and its mission had been at least partly accomplished: a centrist Democrat had been elected president. But when the group saw the foreign policy apparatus being overrun by appointees they regarded as dangerous left-liberals, they abandoned any thought of folding. From their perspective, Vance was more or less neutral, a nonideological member of the foreign policy establishment with no particular axe to grind.[48] Not so with lower-ranking officials who covered human rights issues. Outspoken former civil rights activist Andrew Young became U.S. representative to the UN, where he hung Black Power and Palestine Liberation Organization posters on his office walls. He would charge the United States with holding "hundreds, perhaps thousands, of political prisoners." The representative to the UN's Human Rights Commission was former antiwar activist and Jackson antagonist Allard Lowenstein, assisted by former missionary and leftist human rights activist Brady Tyson, who precipitated a flap by issuing an unauthorized apology for the "despicable" U.S. "subversion" of Allende's government.[49] Less radical but still liberal were Brzezinski's National Security Council Global Issues appointment, former Udall adviser Jessica Tuchman; Patricia Derian at the human rights post at State; and Vietnam doves Anthony Lake and Leslie Gelb as the State Department's Policy Planning director and director of politico-military planning, respectively. Not a single name on a list the coalition had passed on was tapped, save one given a minor post in Micronesia. The horrified neocons heartily agreed with Reagan's charge that the foreign policy organs were infested with "born again McGovernites."[50]

Over the next year, the rift between Carter and the coalition widened. What the Democratic right viewed as insufficient criticism of Soviet human rights violations, along with other defense-related issues—selling fighter jets to Saudi Arabia, cancellation of the neutron bomb, reductions in the defense budget, general timidity toward the Soviets—

convinced the hawks that Carter was too weak to protect American interests. As early as June 1977 the coalition condemned Carter's foreign policy as "the experiment that failed." One of the four principal counts against the administration was its softness on Soviet human rights abuses.[51]

Seeking a concept under which to unify their rising concerns about U.S. foreign policy, the coalition sought to claim an ideological campaign for human rights as its centerpiece—an idea, comparable to Cold War containment, that could fuse "a host of arguments and emotions."[52] In an early 1978 manifesto called "Beyond the Cold War, Beyond Détente: Toward a Foreign Policy of Human Rights," coalition authors Joshua Muravchik and Penn Kemble praised the "new force" provided by a growing international movement for human rights, originating with Soviet dissidents, as a motivating force in the battle of ideas. Human rights "is our alternative to all of the enticing 'isms' that authoritarians put forward to vie for men's allegiance," a draft of the manifesto stated. "It has challenged what appeared to be a deepening cynicism and loss of will" in the West and "offers a way of arousing our own people," for "a renewed sense of pride in the ideals of our nation . . . is breaking through the guilt and cynicism which have overshadowed the American political landscape." The problem with Carter's approach was that it was contradictory and erratic and had not truly made human rights a guiding policy. The coalition draft went so far as to advocate human rights criticism of right-wing allies—always keeping in mind the vastly greater dangers posed by totalitarian repression so as to avoid indulging in "a hollow moralism that rebuke[d] only lesser evils."[53]

If the Democratic right failed in its public relations campaign to claim the human rights mantle, it did foster public qualms about the Carter policy. By 1978 the neocons were up in arms. Jackson's staff, Richard Perle in particular, was "*very* disgruntled, disillusioned with the Administration and downright angry over the way many things are handled," not least human rights, one of Brzezinski's aides reported. The president was using rhetoric to deflect attention from his lack of real pressure on the Kremlin about human rights abuses, and instead the liberals in charge were engaged in "McGovernite harassment against countries such as Chile and Nicaragua." Conservative Democrats were still willing to support Carter if he toughened up, Perle advised, but time was running out.[54]

In January 1980, as Carter sought support in the upcoming presidential election, he held a meeting with a group of neoconservatives, seeking to mend fences. Having abandoned détente in the aftermath of the December 1979 Soviet invasion of Afghanistan, Carter was taking a tough anti-Soviet line, precisely as the neocons wanted, yet the meeting was a dismal failure. Norman Podhoretz proposed a large-scale campaign against human rights abuses in the Soviet Union; Carter, defensive, responded by asking for help in dealing with torture in Uruguay—stunning his interlocutors, who could hardly imagine mentioning a topic so trivial and diversionary alongside the Soviet threat to world survival. Elliott Abrams, who had recently left Moynihan's staff and was reportedly attending in the capacity of an adviser to Jackson, termed the meeting "a disaster, the straw that breaks the camel's back," because Carter had indicated that he was going to "continue to pursue a leftist McGovernite-Andy Young foreign policy."[55] Historian Justin Vaïsse calls this meeting "a momentous event in the history of the neoconservative movement," destroying any chance that the coalition would support Carter in his reelection campaign and paving the way for their abandonment of the Democratic Party.[56]

If Carter failed to satisfy those for whom anticommunism was the central rationale for promoting human rights, he fared little better with liberals. Administration officials repeatedly tried to lower expectations, reminding the public that human rights considerations were always but one component of a larger policy that also depended on national security and economic factors. The results smacked of hypocrisy. Romanian president Nicolae Ceausescu, the shah of Iran, and Somalian dictator Mohammed Siad Barre were among the nasty despots Carter embraced for geopolitical reasons. Carter famously called the shah, who would shortly be deposed in a bloody revolution, a great leader who had made Iran "an island of stability in one of the more troubled areas of the world." He even went so far as to toast the shah, whose notoriously brutal secret police were probably at that moment torturing a political prisoner, for sharing a commitment to "the cause of human rights."[57] The administration refused all but the lightest criticisms of the imprisonment of political

The shah of Iran presenting Carter with a tapestry of George Washington in 1977. Critics charged Carter with cozying up to unsavory dictators if their countries were strategically important. (Jimmy Carter Presidential Library)

dissidents in China in deference to the PRC's sensibilities. Even genocidal regimes could be tolerated: in 1979 the United States supported a successful move to allow Pol Pot's cabal, overthrown by a Vietnamese invasion, to continue to represent Cambodia in the United Nations. In the case of apartheid South Africa, the administration merely continued to uphold UN sanctions on a state that had by then become an international pariah.[58]

Where strong efforts were made to deter human rights violations, they generally occurred in countries of little consequence as measured by traditional yardsticks of U.S. national interests. Paraguay could claim little significance to the United States, and its abuses were therefore met with a solid front: diplomatic isolation, total cutoffs in aid, and blocked loans in international forums. In at least one case, "success" for the human rights policy came alongside ignoring even worse crimes. In Indonesia, the Carter administration and human rights organizations pressed General Suharto's regime to release tens of thousands of political prisoners it had held since the mid-1960s, while skirting the mass killings and forced population transfers that continued after its 1975 invasion of East Timor. In this case the centrality accorded to torture and political imprisonment as the world's most fundamental abuses blinded the administration, and some nongovernmental organizations, to other, far more serious ones.[59] As Tony Lake acknowledged in assessing the administration's record a year into office, the administration had been tougher on countries that tortured than on those that denied political liberties, and Latin America had received disproportionate attention. The administration's policies had downplayed the hard, long-term task of trying to promote political and economic rights.[60] The choices of carrots and sticks were also skewed. Despite Carter's efforts to encourage the use of positive incentives to acknowledge improvements in rights records, rights initiatives continued to rely primarily on threats to cut off aid to induce better behavior among U.S. allies, even when evidence of the efficacy of these threats was lacking.

A proposal backed by Brzezinski to create a quasi-governmental institute designed to promote positive initiatives in human rights fell victim to squabbling between liberals and neoconservatives. The idea to create the Institute for Human Rights and Freedom was first broached by Freedom House, with support from the humanitarian International Rescue Committee. The aim was to set up a body, funded by but run independently of the government, that would give grants to human rights nongovernmental organizations, aid victims, and conduct research on how best to foster human rights. Freedom House head Leonard Sussman envisaged an agency whose goals aligned with those of his own organization: research on political rights and civil liberties. This new agency should not merely foster human rights but also fundamental freedoms, Sussman argued, for "inhumane treatment" such as torture and political imprisonment was a function of political and social structures that should be the target of reform.[61] In early 1978 Brzezinski urged Carter to support such an institute, but the president demurred.[62] Congressmen Fascell and Fraser took up the cause and held hearings. Ultimately, though, the proposal failed on Capitol Hill because, as Perle put it, Jackson and others felt it was "going to be turned over to the McGovernites as their plaything." Perle promised support for the proposal only if

Brzezinski agreed to appoint strong anticommunists who would give the body an appropriately anti-Soviet focus.[63] Under such conditions, the initiative went nowhere.

Critics have made much of the ways that internecine warfare between Brzezinski and Vance, and Carter's frequent failures to adjudicate, undermined the coherence of the administration's foreign policy.[64] When it came to human rights, however, many of the important day-to-day battles over policy occurred at lower levels of the bureaucracy. Midlevel State Department staffers whose main interest was in maintaining good relations with allies clashed repeatedly with the new human rights proponents who came from outside the foreign policy apparatus. Richard Holbrooke, for example, was one of the younger foreign policy specialists Carter had tapped for advice during the campaign, someone with years of involvement in the Vietnam War but at lower levels—not one of the "wise old men" who had been the architects of the war. He had spent six years serving in Vietnam-related peace efforts, eventually coming to believe the war was a mistake but a well-intentioned one. Holbrooke, who would go on to be a liberal advocate of humanitarian intervention in the 1990s, never saw the Vietnam War in McGovernite terms and stayed away from McGovern in 1972, viewing him as too far to the left. In a 1976 *Foreign Policy* article, he disavowed "the Vietnam-based, guilt-ridden anguish of the left" and criticized those who thought "that because America has done some evil things, America itself is an evil force in the world."[65] He distanced himself from Wilsonian idealism, saying "Wilson failed," and described his own approach as a blend of moralism and realism.[66]

The human rights dilemmas of the Carter administration played out in the State Department, pitting officials like Holbrooke, as the new assistant secretary of state for East Asian and Pacific Affairs, against non-establishmentarians like Patricia Derian. Derian took over from the hapless James Wilson just as the head of the State Department's Bureau of Human Rights was elevated to assistant secretary status. She was a "McGovernite": she had opposed the Vietnam War on moral grounds, saying, "We have spoiled ourselves and the American dream" by engaging in "slaughter and murder" to prop up a brutal dictator; she had run McGovern's Mississippi campaign in 1972; and she began 1976 as a Udall supporter before signing on as a deputy director of Carter's campaign.[67] Her influence can be overstated—apparently she did not have the access to the president that some claimed for her—but as the one administration figure whose sole mandate was human rights, her outspoken advocacy did much to keep human rights in the public eye.

Her appointment to the human rights post reveals much about the administration's initial, still-incubating views on human rights. When she was tapped for the post as a reward for her campaign services, Derian had had but one paying job, and her main qualification was her years of experience in Mississippi politics working for civil rights reforms. She declined the post of protocol officer that was first offered to her, and when Vance came up with the human rights position at State, she had never heard of it. But to her and to administration officials, it seemed like a good fit. Human rights abroad seemed roughly analogous to civil rights at home, and the portfolio covered just the kind of "soft" issue that was deemed suitable for a woman. The other major official tasked specifically with human rights was also a woman: Jessica Tuchman as head of the National Security Council's Global Issues Cluster, dubbed "globaloney" by more hard-core security-minded colleagues.[68] As ambassador to the UN, African American Andy Young was a key spokesman on human rights. The gender and race of the administration's top human rights officials surely implied to 1970s America that the issue was not truly mainstream nor on a par with other interests.

Unlike Wilson, Derian was an outsider to the State Department and did little to hide her disdain for its traditionalism. Instead of accommodating to prevailing attitudes among the diplomatic corps, she saw her job as "tilting against gray-flannel windmills," as a colleague put it.[69] It was often hard to tell where she saw the primary field of battle: reforming attitudes and behavior among the traditionalists at State or those of repressive dictators abroad. Her disdain was fully reciprocated by seasoned bureaucrats like Holbrooke, who regarded her as an unsophisticated amateur whose childish naïveté endangered important U.S. interests. By the time Carter left office she had been on the verge of resigning over policy disagreements so many times that she left packing boxes stacked permanently in her office.[70] Her approach to the issue of human rights was that of a purist. "I think we should never fall into a situation where we say whose pain is worse, whose suffering is most severe," she told the press in 1978. "Once you pass a certain level of hunger, of pain, of deprivation or suffering, you have moved over into an area where there is no quantitative or qualitative difference."[71] She staffed her office with people who had worked on congressional human rights initiatives, including John Salzberg and Ted Kennedy's former foreign policy aide, Mark Schneider. Like congressional liberals, she prioritized torture and prolonged political imprisonment and was most active in pressing human rights among U.S. allies on the grounds that that was where American influence was strongest.

Derian's brief was human rights. The outlook of those tasked with the maintenance of good relations with U.S. allies was necessarily quite different. Conflicts were inevitable—and frequent. A telling example was the 1978 debate over whether to ban the sale of tear gas to Iran, when the shah was using it to quell demonstrations. Derian argued for the ban; Under Secretary of State for Security Assistance Lucy Benson opposed it. Benson won.[72]

Derian's most persistent antagonist was Richard Holbrooke, with whom she clashed repeatedly and heatedly over human rights issues that fell within the mandate of his bureau. Holbrooke had written an early speech for candidate Carter that lauded human rights, but worked to keep such references from impinging on major security interests. He succeeded, for example, in deleting criticism of the shah of Iran in a May 1976 speech.[73] As Holbrooke saw it, he was trying to carve out a realistic middle ground, whereas Derian wanted to sacrifice important American interests in the name of human rights. Once out of office Holbrooke vented his fury publicly, denouncing the "great damage" inflicted by Derian's "preachy moral arrogance" and what he saw as unabashed efforts to overthrow friendly foreign governments.[74]

Their disagreements were sharpest over how to deal with Philippine president Ferdinand Marcos. "There's no question that [Holbrooke] was not tough on human rights with Marcos," a colleague recalled.[75] Marcos had ruled the country under martial law since 1972, arresting opponents, curtailing civil liberties, and muzzling the press, but Holbrooke

preferred not to press the Philippine dictator on rights issues when rene-
gotiation of the leases to Subic and Clark Naval Bases was at stake. Derian
sniffed that Holbrooke was seduced by Marcos's flattery and trips on his
yachts; Holbrooke raged at Derian's interference in security issues.
Tempers often flared. When Derian proposed inviting Philippine dissident Benino Aquino to the State Department in 1980, for example, she
recalled that Holbrooke stormed in, "arms akimbo, just a raving, furious
man, telling me that it was bad for the country."[76] Still incensed over an
incident when Salzberg, acting as Fraser's aide during a congressional
trip, had met with South Korean dissidents over Holbrooke's strong
objections, Holbrooke ordered his staff not to talk to the young Quaker.
The order made it impossible for Salzberg, who was assigned to the Asia
desk of Derian's Human Rights Bureau, to do his job. Even Derian's
intercession could not rectify the situation, and Salzberg eventually had
to be transferred to the Africa desk.[77]

Derian had better luck when it came to Latin America, where the
administration's efforts came to focus after its brief fling with an anti-
Soviet approach. Derian's views on Latin America reflected the human
rights movement's view that it was there that human rights were most
seriously threatened. Her first trip official trip was to Argentina, El
Salvador, Bolivia, Brazil, and Uruguay, all under right-wing governments targeted by Amnesty for large-scale rights violations. In June 1977,
First Lady Rosalynn Carter took a tour of Latin America, limited to
countries certified by the State Department as having a positive or substantially improving human rights record. Carter himself, in Brazil in
March 1978, met with government critic and human rights activist
Cardinal Paulo Evaristo Arns, who gave him a list of "disappeared."[78]

Argentina, a particular concern of Derian's, is often cited as a success
story for Carter's human rights policy because in the longer term it produced modest but significant results. It was, as a National Security
Council retrospective noted in 1981, "one of the most difficult and vexing
cases" the administration faced. Its human rights abuses—the worst in
the region—received substantial attention in the U.S. media. The military junta that had seized power in 1976 resorted to "revolting forms of
torture, frequent 'disappearance' of prisoners, and other extrajudicial
means of maintaining the regime in power by crushing its opponents," in

A cartoon shows Carter's human rights program as a "hot air balloon" deflating over issues such as support for the shah of Iran, protection of American jobs, and new Israeli settlements. (Ollie Harrington)

the not-so-dry words of the National Security Council report. Reductions in aid levels, a congressional vote to cut off military assistance effective in 1978, the veto of an Export-Import Bank loan, and public pressure were among the moves that seem to have led the regime to moderate its repression. Carter would shift late in his term toward a more accommodating approach to the junta as Soviet-Argentine ties grew and the Sandinista Revolution in Nicaragua reconfigured U.S. policy in the region, but it seems that modest positive effects remained in place.[79]

One of the Carter years' most significant outcomes for international human rights had almost nothing to do with its policies or actions. This was the new ferment within the Soviet bloc stemming from the 1975 Helsinki Final Act of the Conference on Security and Co-operation in Europe. The dissident activity that it set in motion, and the legitimacy the Final Act bestowed on such activity, played a role in the ultimate collapse of communism in Eastern Europe and the USSR—although whether that role is as significant as some have suggested remains an open question.[80] During the lengthy negotiations leading up to the accords, some West European governments had insisted on including "respect for human rights and fundamental freedoms" as a basic principle of relations among European states. All parties further agreed to act in conformity with the Universal Declaration of Human Rights and to fulfill obligations in the human rights covenants and other instruments to which they were signatories, and in the so-called Basket III provisions a range of contacts and exchanges were permitted.[81] Kissinger had scoffed at these provisions, calling the Europeans' efforts to extract concessions on these matters "one of the weirdest negotiations I have ever seen." "I've told all of them that the Soviet Union won't be overthrown without noticing it," he told the Soviets, "and certainly not because of things like increased circulation of newspapers and so on."[82]

During the election campaign, Carter had criticized Ford for giving too much in exchange for too little, and the widespread perception that Helsinki had ratified Soviet domination of Eastern Europe did much to undermine public support for détente. Yet once signed, the accords unexpectedly opened up new avenues for dissent in Eastern Europe. This outcome had not been anticipated by the Kremlin, which had signed the accords in the expectation that the value of what they gained— recognition of the status quo in Eastern Europe—outweighed the disadvantages imposed by human rights provisions they intended to ignore.

Ultimately, however, the accords sparked an unprecedented campaign of mobilization within the Soviet bloc. In 1976 physicist Yuri Orlov formed the first Helsinki Watch Group in Moscow, aimed at monitoring Soviet compliance, and similar groups were soon formed in Czechoslovakia and Poland and across Western Europe. To almost everyone's surprise, the Helsinki Accords had created a powerful space for transnational human rights organizing. In 1978 Brezhnev lamented that human rights constituted the West's "main line of ideological attack against socialist countries."[83]

In 1978 Random House publisher Robert Bernstein and ACLU head Aryeh Neier founded an American version of the Soviet Helsinki Watch. Bernstein had a passion for human rights born of his commitment to intellectual freedom. He identified strongly with famous middle-aged men who became victims of repression, intellectuals like Sakharov and the Argentine journalist Jacobo Timerman—indeed, he identified so strongly, Neier later recalled, that "when Sakharov was force-fed to break a hunger strike, and when Timerman was tortured, it was as if Bob was also force-fed and tortured."[84] Aided first by a small planning grant and then a $400,000 infusion from the Ford Foundation, and thus freed initially from the need to fund-raise, the group announced that it would monitor human rights violations in the Final Act's thirty-five signatories, focusing on Soviet-bloc countries.[85] It maintained contacts with human rights organizations and activists in those countries, and its published reports were about the status of human rights and the condition of dissidents in those countries. In response to Soviet accusations that Western Helsinki groups were ignoring violations in their own countries, Helsinki Watch made some efforts to document problems at home that fell under the rubric of the Helsinki Accords. Its heart was never in self-criticism, however, and as was the case with so many other groups dedicated to international human rights, its focus was turned resolutely outward.[86]

After merging with similar regional "watch" committees formed in the 1980s, Helsinki Watch, renamed Human Rights Watch, would emerge in 1988 as one of the world's largest and most influential human rights organizations. Dismayed by Amnesty's failure to get involved in the Helsinki process and perceiving Amnesty to be overly slow and conservative in its approach, Bernstein and others positioned Helsinki Watch as a rival to Amnesty and the heir to the Jackson-Vanik amendment.[87] A congressional initiative backed by liberal Republican Millicent Fenwick, a first-term New Jersey congresswoman with an interest in civil and women's rights, resulted in the formation of a commission to work on implementing the Helsinki Accords. With Dante Fascell as chair, the Commission on Security and Cooperation in Europe began to influence U.S. policy late in the Carter years.[88]


Called to testify to Congress about human rights in 1982, Richard Holbrooke spent three days writing and rewriting his statement. Every time he finished a statement about a general principle, he would find he did not agree with it and then revise it, only to find he did not agree with the opposite, either. It had been six years since Holbrooke wrote human rights into one of Carter's campaign speeches, and he had spent four years in Carter's State Department arguing human rights issues as they applied to the countries in his purview. Yet he had emerged with no clear convictions other than that when cases of torture came up, U.S. officials ought to gently remonstrate with their foreign counterparts, and that in other situations, everything depended on the larger context.[89] Such lack of clarity was not limited to Holbrooke; Carter, Vance, and Brzezinski all produced memoirs whose treatment of human rights is muddy and ambivalent. Derian's solution—treat all violations the same, with virtually no regard for other interests—had the virtue of consistency, but was hardly feasible.

Assessments of the achievements of Carter's human rights policy usually begin by praising the administration for raising global awareness of the idea and generating new scrutiny of governments that openly mistreated their citizens. But the new rhetoric was far from universally acclaimed, and allies seemed as likely to find it rebarbative as adversaries. West German chancellor Helmut Schmidt, whose disdain for Carter was legendary, regarded human rights as self-serving and dangerous moralizing that threatened to undermine détente.[90] Relations with allies targeted for criticism or aid cutoffs were complicated by the human rights policy—or "ruined," as Brzezinski ranted in 1978 in reference to Chile, Brazil, Argentina, and Uruguay.[91] But a vocal chorus of nongovernmental organizations, dissidents, and sympathetic politicians around the world praised Carter for raising the world's sensitivity to suffering and the need to factor such suffering into policy.

Longer-term moderation of repression in countries like Argentina and amelioration of repression against specific individuals must also be counted among the policy's successes. Again, however, the successes were achieved with respect to a narrow band of rights, and ignoring other rights was arguably an inevitable product of focusing so much attention and effort on a small group of cause-célèbre abuses. Economic and social rights were the group that most clearly fell by the wayside. In 1977 the Policy Review Committee had recommended that "basic human needs" be considered an integral part of the administration's development and human rights strategies, and Carter had come into office pledging to double foreign aid. Here the gap between rhetoric and reality was huge: with the country's own economic woes rising, Carter did not request significant increases in foreign aid requests, and aid as a percentage of gross domestic product remained low relative to what other developed countries provided.[92]

When it comes to assessing the success of Carter's human rights campaigns as domestic psychotherapy, it is difficult to separate the effects of the human rights emphasis from other developments that painted Carter as a weak and ineffective president. If Americans felt tired of feeling humiliated and scorned in 1976, they were angry about feeling humiliated and weak in 1980, and for the right, human rights were one of the indictments of Carter's weakness. Instead of pride and will and nerve, they saw too much guilt and too much willingness to accept responsibility whenever an ally did something unpleasant. Irving Kristol, for example, condemned the "moral bankruptcy" of Carter's foreign policy for wallowing in "pathological" guilt toward countries the United States had never wronged. The country should be "strong and willing to act decisively," pursuing its interests without handwringing about the need for dialogue and mutual understanding.[93] Jeane Kirkpatrick charged that human rights had "lost" Iran and Nicaragua and weakened U.S. interests around the globe.[94]

Historian Gaddis Smith has suggested that Carter took advantage of a brief window of American guilt to sell human rights. Carter, he writes, was a "prophet assailing American wickedness," much like McGovern, who won the election because he tapped a fleeting mood of national guilt.[95] Yet his Notre Dame speech aside, Carter's promotion of human rights was pitched, as the president himself put it, as a way "to reassure people that we were honest and benevolent and moral."[96] His message about the Vietnam War varied: at one time he expressed regret for not opposing the mistaken war sooner, but in office he resolutely opposed reparations to Vietnam, and in an early speech as president he disclaimed any moral obligation stemming from the war. "The destruction was mutual," the president lectured. "We went to Vietnam without any desire to capture territory or to impose American will on other people. We went there to defend the freedom of the South Vietnamese. I don't feel that we ought to apologize or castigate ourselves or assume the status of culpability."[97]

Americans told pollsters that they wanted to restore their moral standing in the world but not at the cost of important U.S. interests. Carter told them he could do it, and he achieved moderate success. Some of the more left-wing officials in the administration occasionally deviated from the message. Andy Young declared that Americans suffered under "a tremendous amount of guilt" because for so long their foreign aid had supported dictators instead of feeding the hungry—but Young was an outlier who would later be dismissed for overstepping his mandate. Again and again, Carter said that human rights were about being proud again, standing tall, feeling good. He said he had merely tapped into what was already "part of the consciousness of the free people of the greatest nation on Earth, the United States." It was this projection that was most obvious to observers at the time, who endlessly repeated variations on *Newsweek*'s observation that "in an uncertain post-Vietnam era, [human rights promotion] has finally given the U.S. and other democracies something to boast about."[98] Pride, virtue, self-respect, prestige: these were the hallmarks of Carter's human rights push—not guilt, and not atonement.

# Conclusion

## *Universal Human Rights in American Foreign Policy*

S EVEN MONTHS AFTER Carter took office, Donald Fraser told an
audience: "Some people around the world view the notion that the
U.S. is about to become the world's moral leader with disbelief. They
wonder about a nation that plotted assassinations, destabilized governments, and engaged in murderous wars suddenly claiming the right to
pass judgment on the morality of other nations."[1] As the person most
responsible for writing broad human rights considerations into foreign
policy, the Minnesota congressman knew well that it was precisely
because America's self-confidence and reputation were under assault
that a new program was needed. Of all the restorative tonics political
leaders tried in their desperate attempts to salve the country's post-
Vietnam War psychic wounds, international human rights promotion
proved to be among the most palatable and popular. When offered the
choice to pass judgment on the morality of other nations instead of
condemning the morality of their own, Americans responded with
alacrity.

Inspiration from abroad had helped put human rights on the table as
a way out of the country's crisis of confidence. The celebrated discourse
of human rights developed by Soviet dissidents seems to have been a
key influence on Scoop Jackson's attraction to human rights as a way to

legitimize his campaign for Soviet Jewish emigration. Liberals had gained exposure to transnational human rights networks in campaigns against repression in Greece, Brazil, and elsewhere, though they used human rights as their central framing device only after Jackson had demonstrated the political potency of such language. Rising sensitivity to global interdependence and détente's weakening of Cold War fears made a push for morality in foreign relations intellectually credible. At home, Kissinger's stance toward morality, so very much out of keeping with America's traditions and self-conception, was a crucial trigger; he sparked on both sides of the political spectrum an intense longing for a way to explain the American role in the world in terms that were not coldly calculating.

From late 1972, when Jackson placed international human rights squarely on the national agenda, through the mid-1970s, as congressional liberals used the new rubric to restructure foreign aid, the concept gained political traction. A crucial catalyst was the end of U.S. involvement in the Vietnam War at the beginning of 1973, which opened up political space that had been occupied by debate over the war. It also left a reservoir of anger and frustration in Congress that liberals, including Fraser and Senator James Abourezk, used to launch a series of legislative initiatives tying U.S. foreign policy to human rights considerations. Yet in the 1976 presidential race, ideas of international human rights played a surprisingly small role, particularly among the Democrats before Carter's eleventh-hour epiphany. The major liberal presidential candidates were more concerned with retreat and reform at home than with launching a new moral crusade. Until Carter picked up the concept shortly before the election, it resonated most strongly in the anti-détente right-wing factions of both parties—among Jackson Democrats and Reagan Republicans.

For liberals, international human rights shifted the agenda from grand schemes of social transformation to more minimalist goals, better suited to a new, chastened sense of limits. In this regard it is useful to see the liberal human rights movement of the 1970s as a successor to one of the central liberal foreign policy idealisms of the 1960s: modernization theory. The rise of human rights in a pessimistic crisis of modernity in the 1970s was surely yoked to the fall of modernization theory and its optimistic zeal. It is no coincidence that the main arena of debate over human rights was the foreign aid budget (and, later, multilateral development loans).[2] Fraser, liberal human rights' most tireless political advocate in the mid-1970s, had been an equally tireless advocate of developmental modernization in the 1960s. Then he had called for an expansive American role in the internal affairs of other nations: "We must take a far more deliberate and more comprehensive role toward developing nations," he wrote in 1965. "We should systematically try to trigger, to stimulate, and to guide the growth of fundamental social structures and behaviors among large numbers of people in other countries."[3] Fraser proposed not only economic development; he was also a democratizer. The catastrophe of the Vietnam War taught him that such hopes were dangerous, and he moved toward a much narrower, more modest vision of global betterment in the 1970s, one in which democratization fell to the wayside in favor of simply hoping that people were not tortured. For all the condemnation that critics have heaped on modernization theory—its hierarchical racism, hubris, neoimperialist motives, and utter failure to achieve its promises—it arguably offered a more empowering vision for the rest of the world than the minimalist creed of the 1970s.[4]

For Jackson and others on the conservative side of the fence, McGovern-style hand-wringing over the Vietnam War was the problem that needed to be overcome. The country needed to reclaim its proud, proselytizing moral role in the world, and human rights offered a means to do so. Without Carter's razor-thin victory in 1976, Jackson and the neoconservatives might have won the fight to define human rights. In this area, the Jackson wing of the Democratic Party and the Reagan wing of the Republican Party were converging. But Carter won the election, and his administration imbued its human rights program with predominantly liberal content, directing most of its energy against right-wing allies in Latin America, while the neocons resentfully nurtured a different, anti-communist vision of human rights from the sidelines.

In both liberal and conservative guises human rights served to reclaim American virtue from the wreckage of Vietnam. It became an official program of the U.S. government because politicians hoped to do good, but they were also keenly desirous of making Americans feel good. Yet contrary to what some critics would have, it was no grand conspiracy.[5] It was a contingent product of what journalist Theodore White called "the emotional wearing out of a nation" following the civil rights movement, Watergate, and above all, the Vietnam War.[6] By breathing new life into arguments for American activism, human rights promotion dimmed the memory of the terrible harm American activism had so recently inflicted in Indochina.[7] In assessing the effects of Carter's presidency, consider the transformation Fraser described. Just a few years earlier, the country was identified with My Lai, the Phoenix program, carpet bombing, free-fire zones, and the napalming of villages; now it donned the mantle of morality, preaching to the world about evildoers abroad. The full measure of this turnaround, and the capacity of human rights to function as a psychic salve that helped the nation avoid a true reckoning with Vietnam, has yet to be plumbed. Already in 1980 Reagan was calling the war a "noble cause," and the "Vietnam syndrome" was stripped down to a reluctance to intervene militarily where interests were unclear or where an exit strategy was ill defined.[8]

Every president since Carter has grappled with the place of human rights in the foreign policy firmament. Dumped out of office after one term, after watching the Soviets invade Afghanistan and flailing helplessly for a seemingly interminable 444 days while Iranian revolutionaries held American hostages, Carter was widely regarded as a failure. He was associated with, when he was not directly blamed for, what felt like a nadir in American power. "Humiliation" was a word that came up frequently. Human rights promotion was tainted, too. Carter had put the weight of American rhetorical power behind human rights, but the modest payoffs were accompanied by confusion, indecisiveness, and lack of conceptual clarity. Western allies scoffed; repressive allies chafed; communist adversaries bellowed and retreated on arms control. At home the right charged human rights policies with undermining the nation's security; the left fulminated about hypocrisy. Yet the idea of human rights would not go away. It was institutionalized in U.S. diplomacy thanks to new laws. It had become the rallying cry of a global mass movement and of vocal, increasingly powerful pressure groups at home.

Americans may not have been happy with the results of human rights policies in practice, but they remained sympathetic to the idea in principle.

Even Reagan, who tried to be the anti-Carter, had to adopt a human rights program, after first trying to dump the idea. Secretary of State Alexander Haig announced at his first press conference that "international terrorism will take the place of human rights in our concern because it is the ultimate cause of abuses of human rights," and Reagan's first nominee for the State Department's key human rights post, Ernest Lefever, was a staunch opponent of inserting human rights considerations into foreign policy who had once said a certain amount of torture was normal.[9] After Congress scuttled the Lefever nomination, his replacement, Elliott Abrams, cast human rights in neoconservative terms—not surprisingly, since he had worked for Jackson and Moynihan. Reagan's State Department declared that human rights was "central to what America is and stands for" and cannot be "tacked on" to foreign policy because it "is its very purpose," but redefined human rights as democracy promotion (except in U.S. allies).[10] Human rights emphatically did not include economic and social rights.[11]

International human rights promotion was now indistinguishable from anticommunism. Reagan called freedom "the inalienable and universal right of all human beings," and set up the National Endowment for Democracy as a neoconservative version of Amnesty International.[12] Crucial to the Reagan view was drawing a bright red line between the "free world" (a phrase again much in vogue) and the "slave" societies of the communist world. In this view regimes allied with the United States used repression in isolated or aberrant ways and were on the path to democratic reform, however long and tortuous that path might be. Totalitarian regimes of the left, in contrast, could survive only through systematic repression woven into every aspect of life. Expounded in a widely read 1979 article by Jeane Kirkpatrick, the idea had been a staple of Coalition for a Democratic Majority thinking for years.[13] The Reagan administration thus returned to the Cold War practice of overlooking or excusing abuses committed by anticommunist regimes. Human rights activists repeatedly clashed with the administration over policy in El Salvador, Guatemala, Nicaragua, South Korea, and elsewhere, and savvy campaigns against Reagan's policies brought Human Rights Watch new levels of professionalization, funding, and public exposure.[14] Despite the efforts of Reagan administration officials to distance themselves from Carter and the cringing liberal self-hatred they thought Carter represented, they saw human rights—just as Carter had—as a means of restoring the American spirit. The country must reconstitute itself as "a source of hope and inspiration," administration officials proposed, so that Americans could "recapture a sense of worth and purpose here at home."[15]

The end of the Cold War inaugurated a new ascendancy of human rights unmoored from anticommunism. Observers in the 1990s predicted that human rights would now set genuine global standards. In a 1991 speech marking the end of the Gulf War, President George H. W. Bush famously hailed "a new world order": "Now, we can see a new world coming into view. . . . A world where the United Nations, freed from cold war stalemate, is poised to fulfill the historic vision of its founders. A world in which freedom and respect for human rights find a home among all nations."[16] UN reforms long mooted by dreamers now became realities, most notably with the creation of the office of UN High Commissioner of Human Rights. The International Criminal Court, whose aim was to deal with crimes against humanity, was established. Former Chilean dictator Augusto Pinochet—the face of torture in the 1970s—was arrested in Britain under the doctrine of universal jurisdiction when Spain issued a warrant to try him. Though he escaped extradition due to ill health, human rights advocates hailed the end of impunity for the world's worst dictators.

But deeds did not match words. Despite enormous optimism and an explosion of talk about human rights in the 1990s, massive human rights violations occurred while the world stood by and watched. Genocide in Rwanda and ethnic cleansing in Bosnia offered stark reminders that safeguarding human rights was still but one concern among many in international politics. The actions that were taken—sanctions against Serbia, for example—highlighted the messy trade-offs that human rights policies imposed.[17] Liberal internationalists began to call for military intervention in the face of massive human rights abuses, and such calls helped spur the Clinton administration into a brief air war—in what was called a humanitarian war—in Kosovo in 1999. That it was waged by NATO without UN sanction seemed to its formerly multilateralist backers a small price to pay.

The terrorist attacks of 9/11 reconfigured the terrain for human rights yet again. If some liberal hawks who in the 1990s had raised the banner of human rights when clamoring for intervention in the Balkans were dismayed at how readily it could be used to justify preemptive war in Iraq in 2003, many others signed on to George W. Bush's crusade with alacrity. For a brief moment, it seemed as though the rift that Carter had failed to close might at last have been bridged, as neocons and some prominent liberals clasped hands to support a war in the name of human rights. Then the unpleasant reality of war and an ill-planned occupation intervened. The costly, ongoing fighting in Afghanistan and Iraq dimmed the star of the neocons, and disillusioned progressives began to see human rights and humanitarian claims as too readily manipulated to suit unjust causes. Carter's 1977 Presidential Review Memorandum on human rights had commented that "security interests cannot justify torture"—and had even prefaced that statement with "needless to say."[18] But the document was discussing the behavior of others, which is what U.S. international human rights promotion had been about from the beginning, and so the Bush administration's open flouting of antitorture laws when it came to defending U.S. security interests should not have come as a surprise. Though Bush's successor, Barack Obama—the first president too young to have been touched by the Vietnam War—disavowed torture, he has kept up and even expanded other human rights violations (including targeted drone killings), and appears less interested in claiming human rights for new causes than in letting the idea fade.

In assessing the legacy of the American war in Iraq for U.S. international human rights promotion, it is worth remembering a much earlier war also fought in part in the name of human rights: the Spanish-American-Cuban-Filipino War that began in 1898. The use of waterboarding in the war on terror prompted critics to remind us that water torture had been an American practice in fighting the Philippines insurgency a century before, but few noticed the similarities in humanitarian justifications for war.[19] In 1900 the Republican Party celebrated the war against Spain as "a war for liberty and human rights" that had given "to ten millions of the human race . . . 'a new birth of freedom,' and to the American people a new and noble responsibility."[20] In the years leading up to the war, politicians and opinion leaders frequently invoked human rights, the "cause of humanity," and a humanitarian duty to prevent Spanish abuses in Cuba. When Cuban rebels started a guerrilla insurgency to free the island from Spanish rule, Spain fought back by herding hundreds of thousands of Cuban peasants into "reconcentration" camps, burning the surrounding countryside to deprive the rebels of resources, and letting the camp population die of starvation and disease. The new penny press denounced the mass deaths as a crime against humanity, and reports of starving children, with bloated abdomens and swollen eyes, outraged Americans.[21] Calls for intervention were buttressed by references to America's duty to defend freedom, "eternal and worldwide" human rights, humanity, and/or civilization.[22] "A war between the United States and Spain at this time would be fraught with deep significance," declared Populist Congressman Mason Peters. "It would result not only in the freedom of Cuba, but the exaltation of a principle which would be an object lesson to the world for all time," pitting oppression and inhumanity against "civil and religious liberty, equality, human rights, progress. . . . Why need we shrink from such a conflict? Such a war would be a blessing to the world."[23]

When McKinley finally agreed to war, the United States defeated Spain quickly. Cuba was disposed of relatively easily with the establishment of a protectorate, but Filipinos—whose freedom from Spanish rule was a by-product of the war—rebelled when the United States attempted to assert control. The insurrection provoked a fierce, years-long debate over imperialism in the United States. Anti-imperialists objected to the imposition of American rule on a far-off land, often on racist grounds. Asiatic peoples could not "rise" to "the high conception of the rights of man entertained by the Anglo-Saxon," one congressman claimed.[24] Imperialists argued that duty impelled Americans to guide and assist the Filipinos toward liberty and independence. Human rights were not just for Americans, expansionists averred; the nation had a duty to extend such rights beyond its boundaries.[25] "We propose to proclaim liberty and justice and the protection of life and human rights wherever the flag of the United States is planted," Senator Platt declared in 1899, even as a bloody years-long war against insurrectionists began, one that saw widespread torture and atrocities and in which an estimated two hundred thousand civilians would die. The eventual victory of U.S. forces consolidated a half-century of U.S. rule.[26] Anti-imperialist George Boutwell, cataloguing the destruction of life and the denial of civil and political rights to Filipinos, said the war rested on "a criminal view of human rights" and that Americans had been "deceived and misled" into thinking "a war of aggression and conquest" was "a war for civilization and humanity."[27]

It is no coincidence that the neoconservative-leaning historian Robert Kagan has recently tried to rehabilitate the war in Cuba as a humanitarian war, the product of a deeply ingrained American universalism and benevolence, fought for mostly unselfish reasons, and a precocious step toward raising universal standards of behavior that could be adjudicated by force.[28] Historians less enthusiastic about the war's consequences are more cognizant of the clear commercial and military interests, the celebration of militarism, and the underlying racism and social Darwinism that led the nation first to war and then to imperialism. Even Kagan ignores the human rights dimension of the war, for human rights can hardly be reconciled with the outright denials of rights that followed, nor were nineteenth-century castings of the idea, so deeply intertwined with racial hierarchy, Christianity, and notions of civilization, cognates of today's universalist rhetoric.

Human rights (and its older relative, the rights of man) is, then, a compelling, adaptable slogan. Facing another postwar, postoccupation era in which the ideals that justified the spilling of blood seem to many in retrospect to have been tarnished, Americans seem to be losing interest in the idea as a guide to U.S. foreign policy. The cautious optimism of the 1970s and the grandiose hopes of the 1990s have given way to a new ambivalence. The rhetoric of human rights is still the world's moral *lingua franca*; nothing has yet arisen to replace it. But it may be that human rights has been stretched and pulled in so many directions that it will lose its force—until, someday, it rises again.

# Abbreviations

| | |
|---|---|
| Abourezk Papers | James G. Abourezk Papers, University of South Dakota Library, Vermillion, South Dakota |
| ACLU | American Civil Liberties Union |
| ADA | Americans for Democratic Action |
| Ad Hoc Records | Records of the Ad Hoc Committee on the Human Rights and Genocide Treaties, Tamiment Library/ Robert F. Wagner Labor Archive, Bobst Library, New York City |
| AI | Amnesty International |
| AI IS | Amnesty International, International Secretariat Archives, International Institute for Social History, Amsterdam, The Netherlands |
| AI USA | Amnesty International, U.S. Section |
| AI USA Records | Records of Amnesty International USA, Center for Human Rights Documentation and Research, Columbia University |
| AID | U.S. Agency for International Development |
| Becket Papers | Elise G. Becket Papers, Hoover Institution Archives, Stanford, California |
| Biddle Papers | Francis B. Biddle Papers, Georgetown University Library, Washington, D.C. |
| Buckley Papers | William F. Buckley Jr. Papers, Yale University Library, New Haven, Connecticut |

| | |
|---|---|
| Carter Library | Jimmy Carter Presidential Library, Atlanta, Georgia |
| CDM | Coalition for a Democratic Majority |
| Church Papers | Frank Church Papers, Boise State University Library, Boise, Idaho |
| Cong. Rec. | Congressional Record: Proceedings and Debates of the . . . Congress |
| Cranston Papers | Alan Cranston Papers, BANC MSS 78/44c, Bancroft Library, University of California, Berkeley |
| DDRS | Declassified Documents Reference System (Gale) |
| Edwards Papers | Don Edwards Congressional Papers, San Jose State University Library, San Jose, California |
| f. | Folder |
| Ford Library | Gerald Ford Presidential Library, Ann Arbor, Michigan |
| Fraser Papers | Donald M. Fraser Papers, Minnesota Historical Society, St. Paul, Minnesota |
| FRUS | *Foreign Relations of the United States*, Washington, DC: US GPO |
| Grant Papers | Frances R. Grant Papers, Rutgers University Library, New Brunswick, New Jersey |
| HA | Bureau of Human Rights and Humanitarian Affairs, State Department, Record Group 59 |
| Harriman Papers | Averell Harriman Papers, Library of Congress, Washington, D.C. |
| Hoover | Hoover Institution Archives, Stanford, California |
| HRQ | *Human Rights Quarterly* |
| HRW | Human Rights Watch Archives, Center for Human Rights Documentation and Research, Columbia University, New York City, New York |
| ILHR Records | Records of the International League for Human Rights, New York Public Library, New York City, New York |
| ILRM | International League for the Rights of Man (after 1976, the International League for Human Rights) |
| IRC CLA | International Relations Committee, RG 233, Center for Legislative Archives, NARA |
| Jackson Papers | Henry M. Jackson Papers, University of Washington Library, Seattle, Washington |

| | |
|---|---|
| Kennedy Library | John F. Kennedy Presidential Library, Boston, Massachusetts |
| Kissinger Memcons | The Kissinger Transcripts: A Verbatim Record of U.S. Diplomacy, 1969–1977, Digital National Security Archive (ProQuest) |
| Kissinger Telcons | The Kissinger Telephone Conversations: A Verbatim Record of U.S. Diplomacy, 1969–1977, Digital National Security Archive (ProQuest) |
| *LAT* | *The Los Angeles Times* |
| LBJ Library | Lyndon Baines Johnson Presidential Library, Austin, Texas |
| LC | Library of Congress, Washington, D.C. |
| Lister Papers | George Lister Papers, Nettie Lee Benson Latin American Collection, University of Texas, Austin, Austin, Texas |
| McGovern Papers | George McGovern Papers, Princeton University Library, Princeton, New Jersey |
| MFN | Most favored nation |
| Morris Papers | Ivan I. Morris Papers, Columbia University Library, New York City, New York |
| Moynihan Papers | Daniel P. Moynihan Papers, Library of Congress, Washington, D.C. |
| NAACP | National Association for the Advancement of Colored People |
| NARA | National Archives and Records Administration, Washington, D.C. |
| NCC | National Council of the Churches of Christ of the U.S.A. |
| NGO | Nongovernmental organization |
| Nixon Library | Richard Nixon Presidential Library, Yorba Linda, California |
| *NYT* | *New York Times* |
| Rosenblatt Papers | Peter R. Rosenblatt Personal Papers, LBJ Library |
| Sagan Papers | Ginetta Sagan Papers, Hoover Institution Archives, Stanford, California |
| SNCC | Student Non-violent Coordinating Committee |
| Symington Papers | W. Stuart Symington Papers, State Historical Society of Missouri, Columbia, Missouri |
| Timmons Collection | Staff Member and Office Files, William E. Timmons Collection, Nixon Library |

| | |
|---|---|
| Udall Papers | Morris Udall Papers, University of Arizona Library, Tucson, Arizona |
| UDHR | United Nations Universal Declaration of Human Rights |
| UNESCO | United Nations Educational, Scientific, and Cultural Organization |
| US GPO | United States Government Printing Office, Washington, D.C. |
| Vanderbilt News Archive | Vanderbilt University Television News Archive, at tvnews.vanderbilt.edu/ |
| WHCF | White House Central Files |
| *WP* | *Washington Post* |
| *WSJ* | *Wall Street Journal* |

# Notes

## Introduction: Enter Human Rights

1. Milan Kundera, "The Gesture of Protest against a Violation of Human Rights," in *Immortality* (New York: Grove Weidenfeld, 1991).

2. Jerome Shestack, "Sisyphus Endures: The International Human Rights NGO," *New York Law School Law Review* 24 (1978–1979): 89. See also the 1979 observation that "the phrase 'human rights' has made a remarkably sudden entry into our common political vocabulary. Increasingly, the wrongs and injustices of governments are referred to as violations of human rights"; Peter G. Brown and Douglas MacLean, eds., introduction to *Human Rights and U.S. Foreign Policy: Principles and Applications* (Lexington, MA: D.C. Heath, 1979), xv.

3. Samuel Moyn reports that the *New York Times* used the term five times as often in 1977 as in any prior year; Moyn, *The Last Utopia: Human Rights in History* (Cambridge, MA: Harvard University Press, 2010), 4. The *Los Angeles Times* print index had seventeen entries under human rights in 1976 and approximately two hundred in 1977. A similar trajectory is apparent in the *Washington Post* print index: it had no entry for human rights in the years 1972–1974 but began to include the term in 1975, listing thirteen entries. The number of entries under the heading more than quadrupled between 1976 and 1977. (See the appropriate volumes of the *Bell and Howell Newspaper Index* for these newspapers.) A suggestive survey of the Google News Archive confirms these results, with 2,600 hits in 1976 and 14,800 in 1977. It is currently impossible to survey the network news with precision, but the Vanderbilt Television News Archive yields thirty-one keyword hits in 1976 compared to 263 in 1977.

4. Bill Frelick, "Priorities for Amnesty International USA," [c. 1978], I.4.7.8, AI USA Records.

283

5. Ronald Steel, "Motherhood, Apple Pie and Human Rights," *New Republic*, June 4, 1977, 14–15.

6. Frances Fitzgerald, "The Warrior Intellectuals," *Harper's*, May 1976, 47.

7. Donald M. Fraser, "Human Rights and U.S. Foreign Policy: Some Basic Questions regarding Principles and Practice," *International Studies Quarterly* 23, no. 2 (June 1979): 185, 176.

8. See Moyn, *Last Utopia*, 121, 220. Compare Gary J. Bass, "The Old New Thing," *New Republic*, November 11, 2010, 35–39. For a discussion of the differences between American constitutional rights and universal human rights, see Louis Henkin, *The Age of Rights* (New York: Columbia University Press, 1990), 141–156.

9. See the appropriate volumes of *The New York Times Index* (New York: New York Times). Compare the different dates in Elizabeth Borgwardt, "FDR's Four Freedoms as a Human Rights Instrument," *Organization of American Historians Magazine of History* 22, no. 2 (April 2008): 11.

10. *New York Times Index, 1976* (New York: New York Times, 1977), 577–578.

11. The most useful broad, global overviews of the rise of human rights in the 1970s are Jan Eckel, "Rebirth of Politics from the Spirit of Morality: Explaining the Human Rights Revolution of the 1970s," in Jan Eckel and Samuel Moyn, eds., *The Breakthrough: Human Rights in the 1970s* (Philadelphia: University of Pennsylvania Press, forthcoming), 226–260; and Michael Cotey Morgan, "The Seventies and the Rebirth of Human Rights," in Niall Ferguson et al., eds., *The Shock of the Global: The 1970s in Perspective* (Cambridge MA: Harvard University Press, 2010), 237–250.

12. Frederick G. Dutton, *Changing Sources of Power: American Politics in the 1970s* (New York: McGraw-Hill, 1971), 258.

13. Ibid., 165.

14. "The Greening of the Astronauts," *Time*, December 11, 1972, 57.

15. On Holocaust consciousness, see Peter Novick, *The Holocaust in American Life* (New York: Houghton Mifflin, 1999). Hasia R. Diner shows that Novick overstates American Jews' lack of attention to the Holocaust in the postwar years, yet there was clearly a rise in the level of awareness and attention in American society in the 1960s; Diner, *We Remember with Reverence and Love: American Jews and the Myth of Silence after the Holocaust, 1945–1962* (New York: New York University Press, 2009).

16. See, e.g., Merle Curti, *American Philanthropy Abroad: A History* (New Brunswick, NJ: Rutgers University Press, 1963).

17. The existence of two strands has been widely noted. Thus, for example, one scholar-participant writing in the 1980s identified the sources of the divergence as the difference between wanting to be "decent" and wanting to "stand tall"; Lowell W. Livezey, *Nongovernmental Organizations and the Ideas of Human Rights* (Princeton, NJ: Center of International Studies, Princeton University, 1988), xiii.

## Chapter 1: The Postwar Marginality of Universal Human Rights

1. George C. Herring, *From Colony to Superpower: U.S. Foreign Relations since 1776* (Oxford: Oxford University Press, 2008), 285, 337, 351–353.

2. Richard A. Primus, *The American Language of Rights* (Cambridge: Cambridge University Press, 1999), 191, 181–182.

3. Ronald H. Carpenter, *Father Charles E. Coughlin: Surrogate Spokesman for the Disaffected* (Westport, CT: Greenwood Press, 1998), 56, 44, 146; on populists and human rights, see, e.g., Norman Pollack, *The Populist Response to Industrial America: Midwestern Populist Thought* (New York: Norton, 1966), 14–15; Pollack, *The Just Polity: Populism, Law, and Human Welfare* (Urbana: University of Illinois Press, 1987), 200–201; see also "The 'Rights of Man,'" *WP*, September 15, 1924, 6.

4. On human rights as a continuous evolution over millennia, see Micheline R. Ishay, ed., *The Human Rights Reader: Major Political Essays, Speeches, and Documents from the Bible to the Present* (New York: Routledge, 1997).

5. See Samuel Moyn's comparison of this kind of history to the history of the Christian church; Moyn, *Last Utopia: Human Rights in History* (Cambridge, MA: Harvard University Press, 2010), 6.

6. The phrase is Elizabeth Borgwardt's: *A New Deal for the World* (Cambridge, MA: Harvard University Press, 2005), 8.

7. Moyn, *Last Utopia*, 59–60.

8. Roger Normand and Sarah Zaidi, *Human Rights at the UN: The Political History of Universal Justice* (Bloomington: University of Indiana Press, 2008), 90; Franklin D. Roosevelt, State of the Union Address, January 6, 1941, Voices of Democracy: The U.S. Oratory Project, posted 2007, voicesofdemocracy.umd.edu/fdr-the-four-freedoms -speech-text/.

9. Declaration by United Nations, January 1, 1945, Avalon Project, last modified 2008, avalon.law.yale.edu/wwii/washc016.asp.

10. Normand and Zaidi, *Human Rights at the UN*, 93.

11. Ruth B. Russell, *A History of the United Nations Charter: The Role of the United States, 1940–1945* (Washington, DC: Brookings Institution, 1958), 34–39. For the strongest statement of the "transformational" significance of the charter, see Borgwardt, *New Deal for the World*; see also Douglas Brinkley and David R. Facey-Crowther, eds., *The Atlantic Charter* (New York: St. Martin's Press, 1994), 88–89.

12. Moyn, *Last Utopia*, 45.

13. Russell, *History*, 323–329, 423–424; Letter, Albert Volk, "Ideals Little Regarded," *NYT*, January 28, 1945, E8; "Social Plan Vague, Jewish Groups Say," *NYT*, May 6, 1945, 30.

14. "Human Rights Count," *NYT*, January 28, 1945, E8; "Social Plan Vague."

15. G. Daniel Cohen, "The Holocaust and the 'Human Rights Revolution,'" in Akira Iriye, Petra Goedde, and William I. Hitchcock, eds., *The Human Rights Revolution: An International History* (New York: Oxford University Press, 2012), 53–72; Mark Mazower, "The Strange Triumph of Human Rights, 1933–1950," *Historical Journal* 47, no. 2 (2004): 379–398.

16. Borgwardt, *New Deal for the World*, 190–191.

17. Kirsten Sellars, *The Rise and Rise of Human Rights* (Phoenix Mill, UK: Sutton, 2002), 4.

18. Jan Herman Burgers, "The Road to San Francisco: The Revival of the Human Rights Idea in the Twentieth Century," *Human Rights Quarterly* 14 (1992): 447–477; Saul

Dubow, "Smuts, the United Nations and the Rhetoric of Race and Rights," *Journal of Contemporary History* 43, no. 1 (2008): 54–56.

19. Russell, *History*, 780.

20. Charter of the United Nations, June 6, 1945, United Nations, www.un.org/aboutun /charter/.

21. A. H. Robertson and J. G. Merrills, *Human Rights in the World*, 3rd ed. (Manchester, UK: Manchester University Press, 1989), 19–21.

22. Charter of the United Nations, ch. 1.

23. "Degree Conferred on Stettinius Here," *NYT*, October 24, 1944, 13.

24. Treaty of Peace with Bulgaria, February 10, 1947, Avalon Project, last modified 2008, avalon.law.yale.edu/20th_century/usmu012.asp; Stephen D. Kertesz, "Human Rights in the Peace Treaties," *Law and Contemporary Problems* 14, no. 4 (1949): 627–646; "Report of the Political and Territorial Commission for Italy," October 5, 1946, *FRUS, 1946, vol. 4: Paris Peace Conference: Documents* (Washington, DC: US GPO, 1970), 311–312.

25. See, e.g., 95 Cong. Rec. 1085 (February 9, 1949); 95 Cong. Rec. 1698 (March 2, 1949). On Mindszenty, see also Moyn, *Last Utopia*, 71–72.

26. Johannes Morsink, *The Universal Declaration of Human Rights: Origins, Drafting, and Intent* (Philadelphia: University of Pennsylvania Press, 2000), 14–16; Normand and Zaidi, *Human Rights at the UN*, 196.

27. Moyn, *Last Utopia*, 63.

28. Universal Declaration of Human Rights, December 10, 1948, United Nations, www .un.org/en/documents/udhr/.

29. The eight abstentions included Saudi Arabia, apartheid South Africa, and members of the communist bloc.

30. Morsink, *Universal Declaration*, 21–24; Hans von Mangoldt, "The Communist Conception of Civil Rights and Human Rights under International Law," in George Brunner, ed., *Before Reforms: Human Rights in the Warsaw Pact States, 1971–1988* (New York: St. Martin's Press, 1990), 27–57.

31. Quoted in Morsink, *Universal Declaration*, 22.

32. Jennifer Amos, "Embracing and Contesting: Soviet Diplomacy on the Universal Declaration of Human Rights, 1948–1958," in Stefan-Ludwig Hoffmann, ed., *Human Rights in the Twentieth Century* (New York: Cambridge University Press, 2011), 147–165.

33. Bess Furman, "D.A.R. Intensifies War against U.N.," *NYT*, April 22, 1953.

34. Frank E. Holman, *Story of the "Bricker" Amendment (The First Phase)* (New York: Committee for Constitutional Government, 1954), 8.

35. Gladwin Hill, "U.N. Rights Drafts Held Socialistic," *NYT*, September 18, 1948.

36. "U.S. Delay Urged on U.S. Rights Plan," *NYT*, February 1, 1949.

37. Duane Tananbaum, *The Bricker Amendment Controversy: A Test of Eisenhower's Political Leadership* (Ithaca, NY: Cornell University Press, 1988), 13.

38. George Eckel, "Dulles Bars Pacts of U.N. on Rights; Fights Treaty Curb," *NYT*, April 7, 1953.

39. Quoted in "In the Nation," *NYT*, March 3, 1953.

40. Quoted in Tananbaum, *Bricker Amendment*, 6.

41. Tananbaum, *Bricker Amendment*, 3–4.

42. Ibid., 21–22.

43. Robert A. Caro, *Master of the Senate: The Years of Lyndon Johnson* (New York: Alfred A. Knopf, 2002), 527–528.

44. Tananbaum, *Bricker Amendment*, 23–24.

45. John Gunther, *Inside U.S.A.* (London: Hamish Hamilton, [1947]), 436.

46. 97 Cong. Rec. 8255 (July 17, 1951). See also Vernon van Dyke, *Human Rights, the United States, and World Community* (New York: Oxford University Press, 1970), 134–135; Tananbaum, *Bricker Amendment*, 25–26.

47. See Van Dyke, *Human Rights*, 135.

48. Frank E. Holman, "International Proposals Affecting So-Called Human Rights," *Law and Contemporary Problems* 14, no. 3 (1949): 484.

49. Reprinted in 95 Cong. Rec. A1928 (March 29, 1949).

50. Tananbaum, *Bricker Amendment*; Holman, *Story*, 12–13.

51. Furman, "D.A.R. Intensifies War"; Arthur Schlesinger, Jr., "Congress and the Making of Foreign Policy," *Foreign Affairs* 51, no. 1 (October 1972): 97.

52. John W. Bricker, "Is the U.N. Proving Dangerous to American Interests?," *Congressional Digest* 31, no. 2 (February 1952): 52–56.

53. Cited in Natalie Kaufman Hevener and David Whiteman, "Opposition to Human Rights Treaties in the United States: The Legacy of the Bricker Amendment," *HRQ* 10, no. 3 (August 1988): 313.

54. Tananbaum, *Bricker Amendment*, 70.

55. Ibid., 117–120; Richard O. Davies, *Defender of the Old Guard: John Bricker and American Politics* (Columbus: Ohio State University Press, 1993), 173.

56. Tananbaum, *Bricker Amendment*, 128–132.

57. Quoted in ibid., 72.

58. Ibid., 86, 179. Davies provides the most detailed analysis of Harley Kilgore's vote, and concludes that Kilgore was not drunk but perhaps medicated after extensive dental work; Davies, *Defender*, 180–182.

59. Natalie Kaufman Hevener, "Drafting the Human Rights Covenants," *World Affairs* 148 (1986): 234–237. On arguments for and against a split, see Roland Burke, "Some Rights Are More Equal Than Others: The Third World and the Transformation of Economic and Social Rights," *Humanity* 3, no. 3 (2012): 427–448.

60. Roland Burke, "From Individual Rights to National Development: The First UN International Conference on Human Rights, Tehran, 1968," *Journal of World History* 19, no. 3 (2008): 280–281.

61. Liberty Lobby leaflet, "Genocide Treaty Again Threatens," [1971], box 5, Ad Hoc Records.

62. John P. Humphrey, "The Memoirs of John P. Humphrey, The First Director of the United Nations Division of Human Rights," *HRQ* 5 (1983): 402–403.

63. ECOSOC Resolution 1235 (XLII), June 6, 1967, 42 U.N. ESCOR Supp. (No. 1) at 17, U.N. Doc. E/4393, University of Minnesota Human Rights Library, last updated December 24, 2013, www1.umn.edu/humanrts/procedures/1235.html

64. Lowell W. Livezey, *Nongovernmental Organizations and the Ideas of Human Rights* (Princeton, NJ: Center of International Studies, Princeton University, 1988), 93–95.

65. Emanual Muravchik to John Morsell, NAACP, December 30, 1969; Betty Kaye Taylor, "Interim Committee," January 14, 1970; Minutes, Ad Hoc Committee, September 29, 1960, box 1, Ad Hoc Records.

66. James Coriden, ed., *The Case for Freedom: Human Rights in the Church* (Washington, DC: Corpus Books, 1969); J. Bryan Hehir, "Religious Activism for Human Rights: A Christian Case Study," in John Witte, Jr., and J. D. van der Vyver, eds., *Religious Human Rights in Global Perspective*, vol. 1, *Religious Perspectives* (The Hague: M. Nijhoff, 1996), 97–119; on the U.S. Catholic Conference, see Livezey, *Nongovernmental Organizations*, 78ff.

67. Samuel P. Huntington, *The Third Wave: Democratization in the Late Twentieth Century* (Norman: University of Oklahoma Press, 1991), 72–85.

68. Encyclical *Pacem in Terris* of John XXIII, April 11, 1963, The Vatican: John XXIII, Encyclicals, www.vatican.va/holy_father/john_xxiii/encyclicals/documents/hf_j-xxiii _enc_11041963_pacem_en.html. On earlier papal references to human rights, see Moyn, *Last Utopia*, 50–51.

69. Stanley I. Stuber, "Appraisal of the International Year for Human Rights (1968)," [1968], box 4, Ad Hoc Records.

70. Telegram, Pope to Johnson, January 11, 1966, WHCF, Confidential Files IT 47, box 58, LBJ Library.

71. The NCC comprised some thirty Protestant and Orthodox denominations. Livezey, *Nongovernmental Organizations*, 66.

72. Ibid., 68.

73. Quoted in Morris B. Abram, "The U.N. and Human Rights," *Foreign Affairs* 47, no. 2 (January 1969): 364. On the early position of the WCC toward human rights, see Edward Duff, *The Social Thought of the World Council of Churches* (London: Longmans, Green, 1956), 1, 13, 258, 276–278.

74. Livezey, *Nongovernmental Organizations*, 109.

75. Ibid., 38–39.

76. Ibid., 43–51.

77. Moyn, *Last Utopia*, 45.

## Chapter 2: Managing Civil Rights at Home

1. David Hawk résumé, April 2012, www.davidrhawk.com/decemberresume.pdf; David Hawk, e-mail message to author, January 18, 2013; David Hawk Resume, box 4, Morris Papers.

2. David Hawk, interview by author, January 11, 2012.

3. Joshua Rubenstein, former Northeast Regional Director, Amnesty International USA, interview by author, January 8, 2013.

4. For the most forceful presentation of the distinction between 1960s anti-colonialism and 1970s human rights, see Samuel Moyn, *The Last Utopia: Human Rights in History* (Cambridge, MA: Harvard University Press, 2010), 84–119.

5. Rita Hauser, interview by author, December 10, 2012.

6. This finding is based on keyword searches of the ProQuest Historical Newspapers database.

7. W. E. B. Du Bois, "An Appeal to the World: A Statement on the Denial of Human Rights in the Case of Citizens of Negro Descent in the United States of America and an Appeal to the United Nations for Redress," 1947, BlackPast.org, v. 2.0, last modified 2011, www.blackpast.org/?q=1947-w-e-b-dubois-appeal-world-statement-denial -human-rights-minorities-case-citizens-n.

8. Carol Anderson, *Eyes off the Prize: The United Nations and the African American Struggle for Human Rights, 1944-1955* (New York: Cambridge University Press, 2003), 103-112; Nikhl Pal Singh, *Black Is a Country: Race and the Unfinished Struggle for Democracy* (Cambridge, MA: Harvard University Press, 2004), 156-159.

9. Moyn, *Last Utopia*, 104.

10. Address of Mayor Hubert Humphrey to Democratic National Convention, Philadelphia: Civil Rights, July 14, 1948, Minnesota Historical Society Online Collections, ID number por 4186 p66 (Locator Number SV), last modified 2013, www.mnhs.org/library/findaids/00442/pdfa/00442-00187.pdf.

11. Press Release, "Senator Humphrey Introduces Omnibus Human Rights Act of 1959," May 19, 1959; Press Release, "Humphrey Calls for U.S. to Back International Action on Human Rights," June 23, 1958, box 15, Ernest Lefever Papers, Hoover.

12. Andrew M. Manis, *A Fire You Can't Put Out: The Civil Rights Life of Birmingham's Reverend Fred Shuttlesworth* (Tuscaloosa: University of Alabama Press, 1999), 95-96, 463n49.

13. John Dittmer, *The Good Doctors: The Medical Committee for Human Rights and the Struggle for Social Justice in Health Care* (New York: Bloomsbury Press, 2009), 36.

14. James Miller, *"Democracy Is in the Streets": From Port Huron to the Siege of Chicago* (New York: Simon and Schuster, 1987), 33.

15. "Rockefeller Gives Sermon in Harlem on Civil Rights," *NYT*, January 29, 1962, 1.

16. Gerald Benjamin, *Race Relations and the New York City Commission on Human Rights* (Ithaca, NY: Cornell University Press, 1974), 37, 125-129, 259.

17. Harry Edwards, "Why Negroes Should Boycott Whitey's Olympics," *Saturday Evening Post*, March 9, 1968, 6-7; Richard Edward Lapchick, *The Politics of Race and International Sport: The Case of South Africa* (Westport, CT: Greenwood Press, 1975), 102-103, 109; Tommie Smith with David Steele, *Silent Gesture: The Autobiography of Tommie Smith* (Philadelphia: Temple University Press, 2007), 22, 100, 117-119, 161.

18. See Amy Bass, *Not the Triumph but the Struggle: The 1968 Olympics and the Making of the Black Athlete* (Minneapolis: University of Minnesota Press, 2002).

19. "California Oil Slick," *CBS Evening News*, February 5, 1969, record number 202437; "California/Mrs. Evers," *ABC Evening News*, March 16, 1970, record number 9557; and "Computer Intrigue," *ABC Evening News*, September 1, 1970, record number 11938, Vanderbilt News Archive.

20. Human Rights Party of Ann Arbor, Party Platform, February 1972, Liberation News Library, box 3, series 26, Liberation News Archive, Temple University Library, Philadelphia; Human Rights Party of Ann Arbor, Preamble, February 1, 1972, f. 59, box 20, Social Movements Collection, The Vietnam Center and Archive, Texas Tech University, last modified 2013, www.vietnam.ttu.edu/virtualarchive/items.php ?item=14512059003; Willis Frederick Dunbar and George S. May, *Michigan: A*

*History of the Wolverine State* (Grand Rapids, MI: Wm. N. Eerdmans Publishing, 1995), 590.

21. *Democratic Fact Book 1970*, Compiled by the Democratic Senatorial Campaign Committee in Cooperation with the Democratic National Congressional Committee and the Democratic National Committee, in Russell B. Miller, "Papers re his political campaign, 1970," box 2, Cranston Papers.

22. Jerome Shestack, "Foreword," *Human Rights* 1, no. 1 (August 1970): vii–viii.

23. This observation is based on incomplete surveys of material in White House Central Files, Subject Files, HU Human Rights in the Kennedy, Johnson, and Nixon Libraries.

24. Martin Luther King, Jr., "Let My People Go," *Africa Today* 12, no. 10 (December 1965): 10.

25. Thomas F. Jackson, *From Civil Rights to Human Rights: Martin Luther King, Jr., and the Struggle for Economic Justice* (Philadelphia: University of Pennsylvania Press, 2007), 1, 104, 131, 169, 204, 224. For a relatively early linkage of global poverty to the language of human rights, see King, "Let My People Go," 9–11.

26. Quoted in Amy Nathan Wright, "Civil Rights 'Unfinished Business': Poverty, Race, and the 1968 Poor People's Campaign" (Ph.D. diss., University of Texas, Austin, 2007), 151, 143.

27. Malcolm X, "The Ballot or the Bullet," April 3, 1964, in George Breitman, ed., *Malcolm X Speaks: Selected Speeches and Statements* (New York: Merit, 1965), 34–35. See also Mark Ledwidge, *Race and U.S. Foreign Policy: The African-American Foreign Affairs Network* (New York: Routledge, 2012), 138–160.

28. Malcolm X, "The Black Revolution," April 8, 1964, in Breitman, *Malcolm X Speaks*, 55.

29. "Outline for Petition to the United Nations Charging Genocide against 22 Million Black Americans," in John Henrik Clarke, ed., *Malcolm X: The Man and His Times* (New York: Macmillan, 1969), 343–351; Peter Goldman, *The Death and Life of Malcolm X* (London: Victor Gollancz, 1974), 156–158.

30. James Furman, *The Making of Black Revolutionaries* (Seattle: University of Washington Press, 1997), 480–481, 487; Clayborne Carson, *In Struggle: SNCC and the Black Awakening of the 1960s* (Cambridge, MA: Harvard University Press, 1981), 266.

31. See Mary L. Dudziak, *Cold War Civil Rights: Race and the Image of American Democracy* (Princeton, NJ: Princeton University Press, 2000), esp. 132, 185, 208–209.

32. Quoted in Ad Hoc Committee on the Human Rights and Genocide Treaties, "Program Report for White House Conference," [1965?], box 2, Ad Hoc Records.

33. Vernon van Dyke, *Human Rights, the United States, and World Community* (New York: Oxford University Press, 1970), 131.

34. "Human Rights: A Guide for Community Action," [1963], box 4, Ad Hoc Records.

35. Minutes of First Meeting of Commission, February 28, 1968; Sixth Meeting Minutes, December 4, 1968, box 469, Harriman Papers.

36. The President's Commission for the Observance of Human Rights Year, 1968, "To Continue Action for Human Rights: Final Report," [1969], pp. 7–9, f. 12, box 4, Ad

Hoc Records; Committee Report, "For Free Men in a Free World," box 468, Harriman Papers.

37. President's Commission, "To Continue Action," 11.

38. Final Report, 4th Meeting, [1968], box 469, Harriman Papers.

39. President's Commission, "To Continue Action," 38, 49, 52.

40. Ibid., 19.

41. Stanley I. Stuber, "Appraisal of the International Year for Human Rights (1968)," [1968], box 4, Ad Hoc Records.

42. See Roland Burke, *Decolonization and the Evolution of International Human Rights* (Philadelphia: University of Pennsylvania Press, 2010).

43. Van Dyke, *Human Rights*, 36, 205.

44. Transcript, Morris Abram Oral History Interview II, May 3, 1984, by Michael L. Gillette, p. 9, LBJ Library Oral History Collection, last modified October 1, 2008, www.lbjlib.utexas.edu/johnson/archives.hom/oralhistory.hom/abramm/abramm .asp; Morris Abram, "America's Mute Conscience," *NYT*, December 26, 1971, *A6*.

45. On antiapartheid protests linked to Human Rights Day in 1957 and 1966, see Francis Njubi Nesbitt, *Race for Sanctions: African Americans against Apartheid, 1946–1994* (Bloomington: Indiana University Press, 2004), 32–33, 50, 56.

46. Donald R. Culverson, *Contesting Apartheid: U.S. Activism, 1960–1987* (Boulder, CO: Westview, 1999), 42–49, 71–72.

47. Roy Wilkins, NAACP, to Johnson, May 4, 1966, box 250, Subject Files: Countries (CO) Rhodesia, WHCF, LBJ Library.

48. See, e.g., Memo, Rick Haynes to Walt Rostow, April 18, 1966, box 97, National Security File: Country File (Rhodesia), LBJ Library.

49. Dean Acheson, "The Arrogance of International Lawyers," *International Lawyer* 2, no. 4 (July 1968): 591–600; "The Acheson-Goldberg Correspondence on Rhodesia," *Africa Report* 12 (January 1967): 56–57.

50. Arthur J. Goldberg, "Rhodesia Is a Moral Issue," *WP*, January 8, 1967, E3.

51. Anthony Lake, *The "Tar Baby" Option: American Policy toward Southern Rhodesia* (New York: Columbia University Press, 1976), 119–120.

52. Memo, Benjamin Read, Department of State, to Rostow, "Foreign Policy Ideas Developed during Johnson Administration," November 29, 1966, f. "Foreign Policy," box 18, National Security File: Subject File, LBJ Library.

53. Memo, Joseph Sisco, n.d. [1967?], "Major US Accomplishments in UN since 1964," f. "Foreign Policy," box 18, National Security File: Subject File, LBJ Library.

54. Invitation, Recognition Dinner, Detroit Committee for Human Rights Day Observance, 1969, box 4, Ad Hoc Records.

55. Quoted in Burke, *Decolonization*, 103–104.

56. "He Works for Rights," *NYT*, November 19, 1965, 27.

57. Abram to Johnson, December 11, 1968, box 13, IT United Nations 47–9/A, WHCF: Confidential Files, LBJ Library.

58. Morris Abram, "United States and International Human Rights—Retrospect and Prospects," [1968], box 13, IT United Nations 47–9/A, WHCF: Confidential Files, LBJ Library.

59. Sam Pope Brewer, "U.S. Accused of Lagging in Human Rights Support," *NYT*, April 10, 1968, 31.

60. Anthony Lewis, "Words and Deeds," *NYT*, November 20, 1975, 41.

61. Morris B. Abram, "The U.N. and Human Rights," *Foreign Affairs* 47, no. 2 (January 1969): 365.

## Chapter 3: The Trauma of the Vietnam War

1. Barbie Zelizer, *About to Die: How News Images Move the Public* (New York: Oxford University Press, 2010), 236–239.

2. Nixon White House Tape 730-10, June 12, 1972, mp3, 2:02:42, nixontapes.org, last modified 2010, nixontapeaudio.org/chron3/rmn_e730b.mp3 (for similar suspicions about another war atrocity photo, see Telcon, Nixon and Kissinger, December 1, 1969, Kissinger Telcons); George McGovern, *Grassroots: The Autobiography of George McGovern* (New York: Random House, 1977), 245; Television address, October 10, 1972, in George McGovern, *An American Journey: The Presidential Campaign Speeches of George McGovern* (New York: Random House, 1974), 112.

3. Speech at Wheaton College, October 11, 1972, in McGovern, *American Journey*, 208.

4. On war crimes and international law, see Samuel Moyn, "From Antiwar Politics to Antitorture Politics," in Austin Sarat, Lawrence Douglas, and Martha Merrill Umphrey, eds., *Law and War* (Stanford: Stanford University Press, forthcoming).

5. Charles Chatfield, "The Antiwar Movement and America," in Charles DeBenedetti, *An American Ordeal: The Antiwar Movement of the Vietnam War* (Syracuse, NY: Syracuse University Press, 1990), 403–404.

6. Eugene Genovese, "The Spirit of '70," *Newsweek*, July 6, 1970, 19.

7. He also called for an almost unconditional withdrawal from Vietnam. Richard Reeves, *Old Faces of 1976* (New York: Harper and Row, 1976), 113.

8. Democratic Party Platform of 1972, July 10, 1972, The American Presidency Project, copyright 2013, www.presidency.ucsb.edu/ws/?pid=29605; Bruce Miroff, *The Liberals' Moment: The McGovern Insurgency and the Identity Crisis of the Democratic Party* (Lawrence: University Press of Kansas, 2007), 77.

9. Democratic Party Platform of 1972.

10. Republican Party Platform of 1972, August 21, 1972, The American Presidency Project, copyright 2013, www.presidency.ucsb.edu/ws/?pid=25842.

11. This was the result of a 1969 *Fortune* poll, cited in Frederick G. Dutton, *Changing Sources of Power: American Politics in the 1970s* (New York: McGraw-Hill, 1971), 53–54. Polls also showed that less than one-third of the young believed the American way of life was superior to that of any other country.

12. Robert Keatley, "A Foreign Policy for Mr. McGovern," *WSJ*, June 29, 1972, 10.

13. Address Accepting the Presidential Nomination, July 14, 1972, The American Presidency Project, copyright 2013, www.presidency.ucsb.edu/ws/index.php?pid =25967.

14. Arthur M. Schlesinger, Jr., *Journals, 1952–2000* (New York: Penguin Press, 2007), 354.

15. Report on a meeting with Fulbright and others, March 17-18, 1966, box 5, Ad Hoc Records.

16. While not a definitive measure by any means, I have yet to see a book about the antiwar movement that includes "human rights" in its index.

17. On uses of international laws of war, see, e.g., *In the Name of America: The Conduct of the War in Vietnam by the Armed Forces of the United States as Shown by Published Reports, Compared with the Laws of War Binding on the United States Government and on Its Citizens* ([New York]: Clergy and Laity Concerned about Vietnam, 1968), 1–3.

18. "Action Strategies: An Ecumenical Witness," January 1972, quoted in Jill K. Gill, " 'Peace Is Not the Absence of War but the Presence of Justice': The National Council of Churches' Reaction and Response to the Vietnam War" (Ph.D. diss., University of Pennsylvania, 1996), 481–482. See also Edward Fiske, "Religious Assembly Terms Vietnam Policy Immoral," *NYT*, January 17, 1972, 35.

19. On opposition as fueled less by moral concerns than by the cost in American lives and the lack of progress as the war dragged on, see John E. Mueller, *War, Presidents and Public Opinion* (New York: John Wiley and Sons, 1973), 52–63; Howard Schuman, "Two Sources of Antiwar Sentiment in America," *American Journal of Sociology* 78, no. 3 (November 1972): 513–536.

20. Quoted in Terry H. Anderson, "Vietnam Is Here: The Antiwar Movement," in David L. Anderson and John Ernest, eds., *The War That Never Ends: New Perspectives on the Vietnam War* (Lexington: University Press of Kentucky, 2007), 252.

21. "For All Humanity: Report of the Committee on Human Rights of the National Citizens' Commission on International Cooperation," [1966], box 5, Ad Hoc Records.

22. Reports of Interviews with Senators and Representatives, UN-Washington Seminar on Human Rights, 1967, box 5, Ad Hoc Records.

23. ILRM Statement, January 1966, box 36, ILRM.

24. Cover Sheet, May 1, 1968, box 48, ILRM.

25. "Human Rights in the Vietnam War," [1968], box 36, ILRM.

26. "Cruelty in Vietnam Is Laid to Both Sides by Jurists," *NYT*, June 27, 1968, 6; Rusk to William Butler, March 1968, box 37, ILRM.

27. Russell, quoted in Andrew E. Hunt, *The Turning: A History of Vietnam Veterans against the War* (New York: New York University Press, 199736; Fredrik Logevall, "The Swedish-American Conflict over Vietnam," *Diplomatic History* 17, no. 3 (July 1993): 430.

28. David L. Anderson, "Introduction: What Really Happened?," in David L. Anderson, ed., *Facing My Lai: Moving beyond the Massacre* (Lawrence: University Press of Kansas, 1998), 1–17.

29. Seymour Hersh, "The Role of the Press in the Vietnam War," in Anderson, *Facing My Lai*, 54–57, 61–62. See also Clarence R. Wyatt, "The Media and the Vietnam War," in Anderson and Ernest, *War That Never Ends*, 282–283.

30. Telcon, Kissinger and Laird, November 21, 1969, Kissinger Telcons. (Transcriptions of Kissinger's telephone conversations from this period are not fully verbatim.)

31. For a typical example, see "Notes and Comment," *New Yorker*, December 20, 1969, 27–29.

32. "The Great Atrocity Hunt," *National Review*, December 16, 1969, 1252.

33. Hunt, *Turning*, 36.

34. Elliott Meyrowitz and Kenneth J. Campbell, "Vietnam Veterans and War Crimes Hearings," in Melvin Small and William D. Hoover, eds., *Give Peace a Chance: Exploring the Vietnam Antiwar Movement* (Syracuse, NY: Syracuse University Press, 1992), 130n4.

35. "The Clamor over Calley: Who Shares the Guilt?," *Time*, April 12, 1971, 14–21.

36. Meyrowitz and Campbell, "Vietnam Veterans," 131–133. For a meticulously documented account of the extent of American crimes and brutality in the war, see Bernd Greiner, *War without Fronts: The USA in Vietnam*, trans. Anne Wyburd with Victoria Fern (London: Bodley Head, 2009).

37. Hunt, *Turning*, 72–73.

38. William F. Crandell, "They Moved the Town: Organizing Vietnam Veterans Against the War," in Small and Hoover, *Give Peace a Chance*, 147.

39. Neil Sheehan, "Should We Have War Crimes Trials?" *New York Times Book Review*, December 22, 1970, BR1ff; quotation from James Reston, Jr., in *Saturday Review* article published a few days later, cited in Guenter Lewy's apologia for the war, *America in Vietnam* (New York: Oxford University Press, 1978), 316.

40. Meyrowitz and Campbell, "Vietnam Veterans," 135n23, 135n24; Lewy, *America*, 316–317.

41. On this report see Moyn, "From Antiwar Politics."

42. Sheehan, "Should We Have War Crime Trials?" See also Moyn, "From Antiwar Politics."

43. *Hearing on the Nomination of William E. Colby to be Director of Central Intelligence, Before the Comm. on Armed Services of the United States Senate*, 93rd Cong. 36 (1973).

44. TelCon, Nixon and Kissinger, 05438 / 19710408-2206-Nixon_001-053ab, April 8, 1971, Kissinger Telcons.

45. "Nation: Bound to Happen?," *Time*, January 12, 1970, 10, which also notes that only 22 percent clearly expressed moral repugnance. A Harris poll showed that 91 percent of respondents had followed the trial closely, and that 36 percent disagreed and 35 percent agreed with the verdict, with 29 percent undecided; William M. Hammond, *Public Affairs: The Military and the Media, 1968–1973* (Washington, DC: GPO, 1996), 254.

46. "Calley Case/Reaction," *CBS Evening News*, April 2, 1971, record number 216223, Vanderbilt News Archive.

47. "Closing the My Lai Case," *Time*, November 25, 1974, 33–34; Kendrick Oliver, "Atrocity, Authenticity and American Exceptionalism: (Ir)rationalizing the Massacre at My Lai," *Journal of American Studies* 37, no. 2 (2003): 247–268.

48. Greiner, *War without Fronts*, 354–355.

49. Michal R. Belknap, *The Vietnam War on Trial: The My Lai Massacre and the Court-Martial of Lieutenant Calley* (Lawrence: University of Kansas Press, 2002), 256.

50. Russell Baker, "Observer: Mr. President: Save That Illusion," *NYT*, November 30, 1969, E12.

51. Quoted in Robert D. McFadden, "Calley Verdict Brings Home the Anguish of War to Public," *NYT*, April 4, 1971, 56.

52. Nicholas Turse, "'Kill Anything That Moves': U.S. War Crimes and Atrocities in Vietnam, 1965-1973" (Ph.D. diss., Columbia University, 2005), 8.

53. Joseph A. Fry, "Unpopular Messengers: Student Opposition to the Vietnam War," in Anderson and Ernest, *War That Never Ends*, 231.

54. Terry H. Anderson, *The Movement and the Sixties* (New York: Oxford University Press, 1996), 379.

55. David Hawk Resume, box 4, Morris Papers.

56. Richard Cummings, *The Pied Piper: Allard K. Lowenstein and the Liberal Dream* (New York: Grove Press, 1985), 337, 341. For additional biographical information, see James A. Wechsler, "Another Casualty," *New York Post Magazine*, March 12, 1969, 5.

57. Quoted in Cummings, *Pied Piper*, 337.

58. Robert C. Maynard, "250 Student Leaders Balk at Wartime Draft," *WP*, April 23, 1969, A1. See also David Farber's assessment of Hawk as a type of antiwar activist who "lacked interest in fundamental cultural or political critiques" but who "wanted to reform the system"; Farber, "The Counterculture and the Antiwar Movement," in Small and Hoover, *Give Peace a Chance*, 19.

59. Tom Wells, *The War Within: America's Battle over Vietnam* (Berkeley: University of California Press, 1994), 223-225, 330.

60. Quoted in Nancy Zaroulis and Gerald Sullivan, *Who Spoke Up? American Protest against the War in Vietnam, 1963-1975* (Garden City, NY: Doubleday, 1984), 246.

61. Ibid., 245-247, 257-258, 266; James Kirkpatrick Davis, *Assault on the Left: The FBI and the Sixties Antiwar Movement* (Westport, CT: Praeger, 1997), 139.

62. Sidney Peck, quoted in Zaroulis and Sullivan, *Who Spoke Up?*, 265; see also David McReynolds, "Pacifists and the Vietnam Antiwar Movement," in Small and Hoover, *Give Peace a Chance*, 65.

63. DeBenedetti, *American Ordeal*, 263.

64. Cummings, *Pied Piper*, 434-444, 393-395.

65. David Hawk, interview by author, January 11, 2012.

66. See the excellent account in Miroff, *Liberals' Moment*.

67. Diary of Henry Brandon, October 1, 1972, box 8, Henry Brandon Papers, LC.

68. Editorial, "Foreign Policy Void," *NYT*, September 19, 1972, 32; William Greider, "McGovern Calls for Idealism, Would Abandon Power Politics in World Affairs," *WP*, October 6, 1972, A1; Robert Semple, "McGovern's Position on Foreign Policy," *NYT*, September 13, 1972, 33; Keatley, "Foreign Policy for Mr. McGovern," 10.

69. McGovern, Speech Draft, [c. October 1972], pp. 11, 14–17, box 147, Sargent Shriver Papers, Kennedy Library.

70. Semple, "McGovern's Position," 33.

71. Gordon L. Weil, *The Long Shot: McGovern Runs for President* (New York: Norton, 1973), 45.

72. "McGovern Criticizes Soviet," *NYT*, August 17, 1972, 8; "Text of Statement by Senator McGovern Presenting His Views on Foreign Policy," *NYT*, October 6, 1972, 26; but see also "McGovern Backs Limit on Status of Soviet Trade," *NYT*, September 22, 1972, 1.

73. George Lardner, Jr., "McGovern Would End Greek Aid," *WP*, July 23, 1972, A1.

74. Speech, Sargent Shriver, "The Quest for Peace," October 4, 1972, box 147, Sargent Shriver Papers, Kennedy Library.

75. Advertisement, "How George McGovern Won the Election," *NYT*, November 5, 1972, E5. See also Flyer, "Issues and McGovern," 1972, box 97, McGovern Papers.

76. Mercouri to McGovern, July 18, 1972, box 464, McGovern Papers.

77. "Tommy Smothers in Chicago," October 31, 1972, quoted in Miroff, *Liberals' Moment*, 115.

78. Ernest R. May and Janet Fraser, eds., *Campaign '72: The Managers Speak* (Cambridge, MA: Harvard University Press, 1973), 4.

79. Miroff, *Liberals' Moment*, 27.

80. Byron E. Shafter, *Quiet Revolution: The Struggle for the Democratic Party and the Shaping of Post-Reform Politics* (New York: Russell Sage Foundation, 1983); Meany quoted in Anderson, *Movement and the Sixties*, 393, 397.

81. Terry H. Anderson, *The Sixties* (New York: Longman, 1999), 206.

82. May and Fraser, *Campaign '72*, 25.

83. Quoted in Anderson, *Movement and the Sixties*, 402.

84. Speech, Catholic University of America, April 20, 1972, in McGovern, *American Journey*, 192; "magnificent obsession" quoted in Miroff, *Liberals' Moment*, 109.

85. Radio and television address, November 3, 1972, in McGovern, *American Journey*, 135-136.

86. Sandy Berger quoted in Miroff, *Liberals' Moment*, 126.

87. Miroff, *Liberals' Moment*, 129.

88. McGovern, *Grassroots*, 175.

89. Speech, Catholic University, 194.

90. Speech, Wheaton College, October 11, 1972, in McGovern, *American Journey*, 208-212.

91. Speech, Catholic University, 192; Anderson, *Movement and the Sixties*, 394.

92. Quoted in Anderson, *Movement and the Sixties*, 401.

93. "Human Beings Fused Together," *Time*, October 23, 1972, 36; see also Miroff, *Liberals' Moment*, 99.

94. Carter quoted in Anderson, *Movement and the Sixties*, 402; William Greider, "McGovern Keeps His Faith," *WP*, October 17, 1972, A1; McGovern's recollection of Talmadge's words, quoted in Miroff, *Liberals' Moment*, 125; Wattenberg quoted in May and Fraser, eds., *Campaign '72*, 132 (see also Patrick Buchanan, "The Legend of Saint George McGovern," *NYT*, November 24, 1972, 37); McGovern, *Grassroots*, 245; Garry Wills quoted in McGovern, *Grassroots*, 245.

95. Quoted in Anderson, *Movement and the Sixties*, 394; Weil, *Long Shot*, 14-15.

96. "Playboy Interview: George McGovern," *Playboy*, August 1971, 62.

97. McGovern, *Grassroots*, 263.

98. Typescript, James M. Wall, "Politics and Morality: An Exclusive Interview with George McGovern," pp. 12, 14, box 463, McGovern Papers.

99. Patrick Anderson, *Electing Jimmy Carter: The Campaign of 1976* (Baton Rouge: Louisiana State University Press, 1994), 38-39.

## Chapter 4: The Liberal Critique of Right-Wing Dictatorships

1. Samuel P. Huntington, *The Third Wave: Democratization in the Late Twentieth Century* (Norman: University of Oklahoma Press, 1991).
2. The most extensive treatments are in David Weissbrodt, "Donald Fraser," in David P. Forsythe, ed., *Encyclopedia of Human Rights* (New York: Oxford University Press, 2009), vol. 2, 270–273; and Kathryn Sikkink, *Mixed Signals: U.S. Human Rights Policy and Latin America* (Ithaca, NY: Cornell University Press, 2004), 49.
3. Richard Reeves, *Old Faces of 1976* (New York: Harper and Row, 1976), 95. Reeves called him "Donald Fraser of Michigan," confusing Fraser, of Minnesota, with Michigan's well-known labor leader Douglas Fraser.
4. Bill Peterson, "Fraser Faces Tough Populist Coalition in Minneapolis Primary," *WP*, September 10, 1979, A4.
5. Margaret Carpenter, "Donald M. Fraser," in Ralph Nader Congress Project, *Citizens Look at Congress* (Washington, DC: Grossman Publishers, [1972]), 1–4.
6. Arthur T. Hadley, *The Invisible Primary* (Englewood Cliffs, NJ: Prentice-Hall, 1976), 119.
7. Speech, "Constructive Uses of American Power," Urbana, Illinois, August 25, 1966, 147.B.15.3B, Fraser Papers; "Donald MacKay Fraser: An Inventory of His Papers at the Minnesota Historical Society," April 2003, 72–74, Minnesota Historical Society, last modified 2013, www.mnhs.org/library/findaids/00290.pdf.
8. Peterson, "Fraser Faces Tough Populist Coalition."
9. On constituent lack of interest, see Sikkink, *Mixed Signals*, 49.
10. 133 Cong. Rec. 5103 (March 1, 1967).
11. Speech notes, untitled [on morality in international affairs], [c. 1965], 147.B.15.3B, Fraser Papers.
12. Memo, Sherwin J. Markman to LBJ, May 17, 1966, box 97, National Security File: Country File (Rhodesia), LBJ Library.
13. *United States–South African Relations: Hearings Before the Subcomm. on Africa, Comm. on Foreign Affairs, House of Representatives, March 1966*, 89th Cong. 340 (1966).
14. Speech, untitled, Carleton College, January 19, 1964, pp. 22–23, 27, 147.B.15.3B, Fraser Papers.
15. Notes [on trade policy], [1964–1968], 147.B.15.3B, Fraser Papers.
16. Speech notes, untitled, [c. 1965], 1, 147.B.15.3B, Fraser Papers.
17. Speech notes, untitled [1964–1968], pp. 3, 7, 147.B.15.3B, Fraser Papers.
18. Brian E. Butler, "Title IX of the Foreign Assistance Act: Foreign Aid and Political Development," *Law and Society Review* 3, no. 1 (August 1968): 116–117n7, 117n9, 118–124; Thomas Carothers, *Aiding Democracy Abroad: The Learning Curve* (Washington, DC: Carnegie Endowment for International Peace, 1999), 19–23, quotations at 23; Robert A. Packenham, *Liberal America and the Third World: Political Development Ideas in Foreign Aid and Social Science* (Princeton, NJ: Princeton University Press, 1973), 98–109; Elizabeth Fletcher Crook, "Political Development as a Program Objective of U.S. Foreign Assistance: Title IX of the 1966 Foreign

Assistance Act" (Ph.D. diss., Tufts University, 1970), 79–99. On the paternalism of Fraser's views and of Title IX in general, see Roxanne Lynn Doty, *Imperial Encounters: The Politics of Representation in North-South Relations* (Minneapolis: University of Minnesota Press, 1996), 128–137.

19. Carothers, *Aiding Democracy*, 19–23.

20. Samuel P. Huntington, *Military Intervention, Political Involvement, and the Unlessons of Vietnam* (Chicago: Adlai Stevenson Institute of International Affairs, 1968), 28.

21. 133 Cong. Rec. 5131 (March 2, 1967).

22. Donald Fraser, "The Spirit of Title IX," in *Primer on Title IX* (Washington, DC: Agency for International Development, 1968), 21.

23. Donald M. Fraser, "New Directions in Foreign Aid," *World Affairs* 129, no. 4 (1967): 248–249.

24. Speech, "The Missing Dimension in U.S. Foreign Policy," January 1966, 147.B.15.3B, Fraser Papers.

25. "Rough Draft . . . co-op speech," n.d. [c. 1965], 147.B.15.3B, Fraser Papers. See also Donald M. Fraser, "Title IX: The Dynamics of Growth in Developing Nations," *Foreign Service Journal* 47, no. 3 (March 1970): 12–14.

26. Memorandum of Meeting, "Strategy for Securing Support for Political Development Initiatives," October 4, 1966, 147.B.15.3B, Fraser Papers.

27. Butler, "Title IX"; Carothers, *Aiding Democracy*, 24.

28. 114 Cong. Rec. 2313 (February 6, 1968); 114 Cong. Rec. 26221 (September 10, 1968).

29. 116 Cong. Rec. 19442 (June 11, 1970); 116 Cong. Rec. 9094 (March 24, 1970).

30. Carothers, *Aiding Democracy*, 23, 26–28; Princeton Lyman, "An Introduction to Title IX," *Foreign Service Journal* 47, no. 3 (March 1970), 6; Butler, "Title IX."

31. Speech, untitled, Carleton College, January 19, 1964, 147.B.15.3B, Fraser Papers.

32. *United States–South African Relations*, 340.

33. 113 Cong. Rec. 5131 (March 2, 1967).

34. C. M. Woodhouse, *The Rise and Fall of the Greek Colonels* (London: Granada, 1985), 35.

35. Quoted in Keith R. Legg, *Politics in Modern Greece* (Stanford, CA: Stanford University Press, 1969), 238.

36. Ibid., 36–38; Effie G. H. Pedaliu, "Human Rights and Foreign Policy: Wilson and the Greek Dictators, 1967–1970," *Diplomacy and Statecraft* 18 (2007): 185–214. See also Philipp Rock, *Macht, Märkte und Moral: Zur Rolle der Menschenrechte in der Außenpolitik der Bundesrepublik Deutschland in den sechziger und siebziger Jahren* (Frankfurt: Peter Lang, 2010), 45–119.

37. James Becket, "The Greek Case before the European Human Rights Commission," *Human Rights* 1, no. 1 (August 1970): 95; Woodhouse, *Rise and Fall*, 39–40, 51–52, 67–72.

38. Quotation in David F. Schmitz, *The United States and Right-Wing Dictatorships, 1965–1989* (New York: Cambridge University Press, 2006), 77. See also James Edward Miller, *The United States and the Making of Modern Greece: History and Power, 1950–1974* (Chapel Hill: University of North Carolina Press, 2009), 157–175; Woodhouse, *Rise and Fall*, 40.

39. See Policy Planning Staff, "U.S. Policies on Human Rights and Authoritarian Regimes," undated [October 1974], Box 348, Policy Planning Council, Director's Files [Winston Lord], 1969–1977, Entry 5027, RG 59, NARA.

40. Russell Warren Howe and Sarah Hays Trott, *The Power Peddlers: How Lobbyists Mold America's Foreign Policy* (Garden City, NY: Doubleday, 1977), 410–434; Jim Pyrros, "Memories of the Anti-Junta Years," 1991, box 2, Greek Junta Papers, University of Michigan Library.

41. *Colorado Daily*, October 5, 1967, quoted in Steven M. Gillon, *Politics and Vision: The ADA and American Liberalism, 1947–1985* (New York: Oxford University Press, 1987), 206.

42. "Congressman Says U.S. Is Practicing Genocide," *LAT*, February 21, 1970, 8.

43. Pyrros, "Memories"; Maryanne Lyons Kendall, e-mail correspondence with author, July 1, 2012; LuVerne Conway, interview by author, November 11, 2011.

44. See the brief biography of Mercouri at www.melinamercourifoundation.org.gr /page_2_1_en.htm; for Mercouri and congressmen, see Memo, Rostow to Johnson, October 8, 1968, "Partial Resumption of Military Shipments to Greece," *FRUS, 1964–1968*, vol. 16: *Cyprus, Greece, Turkey* (Washington, DC: US GPO, 2000), 767.

45. "Actress Proposes Boycott of Greece," *WP*, December 20, 1967, 9; "A Tribute to Melina Mercouri," [1994], f. 14, box 41, Edwards Papers.

46. "Greek Star Acts as Lobbyist against Junta—On Sunday," *Baltimore Sun*, October 2, 1967.

47. Paul Lyons to Michael Carsiotis, January 29, 1968, f. 1, box 41, Edwards Papers. Amnesty's New York groups held a joint demonstration with the American Committee at the Greek National Tourist Organization on May 29, 1967. *Amnesty Action*, Summer 1967, 7.

48. Pyrros, "Memories," 29.

49. Howe and Trott, *Power Peddlers*, 435.

50. "Tribute to Melina Mercouri," 3.

51. Fraser to Edwards, March 13, 1968, f. 5, box 41, Edwards Papers.

52. Maurice Goldbloom to John Carey, August 20, 1971, box 34, ILRM; Goldbloom to Lyons, ACLU List, May 29, 1968, f. 5, box 41, Edwards Papers.

53. U.S. Committee for Democracy in Greece, Newsletter, n.d. [1968], f. 4, box 41, Edwards Papers; James G. Pyrros, "PASOK and the Greek Americans: Origins and Development," in Nikolaos A. Stavrou, ed., *Greece under Socialism: A NATO Ally Adrift* (New Rochelle, NY: Aristide Caratzas, 1988), 228. Pell objected to his name being released as a member of the committee; Biddle to Pell, January 25, 1968, f. 56, box 8, Biddle Papers.

54. Benenson quoted in Linda Rabben, *Fierce Legion of Friends: A History of Human Rights Campaigns and Campaigners* (Hyattsville, MD: Quixote Center, 2002), 195.

55. See Tom Buchanan, "'The Truth Will Set You Free': The Making of Amnesty International," *Journal of Contemporary History* 37 (2002): 579. See also Rabben, *Fierce Legion*, 180–185.

56. Introduction by the Secretary-General, *Amnesty International Annual Report 1970–1971*, 7, Amnesty International Library, Index No. POL 10/001/1971, last modified

2013,     http://www.amnesty.org/en/library/asset/POL10/001/1971/en/c21872f5-04d5 -465d-aca2-aa97b36c25e3/pol100011971eng.pdf.

57. Jonathan Power, *Against Oblivion: Amnesty International's Fight for Human Rights* (Glasgow: Fontana, 1981), 29–31.

58. See Barbara Keys, "Anti-Torture Politics: Amnesty International, the Greek Junta, and the Origins of the U.S. Human Rights Boom," in Akira Iriye, Petra Goedde, and William I. Hitchcock, eds., *The Human Rights Revolution: An International History*(New York: Oxford University Press, 2012), 201–222.

59. Peter Benenson to Frieda Zimmerman, June 30, 1964, box 29, ILHR.

60. Lyons to Biddle, August 25, 1967, f. 29, box 8, Biddle Papers.

61. Amelia Augustus, interview by author, July 25, 2012. Maryanne Lyons Kendall also cited confusion about the name as a difficulty faced in the late 1960s; Maryanne Lyons Kendall, email message to author, July 1, 2012.

62. *Amnesty International: Movement for Freedom of Opinion and Religion, Annual Report, June 1, 1964–May 31, 1965* (London: Amnesty International, International Secretariat, [1965]), 10, 32; Minutes, Luncheon Meeting, November 10, 1965, f. 10, box 26, Grant Papers.

63. Ibid.; Suggestions for an American Section of AI, November 1965; Minutes, Luncheon Meeting at Freedom House, December 15, 1965, I.1.1, AI USA Records; Memo, Lyons to Supporting Foundations and Sponsors, "Year-End Report," November 15, 1967, f. 29, box 8, Biddle Papers; Memo, Lyons to Board, "Board Meeting Agenda," September 12, 1967, box 29, ILHR Records. See also the not fully accurate "Historical Introduction to Amnesty International USA," in *AI USA: Addendum to the Amnesty International Handbook* (New York: Amnesty International USA, 1978), n.p. On Straight's role see Roland Perry, *Last of the Cold War Spies: The Life of Michael Straight* (Cambridge, MA: Da Capo Press, 2005), 308; and Maryanne Lyons Kendall, e-mail message to author, July 1, 2012.

64. "AIUSA: An Outline for Expansion," [1966], f. 15, box 26, Grant Papers.

65. Maryanne Lyons Kendall, e-mail message to author, July 1, 2012.

66. "Paul Lyons Dies; Chief of Amnesty's U.S. Office, *WP*, April 14, 2000, B7; quotation appears in Lyons to Twentieth Century Fund, September 25, 1967, f. 29, box 8, Biddle Papers; Maryanne Kendall Lyons, e-mail messages to author, July 1, 2012 and July 28, 2012.

67. On Straight's family, see Lew Rockwell, "No Wonder *The New Republic* Hates LRC," *The LRC Blog*, posted March 1, 2009, www.lewrockwell.com/blog/lewrw/archives /25608.html.

68. Lyons to Twentieth Century Fund; Maryanne Lyons Kendall, e-mail correspondence with author, July 1, 2012.

69. Maryanne Lyons to Biddle, November 14, 1967, f. 29, box 8, Biddle Papers.

70. On the initiation of direct mail, see Memo, Lyons to Board, "Funding," May 26, 1967, box 29, ILRM Records. "Grave financial problems" caused by "expensive direct-mail solicitation" are described in E. J. Kahn, Jr., "The Meddlers," *New Yorker*, August 22, 1970, 50.

71. See, e.g., Sagan to Arthur Danto, f. 14, box 89, Sagan Papers. Compare Kenneth Cmiel, "The Emergence of Human Rights Politics in the United States," *Journal of*

*American History* 86, no. 3 (December 1999): 1231–1250, esp. 1243–1245. Richard Viguerie is credited with starting the first direct-mail company in 1965 and thereby with helping to spur a conservative resurgence; Sara Diamond, *Spiritual Warfare: The Politics of the Christian Right* (Boston: South End Press, 1990), 57.

72. Amelia Augustus, interview by author, July 25, 2012.

73. Lyons, "Dear Board Member or Sponsor," [1967], f. 29, box 8, Biddle Papers.

74. See the documents in box 47, Buckley Papers.

75. Stephanie Grant, interview by Ann Marie Clark, quoted in Ann Marie Clark, *Diplomacy of Conscience: Amnesty International and Changing Human Rights Norms* (Princeton, NJ: Princeton University Press, 2001), 12; Jeri Laber, *The Courage of Strangers: Coming of Age with the Human Rights Movement* (New York: PublicAffairs, 2002), 74. Similarly, early press coverage of Amnesty did not cite the concept of human rights: see, e.g., Bernard Weinraub, "Political Prisons Hold Many Types," *NYT*, June 28, 1970, 13. Compare Peter Benenson's use of "the human rights movement" to describe AI and the ILRM: Benenson to Baldwin, July 31, 1964, box 29, ILRM Records.

76. Lyons to Twentieth Century Fund. Compare Paul J. Lyons, "Amnesty for Prisoners of Conscience," *Ave Maria: National Catholic Weekly*, November 5, 1966.

77. *Amnesty Action*, Summer 1967, 4.

78. Memo, Lyons to Biddle, September 15, 1967, f. 29, box 8, Biddle Papers.

79. Lyons to Mrs. G. Campbell Becket, May 2, 1968, 151.H.3.2F, Fraser Papers.

80. Lyons to AI USA Board Members, "Money," August 7, 1967, f. 29, box 8, Biddle Papers. The "tea parties" quotation is in Confidential Memo, Anthony Marreco (Treasurer) to IEC, Re "Amnesty International in America. Visit April 1–23, 1970," 4, f. 48, AI IS.

81. Memo, Marreco, "Amnesty International in America."

82. Ennals to Mark Benenson, January 5, 1970, f. 47, AI IS; Kahn, "Meddlers," 50. According to Amelia Augustus, in 1971 the U.S. section owed the secretariat $21,000. She negotiated cancellation of the accumulated debt in exchange for a promise to pay future levies in full; Amelia Augustus, interview by author, July 25, 2012.

83. Fact Sheet, U.S. Committee for Democracy in Greece, f. 56, box 8, Biddle Papers; Lyons to Fraser, April 18, 1968, f. 5, box 41; Toni Lee to Reuther, December 9, 1968; Goldbloom to Conway, September 19, 1968; Fraser to Lyons, October 1, 1968, f. 4, box 41, Edwards Papers.

84. Memo, Lyons to Board Members and Key List, July 10, 1967, box 29, ILRM Records.

85. Lyons to Fitch, September 20, 1967, box 29, ILRM Records.

86. See also the article in the "For and about Women" section: Carolyn Lewis, "Winds of Freedom Blow at House Party," *WP*, July 31, 1967, B5.

87. Materials relating to these groups are in box 2, Greek Subject Collection, Hoover. The nomenclature in Europe appears to have been similar; e.g., Comité Français pour la Grèce démocratique.

88. See, e.g., 115 Cong. Rec. 13034 (May 20, 1969).

89. *Amnesty Action*, September 1967, 1; Lyons, letter to the editor, *NYT*, January 8, 1968 (letter dated December 29, 1967), 38. See also Lyons, letter to the editor, *NYT*, February 4, 1968, E13; Letter to Rusk, November 17, 1967, and "Dear Friends" letter,

American Committee for Democracy and Freedom in Greece, November 1967, f. 2, box 41, Edwards Papers; 115 Cong. Rec. 3597 (February 17, 1969); Statement of the U.S. Committee for Democracy in Greece, June 9, 1969, box 2, Becket Papers.

90. NCC, "Concerning Greece," November 19, 1969, box 34, ILRM Records; "Greece: Torture," *Newsweek*, December 15, 1969, 52. See also "Warning to the Junta," *NYT*, May 8, 1969, 46; Anthony Lewis, "Greece: Trouble Ahead for the Colonels," *NYT*, November 30, 1969, E7; Thomas Buergenthal, "Findings on Greece," *NYT*, December 12, 1969, 54.

91. Baldwin to Fraser and Reuther, [1968], box 34, ILRM Records.

92. *Hearings on Greece, Spain, and the Southern NATO Strategy, Before the Subcomm. on Europe, Comm. on Foreign Affairs, House of Representatives*, 92nd Cong. 55–64, quotation at 64 (1971).

93. "Dear Friend," U.S. Committee for Democracy in Greece, [1971], box 35, ILRM Records.

94. Howe and Trott, *Power Peddlers*, 435.

95. See the recollections of Rosenthal staffer Clifford Hackett: "The Role of Congress and Greek-American Relations," in Theodore Couloumbis and John O. Iatrides, eds., *Greek-American Relations: A Critical Review* (New York: Pella, 1980), 132–133; Hackett, "Congress and Greek American Relations: The Embargo Example," *Journal of the Hellenic Diaspora* 15 (1988): 5–31.

96. Keys, "Anti-Torture Politics."

97. "Dear Friend" fund-raising letter, May 17, 1968, box 34, ILRM Records.

98. Draft, n.d.; Committee Newsletter [April 1968], p. 2, f. 5, box 41, Edwards Papers.

99. Summary, "First Tuesday: Greek Victims," August 5, 1969, media ID M690805, NBCUniversal Archives, last modified 2011, www.nbcuniversalarchives.com/nbcuni /clip/5112788433_s05.do; NBC News Press Release, f. 35, box 74; George Mougious to Senator Sam Ervin, October 20, 1971, f. 2, box 41, Edwards Papers; Christopher S. Wren, "Government by Torture," *Look*, May 27, 1969, 19ff; "Greece/Repression," *NBC Evening News*, December 12, 1969, record number 443693, Vanderbilt News Archive. See also "Excerpts from Council of Europe's Report on Treatment of Prisoners in Greece," *NYT*, April 16, 1970, 14. Senator Birch Bayh said, "The regime's policy of torture and denial of constitutional rights had been a matter of deep concern to me"; Pell wrote in 1970, "What most distresses me is their past practices of permitting torture"; quoted in *Common Heritage*, April 1970, 18.

100. Thomas Skidmore, *The Politics of Military Rule in Brazil, 1964–1985* (New York: Oxford University Press, 1988), 88–89.

101. James N. Green, *"We Cannot Remain Silent": Opposition to the Brazilian Military Dictatorship in the United States* (Durham, NC: Duke University Press, 2010).

102. Based on *NYT* and *WP* keyword searches in the ProQuest Historical Newspapers database.

103. Ralph della Cava, "Torture in Brazil," *Commonweal*, April 24, 1970, 131ff.

104. See, e.g., "Ex-Prisoners Tell of Brazil Torture," *WP*, January 17, 1971, about an American citizen and a Swiss Brazilian victim.

105. Peter Kami, letter to the editor, *WP*, December 12, 1971, 55.

106. See, e.g., della Cava, "Torture in Brazil," 139.

107. "Oppression in Brazil," *WP*, February 28, 1970, A14 (della Cava also referred to "complicity"; see "Torture in Brazil," 141); on police training see esp. Martha K. Huggins, *Political Policing: The United States and Latin America* (Durham, NC: Duke University Press, 1998); and, e.g., Jack Anderson, "U.S. Is Accused in Brazilian Torture," *WP*, February 1, 1971, D11; Frank Mankiewicz and Tom Braden, "Brazilian Blood on Our Hands," *WP*, March 23, 1971, A19.

108. Jack Anderson, "Hart Quiz to Bare Tortures in Brazil," *WP*, September 28, 1970, B11. See also Anderson, "U.S. Is Accused."

109. Audrey D. Johnston to Church, September 28, 1970, box 45, series 2.2, Church Papers.

110. (Mrs.) Vaughn Thomas, Hyattsville, MD, to Church, n.d., box 45, series 2.2, Church Papers.

111. Victoria Maura, Evergreen Park, IL, to Church, September 28, 1970, box 45, series 2.2, Church Papers.

112. [first name illegible] Goos, Perth Amboy, NJ, to Church, February 1, 1971, box 45, series 2.2, Church Papers.

113. A. Harris, Stockton, CA, to Church, February 3, 1971, box 45, series 2.2, Church Papers.

## Chapter 5: The Anticommunist Embrace of Human Rights

1. George Packer, *The Assassins' Gate: America in Iraq* (New York: Farrar, Straus and Giroux, 2005), 29.

2. Quotation in Richard Perle interview, "Richard Perle: The Making of a Neoconservative," *Think Tank with Ben Wattenberg*, [2003], copyright 2013, www.pbs .org/thinktank/transcript1017.html.

3. Kathryn Sikkink, *Mixed Signals: U.S. Human Rights Policy and Latin America* (Ithaca, NY: Cornell University Press, 2004), 65.

4. KGB reporting of comments made by Natalya Solzhenitsyna, Solzhenitsyn's wife, conveying Solzhenitsyn's views to Sakharov. Joshua Rubenstein and Alexandr Gribanov, eds., *The KGB File of Andrei Sakharov* (New Haven, CT: Yale University Press, 2005), 158.

5. There is little documentary evidence as to why Jackson chose human rights as a framework, but the influence of the dissidents is suggested in 5th Draft, "Beyond the Cold War, Beyond Détente: Toward a Foreign Policy of Human Rights," [January 1978], pp. 3–4, f. Manifesto [2], box 20, Rosenblatt Papers.

6. For historical reasons I quote from the first, hasty English translation: "Excerpts from Nobel Lecture Published by Solzhenitsyn," *NYT*, August 25, 1972, 2. Solzhenitsyn won the prize in 1970 but submitted a lecture for publication only in 1972.

7. Ludmila Alekseyeva, *Soviet Dissent: Contemporary Movements for National, Religious, and Human Rights* (Middletown, CT: Wesleyan University Press, 1985), 269.

8. Benjamin Nathans, "The Dictatorship of Reason: Aleksandr Vol'pin and the Idea of Rights under 'Developed Socialism,'" *Slavic Review* 66, no. 4 (Winter 2007): 630–634.

9. They are also sometimes labeled *zakoniki* (legalists); Emma Gilligan, *Defending Human Rights in Russia* (New York: Routledge, 2004), 10, 89.

10. Benjamin Nathans, "The Disenchantment of Socialism: Soviet Dissidents, Human Rights, and the New Global Morality," in Jan Eckel and Samuel Moyn, eds., *The Breakthrough: Human Rights in the 1970s* (Philadelphia: University of Pennsylvania Press, forthcoming), 33–48.

11. On the primacy of human rights in dissident strategies, see Robert Horvath, "Demise of Soviet Communism," in David P. Forsythe, ed., *Encyclopedia of Human Rights* (New York: Oxford University Press, 2009). See also Andrei D. Sakharov, *Sakharov Speaks* (London: Collins and Harvill, 1974), 138–140.

12. Michael Scammel, *Solzhenitsyn: A Biography* (London: Hutchinson, 1984), 717. The Nobel ceremony occurs on December 10 to mark the day of Alfred Nobel's death.

13. *God prav cheloveka v Sovetskom Soiuze: Khronika tekyshchikh sobytii*, April 30, 1968, vyp. 1, Memorial, www.memo.ru/history/diss/chr/index.htm.

14. Quoted in Peter Reddaway, ed., *Uncensored Russia: The Human Rights Movement in the Soviet Union* (London: Cape, 1972), 15.

15. Quoted in Peter Reddaway, letter to the editor, *Times* (London), December 5, 1968, 11.

16. See, for example, the first five letters in Dokumenty Initsiativnoi gruppy po zashchite prav cheloveka v SSSR, Memorial, www.memo.ru/history/diss/ig/docs/igdocs.html.

17. Quoted in "Soviet Dissidents Appeal to UN," *Times* (London), October 2, 1969, 1. On the UN reaction, see Robert Horvath, "Breaking the Totalitarian Ice: The Initiative Group for the Defense of Human Rights in the USSR," *Human Rights Quarterly*, forthcoming.

18. See the documents in Dokumenty Initsiativnoi gruppy po zashchite prav cheloveka v SSSR, Memorial, www.memo.ru/history/diss/ig/docs/igdocs.html.

19. Anatoly Dobrynin, *In Confidence: Moscow's Ambassador to America's Six Cold War Presidents, 1962–1986* (New York: Random House, 1995), 159, 267.

20. Memo, "Soviet-Jewish Political Prisoners: A Background Survey," October 1970, box 117, Staff Member and Office Files: Leonard Garment, Nixon Library.

21. See, e.g., the refusenik's appeal quoted in *Denial of Human Rights to Jews in the Soviet Union: Hearings Before the Subcommittee on Europe, Committee on Foreign Affairs, House of Representatives, May 17, 1971*, 92nd Cong. 18 (1971).

22. This generalization is based in part on a rough qualitative estimate of the titles turned up in a keyword search of the *NYT* in the ProQuest Historical Newspapers database. See also Edward Bailey Hodgman, "Détente and the Dissidents: Human Rights in U.S.-Soviet Relations, 1968–1980" (Ph.D. diss., University of Rochester, 2003), 121–123. On the identification of dissidents as human rights advocates, see, for example, the feature article "Struggling Now for Human Rights: A Talk with Valery Chalidze," *NYT*, March 4, 1973, 243ff.

23. Thomas J. W. Probert, "The Innovation of the Jackson-Vanik Amendment," in Brendan Simms and D. J. B. Trim, eds., *Humanitarian Intervention: A History* (Cambridge: Cambridge University Press, 2011), 323–342; A. D. Chernin, "Making Soviet Jews an Issue," in Murray Friedman and Albert D. Chernin, eds., *A Second Exodus: The American Movement to Free Soviet Jews* (Hanover, NH: Brandeis University Press, 1999), 57.

24. "Official Approaches since 1959 to Soviet Officials concerning Jews in the USSR and Soviet Responses," Enclosure 5 [May 6, 1969], box 116, Staff Member and Office Files: Leonard Garment, Nixon Library.

25. "Department Supports Congressional Resolution on Soviet Jewry," *Department of State Bulletin* 65, no. 1693 (1971): 661.

26. American Jewish Committee, "The World of the 1970s: A Jewish Perspective," [1971], p. 37, American Jewish Committee Archives, copyright 2006, www.ajcarchives.org /ajcarchive/DigitalArchive.aspx.

27. *The Jacob Blaustein Institute for the Advancement of Human Rights of the American Jewish Committee, 1971–1992* (New York: American Jewish Committee, Institute of Human Relations, [1992]).

28. *Congress and the Nation* (Washington, DC: Congressional Quarterly Service, 1969–1972), vol. 3: 888.

29. Ronald I. Rubin, "Soviet Jewry and the United Nations: The Politics of Non-governmental Organizations," *Jewish Social Studies* 29, no. 3 (July 1967): 139–154.

30. Javits's 1965 remarks reproduced in *Denial of Human Rights*, 37.

31. See, e.g., Noble Melencamp to John Rothmann, October 27, 19769, box 38, WHCF-HU Human Rights, Nixon Library.

32. *Antireligious Activities in the Soviet Union and in Eastern Europe: Hearings Before the Subcomm. on Europe, House Comm. on Foreign Affairs, May 10, 11, and 12, 1965*, 89th Cong. 52 (1965).

33. Paula Stern, *Water's Edge: Domestic Politics and the Making of American Foreign Policy* (Westport, CT: Greenwood Press, 1979), 9.

34. All of these men signed a 1967 appeal for Soviet Jews; Chernin, "Making Soviet Jews," 48–49.

35. Martin Luther King, Jr., telephone address to American Jewish Conference on Soviet Jewry, December 11, 1966, Freedom 25 Blog, posted November 19, 2012, freedom25 .net/Images/MLK-Speech.pdf.

36. Jordan Chandler Hirsch, "The Gateway: The Soviet Jewry Movement, the Right to Leave, and the Rise of Human Rights on the International Stage" (senior thesis essay, Columbia University, 2010), 36; "Jews Protest at Russian Mission," November 7, 1967, NBC News, media ID 00Z0174, NBCUniversal Archives, last modified 2011, www .nbcuniversalarchives.com/nbcuni/clip/5112496923_s01.do. On American Jewish groups' use of human rights rhetoric to press the cause of Soviet Jews, see also Marc E. Frey, "Challenging the World's Conscience: The Soviet Jewry Movement, American Political Culture, and U.S. Foreign Policy, 1952–1967" (Ph.D. diss., Temple University, 2002), 17–19, 35, 44–48, 76, 90, 109, 128, 201–2.

37. "Freedom Bus Riders Tell Plight of Soviet Jews," *Milwaukee Sentinel*, November 5, 1971, 6.

38. Chernin, "Making Soviet Jews," 50.

39. Abraham Ribicoff to Nixon, April 21, 1969, box 38, WHCF-HU Human Rights, Nixon Library.

40. Morris Abram, "The Right to Leave," *NYT*, January 22, 1971, 39.

41. See, e.g., Tad Szulc, "U.S. Sees Signing of Trade Accord with Soviet in '72," *NYT*, September 15, 1972, 1.

42. *Denial of Human Rights*, 1–2.

43. Ibid., 13. See also *Soviet Jewry: Hearings Before the Subcomm. on Europe, Committee on Foreign Affairs, House of Representatives, November 9 and 10, 1971*, 92nd Cong. 117, 127 (1972).

44. Richard Reeves, *Old Faces of 1976* (New York: Harper and Row, 1976), 59.

45. Robert G. Kaufman, *Henry M. Jackson: A Life in Politics* (Seattle: University of Washington Press, 2000), 219.

46. Reeves, *Old Faces*, 64, 67.

47. Untitled memo, n.d., box 110, Timmons Collection.

48. Kaufman, *Henry M. Jackson*, 179.

49. See, e.g., Dan Morgan, "Jackson Emerges as Leader of Foreign Policy Opposition," *NYT*, October 22, 1973, A2.

50. Reeves, *Old Faces*, 52. See also Kaufman, *Henry M. Jackson*, 184.

51. Quoted in Kaufman, *Henry M. Jackson*, 209.

52. Reeves, *Old Faces*, 67.

53. Charles Horner, "Human Rights and the Jackson Amendment," in Dorothy Fosdick, ed., *Staying the Course: Henry M. Jackson and National Security* (Seattle: University of Washington Press, 1987), 125.

54. Report, "Senator Henry Jackson, Voting Analysis—91st Congress," [c. 1971], box 110, Timmons Collection.

55. Reeves, *Old Faces*, 66; Jules Witcover, *Marathon: The Pursuit of the Presidency, 1972–1976* (New York: Viking, 1977), 160–161. Jackson had so enraged antiwar leader Allard Lowenstein that Lowenstein considered moving to Seattle to run against him in the 1970 Senate race. Kaufman, *Henry M. Jackson*, 218.

56. Justin Vaïsse, *Neoconservatism: The Biography of a Movement*, trans. Arthur Goldhammer (Cambridge, MA: Harvard University Press, 2010), 87.

57. Bruce Miroff, *The Liberals' Moment: The McGovern Insurgency and the Identity Crisis of the Democratic Party* (Lawrence: University Press of Kansas, 2007), 264. As Justin Vaïsse notes, "The most ardent hawks in this period were to be found among Democrats"; Vaïsse, *Neoconservatism*, 10.

58. Quoted in Ben J. Wattenberg, *Fighting Words: A Tale of How Liberals Created Neoconservatism* (New York: St. Martin's Press, 2008), 136.

59. Jackson, "Foreign Policy," National War College, April 1965, quoted in Kaufman, *Henry M. Jackson*, 174.

60. Quoted in Peter J. Ognibene, *Scoop: The Life and Politics of Henry M. Jackson* (New York: Stein and Day, 1975), 193.

61. Quoted in Reeves, *Old Faces*, 138.

62. Quoted in Kaufman, *Henry M. Jackson*, 230, 223, 236.

63. Norman Podhoretz, *The Present Danger: "Do We Have the Will to Reverse the Decline of American Power?"* (New York: Simon and Schuster, 1980), 31.

64. Vaïsse, *Neoconservatism*, 92–93.

65. See, e.g., Kaufman, *Henry M. Jackson*, 205.

66. Henry M. Jackson, "The Four Freedoms in Today's World," December 4, 1971, f. 3, box 9, Jackson Papers.

67. Kaufman, *Henry M. Jackson*, 83–84; Joshua Muravchik, interview by author, January 30, 2013.

68. Stephen S. Rosenfeld, "The Politics of the Jackson Amendment, 'A Piece of Political Baggage with Many Different Handles,'" *Present Tense* 1, no. 4 (Summer 1974): 17.

69. Reeves, *Old Faces*; Ognibene, *Scoop*, 194.

70. Reeves, *Old Faces*, 137, 93, 56.

71. Kaufman, *Henry M. Jackson*, 254–257.

72. Bernard Gwertzman, "Questions and Answers on Soviet Trade and Emigration," *NYT*, October 3, 1973, 12.

73. Henry Kissinger, *White House Years* (New York: Little, Brown, 1979), 1270. See also Kaufman, *Henry M. Jackson*, 250–251.

74. Dobrynin, *In Confidence*, 268–269.

75. Rosenfeld, "Politics of the Jackson Amendment," 17.

76. Quoted in William Korey, "Jackson-Vanik: A 'Policy of Principle,'" in Friedman and Chernin, *Second Exodus*, 98.

77. Memo, Larry Brady to Peter M. Flanigan, September 22, 1972, box 48, Timmons Collection.

78. Rosenfeld, "Politics of the Jackson Amendment," 17–18.

79. CREEP Memo, David Korn to Howard Cohen, August 30, 1972, box 118, Staff Member and Office Files: Leonard Garment, Nixon Library.

80. Rosenfeld, "Politics of the Jackson Amendment," 17–18.

81. Petrus Buwalda, *They Did Not Dwell Alone: Jewish Emigration from the Soviet Union, 1967–1990* (Baltimore: Johns Hopkins University Press, 1997), 95.

82. Hirsch, "Gateway," 61, 65.

83. Republican Party Platform of 1972, August 21, 1972, The American Presidency Project, last modified 2013, www.presidency.ucsb.edu/ws/?pid=25842.

84. Charles Horner, e-mail message to author, February 3, 2013.

85. 118 Cong. Rec. 33658 (October 4, 1972). On Jackson's ideas see John Sinclair Petifer Robson, "Henry Jackson, the Jackson-Vanik Amendment and Detente: Ideology, Ideas, and United States Foreign Policy in the Nixon Era" (Ph.D. diss., University of Texas at Austin, 1989).

86. Press Release, "East-West Trade and Fundamental Human Rights," September 27, 1972, box 48, Timmons Collection. See the text of the speech in Dorothy Fosdick, ed., *Henry M. Jackson and World Affairs: Selected Speeches, 1953–1983* (Seattle: University of Washington Press, 1990), 179–184. The "wicked" and "barbaric" exit tax amounted to "trade in human beings," he said, conjuring up America's history of slavery.

87. Jackson, April 10, 1973, quoted in 119 Cong. Rec. 11549 (1973). The wording in his announcement of mid-March used similar terms. 119 Cong. Rec. 8071 (March 15, 1973).

88. Korey, "Jackson-Vanik," 97; 119 Cong. Rec. 31802 (September 27, 1973); Stephen Isaacs, "Soviets Agree to Ease Curbs on Emigrants," *WP*, October 19, 1974, A1.

89. Henry M. Jackson, "First, Human Détente," *NYT*, September 9, 1973, 219; Speech, Pacem in Terris Conference, Washington, DC, October 11, 1973, in Fosdick, *Henry M. Jackson*, 188.

90. 118 Cong. Rec. 30718 (September 14, 1972).

91. 118 Cong. Rec. 33661–33663 (October 4, 1972).

92. Text from September 12, 1972, in 119 Cong. Rec. 8075 (1973). Compare a later speech that repeatedly referred to human rights: 119 Cong. Rec. 8073 (March 15, 1973).

93. 119 Cong. Rec. 21246 (June 25, 1973); see also 119 Cong. Rec. 6797–6798 (March 7, 1973), 7064–7065 (March 8, 1973), and 10406 (March 29, 1973).

94. Dusko Doder, "Jackson Attacks Soviet Détente in Scathing Speech," *NYT*, June 5, 1973, A12; see also "Freedom of Emigration," *Nation*, December 24, 1973, 676–677; "Détente and Human Rights," *International Herald Tribune*, August 29, 1973.

95. The exit tax was dropped six months after being introduced, and emigration levels hit nearly thirty-five thousand in 1973; Fosdick, ed., *Henry M. Jackson*, 185.

96. Stern, *Water's Edge*, 55, 87.

97. See, e.g., Tom Braden, "Sen. Kennedy: Seeking Options for Détente," *NYT*, April 20, 1974, A19.

98. Telcon, Kissinger and Joseph Alsop, October 5, 1972, Kissinger Telcons. Reports of indiscriminate killing of civilians by the Pakistani Army led to a March 1972 ban on aid to Pakistan and India while the two nations were at war; *Congress and the Nation*, vol. 3, 886.

99. Kissinger and Perle quoted in "What Price the Jackson Amendment?," *Time*, October 1, 1973, 39–40.

100. Telcon, Kissinger and George Kennan, September 14, 1973, Kissinger Telcons.

101. Sakharov, "A Letter to the Congress of the United States," September 14, 1973, in Sakharov, *Sakharov Speaks*, 212–215; see also 119 Cong. Rec. 29803–29804 (September 17, 1973). The *WP* ad is described in 119 Cong. Rec. 30784 (September 20, 1973).

102. Quotations are from the summary of the NBC News report, "Sen. Jackson re: Soviet Emigrants," September 10, 1973, NBCUniversal Archives, last modified 2011, www .nbcuniversalarchives.com/nbcuni/clip/5112772478_s01.do.

103. 119 Cong. Rec. 21147–21150 (June 25, 1973). Jim Pyrros nevertheless recollected that it was a "breakthrough" for the antijunta cause when Jackson came on board in 1973. Pyrros to Orestis Vidalis, May 28, 1997, manuscript provided to the author.

104. Between 1968 and 1970, about four thousand Jews had left. In 1971 the number rose to about thirteen thousand; in 1972 to thirty-two thousand; in 1973 it reached a peak of thirty-five thousand. With the collapse of the trade agreement, that number dropped by nearly fifteen thousand the next year.

105. Press Release, "East-West Trade and Fundamental Human Rights."

## Chapter 6: A New Calculus Emerges

1. "Kissinger and Tho End Talks with Handshakes and Smiles," *NYT*, January 24, 1973, 73; "End of a Nightmare," *NYT*, January 24, 1973, 40; "Vietnam Agreement . . . ," *NYT*, January 25, 1973, 38.

2. On Jackson's hold on the human rights debate in 1973, see, e.g., Richard Holbrooke, "Washington Dateline: The New Battlelines," *Foreign Policy* 13 (Winter 1973–1974): 184.

3. *Nomination of Henry A. Kissinger: Hearings Before the Committee on Foreign*

*Relations, U.S. Senate, September 7, 10, 11, and 14, 1973*, 93rd Cong. 155–158 (1973). See also Press Release, "Fraser Expresses Reservations about Kissinger Nomination," September 14, 1973, 149.C.13.6F, Fraser Papers. For further evidence of Fraser's concern with the reassertion of congressional power around this time, see Donald M. Fraser and Iric Nathanson, "Rebuilding the House of Representatives," in Norman J. Ornstein, ed., *Congress in Change: Evolution and Reform* (New York: Praeger Publishers, 1975), 288.

4. Holbrooke, "Washington Dateline," 184.
5. *Newsweek*, June 10, 1974 (cover); "Superstar Statecraft: How Henry Does It," *Time*, April 1, 1974, 32–40.
6. *Nomination of Henry A. Kissinger*, 166–169.
7. Ibid., 175–178.
8. Ibid., 186. On the Lawyers Committee, see Samuel Moyn, "From Antiwar Politics to Antitorture Politics," in Austin Sarat, Lawrence Douglas, and Martha Merrill Umphrey, eds., *Law and War* (Stanford: Stanford University Press, forthcoming).
9. See, e.g., "Sakharov: A Warning Defied," *NYT*, August 26, 1973, 173.
10. *Nomination of Henry A. Kissinger*, 40.
11. Ibid., 229.
12. Ibid., 39–41, 116–117, 85–86, 143.
13. Nixon White House Tapes, March 1, 1973, quoted in Adam Nagourney, "In Tapes, Nixon Rails against Jews and Blacks," *NYT*, December 10, 2010, A13. "The emigration of Jews from the Soviet Union is not an objective of American foreign policy," Mr. Kissinger said. "And if they put Jews into gas chambers in the Soviet Union, it is not an American concern. Maybe a humanitarian concern."
14. *Nomination of Henry A. Kissinger*, 241.
15. See, e.g., Clare Apodaca, *Understanding U.S. Human Rights Policy: A Paradoxical Legacy* (New York: Routledge, 2006), 34–35; David Weissbrodt, "Human Rights Legislation and U.S. Foreign Policy," *Georgia Journal of International and Comparative Law* 7 (1977): 241; Robert A. Pastor, *Congress and the Politics of U.S. Foreign Economic Policy, 1929–1976* (Berkeley: University of California Press, 1980), 304; Mark L. Schneider, "A New Administration's New Policy: The Rise to Power of Human Rights," in Peter G. Brown and Douglas MacLean, eds., *Human Rights and U.S. Foreign Policy: Principles and Applications* (Lexington, MA: D.C. Heath, 1979), 7; Lars Schoultz, *Human Rights and United States Policy toward Latin America* (Princeton, NJ: Princeton University Press, 1981), 194–195.
16. Robert Sherrill quoted in Mark J. Green, *Who Runs Congress?*, rev. ed. (New York: Bantam Books, 1975), 206.
17. Telcon, Bruce Harlow and Kissinger, September 14, 1973, Kissinger Telcons.
18. Jack Nelson, "Abourezk Fights to End Aid to Foreign Police," *WP*, September 22, 1974, F1; James G. Abourezk, *Advise and Dissent: Memoirs of South Dakota and the U.S. Senate* (Chicago: Lawrence Hill Books, 1989), 131.
19. Statement before the Senate Armed Services Committee, March 19, 1974, f. 51, box 713, Abourezk Papers.
20. *Foreign Economic Assistance, 1973: Hearings Before the Comm. on Foreign Relations, U.S. Senate, June 26 and 27, 1973*, 93rd Cong. 244–245 (1973).

21. "The Cages of Con Son Island," *Time*, July 20, 1970, 22; "South Vietnam: School of Hard Knocks," *Newsweek*, July 23, 1973, 11.

22. "Vietnam/Political Prisoners," *ABC Evening News*, March 9, 1973, record number 25261, Vanderbilt News Archive.

23. Quoted in Anthony Lewis, "Whom We Welcome," *NYT*, March 31, 1973, 35.

24. *Foreign Economic Assistance, 1973*, 244–250.

25. 119 Cong. Rec. 23804–23805 (July 13, 1973).

26. 119 Cong. Rec. 32284–32286 (October 1, 1973).

27. "Viet Prison Cruelty Is Debated," *WP*, January 12, 1974, A15; "Militant Antiwar Movement Shifts Tactics, Not Targets," *WP*, June 2, 1974, G6; " 'The Movement,' with the War Ebbing, Ponders Its Role in a Nation at Peace," *NYT*, February 18, 1973, 60; "Antiwar Groups to Oppose U.S. Aid to Saigon Prisons," *NYT*, September 19, 1973, 17; "Senate Liberals Will Seek to End Aid to Saigon Police," *NYT*, September 16, 1973, 1; Bill Zimmerman, *Troublemaker: A Memoir from the Front Lines of the Sixties* (New York: Doubleday, 2011), 359–364.

28. Tom Cornell quoted in Nancy Zaroulis and Gerald Sullivan, *Who Spoke Up? American Protest against the War in Vietnam, 1963–1975* (Garden City, NY: Doubleday, 1984), 405.

29. Zaroulis and Sullivan, *Who Spoke Up?*, 413.

30. Anthony Lewis, "Peace with Honor," *NYT*, July 16, 1973, 29.

31. For details see *Congress and the Nation* (Washington, DC: Congressional Quarterly Service, 1977), vol. 4, 890–895.

32. A useful survey of the arguments for and against can be found in the debate in the Senate: 119 Cong. Rec. 32593–32598 (October 2, 1973). Liberal disenchantment with foreign aid can be seen in the fact that Abourezk and other liberals including Frank Church and William Fulbright voted against the 1973 bill.

33. Patricia Weiss Fagen, "U.S. Foreign Policy and Human Rights: The Role of Congress," in Antonio Cassese, ed., *Parliamentary Control over Foreign Policy: Legal Essays* (Germantown, MD: Sijthoff and Noordhoff, 1980), 109–121.

34. John F. Lehman, *The Executive, Congress, and Foreign Policy: Studies of the Nixon Administration* (New York: Praeger, 1976), 179.

35. Mary Russell, "House Passes Aid Bill by Only 5 Votes," *WP*, July 27, 1973, A1; Sandy Vogelgesang, *American Dream, Global Nightmare: The Dilemma of U.S. Human Rights Policy* (New York: W. W. Norton, 1980), 200–201. On the "basic needs" approach, see Gilbert Rist, *The History of Development: From Western Origins to Global Faith* (London: Zed, 1997), 162–170.

36. 119 Cong. Rec. 23804–23805 (July 13, 1973).

37. "Senate Liberals Will Seek to End Aid."

38. 119 Cong. Rec. 32286–32287 (October 1, 1973); see also Michael Harrington's amendment in the House to cut off police and prison aid to South Vietnam: 119 Cong. Rec. 26199 (July 26, 1973).

39. Fred Branfman, "Caged by Saigon," *NYT*, September 27, 1973, 39.

40. 119 Cong. Rec. 17838–17841 (June 4, 1973); *Treatment of Political Prisoners in South Vietnam by the Government of the Republic of South Vietnam: Hearing Before the*

*Subcommittee on Asian and Pacific Affairs, House of Representatives, September 13, 1973,* 93rd Cong. 1 (1973).

41. 119 Cong. Rec. 32287 (October 1, 1973).

42. On Morgan, see, e.g., Laurence Stern, "Washington Dateline: Two Henrys Descending," *Foreign Policy* 18 (Spring 1975): 172.

43. Thomas M. Franck and Edward Weisband, *Foreign Policy by Congress* (New York: Oxford University Press, 1979), 229; Julian E. Zelizer, *On Capitol Hill: The Struggle to Reform Congress and Its Consequences, 1948-2000* (Cambridge: Cambridge University Press, 2004), 1-5, 127, 138; Cecil V. Crabbe and Pat M. Holt, *Invitation to Struggle: Congress, the President and Foreign Policy* (Washington, DC: Congressional Quarterly Press, 1980), 55, 192-193, 237; David J. Vogler, *The Politics of Congress,* 2nd ed. (Boston: Allyn and Bacon, 1977), 171-177, 200.

44. Ornstein, *Congress in Change,* 103.

45. Ibid.; Robert David Johnson, *Congress and the Cold War* (New York: Cambridge University Press, 2006), 179-180; James M. McCormick, "Decision Making in the Foreign Affairs and Foreign Relations Committees," in Randall Ripley and James Lindsay, eds., *Congress Resurgent: Foreign and Defense Policy on Capitol Hill* (Ann Arbor: University of Michigan Press, 1993), 127, 138; Robert B. Boettcher, "The Role of Congress in Deciding United States Human Rights Policies," in Natalie Kaufman Hevener, ed., *The Dynamics of Human Rights in U.S. Foreign Policy* (New Brunswick, NJ: Transaction Books, 1984), 280.

46. See the subcommittee hearings listed in the Library of Congress catalog.

47. Boettcher, "Role of Congress," 280.

48. Ibid., 281; Ornstein, *Congress in Change,* 104; Draft letter to new members of House Foreign Affairs Committee, December 31, 1974, 151.H.4.2F, Fraser Papers.

49. See the various documents in the subcommittee folder in 152.K.8.12F, Fraser Papers.

50. Anthony Lake, *The "Tar Baby" Option: American Policy toward Southern Rhodesia* (New York: Columbia University Press, 1976), 2, 111, 198, 215-216; Memo "re Proposed Joint hearing on Rhodesia," January 11, 1973, 152.K.8.12F; Draft letter to new members.

51. Bob Boettcher to Fraser, "IOM Activities during 93rd Congress," January 11, 1973, 151.I.11.8F, Fraser Papers.

52. Mark Benenson, "A Proposal," *Christian Science Monitor,* September 9, 1972, 16.

53. John Salzberg, "The United Nations Sub-Commission on Prevention of Discrimination and Protection of Minorities: A Functional Analysis of an Independent Expertbody Promoting Human Rights" (Ph.D. diss., New York University, 1973).

54. John Salzberg, interview with author, November 8, 2008; John Salzberg, letter to the editor, *NYT,* May 22, 1966, 217.

55. Salzberg, interview with author; John Salzberg, letter to the editor, *NYT,* September 20, 1971, 24.

56. Press Release, "Fraser Announces Human Rights Hearings," September 13, 1973, 149.C.13.6F, Fraser Papers.

57. *International Protection of Human Rights, The Work of International Organizations and the Role of U.S. Foreign Policy: Hearings Before the Subcomm. on International*

*Organizations and Movements, Comm. on Foreign Affairs, House of Representatives,*
*August 1; September 13, 19, 20, 27; October 3, 4, 10, 11, 16, 18, 24, 25; November 1;*
*December 7, 1973,* 93rd Cong. 17, 31 (1974).

58. Ibid., 484.

59. Fraser quoted in Kathryn Sikkink, *Mixed Signals: U.S. Human Rights Policy and Latin America* (Ithaca, NY: Cornell University Press, 2004), 65.

60. *International Protection of Human Rights,* 16.

61. Boettcher, "Role of Congress," 280.

62. Press Release, "Fraser Announces Human Rights Hearings."

63. John Salzberg, "A View from the Hill," in David D. Newsom, ed., *The Diplomacy of Human Rights* (Lanham, MD: University Press of America, 1986), 15.

64. Salzberg, interview with author.

65. *International Protection of Human Rights,* 37–38.

66. Press release, "Fraser Honored for Efforts on Behalf of International Human Rights," December 10, 1973, 151.H.4.2F, Fraser Papers.

67. Eldridge quoted in Sikkink, *Mixed Signals,* 68.

68. Draft letter to new members; and Fraser to Morgan, November 18, 1974, 151.H.4.2.F, Fraser Papers.

69. Based on a Library of Congress catalog survey of the subcommittee's publications. See also Memo, John Salzberg, "Draft Outline of 1975 International Human Rights Program," December 18, 1974, 151.H.4.2F, Fraser Papers.

70. Boettcher, "Role of Congress," 281.

71. Press Release, "Fraser Appointed to U.N. Human Rights Commission," February 8, 1974, 151.H.4.2.F, Fraser Papers; Minnpapers Report, "Fraser for Friday PMS," November 13, 1975, 151.H.3.3B, Fraser Papers; 120 Cong. Rec. 31489 (September 17, 1974); Edwards to Sagan, September 21, 1973, f. 5, box 53, Sagan Papers. See also Donald M. Fraser and John P. Salzberg, "International Political Parties as a Vehicle for Human Rights," *Annals of the American Academy of Political Science* 442 (March 1979): 63–68.

72. Boettcher, "Role of Congress," 282.

73. On Salzberg's role, see ibid., 281.

74. John Barnes, "Slaughterhouse in Santiago," *Newsweek,* October 8, 1973, 53–54.

75. Memo, R. Michael Finlay to Dante Fascell, "Correspondence on Chile," October 20, 1973, Subcommittee on Inter-American Affairs, 93rd Cong., IRC CLA. See also "Talking Points on House Resolution 584, Concerning Protection of Human Rights in Chile," [1973], box 8, Subcommittee on Inter-American Affairs, 93rd Cong., IRC CLA.

76. John Maxwell to Fascell, March 21, 1974, box 9, Subcommittee on Inter-American Affairs, 93rd Cong., IRC CLA.

77. See, e.g., 119 Cong. Rec. 31694–31695 (September 26, 1973).

78. "Human Rights in Chile," *WP,* October 5, 1973, A28.

79. H.R. Res. 575, October 2, 1973, Subcommittee on Inter-American Affairs, 93rd Cong, box 9, IRC CLA. See also the resolution introduced by Fraser, Kastenmeier, McCloskey, Reid, Steiger, Obey, Moakley, Whalen, and Young on September 20; Press Release, "House Members Urge Protection of Human Rights in Chile," September 20, 1973, 149.C.13.6F, Fraser Papers.

80. 119 Cong. Rec. 30615 (September 20, 1973); Sikkink, *Mixed Signals,* 57–58; Mark

Schneider biographical information at "Mark Schneider," International Crisis Group, copyright 2013, www.crisisgroup.org/en/about/staff/advocacy/washington /mark-schneider.aspx.

81. Press Release, "House Members Urge Protection."
82. Paul E. Sigmund, *The United States and Democracy in Chile* (Baltimore: Johns Hopkins University Press, 1993), 89.
83. Ibid.
84. 119 Cong. Rec. 40865 (December 11, 1973). The ban on aid to Chile failed 102 to 304. Ibid., 40866.
85. "Sato, Ireland's MacBride Win 1974 Nobel Peace Prize," *WP*, October 9, 1974, A1; "Kissinger, Tho Award Draws International Criticism," *WP*, October 18, 1973, A28.
86. Moses Moskowitz, *International Concern with Human Rights* (Leiden: Sijthoff, 1974), vi; Samuel Moyn, *The Last Utopia: Human Rights in History* (Cambridge, MA: Harvard University Press, 2010), 122–124.
87. Tom Wicker, "Kissinger's Question," *NYT*, September 14, 1973, 39.
88. "Freedom of Emigration," *Nation*, December 24, 1973, 677; 138 Cong. Rec. 31694 (September 26, 1973). Such connections were also drawn by ordinary Americans; see, e.g., Joanne Laws to Symington, January 24, 1974, f. 6250, Symington Papers; Patricia Kelly to Fraser, April 20, 1974, 149.G.13.7, Fraser Papers.

## Chapter 7: Insurgency on Capitol Hill

1. Rosenthal and Fraser had solicited Solzhenitsyn's views; "Translation of Solzhenitsyn Letter," April 3, 1974, 149.C.13.6F, Fraser Papers.
2. Drinan quoted in Yves Delazay and Brian Garth, "From the Cold War to Kosovo: The Rise and Renewal of the Field of International Human Rights," *Annual Review of Law and Social Science* 2 (December 2006): 240; James Abourezk, e-mail message to author, November 5, 2012.
3. *Human Rights in the World Community: A Call for U.S. Leadership: Report of the Subcomm. on International Organizations and Movements, Comm. on Foreign Affairs, House of Representatives, March 27, 1974*, 93rd Cong. 9 (1974).
4. Marianne Means, "Human Rights Becomes Issue between House, Diplomats," *Reading Eagle*, April 18, 1974, 4.
5. Compare "The Question of Stockpiling Grain Debated in Senate," *NYT*, March 27, 1974, 24.
6. "Human Rights Emphasis Urged for U.S. Diplomacy," *Boston Globe*, March 27, 1974, 1; Darius Jhabvala, "A 'Moral' Foreign Policy," *St. Louis Post-Dispatch*, April 7, 1974; "House Unit Stresses Humanity," *WP*, March 27, 1974, A2; "U.S. Urged to Act on Human Rights," *NYT*, March 28, 1974, 17.
7. *Human Rights in the World Community*, 124, 12–13.
8. Lars Schoultz, *Human Rights and United States Policy toward Latin America* (Princeton, NJ: Princeton University Press, 1981), 123.
9. John Salzberg, "A View from the Hill," in David D. Newsom, ed., *The Diplomacy of Human Rights* (Lanham, MD: University Press of America, 1986), 17; Patrick Breslin, "Human Rights: Rhetoric or Action?," *WP*, February 27, 1977, 33.

10. James Wilson, "Diplomatic Theology—An Early Chronicle of Human Rights at State," [August 1977], pp. 30, 7, James Wilson Papers, 1958–77, Human Rights and Humanitarian Affairs, Ford Library; Memorandum, "Ronald Palmer," March 17, 1976, box 4, Morris Papers; Fraser to Kissinger, June 27, 1974, Papers of George Lister, Human Rights Bureau, University of Texas, Austin, www.utexas.edu/law/centers /humanrights/lister/assets/pdf/Human%20Rights%20Bureau/frasertokissinger june271974.pdf?id=txu-blac-glp-304; and Memo, George Lister to Bill Rogers, "Your Meeting with Fraser," October 9, 1974, Papers of George Lister, Human Rights Bureau, University of Texas, Austin, www.utexas.edu/law/centers/humanrights /lister/assets/pdf/Human%20Rights%20Bureau/listertorogersoct91974.pdf?id=txu -blac-glp-305 .

11. Charles Stuart Kennedy's comment in "Interview with James M. Wilson, Jr.," March 31, 1999, Foreign Affairs Oral History Collection of the Association for Diplomatic Studies and Training (FAOHC), Library of Congress, last updated August 13, 2012, hdl.loc.gov/loc.mss/mfdip.2004wil14.

12. Charles Stuart Kennedy, "Interview with Ronald D. Palmer," May 15, 1992, FAOHC, last updated August 13, 2012, hdl.loc.gov/loc.mss/mfdip.2004palo3.

13. Wilson, "Diplomatic Theology," 4; Schoultz, *Human Rights*, 125.

14. Thomas M. Franck and Edward Weisband, *Foreign Policy by Congress* (New York: Oxford University Press, 1979), 3, 85.

15. J. William Fulbright, *The Crippled Giant: American Foreign Policy and Its Consequences* (New York: Random House, 1972), 165, 173.

16. Randall Bennett Woods, *J. William Fulbright, Vietnam, and the Search for a Cold War Foreign Policy* (Cambridge: Cambridge University Press, 1998), 279; quotation in Bill Kauffman, *America First! Its History, Culture and Politics* (Amherst, NY: Prometheus Books, 1995), 152.

17. Statement by Fulbright, "Human Rights Conventions," January 1968, box 97, Staff Member and Office Files: Leonard Garment, Nixon Library; Fulbright to Herschel Halbert, December 13, 1967, box 468, Harriman Papers.

18. Quoted in Richard Reeves, *Old Faces of 1976* (New York: Harper and Row, 1976), 136.

19. James Abourezk, e-mail message to author, November 5, 2012; Schoultz, *Human Rights*, 198–201.

20. Franck and Weisband, *Foreign Policy by Congress*, 229–231.

21. Robert David Johnson, *Congress and the Cold War* (New York: Cambridge University Press, 2006), xxiii–xxiv.

22. Donald M. Fraser, "Human Rights and U.S. Foreign Policy: Some Basic Questions regarding Principles and Practice," *International Studies Quarterly* 23, no. 2 (June 1979): 179.

23. Don Ostrom to Don Edwards, July 21, 1967, box 41, Edwards Papers.

24. Press Release, "Fraser Amendment Prohibits Military Assistance to Anti-Democratic Governments," October 16, 1969, 151.H.4.2F, Fraser Papers.

25. Committee on Foreign Affairs, Amendment to H.R. 11792, October 1, 1973, 151.H.4.2.F, Fraser Papers.

26. Draft transcript [June 1974], 151.H.4.2F, Fraser Papers; Arthur W. Rovine, "Contemporary Practice of the United States Relating to International Law," *The American Journal of International Law* 68, no. 1 (1974): 143–144; Salzberg, "View from the Hill"; David Weissbrodt, "Human Rights Legislation and U.S. Foreign Policy," *Georgia Journal of International and Comparative Law* 7 (1977): 241n39; Ingersoll to Morgan, June 27, 1974, 149.G.13.8F, Fraser Papers.

27. 120 Cong. Rec. 23141 (July 15, 1974).

28. *Foreign Assistance Authorization: Hearings Before the Committee on Foreign Relations, United States Senate, June and July 1974*, 93rd Cong. 267–272 (1974).

29. Ibid., 345, 342. See also James S. Rausch, U.S. Catholic Conference, to Nixon, February 14, 1974, box 1, HU Human Rights, White House Subject Files, Nixon Library.

30. Memo, Salzberg to Fraser and Robert Boettcher, July 3, 1974; and "Executive Branch Action on Section 32," June 13, 1974, 149.G.13.8F, Fraser Papers; John Salzberg and Donald D. Young, "The Parliamentary Role in Implementing International Human Rights: A U.S. Example," *Texas International Law Journal* 12 (Spring–Summer 1977): 271. The language appeared in ECOSOC Resolution 1503.

31. Quoted in Weissbrodt, "Human Rights Legislation," 242n41.

32. Memo, "Summary of July Foreign Assistance Act Mark-Up Sessions," August 20, 1974, 149.G.13.8F, Fraser Papers.

33. 120 Cong. Rec. 39135 (December 11, 1974); Stephen B. Cohen, "Conditioning U.S. Security Assistance on Human Rights Practices," *American Journal of International Law* 76 (April 1982): 252; Kathryn Sikkink, *Mixed Signals: U.S. Human Rights Policy and Latin America* (Ithaca, NY: Cornell University Press, 2004), 69–70.

34. 120 Cong. Rec. 39135–39136 (December 11, 1974).

35. Salzberg, "View from the Hill," 19.

36. 120 Cong. Rec. 38087–38089 (December 4, 1974); Press Release, untitled, December 4, 1974, box 264, Cranston Papers.

37. It would have left Abourezk's wording and added a new subsection cutting off economic and military aid to any country unless the president certified that it did "not violate human rights with respect to" political or religious arrest or persecution; denial of the right to a fair and prompt trial; or torture; S. 3394, referred to the Senate Committee on Foreign Relations, 149.G.13.8F, Fraser Papers. Based on the absence of any reference to the amendment in the *Congressional Record*, it appears Javits backed off his amendment.

38. Telegram, Washington to Brasilia, "Tunney Amendment of Military Assistance," June 26, 1972; Telegram, Washington to Brasilia, "Allegations of Torture in Brazil," June 28, 1972, Pol 29 Brazil, State Department Decimal Files, NARA.

39. 22 USC §2304.

40. Memorandum of Conversation of October 8, 1976 Meeting with Indian Foreign Minister Chavan, October 12, 1976, Doc. 237, *FRUS, 1969–1976*, Vol. E-8: *Documents on South Asia, 1973–1976* (Washington, DC: US GPO, 2007), history.state.gov /historicaldocuments/frus1969-76ve08.

41. Henry Kissinger, *White House Years* (Boston: Little, Brown, 1979), 1016.

42. Quoted (in order) in Jeremi Suri, "Détente and Human Rights: American and West European Perspectives on International Change," *Cold War History* 8, no. 4 (November 2008): 529; Hugh M. Arnold, "Henry Kissinger and Human Rights," *Universal Human Rights* 2, no. 4 (October–December 1980): 63; Minutes of the Secretary's Staff Meeting, October 22, 1974, Doc. 244, *FRUS, 1969–1976*, Vol. *E-3: Documents on Global Issues, 1973–1976* (Washington, DC: US GPO, 2009), history .state.gov/historicaldocuments/frus1969-76ve03; Jeremi Suri, *Henry Kissinger and the American Century* (Cambridge: Harvard University Press, 2007), 251.

43. Richard M. Nixon, *U.S. Foreign Policy for the 1970's: Building for Peace; A Report to the Congress by Richard Nixon, February 25, 1971* (Washington, DC: GPO, 1971), 18.

44. Wilson, "Diplomatic Theology," 36–37; Memorandum of Conversation, "U.S.-Chilean Relations," June 8, 1976, National Security Archive, posted December 12, 2006, www.gwu.edu/~nsarchiv/NSAEBB/NSAEBB212/19760608%20US-Chilean %20Relations.pdf.

45. Wilson, "Diplomatic Theology," 20–21; Memorandum of Conversation, Secretary's Meeting with Foreign Minister Carvajal, September 29, 1975, National Security Archive, posted February 3, 2004, www.gwu.edu/~nsarchiv/NSAEBB/NSAEBB110 /chile08.pdf.

46. Telcon, Kissinger and Harry Shlaudeman, June 20, 1976, Kissinger Telcons.

47. See, e.g., Sikkink, *Mixed Signals*, 107–120.

48. Memorandum of Conversation, Secretary's Meeting with Argentine Foreign Minister Guzzetti, October 7, 1976, National Security Archive, posted December 4, 2003, www.gwu.edu/~nsarchiv/NSAEBB/NSAEBB104/Doc6%20761007.pdf.

49. Policy Planning Staff, "U.S. Policies on Human Rights and Authoritarian Regimes," undated [October 1974], Box 348, Policy Planning Council, Director's Files [Winston Lord], 1969–1977, Entry 5027, RG 59, NARA. For a summary, see "Summary of Paper on Policies on Human Rights and Authoritarian Regimes," October 1974, Doc. 243, *FRUS, 1969–1976*, Vol. *E-3*, history.state.gov/historicaldocuments/frus1969-76ve03 /d243.

50. Wilson, "Diplomatic Theology," 4.

51. See, for example, Department of State, The Secretary's Regionals' and Principals' Staff Meeting, December 23, 1974, National Security Archive, posted February 3, 2004, www.gwu.edu/~nsarchiv/NSAEBB/NSAEBB110/chile07.pdf.

52. Minutes of the Secretary's Staff Meeting, October 22, 1974.

53. Ibid.

54. "Pat M. Holt, Chief of Staff, Foreign Relations Committee," pp. 253–254, Oral History Interviews, Senate Historical Office, www.senate.gov/artandhistory/history/oral _history/Pat_M_Holt.htm.

55. Ibid., 245.

56. Rose Styron, "Terror in Chile II: The Amnesty Report," *New York Review of Books* 21, no. 9 (May 30, 1974).

57. *Refugee and Humanitarian Problems in Chile: Hearings Before the Subcomm. to Investigate Problems Connected with Refugees and Escapees, Comm. on the Judiciary, Senate, Part II, 23 July 1974* 93rd Cong. 62 (1974).

58. The Secretary's Principals and Regionals Staff Meeting, December 23, 1974, p. 26; The Secretary's Principals and Regionals Staff Meeting, December 20, 1974, pp. 27–29, NSA EBB 110.

59. Seymour Hersh, "CIA Chief Tells House of $8 Million Campaign against Allende in 1970–73," *NYT*, September 8, 1973, 1; Hersh, "Kissinger Called Chile Strategist," *NYT*, September 15, 1974, 1.

60. Quoted in "Kissinger Said to Rebuke U.S. Ambassador to Chile," *NYT*, September 27, 1974, 18; Robert A. Pastor, *Congress and the Politics of U.S. Foreign Economic Policy, 1929–1976* (Berkeley: University of California Press, 1980), 308.

61. 120 Cong. Rec. 32653 (September 25, 1974). See also 120 Cong. Rec. 39896 (December 13, 1974).

62. John Salzberg and Bob Boettcher to Fraser, "Kissinger, Popper and Human Rights in Chile," September 27, 1974, 151.H.3.3B, Fraser Papers.

63. Seymour Hersh, "Kissinger Is Challenged on Chile Policy," *NYT*, September 28, 1974; Memo, Fraser, September 27, 1974, 151.H.3.3B, Fraser Papers.

64. The Secretary's Principals and Regionals Staff Meeting, December 23, 1974, NSA EBB 110.

65. *Foreign Assistance Authorization*, 345, 342.

66. Philip L. Ray, Jr., and J. Sherrod Taylor, "The Role of NGOs in Implementing Human Rights in Latin America," *Georgia Journal of International and Comparative Law* 7 (1977): 486.

67. Kenneth Meyers to W. Stuart Symington, [c. March 1974], f. 6250, Symington Papers.

68. Elizabeth Mohler to Symington, October 26, 1975, f. 6268, Symington Papers.

69. Weissbrodt, "Human Rights Legislation," 243; Cohen, "Conditioning U.S. Security Assistance," 254–255.

70. Weissbrodt, "Human Rights Legislation," 243; "House Votes to Ban Foreign Aid for Human-Rights Violations," *NYT*, September 11, 1975, 18.

71. John Salzberg, interview by author, November 6, 2008; Schoultz, *Human Rights*, 196–197.

72. Schoultz, *Human Rights*, 196–198.

73. Lord to Kissinger, "Security Assistance and the Human Rights Reports to Congress," September 20, 1975, box 5, Human Rights Subject File, HA, NARA.

74. Policy Planning Staff, "Security Assistance and the Human Rights Report to the Congress," [September 19, 1975], box 5, Human Rights Subject File, HA, NARA.

75. "Human Rights Today," undated [1975], "General" folder, box 1, Human Rights Subject File, HA, NARA; Wilson, "Diplomatic Theology," 8.

76. Cranston to Kissinger, November 5, 1975, box 5, HA, NARA; Wilson, "Diplomatic Theology," 17–18; Memo, Maw to Kissinger, "Report to Congress on Human Rights," July 16, 1975, box 1, HA, NARA.

77. Wilson, "Diplomatic Theology," 18–21; Runyon to All Assistant Legal Advisers, p. 2; and "Korea" [country report], [1975], box 5, HA, NARA.

78. Salzberg to Fraser, September 29, 1975, 151.H.4.2F, Fraser Papers.

79. Bernard Gwertzman, "U.S. Blocks Rights Data on Nations Getting Arms," *NYT*, November 19, 1975, 1.

80. "Interview with James M. Wilson, Jr."

81. Gwertzman, "U.S. Blocks Rights Data," 1.

82. Quoted in Wilson, "Diplomatic Theology," 24.

83. Gwertzman, "U.S. Blocks Rights Data," 1; William H. Lewis to Marilyn Berger of the *Washington Post*, December 6, 1975, box 5, HA, NARA.

84. Gwertzman, "U.S. Blocks Rights Data"; Marilyn Berger, "Aid Ban Urged for Nations Violating Human Rights, Lands," *WP*, November 20, 1975, A3.

85. Ford's veto cited the human rights machinery as one of his objections; Bernard Gwertzman, "President Vetoes Aid Bill, Charging It Restricts Him," *NYT*, May 8, 1976, 1.

86. Salzberg and Young, "Parliamentary Role," 273.

87. Cranston had pushed for a semi-independent director of human rights to act as a kind of watchdog on the department, but the end result was a position subordinate to the secretary of state; Wilson, "Diplomatic Theology," 27–28.

88. Barbara Keys, "Congress, Kissinger, and the Origins of Human Rights Diplomacy," *Diplomatic History* 34, no. 4 (November 2010): 823–851.

89. Airgram, Santiago to Washington, May 17, 1975, "FY 1976–77 CASP for Chile," in Peter Kornbluh, *The Pinochet File: A Declassified Dossier on Atrocity and Accountability* (New York: New Press, 2003), 306.

90. Judith Innes de Neufville, "Human Rights Reporting as a Policy Tool: An Examination of the State Department Country Reports," *Human Rights Quarterly* 8, no. 4 (November 1986): 681; Joshua Muravchik, *The Uncertain Crusade: Jimmy Carter and the Dilemmas of Human Rights Policy* (Lanham, MD: Hamilton Press, 1986), 41, 231–232.

91. See Brad Simpson, "Denying the 'First Right': The United States, Indonesia, and the Ranking of Human Rights by the Carter Administration, 1976–1980," *International History Review* 31, no. 4 (2009): 798–826.

92. Sonia Cardenas, "Norm Collision: Explaining the Effects of International Human Rights Pressure on State Behavior," *International Studies Review* 6 (2004): 213–231.

93. Sandra Vogelgesang, "What Price Principle? U.S. Policy on Human Rights," *Foreign Affairs* 56 (Spring 1978): 825, 830, 838.

94. Tom Jones to David Weissbrodt, July 21, 1974, II.1.5, AI USA Records.

95. "Human Rights Today."

96. In a winter 1972 article, Lincoln Bloomfield did not mention human rights, though he concluded by saying that only by adopting "humane" foreign policies would it be possible to "cure the sickness that has crept into the veins of American foreign policy" as a result of the war in Vietnam; "Foreign Policy for Disillusioned Liberals," *Foreign Policy* 9 (Winter 1972–1973): 68. In an article written three years later, Edward Kolodziej discussed cutoffs in aid but did not use the term "human rights"; "Congress and Foreign Policy: The Nixon Years," *Proceedings of the Academy of Political Science* 32, no. 1 (1975): 167–179

97. Tom Harkin, "Human Rights and Foreign Aid: Forging an Unbreakable Link," in Peter G. Brown and Douglas MacLean, eds., *Human Rights and U.S. Foreign Policy: Principles and Applications* (Lexington, MA: D.C. Heath, 1979), 26.

## Chapter 8: The Human Rights Lobby

1. Darren G. Hawkins, *International Human Rights and Authoritarian Rule in Chile* (Lincoln: University of Nebraska Press, 2002), 56–57.
2. Justin Vaïsse, *Neoconservatism: The Biography of a Movement*, trans. Arthur Goldhammer (Cambridge, MA: Harvard University Press, 2010).
3. Vania Markarian, *Left in Transformation: Uruguayan Exiles and the Latin American Human Rights Networks, 1967–1984* (New York: Routledge, 2005), 104.
4. David Weissbrodt, "The Influence of Interest Groups on the Development of United States Human Rights Policies," in Natalie Kaufman Hevener, ed., *The Dynamics of Human Rights in U.S. Foreign Policy* (New Brunswick, NJ: Transaction Books, 1984), 242–243. On the rise of groups devoted to Latin America, see Vanessa Walker, "Ambivalent Allies: Advocates, Diplomats, and the Struggle for an 'American' Human Rights Policy" (Ph.D. diss., University of Wisconsin, Madison, 2011). An excellent account of human rights nongovernmental organizations can be found in Lars Schoultz, *Human Rights and United States Policy toward Latin America* (Princeton, NJ: Princeton University Press, 1981), 74–88. For a sharp critique of the Working Group and Chagnon in particular as procommunist, see Joshua Muravchik, *The Uncertain Crusade: Jimmy Carter and the Dilemmas of Human Rights Policy* (Lanham, MD: Hamilton Press, 1986), 168–169.
5. Schoultz, *Human Rights*, 75–76.
6. Lowell Livezey, *Nongovernmental Organizations and the Ideas of Human Rights* (Princeton, NJ: Center of International Studies, Princeton University, 1988), 118–122.
7. Quoted in Muravchik, *Uncertain Crusade*, 169.
8. Jan Eckel, "'Utopie der Moral, Kalkül der Macht': Menschenrechte in der globalen Politik seit 1945," *Archiv für Sozialgeschichte* 49 (2009): 460; Samuel Moyn, *The Last Utopia: Human Rights in History* (Cambridge, MA: Harvard University Press, 2010), 146–147.
9. Ginger McRae to Rick Wright, "Meeting with Charles Runyon," October 6, 1976, II.1.5, AI USA Records.
10. Lister to Fraser, October 30, 1992, 7.20, Lister Papers.
11. Gregory Krauss, "Impacting Foreign Policy as a Mid-Level Bureaucrat: The Diplomatic Career of George Lister" (M.P.Aff. thesis, University of Texas, Austin, 2007), 67, 80, 85.
12. See, e.g., Lister to Rogers, August 5, 1975; and Lister to Rogers, June 24, 1975, 12.10, Lister Papers.
13. Krauss, "Impacting Foreign Policy," 88–89.
14. Hawk continued, "As weird and often pernicious as America is, when there is something substantive and meaningful happening (as human rights just might) it can be an exciting and fun place to be." Hawk to Stephanie Grant, February 27, 1976, box 4, Morris Papers.
15. Memo, Hawk to Board, March 1976, box 4, Morris Papers.
16. David Ottaway, "The Growing Lobby for Human Rights," *WP*, December 12, 1976, 31.

17. See, e.g., David Weissbrodt, "Human Rights Legislation and U.S. Foreign Policy," *Georgia Journal of International and Comparative Law* 7 (1977); David P. Forsythe, "Humanizing American Foreign Policy: Non-profit Lobbying and Human Rights" (working paper, Institute for Social and Policy Studies, [1980]), 20.

18. Sagan to Max Palevsky, January 10, 1974, f. 4, box 90, Sagan Papers.

19. See, e.g., Ernest R. May and Janet Fraser, eds., *Campaign '72: The Managers Speak* (Cambridge, MA: Harvard University Press, 1973), 130. On confusion over the name, see, e.g., Memo, Sagan to Advisory Board, "KCBS Broadcast Confusing AI and 'Amnesty,'" October 1, 1974, box 36, Sagan Papers.

20. Memo, Mark Benenson to Directors, May 28, 1970, f. 70, box 78, Buckley Papers.

21. "Executive Director's Annual Report," *Amnesty Action*, February 1974, 1.

22. Publicity, 1973, box 4, Morris Papers.

23. Ginetta Sagan to Morris, May 11, 1974, box 4, Morris Papers. Many of the new members were temporary, and a 1974 report noted that "AI remains a small, relatively unknown organization"; Lorrin Rosenbaum, "Proposal to Amnesty International," August 28, 1974, box 36, Sagan Papers. In early 1974, West Germany had 455 adoption groups, compared to 75 in the United States, of which perhaps 40 percent existed only on paper; handwritten notes, n.d., box 4; Hawk to Board, March 1976, box 4, Morris Papers.

24. Memo, Lyons to Board, "International Executive Committee Meeting, London, March 22-23, 1969"; "Background and Financial Data," box 58, Buckley Papers. This was done partly based on an interpretation of the tax-exempt status rules; Confidential Memo, Anthony Marreco (Treasurer) to IEC, Re: "Amnesty International in America, Visit April 1-23, 1970," p. 5, f. 48, AI IS.

25. On the debt, see "Statement of Taxes, Payables, and Unrecorded Accounts Payable," July 31, 1969, box 58, Buckley Papers; Confidential Memo, Marreco to IEC; Amelia Augustus, interview by author, July 26, 2012. Details of Lyons's ouster can be found in f. 69, box 78, Buckley Papers. On shared space with the ILRM, see Benenson to Buckley, March 9, 1970, f. 69, box 78, Buckley Papers. On Benenson's lifetime NRA membership, see Benenson to Buckley, March 2, 1972, f. 71, box 78, Buckley Papers.

26. Mark K. Benenson, "Dear Friend," [c. 1969], box 2, Becket Papers.

27. Amelia Augustus résumé, f. 71, box 78, Buckley Papers; Martin Ennals to Mark Benenson, January 5, 1970, f. 47, AI IS; Benenson to Directors, March 6, 1971, f. 71, box 78, Buckley Papers; Resignation Letter, Augustus to AI USA Board, July 17, 1974, box 4, Morris Papers; AI USA Minutes, April 20, 1972, I.1.1, AI USA; Amelia Augustus, interview by author, July 26, 2012.

28. Kay Holmes, "The Politics of Conscience," *Ms.*, November 1973, 32.

29. Amelia Augustus, interview by author, July 26, 2012.

30. Ivan Morris to Martin Ennals, October 30, 1974; and Morris to Board of AIUSA, "Termination of Contract," July 1, 1974, box 4, Morris Papers; Amelia Augustus, interview by author, July 26, 2012.

31. Gottlieb to Barbara Sproul, August 21, 1974, box 4, Morris Papers.

32. Anthony Lewis, "The Meaning of Torture," *NYT*, May 30, 1974, 37.

33. Colman McCarthy, "Aiding Political Prisoners," *WP*, May 17, 1974, A30; 120 Cong. Rec. 15375 (May 20, 1974).

34. Ottaway, "Growing Lobby."

35. Wendy Turnbull to Charles Robinson, May 26, 1976; AIUSA Budget, 1975–1976, n.d.; Memo, Michaelson to Mark Benenson, May 7, 1975, box 4, Morris Papers.

36. Morris to Wright, July 2, 1976; and Memo, Hawk to Board, March 1976, box 4, Morris Papers.

37. Norman Marsh quoted in Linda Rabben, *Fierce Legion of Friends: A History of Human Rights Campaigns and Campaigners* (Hyattsville, MD: Quixote Center, 2002), 185.

38. Laurie S. Wiseberg and Harry M. Scoble, "The International League for Human Rights: The Strategy of a Human Rights NGO," *Georgia Journal of International and Comparative Law* 7 (1977), 289–313.

39. Mark Benenson, AI USA, to Stephanie Grant, London, f. 21, box 36, Grant Papers.

40. Peter Benenson quoted in Rabben, *Fierce Legion*, 192.

41. *Bulletin of the International League for the Rights of Man*, November 1972, 1, box 1, Becket Papers.

42. Ann Marie Clark, *Diplomacy of Conscience: Amnesty International and Changing Human Rights Norms* (Princeton: Princeton University Press, 2001), 40–46.

43. "Power problems" appears in "Reports to the Executive Committee and David [Hawk] from Ginetta [Sagan] and Sally [Lilienthal] asking for specific action in reference to the Los Angeles office," [c. May 1, 1976], box 4, Morris Papers.

44. Lyons to Benenson, July 23, 1970; Memo, Benenson to Board, May 28, 1970; and Arne Haaland to IEC on Meeting of AI USA Board, July 20, 1970, f. 70, box 78, Buckley Papers.

45. Memo, Benenson to Board, May 28, 1970.

46. Ibid.; Benenson to Board, March 6, 1971, f. 71, box 78, Buckley Papers; Stephen Hopgood, *Keepers of the Flame: Understanding Amnesty International* (Ithaca, NY: Cornell University Press, 2006), 107.

47. Minutes, May 4, 1970; Benenson to Board, May 16, 1971, I.1.1, AI USA Records.

48. Vincent McGee, AIUSA Planning Meeting, AIUSA/International Movement, April 13, 1979, I.4.7, AI USA Records.

49. Wendy Turnbull to Thomas C. Jones, Jr., June 8, 1976, box 4, Morris Papers.

50. Thomas C. Jones, Jr. to Pat Stocker, June 4, 1976, box 4, Morris Papers. See also Edy Kaufman to Rose Styron, May 24, 1976; and Jones to Kaufman, June 11, 1976, box 4, Morris Papers.

51. Robert Karen, "Amnesty International: Against the Tide of Torture," *Nation*, November 30, 1974, 552.

52. Advertisement, *Matchbox* 1, no. 1 (Spring/Summer 1974), 30.

53. Untitled report, May 4, 1974, box 4, Morris Papers.

54. ANACAPA Fund, AIUSA Exhibit 1: Follow-up to 1976 Mailings, November 1976, I.4.7, AI USA Records. McGovern's campaign had targeted many of the same groups in 1972; see Leo Cherne, "Why This Democrat Is Voting for Nixon," [c. 1972], box 59, William R. Kintner Papers, Hoover.

55. George Nash, "The Ordeal of Amnesty International," *National Review*, December 6, 1974, 1427.

56. William F. Buckley, Jr., "On the Right: Amnesty," *New York Post*, April 9, 1970, 49.

57. Lyons to Buckley, November 20, 1968, box 47, Buckley Papers. See also Lyons to Buckley, January 16, 1969, box 58, Buckley Papers.

58. Buckley to Benenson, May 24, 1971; Buckley to Benenson, July 29, 1971; and Benenson to Buckley, July 2, 1971, f. 71, box 78, Buckley Papers; see also Nash, "Ordeal," 1408.

59. Tibor Szamuely, "Partial Amnesty," *Encounter* 34, no. 6 (June 1970): 33–37; Nash, "Ordeal," 1407ff; M. Stanton Evans, "Dark Horses," *National Review*, January 25, 1980, 113. See also Ottaway, "Growing Lobby."

60. Andrew Blane, "The Individual in the Cell: A Rebuttal to 'Politics and Amnesty International,'" *Matchbox*, Winter 1979, 6ff.

61. Draft Resolution [1973], II.1.1, AI USA Records.

62. Draft Resolution for International Council, December 17, 1974, II.1.1, AI USA Records.

63. Hawk to Board, March 1976, box 4, Morris Papers. As of March 1976, 55 percent of groups were in the west, 45 percent in the east.

64. Jeri Laber, *The Courage of Strangers: Coming of Age with the Human Rights Movement* (New York: PublicAffairs, 2002), 71; "rich New Yorkers" quoted in Hopgood, *Keepers of the Flame*, 111. On Morris see H. Paul Varley, "A Remembrance of Ivan Morris," *Journal of Japanese Studies* 3, no. 1 (Winter 1977): 135–143.

65. Opening Remarks [Event c. 1975], box 4, Morris Papers.

66. Karen, "Amnesty International," 550–553. Like Lyons, Sagan consciously identified as a human rights activist. See, e.g., Sagan to Bob Dylan, n.d. [c. 1973], f. 17, box 89, Sagan Papers.

67. See the finding aid to the Ginetta Sagan Papers at the Hoover Institution Archives, which says that AI officially recognized her group in 1971. In a letter to Morris, Sagan said she began the group in June 1972; Draft, Sagan to Morris, June 1976, box 202, Sagan Papers.

68. David Hawk, interview by author, January 11, 2012.

69. Quoted in "Ginetta Sagan Dies; Torture Victim Fought for Political Prisoners," *LAT*, August 30, 2000, 3.

70. Ginetta Sagan, "A Personal Matter," *Matchbox*, Spring/Summer 1974, 10.

71. Joan Baez, *And a Voice to Sing With: A Memoir* (New York: Summit, 1987), 179.

72. David Hajdu, *Positively 4th Street: The Lives and Times of Joan Baez, Bob Dylan, Mimi Baez Fariña, and Richard Fariña* (New York: Farrar, Straus and Giroux, 2001), 263–266.

73. "The Mellowing of Joan Baez," *Chicago Tribune*, September 26, 1976, 76.

74. Baez, *And a Voice*, 179–183.

75. Sagan to AI London, May 22, 1974, f. 1, box 90, Sagan Papers.

76. James S. Baugess and Abbe Allen DeBolt, eds., *Encyclopedia of the Sixties: A Decade of Culture and Counterculture* (Santa Barbara, CA: Greenwood, 2012), 48.

77. Baez, *And A Voice*, 179–183; "Joan Baez Scheduled for Charity Concert," *LAT*, August 9, 1973, C24.

78. Sagan to Ennals, January 8, 1974, f. 17, box 89, Sagan Papers.

79. Letter [Sagan?] to Jim Seymour, April 12, 1974, f. 7, box 89, Sagan Papers.

80. Dan Hirsch, Office Report, June 4, 1976; and Sagan to Morris, May 11, 1974, box 4, Morris Papers.

81. Nash, "Ordeal," 1408.

82. Sagan to Buckley, January 30, 1975, f. 74, box 78, Buckley Papers.

83. Sagan to Buckley, October 3, 1975, f. 74, box 78, Buckley Papers.

84. Sagan to Palevsky, December 20, 1973, f. 4, box 90, Sagan Papers.

85. Jean-Pierre Debris and André Menras, *Rescapés des Bagnes de Saigon: Nous Accusons* (Paris: Les Editeurs Français Réunis, [1973]). See also the review by Joseph Buttinger, "Thieu's Prisoners," *New York Review of Books*, 20, no. 10 (June 14, 1973): 20–24; Flyer, untitled, [March 1973?], box 36; and [Sagan?] to Don and Marian Eldridge, n.d. [1973], f. 17, box 89, Sagan Papers; "Witnesses from a Prison in S. Vietnam," *Amnesty Action*, March 1973, 1.

86. See, e.g., Lynne Shatzkin Coffin to Executive Committee, and Hanna Grumwald, "March California Trip," May 6, 1976, box 4, Morris Papers.

87. On AI's use of the politics of image along with the politics of information, see Kenneth Cmiel, "The Emergence of Human Rights Politics in the United States," *Journal of American History* 86, no. 3 (December 1999): 1231–1250. On AI USA's attitude toward overt lobbying, see, e.g., Memo to Mark Benenson, May 7, 1975, box 5, Morris Papers. On human rights covert lobbying, see Forsythe, "Humanizing American Foreign Policy," 5-6.

88. Cmiel, "Emergence," 1247.

89. Memo, Joshua Rubenstein, New England Coordinator, to Long-Range Planning Meeting, [1977], I.4.7, AI USA Records.

90. Wendy Turnbull to Charles Robinson, May 26, 1976, box 4, Morris Papers.

91. For critiques along these lines, see Cosmas Desmond, *Persecution East and West: Human Rights, Political Prisoners and Amnesty* (New York: Penguin, 1983), 19, 23, 26, 34; Wendy Brown, " 'The Most We Can Hope For . . .': Human Rights and the Politics of Fatalism," *South Atlantic Quarterly* 103, no. 2/3 (2004): 451–463.

92. Sherman Carroll to David Hawk and Bob Maurer, "Report on AI Trade and Aid Seminar," March 6, 1978, II.2.6, AI USA Records.

93. Ginetta Sagan, "Dear Friend" fund-raising letter, [c. 1973], f. AI Various, box 14, Sagan Papers.

94. Letter, n.d., II.1.1, AI USA.

95. *Amnesty Action*, March 1974, box 36, Sagan Papers. See also Moyn, *Last Utopia*, 147.

96. Sagan, "Dear Fellow Human," [1973], f. 1, box 54, Grant Papers.

97. West Coast Office fund-raising letter, "Dear Friend," [c. 1976], p. 4, 2.26.41, Allard Lowenstein Papers, University of North Carolina, Louis Round Wilson Special Collections Library, Chapel Hill, NC.

98. AI Brochure, [c. 1978], box 14, Sagan Papers; "Dear Fellow Human."

99. Ginetta Sagan, "Dear Friend" fund-raising letter. It was such a compelling formula that at least one other organization copied it; see Jon Sawyer to Safe Return, August 8, 1975, box 36, Sagan Papers.

100. Forsythe, "Humanizing American Foreign Policy," 9, 13, 21, quotation at 26.

101. Ennals to Simon, February 24, 1976; Ennals to Simon, March 26, 1976; Manuel Trucco to Mary McCrory [sic], May 18, 1976; and "Actions by the Treasury Department to Promote Observance of Fundamental Human Rights by Foreign Governments," [1976], drawer 18, William E. Simon Papers, Lafayette College Library, Euston, PA.

102. Wiseberg and Scoble, "International League," 301.

103. Quoted in Nash, "Ordeal," 1408; Sagan to Hawk, December 8, 1975, box 52, Sagan Papers.

104. Fraser to Kissinger, June 28, 1974, 151.H.4.2.F, Fraser Papers.

105. Memo, Stephanie Grant, "Guidelines for Approaching Washington," [c. 1975], box 4, Morris Papers.

106. "Report of the Amnesty International (U.S.A.) Washington Committee," n.d. [1976]; Memo, Rick Sloan to Rick Wright, "AI's Role in the 502B Process," October 7, 1976; and Memo, Rick Sloan to Rick Wright, AI Washington Office, "Americans for Democratic Action and the Center for International Policy's Role in the 502B Process," October 8, 1976, II.1.5, AI USA Records.

107. Donald Culverson, "The Politics of the Anti-apartheid Movement in the United States, 1969-1986," *Political Science Quarterly* 111, no. 1 (1996): 136-138.

108. Draft Outline of Proposed AIUSA Washington, D.C. Liaison, f. 9, box 53, Sagan Papers; Wendy Turnbull, Schedule of Trip to Washington, June 17, 1977, II.4.14, AI USA Records.

109. Memo, Ginger McRae to Executive Committee, August 22, 1977, II.1.5, AI USA Records.

110. "March to End Torture," *Amnesty International [U.S.A.] Newsletter*, March 1976, 2.

111. Memo, to House and Senate Conferees on the Appropriations Bill for Foreign Assistance and Related Programs, FY 1977, "Prohibition of Military Aid to Uruguay," September 14, 1976; and AI Washington, Uruguay: Background Paper, September 1976, f. 17, box 23, Americans for Democratic Action Records, Wisconsin Historical Society, Madison.

112. Joshua Rubenstein, interview by author, November 28, 2012; see also Schoultz, *Human Rights*, 84.

113. Schoultz, *Human Rights*, 106-108. Thomas Hammarberg wrote in Amnesty's 1978 annual report that Amnesty did not "propose" boycotts or cuts in aid. "That kind of economic pressure," Hammarberg stated, "is not within our mandate and is not our way of working"; *Amnesty International Report 1978* (London: Amnesty International, 1979), 3.

114. Memo, Rick Sloan to Rick Wright, "Americans"; and Bruce Cameron, "Partial Chronology Pertaining to Fall 1976 502-B Reports," [1976], II.1.5, AI USA Records.

115. AI Pacific Regional Conference Report (1976), quoted in Draft Report, AI Seminar, "Human Rights and Economic Pressures," London, January 28-29, 1978, 3, II.2.6, AI USA Records.

116. Draft Report, AI Seminar, 24-24, 37, 53-54, 56, 59-61; on Hammarberg, see also Hopgood, *Keepers of the Flame*, 92.

117. Forsythe, "Humanizing American Foreign Policy," 16.

118. Laber, *Courage of Strangers*, 84.

119. "The Threes," quoted in Rabben, *Fierce Legion*, 197.

120. Jan Eckel, "Rebirth of Politics from the Spirit of Morality: Explaining the Human Rights Revolution of the 1970s," in Jan Eckel and Samuel Moyn, eds., *The Breakthrough: Human Rights in the 1970s* (Philadelphia: University of Pennsylvania Press, forthcoming), 226-260.

121. Ginetta Sagan, "Dear Friend" fund-raising letter.

122. On Amnesty's reliance on "thin description," see Cmiel, "Emergence."

123. See, e.g., Epidemic: Torture, [1973?], II.2.11, AI USA Records; "Amnesty and Torture," n.d., 3, f. 1234, AI IS.

124. Leonard Sussman to Paul Hirsch, May 10, 1977, f. 27, box 31, Grant Papers.

## Chapter 9: A Moralist Campaigns for President

1. Anthony Lewis, "How to Deal With Thugs," *NYT*, January 5, 1976, 29.

2. Carl Bon Tempo, "Human Rights and the U. S. Republican Party in the Late 1970s," in Jan Eckel and Samuel Moyn, eds., *The Breakthrough: Human Rights in the 1970s* (Philadelphia: University of Pennsylvania Press, forthcoming); "Campaign 1976/ Republican Convention/Platform/ERA," *ABC Evening News*, August 11, 1976, record number 44771, Vanderbilt News Archive.

3. Euel W. Elliott, *Issues and Elections: Presidential Voting in Contemporary America—A Revisionist View* (Boulder, CO: Westview, 1989), 44–47.

4. William Safire, "Super Yalta," *NYT*, July 28, 1975, 21; "Jerry, Don't Go," *WSJ*, July 23, 1975, 14.

5. Typescript, Paul Winkeller, "How Jimmy Carter Was Introduced to America on TV News," [c. 1976], 13, f. 13, box 161, Theodore White Papers, Harvard University Archives.

6. Ron Nessen, *It Sure Looks Different from the Inside* (New York: Simon and Schuster, 1978), 345. When the Nixon administration had failed to condemn Solzhenitsyn's 1974 expulsion from the Soviet Union, Jackson used the occasion to charge that détente ignored human rights. Henry Jackson, "Jackson Attacks Nixon Stance on Solzhenitsyn," *LAT*, March 4, 1974, A5.

7. "Solzhenitsyn's Views Dangerous—Kissinger," *Chicago Tribune*, June 17, 1975, 1; Jussi Hanhimäki, *The Flawed Architect: Henry Kissinger and American Foreign Policy* (New York: Oxford University Press, 2004), 434, 436.

8. Daniel Patrick Moynihan, "The United States in Opposition," *Commentary* (March 1975): 31–44.

9. Moynihan to Rumsfeld, March 17, 1975, in Steven R. Weisman, ed., *Daniel Patrick Moynihan: A Portrait in Letters of an American Visionary* (New York: PublicAffairs, 2010), 375.

10. Daniel Patrick Moynihan with Suzanne Weaver, *A Dangerous Place* (London: Secker and Warburg, 1979), 72.

11. Ibid., 8.

12. Ibid., 119.

13. Speech quoted in Moynihan, *Dangerous Place*, 158–161. See also Moynihan to Kissinger, September 9, 1975, in Weisman, *Daniel Patrick Moynihan*, 378–379.

14. "Moynihan Calls on U.S. to Start 'Raising Hell' in U.N.," *Times* (London), May 3, 1975.

15. Press Release, Moynihan Statement on the UN Resolution, November 10, 1975, American Jewish Committee Archives, copyright 2006, www.ajcarchives.org/ajcarchive /DigitalArchive.aspx.

16. Daniel Jonathan Sargent, "From Internationalism to Globalism: The United States and the Transformation of International Politics in the 1970s" (Ph.D. diss., Harvard University, 2008), 454–477; Moynihan, *Dangerous Place*, 11–12, 72–74.

17. *Time*, January 26, 1976 (cover); "Moynihan's Tactics Anger Diplomats, Please Americans," *Boston Globe*, November 21, 1975, 2; [Summary, Opinion Research Corporation Poll, January 12, 1976], I:340, Moynihan Papers.

18. Ben J. Wattenberg, *Fighting Words: A Tale of How Liberals Created Neo-conservatism* (New York: St. Martin's Press, 2008), 128–130.

19. Moynihan, *Dangerous Place*, 278.

20. Moynihan to William D. Rogers, February 9, 1976, I:342, Moynihan Papers.

21. "Academy Steps Up Human Rights Drive," *Science News*, May 7, 1977, 294.

22. Laurie S. Wiseberg and Harry M. Scoble, "The International League for Human Rights: The Strategy of a Human Rights NGO," *Georgia Journal of International and Comparative Law* 7 (1977): 290.

23. William Korey, *Taking On the World's Repressive Regimes: The Ford Foundation's International Human Rights Policies and Practices* (New York: Palgrave Macmillan, 2007), 36; William D. Carmichael, "The Role of the Ford Foundation," in Claude E. Welch, Jr., ed., *NGOs and Human Rights: Promise and Performance* (Philadelphia: University of Pennsylvania Press, 2001), 249–251.

24. Leslie Gelb, "Kissinger Aides Find Americans Distrust Policy," *NYT*, September 16, 1976, 81; 122 Cong. Rec. 33230–33231 (September 29, 1976).

25. Samuel Moyn, *The Last Utopia: Human Rights in History* (Cambridge, MA: Harvard University Press, 2010), 152–155; Hugh M. Arnold, "Henry Kissinger and Human Rights," *Universal Human Rights* 2, no. 4 (October–December 1980): 57–71, 61–62; *The Presidential Campaign 1976, vol. 1, Jimmy Carter,* comp. Committee on House Administration, U.S. House of Representatives (Washington, DC: Government Printing Office, 1978–1979). On Kissinger's private views, see, e.g., Telcon, Kissinger and Harry Shlaudeman, June 30, 1976, Kissinger Telcons. For Kissinger's public addresses during the Ford years, see "The Public Papers of Secretary of State Henry Kissinger, 1974–1977," Gerald R. Ford Presidential Digital Library, www.fordlibrarymuseum.gov/library/hakpp.asp.

26. John B. Dunlop, "Solzhenitsyn's Reception in the United States," in John B. Dunlop, Richard S. Haugh, and Michael Nicholson, eds., *Solzhenitsyn in Exile: Critical Essays and Documentary Materials* (Stanford, CA: Hoover Institution Press, 1985), 30–37.

27. Arnold, "Henry Kissinger," 62–69; "Text of Kissinger's Address in Zambia on U.S. Policy toward Southern Africa," *NYT*, April 28, 1976, 16; "Kissinger in Latin America, Makes Appeal on Rights," *NYT*, June 7, 1976, 3; "Kissinger Assails Chile over Curbs," *NYT*, June 9, 1976, 81; "Fateful Meeting," *NYT*, September 1, 1976, 32.

28. National Security Council, Briefing Book 1, Second Debate, September 30, 1976, pp. 10–13, Gerald R. Ford Presidential Digital Library, www.fordlibrarymuseum.gov/library/document/0010/1554428.pdf. On how human rights "eluded" Ford, see Moynihan, *Dangerous Place*, 230.

29. "The Making of an Image," *WSJ*, September 28, 1976, 48; "Peace," Ford Commercial, 1976, Museum of the Living Image, The Living Room Candidate: Presidential

Campaign Commercials, 1952-2012, copyright 2012, www.livingroomcandidate.org /commercials/1976/peace.

30. Draft outline, Foreign Policy and National Defense, 1976 Republican Platform, box 28, Michael Raoul-Duval Files, Ford Library.

31. Republican Party Platform of 1976, August 18, 1976, The American Presidency Project, copyright 2013, www.presidency.ucsb.edu/ws/?pid=25843; Jules Witcover, *Marathon: The Pursuit of the Presidency, 1972-1976* (New York: Viking, 1977), 485; Kiron Skinner, Serhiy Kudelia, Bruce Bueno de Mesquita, and Condoleezza Rice, *The Strategy of Campaigning: Lessons from Ronald Reagan and Boris Yeltsin* (Ann Arbor: University of Michigan Press, 2007), 118; Bon Tempo, "Human Rights."

32. Quoted in Shirley Craig, *Reagan's Revolution: The Untold Story of the Campaign That Started It All* (Nashville, TN: Nelson Current, 2005), 324.

33. Memo, Mike Duval to Dick Cheney, with attached compromise amendment, August 17, 1976, box 28, Michael Raoul-Duval Files, Ford Library; Craig, *Reagan's Revolution*, 304-305, 311, 322-324; William Safire, "Henry's Private Scorn," *NYT*, October 18, 1976, 28; Jonathan Moore and Janet Fraser, eds., *Campaign for President: The Managers Look at '76* (Cambridge, MA: Ballinger Publishing, 1977), 57.

34. Republican Party Platform of 1976. On the South Korea revelations, see Transcript, Secretary of State's Staff Meeting, May 14, 1976, pp. 42-50, Kissinger Memcons.

35. Bon Tempo, "Human Rights."

36. ADA, "The International Human Rights Crisis and the 1976 Presidential Campaign," Resolution Adopted 1976; and Memo from Staff to Foreign and Military Policy Commission, "The International Human Rights Crisis and the 1976 Presidential Campaign (new resolution)," Domestic Policy Staff, Al Stern Files, "Human Rights," box 3, Carter Library.

37. David Ottaway, "The Growing Lobby for Human Rights," *WP*, December 12, 1976, 31.

38. Donald Fraser, Pete McCloskey, Jonathan Bingham, and Millicent Fenwick, "Dear Colleague" letter with enclosed "Human Rights Statement," September 7, 1976, 151.H.4.2.F, Fraser Papers.

39. Fraser to Morgan, March 29, 1976, 151.H.4.2.F, Fraser Papers.

40. Common Cause, "Presidential Candidates' Positions: International Problems and National Security," April 1976, p. 4 of 45, f. 25, box 6, series 5.5, Church Papers.

41. Lecture, "America and Freedom's Future," Kansas State University, January 21, 1976, f. 81, box 11, 3560-3566, Jackson Papers; Peter Milius, "Jackson Hits U.N. 'Hypocrisy,'" *WP*, April 20, 1976, A4.

42. Milius, "Jackson Hits"; "Press Human Rights, Jackson Urges," *LAT*, April 20, 1976, B17; Peter Goldman et al., "The Scoop on Scoop," *Newsweek*, February 16, 1976, 33; Moynihan, *Dangerous Place*, 281.

43. Leslie Gelb, "Presidential Challengers Diverge on Foreign Policy," *NYT*, April 6, 1976, 21.

44. McGovern endorsed Udall in Massachusetts (the only state he carried in 1972) but was so annoyed by a scoffing remark of a Udall aide that he decided to stay on the sidelines for the remainder of the race; Donald W. Carson and James W. Johnson, *Mo: The Life*

*and Times of Morris K. Udall* (Tucson: University of Arizona Press, 2001), 169–170. On Udall, see Barry Farrell, "Morris Udall: Playing by Winners' Rules," *Progressive* 39, no. 12 (1975): 25–30; Ed Johnson, "Udall: A Long Campaign for Recognition," *Congressional Quarterly Weekly Report*, November 22, 1975, 2533–2538; Larry L. King, "The Road to Power in Congress: The Education of Mo Udall—And What It Cost," *Harper's Magazine*, June 1971, 39ff.

45. When Ron Ridenhour sent letters to members of Congress and government officials trying to call attention to the massacre at My Lai, Udall was one of the few recipients to follow up; Carson and Johnson, *Mo*, 89–92.

46. [Don Edwards], "A Tribute to Melina Mercouri," [1994], f. 41, box 41, Edwards Papers; Carson and Johnson, *Mo*, 76.

47. Udall, Letter, December 26, 1973, f. 16, box 123, Udall Papers.

48. Carson and Johnson, *Mo*, 145.

49. James Ayars to Udall, December 1975, f. 5, box 43, Udall Papers.

50. Draft [foreign policy address], untitled [c. 1976], p. 6; and "Congressman Morris K. Udall on Foreign Policy," [n.d.], f. 5, box 43, Udall Papers. See also Johnson, "Udall," 2533–2538.

51. Jessica Tuchman, Outline of Foreign Policy Talk, September 22, 1975, p. 3, f. 5, box 43, Udall Papers.

52. Address, World Affairs Council [c. 1975], p. 6, f. 5, box 43, Udall Papers; Gelb, "Presidential Challengers." On McGovern's use of the same phrase, see his Address Accepting the Presidential Nomination at the Democratic National Convention, July 14, 1972, The American Presidency Project, copyright 2013, www.presidency.ucsb .edu/ws/?pid=25967.

53. Speech, "A New American Foreign Policy—As If the People Mattered," [c. 1976], f. 7, box 23, series 8.1, Church Papers.

54. Notes, March 19, 1976, f. 1, box 161, Theodore White Papers, Harvard University Archives.

55. See, e.g., Foreign Policy Address at Lewis and Clark College, May 12, 1976, f. 5, box 7, series 7.9, Church Papers. See also Brochure, "Frank Church on Foreign Policy," f. 5, box 7, series 7.9, Church Papers; LeRoy Ashby, *Fighting the Odds: The Life of Senator Frank Church* (Pullman: Washington State University Press, 1994), 503–504.

56. Speech, "A New American Foreign Policy."

57. Speech, "Covert Action: Swampland of American Foreign Policy," Pacem in Terris IV, December 4, 1975, p. 7, f. 4, box 8, series 5.5, Church Papers.

58. 117 Cong. Rec. 38252–38258 (October 29, 1971).

59. Notes, "Foreign Policy" [1976], p. 4, f. 17, box 7, series 5.5, Church Papers.

60. Brochure draft, n.d., p. 5, f. 17, box 7, series 5.5, Church Papers.

61. Address at the Democratic National Convention, July 1976, f. 3, box 8, series 5.5, Church Papers.

62. Robert G. Kaufman, *Henry M. Jackson: A Life in Politics* (Seattle: University of Washington Press, 2000), 238, citing an interview with Richard Perle.

63. Martin Schram, *Running for President, 1976: The Carter Campaign* (New York: Stein and Day, 1977), 54.

64. *Presidential Campaign 1976, vol. 1 pt. 1*, 83–84.

65. Witcover, *Marathon*, 144.

66. Charles Mohr, "Carter Credibility Issue: Calley and Vietnam War," *NYT*, May 21, 1976, 54; James Wooten, *Dasher: The Roots and Rising of Jimmy Carter* (London: Weidenfeld and Nicolson, 1978), 350; Kandy Stroud, *How Jimmy Won: The Victory Campaign from Plains to the White House* (New York: William Morrow, 1977), 12; Elizabeth Drew, *American Journal: The Events of 1976* (New York: Random House, 1977), 224.

67. Witcover, *Marathon*, 106, 143.

68. Richard Reeves, *Old Faces of 1976* (New York: Harper and Row, 1976), 14–15.

69. A. Glenn Mower, Jr., *Human Rights and American Foreign Policy: The Carter and Reagan Experiences* (New York: Greenwood Press, 1987), 18–19; Bruze Mazlish and Edwin Diamond, *Jimmy Carter: A Character Portrait* (New York: Simon and Schuster, 1979), 162–164.

70. *Presidential Campaign 1976, vol. 1, pt. 1*, 85.

71. Jimmy Carter, interview by Jack Bass and Walter De Vries, 1974, Southern Oral History Program Collection (#A-0066), Southern Historical Collection, University of North Carolina, Chapel Hill, dc.lib.unc.edu/cdm/compoundobject/collection/sohp /id/8503/rec/7; see also Simon Stevens, "'From the Viewpoint of a Southern Governor': The Carter Administration and Apartheid, 1977–1981," *Diplomatic History* 36, no. 5 (November 2012): 845–848.

72. Moyn, *Last Utopia*, 155.

73. Schram, *Running for President*; Witcover, *Marathon*; Ronald R. Stockton and Frank Whelon Wayman, *A Time of Turmoil: Values and Voting in the 1970s* (East Lansing: Michigan State University Press, 1983); Marlene M. Pomper, ed., *The Election of 1976: Reports and Interpretations* (New York: David McKay, 1977); Richard Reeves, *Convention* (New York: Harcourt Brace Jovanovich, 1977). See also Moore and Fraser, *Campaign for President*. Drew, *American Journal*, mentions human rights only in the context of domestic issues; 275. See also Louis Wiznitze, *Jimmy Carter, ou L'irrésistible ascension* (Lausanne: Favre, 1976), 159–165.

74. Briefing Book (1), Second Debate: Carter of Foreign Policy, October 6, 1976, Gerald R. Ford Presidential Digital Library, www.fordlibrarymuseum.gov/library/document /0010/1554419.pdf. Near the end of the briefing book, there was a brief section titled "Human Rights" that consisted of the B'nai B'rith speech: Briefing Book (2): Second Debate: Carter of Foreign Policy, Gerald R. Ford Presidential Digital Library, www .fordlibrarymuseum.gov/library/document/0010/6283006.pdf.

75. Gaddis Smith, *Morality, Reason, and Power: American Diplomacy in the Carter Years* (New York: Hill and Wang, 1986), 28.

76. Carter, "I See an America . . . ," June 1, 1976, in *Presidential Campaign 1976, vol. 1, pt. 1*, 199.

77. Quoted in Drew, *American Journal*, 41.

78. Jimmy Carter, *Why Not the Best?* (Nashville, TN: Broadman Press, 1975), 123. See also Arthur Schlesinger, "Human Rights and the American Tradition," *Foreign Affairs* 57, no. 3 (1978): 503–526.

79. Drew, *American Journal*, 275. For a cogent argument about the domestic components of Carter's human rights vision, see John Dumbrell, *The Carter Presidency: A*

*Re-evaluation*, 2nd ed. (Manchester, UK: Manchester University Press, 1995), 20, 63–109.

80. Hodding Carter III, "Carter," *WP*, April 26, 1976, A23.

81. Acceptance Speech, Democratic National Convention, in Jimmy Carter, *A Government as Good as Its People* (New York: Simon and Schuster, 1977), 131.

82. Formal Announcement, December 12, 1974, in *Presidential Campaign 1976, vol. 1, pt. 1*, 3; see also 70.

83. "New Approach to Foreign Policy," May 28, 1975, in *Presidential Campaign 1976, vol. 1, pt. 1*, 70.

84. Patrick Anderson, *Electing Jimmy Carter: The Campaign of 1976* (Baton Rouge: Louisiana State University Press, 1994), 41–42; "Carter/Foreign Policy," *CBS Evening News*, June 23, 1976, record number 246567, Vanderbilt News Archive.

85. Democratic Advisory Council of Elected Officials, *Priorities for '76: A Choice for the Democratic Party* (Washington, DC: Democratic National Committee, [1976]), 80, 86, 99.

86. Rowland Evans and Robert Novak, "The Hostility toward Solzhenitsyn," *WP*, September 2, 1976, A15; Democratic Party Platform of 1976, July 12, 1976, The American Presidency Project, copyright 2013, www.presidency.ucsb.edu/ws/?pid =29606; Moynihan, *Dangerous Place*, 282–283.

87. Stephen S. Rosenfeld, "Secretary of State Scoop Jackson?," *WP*, June 18, 1976, A27; "CDM's Foreign Policy Amendments," *Political Observer*, July 1976, p. 2, box 1, Rosenblatt Papers.

88. Penn Kemble, "Platform Goals: Economic Progress and International Human Rights," *Political Observer*, July 1976, p. 2, box 1, Rosenblatt Papers.

89. Daniel P. Moynihan, "The Politics of Human Rights," *Commentary* (August 1977): 22; Moynihan, *Dangerous Place*, 282–283. On Moynihan's sense that CDMers' efforts in the platform-drafting put human rights on the party's agenda, see Weisman, *Daniel Patrick Moynihan*, 392. See also Justin Vaïsse, *Neoconservatism: The Biography of a Movement,* trans. Arthur Goldhammer (Cambridge, MA: Harvard University Press, 2010), 125.

90. Rowland Evans and Robert Novak, "Abzug-Moynihan Fight Centers on National Security Issue," *Boston Globe*, August 26, 1976, 31.

91. Kemble, "Platform Goals," 1.

92. Ben Wattenberg, "Freedom as a Foreign Policy Base," *NYT*, July 13, 1976, 32.

93. Rosenfeld, "Secretary of State"; Moynihan, "Politics," 19; Acceptance speech, Democratic National Convention, in Carter, *Government as Good*, 131. A June speech to the Foreign Policy Association covered human rights in somewhat more detail, but still as a minor issue, not a central element of foreign policy.

94. Campaign brochure quoted in Mary E. Stuckey, *Jimmy Carter, Human Rights, and the National Agenda* (College Station: Texas A&M University Press, 2008), xvii; see also, e.g., "The Democratic Nominee—'If I Were President . . . ,'" *National Journal*, July 17, 1976, 990–991.

95. Kenneth E. Morris, *Jimmy Carter, American Moralist* (Athens: University of Georgia Press, 1996), 3, 76, 102.

96. Peter G. Bourne, *Jimmy Carter: A Comprehensive Biography from Plains to Post-presidency* (New York: Scribner, 1997), 383; "Carter Speaks on Human Rights," *WP*, September 9, 1976, A8.

97. Speech to B'nai B'rith Convention, Washington, D.C., September 8, 1976, in *Presidential Campaign 1976*, vol. 1, pt. 2, 709–714; Charles Mohr, "Carter Suggests That U.S. Foster Rights Overseas," *NYT*, September 9, 1976, 81.

98. Speech Draft/Holbrooke, September 1–2, 1976, box 20, Human Rights 8/76, Stuart Eizenstat Subject Files, 1976 Campaign Committee to Elect Jimmy Carter, Carter Library.

99. Sidney Kraus, ed., *The Great Debates: Carter vs. Ford, 1976* (Bloomington: Indiana University Press, 1979), 476–480, 492.

100. Ibid., 482; John Robert Greene, *The Presidency of Gerald R. Ford* (Lawrence: University Press of Kansas, 1995), 184–186.

101. 123 Cong. Rec. 1071–1073 (January 13, 1977); "Candidates Woo Catholics and Bishops: Carter Visits Notre Dame," *Boston Globe*, October 11, 1976, 1–2.

102. Elizabeth Drew, "A Reporter at Large: Human Rights," *New Yorker*, July 18, 1977, 37.

103. Stephen Rosenfeld, "A Carter Challenge to Ford's Foreign View," *NYT*, June 25, 1976, A27.

104. Quoted in Michael Janeway, "Campaigning: Democratic Convention Notes," *Atlantic Monthly* 238, no. 4 (October 1976): 12.

105. Rally in Portland, Oregon, September 27, 1976, in Carter, *Government as Good*, 196–197.

106. Speech to the Foreign Policy Association, June 23, 1976, in Carter, *Government as Good*, 116.

107. *Presidential Campaign, 1976*, vol. 1, pt. 2, 351.

108. Rally in Portland.

109. Quoted in Dumbrell, *Carter Presidency*, 113.

## Chapter 10: "We Want to Be Proud Again"

1. Jimmy Carter, Inaugural Address, January 20, 1977, The American Presidency Project, copyright 2013, www.presidency.ucsb.edu/ws/?pid=6575. The quotation in the chapter title is from Jimmy Carter, "Our Nation's Past and Future": Address Accepting the Presidential Nomination, Democratic National Convention, July 15, 1976, The American Presidency Project, www.presidency.ucsb.edu/ws/?pid=25953.

2. Elizabeth Drew, "A Reporter at Large: Human Rights," *New Yorker*, July 18, 1977, 36.

3. James Wooten, *Dasher: The Roots and the Rising of Jimmy Carter* (London: Weidenfeld and Nicolson, 1978), 54. Note that Ford's autobiography was titled *A Time to Heal*.

4. "Carter Spins the World," *Time*, August 8, 1977, 18.

5. Daniel Yankelovich, "Farewell to 'President Knows Best'", *Foreign Affairs* 57, no. 3 (1979): 674, 680; Ole Holsti, "Public Opinion on Human Rights in American Foreign Policy," in David P. Forsythe, ed., *The United States and Human Rights: Looking Inward and Outward* (Lincoln: University of Nebraska Press, 2000), 131–174.

6. "Thirsty . . ." in Irving Kristol, "The Human Rights Muddle," *WSJ*, March 20, 1978, 12; "perfect prescription . . ." in Drew, "Reporter," 41.

7. Norman Gelman to Muravchik, January 12, 1978, F. Manifesto [2], box 20, Rosenblatt Papers.

8. Lincoln Bloomfield, "The Carter Human Rights Policy: A Provisional Appraisal," January 11, 1981, 1, 5, 28, Subject File "NSC Accomplishments—Human Rights: 1/81," box 34, Zbigniew Brzezinski Collection, Carter Library.

9. Gaddis Smith argues that if not for the Iranian Revolution, Carter might have won a second term; *Morality, Reason, and Power: American Diplomacy in the Carter Years* (New York: Hill and Wang, 1986), 244.

10. Kristol, "Human Rights Muddle," 12.

11. Leslie Gelb, "Abroad: Moscow May No Longer Get All the Attention," *NYT*, November 7, 1976, E2. Having failed to mention human rights in a long editorial at the end of December, the *Times* nevertheless did not hesitate to claim to have known all along it would be a top theme. Compare "A New Beginning: Foreign Policy," *NYT*, December 30, 1976, 15; "Human Rights: The President's Promise," *NYT*, January 27, 1977, 34.

12. Quoted in Drew, "Reporter," 37.

13. Cyrus Vance, "Overview of Foreign Policy Issues and Positions," [October 1976], in Vance, *Hard Choices: Critical Years in America's Foreign Policy* (New York: Simon and Schuster, 1983), 441–462.

14. Cyrus Vance, Draft for Inaugural Address, [December 31, 1976], Inaugural Speech—Drafts, Notes, and Suggestions (2), Carter Library.

15. See, e.g., Vance, *Hard Choices*, 436.

16. Memo, Zbigniew Brzezinski, Richard N. Gardner, and Henry Owen, "Foreign Policy Priorities, November 3, 1976–May 1, 1977: A Memorandum to the President-Elect," November 3, 1977, Transition: Foreign Policy Priorities, 11/76, container 41, Subject Files, Plains Files, Carter Library.

17. Brzezinski to Anderson, December 14, 1976, p. 2, Inaugural Speech—Drafts, Notes, and Suggestions (2), Carter Library; "Speech Drew on a Variety of Sources," *NYT*, January 21, 1977, 27. See also Zbigniew Brzezinski, *Power and Principle: Memoirs of the National Security Adviser, 1977–1981*, rev. ed. (New York: Farrar, Straus and Giroux, 1985), 125.

18. Second Draft, n.d., p. 10, Inaugural Speech Drafts—Notes and Suggestions (1), Office of the Staff Secretary, Carter Library.

19. Jimmy Carter, Inaugural Address, 1977; various drafts in Inaugural Speech Drafts—Notes and Suggestions (1), Office of the Staff Secretary, Carter Library.

20. Jimmy Carter, "United States Foreign Policy Remarks to People of Other Nations on Assuming Office," January 20, 1977, The American Presidency Project, copyright 2013, www.presidency.ucsb.edu/ws/?pid=7144.

21. Betty Glad, *An Outsider in the White House: Jimmy Carter, His Advisors, and the Making of American Foreign Policy* (Ithaca, NY: Cornell University Press, 2009), 2, 29–40.

22. Zbigniew Brzezinski, *Between Two Ages: America's Role in the Technetronic Era* (New York: Viking, 1970), 18–22, 66, 272.

23. Carl Bon Tempo, "From the Center-Right: Freedom House and Human Rights in the 1970s and 1980s," in Akira Iriye, Petra Goedde, and William I. Hitchcock, eds., *The Human Rights Revolution: An International History* (New York: Oxford University Press, 2012), 230.

24. Joshua Muravchik, interview by author, January 30, 2013. Brzezinski's name was on what appears to be a draft list of suggested appointments the CDM provided to the Carter team. See "List of CDM recommendations for appointment in the Carter administration (1976)," Companion Website to Justin Vaïsse, *Neoconservativism: The Biography of a Movement,* last modified August 4, 2009, neoconservatism.vaisse .net/doku.php?id=list_of_cdm_recommendations_for_carter_nominations_1976. Muravchik, who shepherded the list to CDMers for consultation, does not recall Brzezinski's name on any drafts and says it would not have been on a final version. On the list, see also Ben J. Wattenberg, *Fighting Words: A Tale of How Liberals Created Neo-conservatism* (New York: St. Martin's Press, 2008), 164–165; Jay Winik, *On the Brink: The Dramatic, Behind-the-Scenes Saga of the Reagan Era and the Men and Women Who Won the Cold War* (New York: Simon and Schuster, 1996), 83–85; Joshua Muravchik, *The Uncertain Crusade: Jimmy Carter and the Dilemmas of Human Rights Policy* (Lanham, MD: Hamilton Press, 1986), 6–9.

25. Brzezinski, *Power and Principle,* 124–129; Bloomfield, " Carter Human Rights Policy," 12.

26. Drew, "Reporter"; Peter G. Bourne, *Jimmy Carter: A Comprehensive Biography from Plains to Post-presidency* (New York: Scribner, 1997), 384.

27. Quoted in Drew, "Reporter," 41.

28. Jimmy Carter, *Keeping Faith: Memoirs of a President* (New York: Bantam Books, 1982),149.

29. Ibid., 148.

30. Caddell to Carter, "Thoughts for Inaugural Speech," January 5, 1977, Inaugural Speech Drafts—Notes, and Suggestions [2], Office of the Staff Secretary, Carter Library.

31. Quoted in Drew, "Reporter," 36.

32. Sandy Vogelgesang, *American Dream, Global Nightmare: The Dilemma of U.S. Human Rights Policy* (New York: W. W. Norton, 1980), 184.

33. Cyrus Vance, "Human Rights and Foreign Policy," *Bulletin of the Department of State* 76 (1977): 505–508.

34. Quoted in Muravchik, *Uncertain Crusade,* 99.

35. Presidential Directive/NSC-30, February 17, 1978, "Human Rights," Jimmy Carter Library, last modified October 19, 2010, www.jimmycarterlibrary.gov/documents /pddirectives/pd30.pdf. On the bureaucratic delays, see Bloomfield, "Carter Human Rights Policy," 8.

36. Vance, "Human Rights and Foreign Policy," 505–508.

37. The document is summarized in Brzezinski, *Power and Principle,* 53–55.

38. Griffin Smith to Jim Fallows, n.d. [1977], Notre Dame Speech May 22, 1977 [2], Records of the Speechwriter's Office, Carter Library.

39. Bernard Gwertzman, "Carter Urges U.N. to Step Up Efforts for Human Rights," *NYT,* March 18, 1977, 1.

40. John Osborne, "Carter's New World," *New Republic,* June 4, 1977, 8–11; Jimmy Carter, Commencement Address at the University of Notre Dame, May 22, 1977, The American Presidency Project, copyright 2013, www.presidency.ucsb.edu/ws/?pid=7552.

41. Carter, Commencement Address at Notre Dame; Arthur Herman, "The Return of Carterism?," *Commentary* (January 2009): 19.

42. Daniel Patrick Moynihan, "A New American Foreign Policy," *New Republic,* February 9, 1980, 17–21.

43. Brzezinski, *Power and Principle*; "Daring to Talk about Human Rights," *Time,* February 7, 1977, 48.

44. Anatoly Dobrynin, *In Confidence: Moscow's Ambassador to America's Six Cold War Presidents* (New York: Random House, 1995), 390.

45. Powell to Carter, February 21, 1977, NSA EBB 291.

46. Bloomfield, "Carter Human Rights Policy," 22.

47. Rowland Evans and Robert Novak, "Goal of Resurrected Coalition Will Be to Influence Carter," *Boston Globe,* July 11, 1977, 19; "Democratic Group Backs Carter on Human Rights," *NYT,* May 15, 1977, 25; CDM Press Release, May 14, 1977, quoted in Justin Vaïsse, *Neoconservatism: The Biography of a Movement,* trans. Arthur Goldhammer (Cambridge, MA: Harvard University Press, 2010), 130.

48. Muravchik, *Uncertain Crusade,* 9.

49. Bartlett C. Jones, *Flawed Triumphs: Andy Young at the United Nations* (Lanham, MD: University Press of America, 1996), 36, 121.

50. Ronald Reagan, "Argentina's View on Human Rights," *Miami News,* October 20, 1978, 13.

51. Vaïsse, *Neoconservatism,* 133.

52. Penn Kemble, Draft Statement, "Launching the 'Liberty Party,'" [August 1977], p. 3, f. Manifesto [1], box 20, Rosenblatt Papers.

53. 5th Draft, "Beyond the Cold War, Beyond Détente: Toward a Foreign Policy of Human Rights," pp. 1, 3–4, 8–10, f. Manifesto [2], box 20, Rosenblatt Papers.

54. Memo, Paul B. Henze to Brzezinski, "Conversation with Dick Perle re Human Rights Foundation, Strategic Issues, Etc.," June 15, 1978, 274124-i1-4, DDRS.

55. Kiron Skinner, Serhiy Kudelia, Bruce Bueno de Mesquita, and Condoleezza Rice, *The Strategy of Campaigning: Lessons from Ronald Reagan and Boris Yeltsin* (Ann Arbor: University of Michigan Press, 2007), 149.

56. Vaïsse, *Neoconservatism,* 133–134.

57. Glad, *Outsider,* 239; Karen Elliott House, "U.S. Officials Worry over Inconsistencies in Human-Rights Plan," *WSJ,* May 11, 1978, 1.

58. A useful, brief overview of human rights policy is in Burton I. Kaufman and Scott Kaufman, *The Presidency of James Earl Carter Jr.,* 2nd ed. (Lawrence: University of Kansas Press, 2006), 43–61. On South Africa see Simon Stevens, "'From the Viewpoint of a Southern Governor': The Carter Administration and Apartheid, 1977–1981," *Diplomatic History* 36, no. 5 (November 2012): 843–880.

59. Bradley R. Simpson, "Denying the 'First Right': The United States, Indonesia, and the Ranking of Human Rights by the Carter Administration," *International History Review* 31, no. 4 (December 2009): 798–826.

60. Memo, Lake to Vance, "The Human Rights Policy: An Interim Assessment," January 20, 1978, 243764-ii-25, DDRS.

61. *Institute for Human Rights and Freedom: Hearing Before the Comm. on Foreign Relations, June 29, 1978,* 95th Cong. 21-25 (1978).

62. Memo, Brzezinski to Carter, "Human Rights Foundation," January 24, 1978, 245306-ii-4; Brzezinski to Carter, December 3, 1977, 243986-ii-1, DDRS; Bloomfield, "Carter Human Rights Policy," 25-26.

63. Memo, Paul B. Henze to Brzezinski, "Conversation with Dick Perle re Human Rights Foundation, Strategic Issues, Etc.," June 15, 1978, 274124-ii-4, DDRS. See also Hauke Hartman, "US Human Rights Policy under Carter and Reagan, 1977-1981," *Human Rights Quarterly* 23 (2001): 414-415.

64. See, e.g., Scott Kaufman, *Plans Unraveled: The Foreign Policy of the Carter Administration* (DeKalb: Northern Illinois University Press, 2008), 240.

65. Richard Holbrooke, "A Sense of Drift, A Time for Calm," *Foreign Policy* 23 (Summer 1976): 98-99; George Packer, "The Last Mission: Richard Holbrooke's Plan to Avoid the Mistakes of Vietnam in Afghanistan," *New Yorker*, September 28, 2009, copyright 2013, www.newyorker.com/reporting/2009/09/28/090928fa_fact_packer.

66. Roger Cohen, "Taming the Bullies of Bosnia," *NYT Magazine*, December 17, 1995, 58.

67. Quoted in John Kelly Damico, "From Civil Rights to Human Rights: The Career of Patricia M. Derian" (Ph.D. diss., Mississippi State University, 1999), 90; "On-the-Job Human Rightist," *WP*, August 11, 1977, B1.

68. John Dumbrell, *The Carter Presidency: A Re-evaluation*, 2nd ed. (Manchester, UK: Manchester University Press, 1995), 182.

69. Quoted in "A Farewell to Derian," *WP*, January 15, 1981, D3.

70. "Human Rights and Mrs. Derian," *NYT*, May 31, 1980, 16.

71. Transcript, Briefing by Vance, Brzezinski, Derian, and Wexler, December 6, 1978, 149.C.12.4F, Fraser Papers.

72. Glad, *Outsider*, 245.

73. Bourne, *Jimmy Carter*, 383-384.

74. *Reconciling Human Rights and U.S. Security Interests in Asia: Hearings Before the Subcomm. on Asian and Pacific Affairs and on Human Rights and International Organizations of the Comm. on Foreign Affairs, House of Representatives*, 97th Cong. 3-5, 14, 480 (1983).

75. Quoted in Derek Chollet and Samantha Power, eds., *The Unquiet American: Richard Holbrooke in the World* (New York: PublicAffairs, 2011), 125.

76. Quoted in Cohen, "Taming the Bullies."

77. John Salzberg, interview by author, November 8, 2008; Raymond Bonner, *Waltzing with a Dictator: The Marcoses and the Making of American Policy* (New York: Random House, 1987), 187-188.

78. Glad, *Outsider*, 242.

79. Bloomfield, "Carter Human Rights Policy," 20-21; Kathryn Sikkink, *Mixed Signals: U.S. Human Rights Policy and Latin America* (Ithaca, NY: Cornell University Press, 2004), 130-137; William Michael Schmidli, "Institutionalizing Human Rights in U.S.

Foreign Policy: U.S.-Argentine Relations, 1976–1980," *Diplomatic History* 35, no. 2 (April 2011): 351–377.

80. See especially Daniel C. Thomas, *The Helsinki Effect: International Norms, Human Rights, and the Demise of Communism* (Princeton, NJ: Princeton University Press, 2001).

81. Ibid., 27–53; The Final Act of the Conference on Security and Cooperation in Europe, August 1, 1975, 14 I.L.M. 1292 (Helsinki Declaration), available at University of Minnesota Human Rights Library last updated December 24, 2012, www1.umn.edu /humanrts/osce/basics/finact75.htm.

82. Meeting with Foreign Minister Gromyko, September 20, 1974, 15, Kissinger-Scowcroft West Wing Office File: USSR–Gromyko File (19), Office of the Assistant to the President for National Security Affairs, Henry Kissinger and Brent Scowcroft: Files (1972) 1974-77, Temporary Parallel File, Ford Library. See also Jussi Hanhimäki, "'They Can Write It in Swahili': Kissinger, the Soviets, and the Helsinki Accords, 1973-5," *Journal of Transatlantic Studies* 1, no. 1 (2003): 37–38, 55.

83. Richard Davy, "Helsinki Myths: Setting the Record Straight on the Final Act of the CSCE, 1975," *Cold War History* 9, no. 1 (2009), 1–22; Svetlana Savranskaya, "Unintended Consequences: Soviet Interests, Expectations and Reactions to the Helsinki Final Act," in Oliver Bange and Gottfried Niedhart, eds., *Helsinki 1975 and the Transformation of Europe* (New York: Berghahn, 2008), 176, 181; Brzezinski quoted in G. S. Ostapenko, *Bor'ba SSSR v OON za sotsial'no-ekonomicheskie prava cheloveka, 1945-1977 gg.* (Moscow: Nauka, 1981), 5–6.

84. Aryeh Neier, *Taking Liberties: Four Decades in the Struggle for Rights* (New York: PublicAffairs, 2003), 154.

85. Jeri Laber, *The Courage of Strangers: Coming of Age with the Human Rights Movement* (New York: PublicAffairs, 2002), 98.

86. See, e.g., Helen Sen to Executive Committee, September 8, 1980, I.1.67, HRW: Helsinki Watch Records.

87. Claude E. Welch, Jr., "Amnesty International and Human Rights Watch: A Comparison," in Claude E. Welch, Jr., ed., *NGOs and Human Rights: Promise and Performance* (Philadelphia: University of Pennsylvania Press, 2001), 94–95.

88. Amy Schapiro, *Millicent Fenwick: Her Way* (New Brunswick, NJ: Rutgers University Press, 2003), 172–176; Sarah B. Snyder, *Human Rights Activism and the End of the Cold War: A Transnational History of the Helsinki Network* (Cambridge: Cambridge University Press, 2011), 46–51.

89. *Reconciling Human Rights*, 59, 11.

90. Helmut Schmidt, *Men and Powers: A Political Retrospective* (New York: Random House, 1989), 182; Smith, *Morality, Reason*, 247.

91. Bloomfield to Brzezinski, Classified Annex, January 16, 1981, Subject File "NSC Accomplishments—Human Rights: 1/81," box 34, Zbigniew Brzezinski Collection, Carter Library.

92. Bloomfield, "Carter Human Rights Policy," 10; David P. Forsythe, *Human Rights and World Politics* (Lincoln: University of Nebraska Press, 1983), 182.

93. Irving Kristol, "Foreign Policy: End of an Era," *Wall Street Journal*, January 18, 1979, 16.

94. Jeane Kirkpatrick, "Dictatorships and Double Standards," *Commentary* (November 1979), www.commentarymagazine.com/article/dictatorships-double-standards/.

95. Smith, *Morality, Reason*, 242.

96. Jimmy Carter, interview with Stephen H. Hochman, et al., November 29, 1982, in Don Richardson, ed., *Conversations with Carter* (Boulder, CO: Lynne Rienner, 1998), 252.

97. Quoted in Don Irwin, "U.S. Owes No Debt to Hanoi, Carter Says," *LAT*, March 25, 1977, B1.

98. Yankelovich, "Farewell," 680; Rowland Evans and Robert Novak, "Brady Tyson— Chapter II," *WP*, 6 May 1977, A21; Jimmy Carter, Yazoo City, Mississippi, Remarks and a Question-and-Answer Session at a Public Meeting, July 21, 1977, The American Presidency Project, www.presidency.ucsb.edu/ws/?pid=7854 (note that in the same speech he said the United States was "trying to look good in the eyes of the world"); "The Push for Human Rights," *Newsweek*, June 20, 1977, 46.

## Conclusion: Universal Human Rights in American Foreign Policy

1. "Human Rights and U.S. Foreign Policy," Address before the ABA International Law Section and the American Foreign Law Association, August 10, 1977, 151.H.4.2F, Fraser Papers.

2. The Netherlands, which adopted a human rights stance in foreign policy in 1973, also made human rights a factor in cutoffs of development aid. J. J. C. Voorhoeve, *Peace, Profits and Principles: A Study of Dutch Foreign Policy* (The Hague: M. Nijhoff, 1979), 267-268.

3. Donald M. Fraser, "Political Development: The Missing Dimension of U.S. Policy toward Developing Nations," Speech at the Cooperative Forum, November 4, 1965, p. 2, quoted in Elizabeth Fletcher Crook, "Political Development as a Program Objective of U.S. Foreign Assistance: Title IX of the 1966 Foreign Assistance Act" (Ph.D. diss., Tufts University, 1970), 84.

4. Compare Nils Gilman, *Mandarins of the Future: Modernization Theory in Cold War America* (Baltimore: Johns Hopkins University Press, 2003), 22, 244-249, 273-276.

5. See, for example, James Peck, *Ideal Illusions: How the U.S. Government Co-Opted Human Rights* (New York: Henry Holt, 2010).

6. Undated notes, [c. Nov 1976], f. 13, box 161, Theodore White Papers, Harvard University Archives.

7. See also Stephen Holmes, "War of the Liberals," *Nation*, November 14, 2005, 29-40.

8. Rowland Evans and Robert Novak, "Making Reagan 'Fail-Safe,'" *WP*, August 22, 1970, A15.

9. "Excerpts from Haig's Remarks at First News Conference as Secretary of State," *NYT*, January 29, 1981, A10; the torture remark was reportedly offered in congressional testimony but not included in the printed text; Lister to Jack B. Kubisch, "Lefever and Roett Testify before House Subcommittee on Inter-American Affairs," August 7, 1974, box 67, Unprocessed Files, Lister Papers.

10. "Excerpts from State Department Memo on Human Rights," *NYT*, November 5, 1981, A10.

11. "For the Record," *WP*, June 4, 1981, A18.

12. Ronald Reagan, Address to Members of the British Parliament, June 8, 1982, Miller Center of Public Affairs, University of Virginia, copyright 2013, millercenter.org /president/speeches/detail/3408. Notably, though, it was during the Reagan years that the United States signed the UN's Convention against Torture and ratified the 1948 UN Convention on Genocide.

13. Jeane Kirkpatrick, "Dictatorships and Double Standards," *Commentary* (November 1979), www.commentarymagazine.com/article/dictatorships-double-standards/.

14. Aryeh Neier, *The International Human Rights Movement: A History* (Princeton, NJ: Princeton University Press, 2012), 204–232.

15. Draft 2, "Human Rights and American Foreign Policy: First Principles," May 21, 1981, box 1, Subject HU Human Rights, White House Office Records Management, Ronald Reagan Presidential Library, Simi Valley, California.

16. George H. W. Bush, "Address before a Joint Session of the Congress on the End of the Gulf War," March 6, 1991, Miller Center of Public Affairs, University of Virginia, copyright 2013, millercenter.org/president/speeches/detail/3430.

17. On the West's vacillations over human rights during the breakup of Yugoslavia, see Peter Russell, "Human Rights, Western Foreign Policy, and the Dissolution of Yugoslavia, 1989–1994" (Ph.D. diss., University of Melbourne, 2010).

18. Presidential Review Memorandum/NSC-28, "Human Rights," July 7, 1977, 30, Jimmy Carter Library, last modified October 19, 2010, www.jimmycarterlibrary.gov /documents/prmemorandums/prm28.pdf

19. See, e.g., Paul Kramer, "The Water Cure," *New Yorker*, February 25, 2008, copyright 2013, www.newyorker.com/reporting/2008/02/25/080225fa_fact_kramer.

20. Republican Party Platform of 1900, June 19, 1900, The American Presidency Project, www.presidency.ucsb.edu/ws/index.php?pid=29630. Such rhetoric was common; see, e.g., "Muddying the Issues," *Atlanta Constitution*, January 12, 1899, 4.

21. Robert Kagan, *Dangerous Nation* (New York: Knopf, 2006), 390–391.

22. "In a Heroic Contest," *Chicago Daily Tribune*, March 1, 1898, 7; "The American Policy," *Atlanta Constitution*, September 6, 1899; "Our Duty Becoming Clearer," *LAT*, March 6, 1898, 2; Charles S. Olcott, *The Life of William McKinley*, vol. 2 (Boston: Houghton Mifflin, 1916), 290; 31 Cong. Rec. 40 (1897); "Absent Democrats Called In," *Charlotte Daily Observer*, February 24, 1900, 1. On how liberty, democracy, and notions of rights figured in the imperialism debate, see Fabian Hilfrich, *Debating American Exceptionalism: Empire and Democracy in the Wake of the Spanish-American War* (New York: Palgrave Macmillan, 2012), 13–38.

23. 31 Cong. Rec. 3255 (1898).

24. 35 Cong. Rec. 1575 (1902).

25. 27 Cong. Rec. 326 (1895).

26. 32 Cong. Rec. 503 (1899).

27. Geo. S. Boutwell, *The Crisis of the Republic* (Boston: Dana Estes, 1900), 196–198, 208; Thomas H. Brown, *George Sewall Boutwell: Human Rights Advocate* (Groton, MA: Groton Historical Society, 1989), 118.

28. Kagan, *Dangerous Nation*, 357–416, esp. 394, 415–416. The book goes up only to the outbreak of war; a sequel is in the works.

# Bibliographical Essay

The great international historian Ernest May used to say that in writing his history of the 1898 Spanish-American War, he had read every relevant document in the archives and newspapers of five countries. Such thoroughness is impossible for historians of more recent decades, who must instead seek ways not to drown in a flood of paper (and pdfs). The documentary abundance for U.S. history in the 1970s is especially overwhelming, for U.S. government declassification has now moved nearly to the end of the decade, and the passage of time has ensured that the store of personal papers of its major figures is now enormous, even as many participants are still around to share their recollections.

This book tapped the archival cornucopia by drawing on dozens of personal collections, five presidential libraries, State Department and congressional archives, the records of assorted organizations, and a variety of smaller collections. The papers of presidential candidates and members of Congress who played both major and minor roles in the story were essential: James Abourezk (University of South Dakota), Edward William Brooke (Library of Congress), Frank Church (Boise State University), Richard Clark (University of Iowa), Alan Cranston (Bancroft Library, University of California, Berkeley), Don Edwards (San Jose State University), Donald Fraser (Minnesota Historical Society), Henry M. Jackson (University of Washington), George McGovern

(Princeton University), Sargent Shriver (John F. Kennedy Library), Stuart Symington (University of Missouri), and Morris Udall (University of Arizona). At the time of writing, the papers of Edward Kennedy were still being processed at the John F. Kennedy Library. Future scholars may find in them reason to assign him a greater role in human rights history than I have given him here.

The archives of organizations and the personal papers of journalists, scholars, former officials, and human rights activists filled in other parts of the story. The papers of William R. Kintner and Ernest Lefever at the Hoover Institution Archives, Averell Harriman and Daniel Patrick Moynihan at the Library of Congress, George Lister at the University of Texas at Austin, Dorothy Schiff at the New York Public Library, and Theodore White at the Harvard University Archives helped flesh out aspects of the 1960s and 1970s. The history of Amnesty International's U.S. section is documented in the International Secretariat Archives at the International Institute for Social History in Amsterdam and the AI USA collection at Columbia University. The years before 1974, however, are relatively sparsely covered in these collections. To get at the period between 1965 to 1974 in the United States, it helps to turn to the personal papers of Francis Biddle at Georgetown and Elise G. Becket at the Hoover Institution Archives, and—with much greater thoroughness—the papers of Ivan Morris at Columbia, William F. Buckley Jr. at Yale, and Frances Grant at Rutgers. Grant's papers also cover Freedom House activities in the early and mid-1970s. On the activities of AI USA's vigorous West Coast branch, the papers of Ginetta Sagan at the Hoover Institution are rich and voluminous. The roles of Michael Straight and Mark Benenson, two crucial figures in AI USA's early history, deserve further exploration.

Helsinki Watch records are held in the collection of its successor, Human Rights Watch, at Columbia. Records relating to other groups and campaigns include the Ad Hoc Committee on the Human Rights and Genocide Treaties at the Tamiment Library of New York University, the Greek Junta Papers at the University of Michigan, the International League for Human Rights at the New York Public Library, and the Liberation News Archive at Temple University. The latter holds publications from many of the country-specific human rights groups whose activities deserve further exploration. The activities of the Coalition for a Democratic Majority are documented in the Peter Rosenblatt papers at the Lyndon Baines Johnson Library. I failed to find good materials on the liberal side of the 1976 Democratic Party platform foreign policy debates in the National Archives' Democratic National Committee materials and in the papers of participants like Bella Abzug (held at Columbia). (Future researchers will undoubtedly step in to flesh out the role of religious and peace groups, many of which are richly documented in the Swarthmore College Peace Collection.)

Participants who shared their recollections with me in interviews or by email include James Abourezk, Amelia Augustus, LuVerne Conway, Donald Fraser, Rita Hauser, David Hawk, Maryanne Lyons Kendall, Jessica Tuchman Mathews, Joshua Muravchik, James Pyrros, Joshua Rubenstein, and John Salzberg. Charles Horner and Bill Zimmerman responded with answers to small questions of fact. From James Abourezk to Bill Zimmerman, many of the names in the index to this book have produced memoirs. Don Fraser, David Hawk, and Ginetta Sagan are lamentable exceptions.

Although excellent work has been done on American engagement with international human rights in the 1940s—see in particular Elizabeth Borgwardt's *A New Deal for the World: America's Vision for Human Rights* (Cambridge, MA: Harvard University Press, 2006)—there is to my knowledge little scholarship on changing definitions and usage of human rights and rights-related talk in the long span of U.S. history. The literature on the civil rights movement has been attuned to the international interests and connections of some sections of the movement, but as yet has not paid much attention to rhetoric about human rights as distinct from civil rights. The contemporary fascination with human rights may change that. For now, Carol Anderson, *Eyes off the Prize: The United Nations and the African American Struggle for Human Rights, 1944–1955* (New York: Cambridge University Press, 2003), and Thomas F. Jackson, *From Civil Rights to Human Rights: Martin Luther King, Jr., and the Struggle for Economic Justice* (Philadelphia: University of Pennsylvania Press, 2007), are among the best places to start.

Studies of the anti–Vietnam War movement almost never mention human rights, even if they often discuss issues that now fall under that rubric. In general, historians have attended far less to why people opposed the war than to how they did it, charting in great detail the loud and colorful protest actions and strategies and devoting considerably less space to parsing the question of motives. Charles DeBenedetti, *An American Ordeal: The Antiwar Movement of the Vietnam War* (Syracuse, NY: Syracuse University Press, 1990), remains the classic study. An eye-opening intellectual history of legal antiwar reasoning is

Samuel Moyn's "From Antiwar Politics to Antitorture Politics," in Lawrence Douglas and Austin Sarat, eds., *Law and War* (Stanford, CA: Stanford University Press, forthcoming). My reading of McGovern's rhetoric of guilt owes much to Bruce Miroff's excellent *The Liberals' Moment: The McGovern Insurgency and the Identity Crisis of the Democratic Party* (Lawrence: University Press of Kansas, 2007). In the large literature on modernization and development, see Nils Gilman, *Mandarins of the Future: Modernization Theory in Cold War America* (Baltimore: Johns Hopkins University Press, 2003), and Gilbert Rist, *The History of Development: From Western Origins to Global Faith* (London: Zed, 1997).

The seventies are now in vogue in American historical scholarship. Among the broad surveys, Thomas Borstelmann's *The 1970s: A New Global History from Civil Rights to Economic Inequality* (Princeton, NJ: Princeton University Press, 2012) offers a new perspective; on the United States, see Bruce J. Shulman, *The Seventies: The Great Shift in American Culture, Society, and Politics* (New York: Free Press, 2001). The essays in Niall Ferguson et al., eds, *The Shock of the Global: The 1970s in Perspective* (Cambridge, MA: Harvard University Press, 2010) point to a new reading of the 1970s. Of the many studies that touch on Soviet Jewish emigration and the Jackson-Vanik amendment, Paula Stern, *Water's Edge: Domestic Politics and the Making of American Foreign Policy* (Westport, CT: Greenwood Press, 1979), remains the best legislative history. Gail Beckerman's recent study highlights transnational connections: *When They Come for Us We'll Be Gone: The Epic Struggle to Save Soviet Jewry* (Boston: Houghton Mifflin Harcourt, 2010), but on Beckerman's assessment of Jackson-Vanik's results, see the review by Benjamin Nathans, "The Wild Desire to Leave," *Nation*, November 29, 2010, 34–36. There is now a cottage industry devoted to the study of neoconservatism and its roots. Justin Vaïsse's *Neoconservatism: The Biography of a Movement*, trans. Arthur Goldhammer (Cambridge, MA: Harvard University Press, 2010) provides the deepest coverage of the movement's 1970s turn to foreign relations and human rights.

Donald Fraser has not been ignored by scholars: the role of his subcommittee hearings in laying the groundwork for liberal human rights legislation is mentioned in probably hundreds of books and articles. Yet as far as I know, no one has ever probed why Fraser held those hearings or explored in detail his subsequent trajectory, and his 1960s political development efforts have faded from memory. The lack of sustained attention to Fraser, James Abourezk, and Tom Harkin presents a sharp contrast to the many detailed studies of the Jackson-Vanik amendment's origins and legislative history. Henry Jackson was a presidential candidate, a polarizing national politician, and a heroic figure to a significant group of intellectuals, whereas the members of Congress who sparked the liberal human rights impulse inspired neither great devotion nor great antipathy—nor did they go on to national heights. To understand their roles, the large body of work that David P. Forsythe has produced since the 1970s is a good starting point, including *Human Rights and U.S. Foreign Policy: Congress Reconsidered* (Gainesville University Presses of Florida, 1988) and *Human Rights and World Politics* (Lincoln: University of Nebraska Press, 1983). Sandy Vogelgesang, who served on the State Department's Policy Planning Staff in the 1970s, wrote a history with insider depth in *American Dream, Global Nightmare: The Dilemma of U.S. Human Rights Policy* (New York: W. W. Norton, 1980). James N. Green's study of U.S. activism on Brazil is the first to plumb grassroots American human rights activism in these years: *"We Cannot Remain Silent": Opposition to the Brazilian Military Dictatorship in the United States* (Durham, NC: Duke University Press, 2010).

Lars Schoultz, *Human Rights and United States Policy toward Latin America* (Princeton, NJ: Princeton University Press, 1981), remains the most thorough account of U.S. human rights policies and organizations in the 1970s, with an intimate knowledge born of close, firsthand observations and interviews that still renders it invaluable. Because Latin America was a crucial focus in these years, his book indirectly provides an accounting of the rise of human rights more generally. More recently, Kathryn Sikkink, *Mixed Signals: U.S. Human Rights Policy and Latin America* (Ithaca, NY: Cornell University Press, 2004), covers the longer term, from Nixon to Clinton. Also important is David F. Schmitz, *The United States and Right-Wing Dictatorships, 1965–1989* (New York: Cambridge University Press, 2006).

Almost nothing has been written on Amnesty's first decade in the United States. The best account remains Kenneth Cmiel, "The Emergence of Human Rights Politics in the United States," *Journal of American History* 86 (1999): 1231–1250. Still useful are classic articles by David Weissbrodt (who worked for Amnesty USA), "The Role of International Non-Governmental Organizations in the Implementation of Human Rights," *Texas International Law Journal* 12 (1977): 293–320; and cofounders of the Human Rights Internet, Laurie Wiseberg and Harry M. Scoble, "Human Rights and Amnesty International," *Annals of the American Academy of Political and Social Science* 413 (May 1974): 11–26. William Korey's *NGOs and the Universal Declaration of Human Rights: A Curious Grapevine* (New York: St. Martin's Press, 1998) is best read as a kind of official history of human rights NGOs written by a participant. Lowell W. Livezey, *Nongovernmental Organizations and the Ideas of Human Rights* (Princeton, NJ: Center of International Studies, Princeton University, 1988) remains valuable. On Amnesty the international organization (rather than its U.S. branch), see Stephen Hopgood, *Keepers of the Flame: Understanding Amnesty International* (Ithaca, NY: Cornell University Press, 2006), and Ann Marie Clark, *Diplomacy of Conscience: Amnesty International and Changing Human Rights Norms* (Princeton, NJ: Princeton University Press, 2001).

The definitive survey of Carter's human rights policy remains to be written, though there is a small mountain of articles, dissertations, and books that cover aspects of it. Joshua Muravchik, a member of the Coalition for a Democratic Majority and neoconservative critic of Carter, wrote a critique that is in itself a fascinating historical document: *The Uncertain Crusade: Jimmy Carter and the Dilemmas of Human Rights Policy* (Lanham, MD: Hamilton Press, 1986). John Dumbrell presents a more sympathetic view in *The Carter Presidency: A Re-evaluation*, 2nd ed. (Manchester, UK: Manchester University Press, 1995); most up-to-date is Scott Kaufman, *Plans Unraveled: The Foreign Policy of the Carter Administration* (DeKalb: Northern Illinois University Press, 2008). The works of David Forsythe, mentioned above, include good coverage of the Carter administration. The rapidly growing literature on the Helsinki Accords and their aftermath is testament to their putative role in ending the Cold War; see Daniel C. Thomas, *The Helsinki Effect: International Norms, Human Rights, and the Demise of Communism* (Princeton, NJ: Princeton University Press, 2001), and Sarah B. Snyder, *Human Rights Activism and the End of the Cold War: A Transnational History of the Helsinki Network* (Cambridge: Cambridge University Press, 2011).

For a broad history of human rights, Samuel Moyn's powerfully argued *The Last Utopia* (Cambridge, MA: Harvard University Press, 2010), which takes issue with much of the received wisdom in the field, is essential reading. It landed on top of a small heap of human rights histories with the force of a grenade and has provoked debates that are reshaping the landscape in ways that are still settling out. His superb chapter on the 1970s makes a case for the decade as the moment when human rights took off—"seemingly from nowhere"—as a consequence of the failures of earlier idealistic internationalisms. (A sequel is in the works.) For an introduction to one of the key fault lines in the debates over human rights history, read Moyn's "Spectacular Wrongs," *Nation*, September 24, 2008, 30–40, in conjunction with Gary J. Bass, "The Old New Thing," *New Republic*, November 11, 2010, 35–39, and Philip Alston, "Does the Past Matter? On the Origins of Human Rights," *Harvard Law Review* 126 (2013): 2043–2081.

Against more hagiographic accounts of the rise of human rights, Kirsten Sellars, *The Rise and Rise of Human Rights* (Phoenix Mill, UK: Sutton, 2002), and James Peck, *Ideal Illusions: How the U.S. Government Co-opted Human Rights* (New York: Henry Holt, 2010), both emphasize the instrumental domestic roots of human rights as a U.S. foreign policy paradigm.

The beginning of a wave of new scholarship on recent human rights history can be discerned in three major collections: Stefan-Ludwig Hoffmann, ed., *Human Rights in the Twentieth Century* (New York: Cambridge University Press, 2011); Akira Iriye, Petra Goedde, and William I. Hitchcock, eds., *The Human Rights Revolution: An International History* (New York: Oxford University Press, 2012); and Jan Eckel and Samuel Moyn, eds., *The Breakthrough: Human Rights in the 1970s* (Philadelphia: University of Pennsylvania Press, forthcoming). Jan Eckel's sweeping, richly nuanced, and deeply researched forthcoming study promises to be pathbreaking; it is previewed in "Utopie der Moral, Kalkül der Macht: Menschenrechte in der globalen Politik seit 1945," *Archiv für Sozialgeschichte* 49 (2009): 437–484.

Much of the best scholarship on human rights in the 1970s and beyond is now in the making. In the near future, new books by Mark Bradley, Jan Eckel, Patrick Kelly, Ben Nathans, Joe Renouard, Daniel Sargent, Lynsay Skiba, William Schmidli, Brad Simpson, Sarah Snyder, Simon Stevens, and Vanessa Walker, among others, promise to make human rights history one of the discipline's most exciting fields of study.

# Acknowledgments

The Internet has revolutionized the process of historical research, making it possible to combine traditional legwork in one's local libraries (when they still exist as places that house books) with access to a dizzying quantity of documents, databases, finding aids, and other online sources just by sitting at a computer. For most historians, however, it remains crucial to go places, and travel has been essential to me as an international historian working in Australia. So I begin by thanking the providers of the funds that made so much of my research possible. The Faculty of Arts and the University of Melbourne were both extraordinarily generous in providing early career funding to sustain several lines of research, of which this book is the first (but not the last!) major end product. An Australian Research Council Discovery Project award for a project on antitorture campaigns generated synergies with this project that allowed me to expand my ambitions for this book. I am particularly grateful to Joy Damousi, who as head of my unit created conducive conditions for research during a crucial early year and helped me secure a University of Melbourne Career Interruptions grant. A grant from the U.S. Studies Centre in Sydney provided additional support. Publication costs were supported by the School of Historical and Philosophical Studies and the Faculty of Arts Publication Subsidy Scheme.

A semester at the Center for the Study of Law and Society at the University of California at Berkeley in 2009 helped generate momentum. While working on a new project at the Center for European Studies at Harvard in 2012, I also put the finishing touches on this book. Access to Harvard's wondrous resources made both research and writing speed along with relative ease. I thank both institutions and the colleagues I met there for making those experiences pleasant and invigorating.

Sam Moyn deserves special mention for assistance and inspiration. His brilliant book, *The Last Utopia*, appeared when I had just started to draft my manuscript. The questions it raised and its provocative arguments, even (or especially) when I disagreed with them, nudged my thinking in new and productive directions, as did the flood of discussion and debate his book generated. He has been generous in his enthusiasm for the project and in reading draft chapters. Sam and Jan Eckel organized a 2010 workshop on human rights in the 1970s at the Freiburg Institute for Advanced Study, which helped bring the decade into view for me. I am grateful to them for inviting me and to fellow participants for unusually stimulating discussions.

Since I moved to Melbourne seven years ago, Roland Burke has been a steady source of good humor and encyclopedic historical knowledge on many topics, not least of which is human rights. My own grasp of the history of human rights would be poorer had he not been around. In the final weeks of writing, he was especially generous in answering last-minute questions about matters large and small. I am grateful to Alison Duxbury, Robert Horvath, and Peter Russell for similar human rights–related inspiration and conversation. Robert G. Kaufman, Bruce Miroff, Daniel Sargent, and Sarah Snyder are among those who shared insights, work in progress, documents, or archival tips. Frank Costigliola's brilliantly original work convinced me of the importance of explicit attention to emotions. I am especially grateful to those who slogged through draft chapters and emerged with corrections and useful suggestions for improvement: Carl Bon Tempo, Roland Burke, Jan Eckel, David Farber, David Goodman, Robert Horvath, Scott Kaufman, Sam Moyn, Ben Nathans, and Chips Sowerwine. Gabriele Kenaston, my dear friend and fellow writer (and sufferer of the afflictions thereof), provided long-distance encouragement (and distraction) and in-person support during research trips to the Bay Area. Other friends and relatives—Cheri Shimeta Hall, Bill Shimeta, Mike and Laurie Shimeta, and Brian Hentschel—helped along the way, especially during research trips.

My research assistants, first Noah Riseman and then Prue Mann, did more than gather books and articles for me; they provided moral support and valuable insights into sometimes mysterious Australian practices. The very capable Bronwyn Lowe stepped in to help during the final crunch month.

Among the many librarians and archivists who helped along the way, I am especially grateful to Debbie Miller at the Minnesota Historical Society, Dan Dailey at the University of South Dakota Archives, Lauren Lehman at the State Historical Society of Missouri, David Kuzma at Rutgers, Scott Cossell at the University of South Dakota Library, and Diane Shaw at Lafayette College. Thanks, too, to the excellent staff at the Library of Congress Manuscripts Division, including Jeff Flannery, Bruce Kirby, and Lewis Wyman, for making it such an extraordinarily pleasant and well-run facility for research. Jim Berryman, the indefatigable American specialist at the Baillieu Library in Melbourne, went out of his way to assist at key moments. Richard Serle's ever-helpful administration of the wonderful Pitt bequest ensured the Baillieu Library was stocked with key books.

It is always a pleasure to work with Harvard University Press. Joyce Seltzer has been what every writer hopes for: an enthusiastic editor with valuable suggestions for writing a better book. The significant improvements between the penultimate and the final draft are largely due to her clearheaded vision of what matters. Brian Distelberg and the rest of the staff were marvelously efficient and knowledgeable.

Some of the ideas and information in Chapter 7 are treated in different form in my article "Congress, Kissinger, and the Origins of Human Rights Diplomacy," *Diplomatic History* 34, no. 4 (November 2010): 823–851. The role of torture in shaping American views of the Greek junta after 1967, touched on briefly in Chapter 4, is covered in depth in my essay "Anti-Torture Politics: Amnesty International, the Greek Junta, and the Origins of the U.S. Human Rights Boom," in Akira Iriye, Petra Goedde, and William I. Hitchcock, eds., *The Human Rights Revolution: An International History* (New York: Oxford University Press, 2012), 201–222.

My husband, Jeff Shimeta, held down the fort in so many ways and let me commandeer the desk *and* the kitchen table for much of the last six weeks of writing. My son, McKinley, cheerfully tagged along on research trips around the world beginning when he was nine, spending many long days in archival reading rooms. I still do not understand how he failed to succumb to the pleasures of writing book reports on Nixon and Reagan, but he found his own creative ways to pass the time. I appreciate his patience and his company, and his occasional willingness to talk about history instead of physics (or Harry Potter). This book is dedicated to him.

# Index

Abourezk, James, 148, 155, 180, 187; Foreign Assistance Act Section 32 political prisoners amendment offered by, 133, 136, 138–141, 161–165, 227; maverick style of, 134; McGovern compared to, 134–135; aid to right-wing dictatorships opposed by, 135, 139–140; international human rights concerns of, 136, 140, 162, 172, 180

Abram, Morris, 31, 43, 46–47, 111–112

Abrams, Elliott, 103, 256, 273

Abzug, Bella, 116, 219, 235

Acheson, Dean, 45

Addams, Jane, 16

African Americans. *See* Civil rights; Civil rights movement

AFL-CIO, 69, 87, 208, 217

Agency for International Development (AID), 81, 83, 100

AI USA. *See* Amnesty International, U.S.A. office

Alabama Christian Movement for Human Rights, 36

Allende Gossens, Salvador, 148, 149, 169, 170, 254

Alliance for Progress in Latin America, 40

American Bar Association, 22–24, 40

American Federation of Labor, 20, 26

American Friends Service Committee, 29–30, 131, 172

American Jewish Committee, 28, 41, 91, 110, 208

American Jewish Conference for Soviet Jewry, 111–112

American Jewish Congress, 20, 26, 41, 208

American Jews, 12–13; Holocaust awareness and, 28–29, 108; Soviet Jews aided by, 109–112

Americans for Democratic Action, 44, 87, 91, 122, 180, 192, 207, 209, 225

*Amnesty Action*, 96, 189

Amnesty International, 32, 76, 102, 140, 146, 163; success and growth of, 2–3; origins of, 89; aims and style of, 181, 200–201, 212; global spread of, 93; London and AI USA friction between, 93–94, 191–192; *Report on Torture* of, 137, 194; Nobel Peace Prize of, 151–152; use of public opinion by, 190; role of women in, 190; power struggles within, 191; foreign aid debate of, 210–211; achievements of, 201–202, 212–213; West Germany section of, 202; Freedom House distancing itself from, 213. *See also* Benenson, Peter

Amnesty International, U.S.A. office (AI USA), 250; Hawk's background and rise in, 65–66; early years of, 87–89, 168–169; liberal influence in, 89–90, 198–199; origin and growth of, 89–91, 181, 183–185; first

Amnesty International, U.S.A. office
(AI USA) *(continued)*
board of, 91; early struggles of, 91–92, 185–
186; human rights ideas of, 92–93, 96;
Paul Lyons on purpose of, 93; London
office friction with, 93–94, 191–192; opposition to Greek junta, 94–97; aims of, 181;
activities of, 184, 200, 225; independence
of, 185; funding strategies of, 185–187;
membership growth of, 187, 189; ILRM
compared to, 190; organizational influence
of, 191; nonpartisanship claims of, 192, 201;
direct-mailing by, 192–193, 200–203; conservatives working with, 193–194; New
York branch of, 195; West Coast branch
of, 195–200; role of women in, 195; Sagan's
impact on, 196; Baez organizing concerts
for, 197–198; Hawk hired by, 65–66, 199–
200; achievements of, 201–202, 212–213;
appeals to prospective members by, 202–
205; Fraser's support of, 207; Washington
office of, 207–208; Uruguay campaign of,
208–209; lobbying and influence of,
209–211
Amnesty International Development, 191
Anderson, Jack, 101, 171
Anderson, Patrick, 74, 234
Anger, 8, 10, 64, 74, 101, 134, 139, 155, 218, 270
Anticommunism, 2–3, 10, 13, 51, 79, 81, 84,
97, 103–104, 135, 138, 224–225, 228, 243,
252, 256, 274
Apartheid, in South Africa, 28, 33, 38,
43–44, 84, 145, 222, 257, 291
Aquino, Benino, 262
Argentina, 67, 130, 206, 208, 209, 210, 225;
Ford/Kissinger policies towards, 166–167;
Carter policies toward, 262–264, 266,
267
Arns, Paulo Evaristo, 262
Ashbrook, Josh, 172
Atlantic Charter, 18–19
Augustus, Amelia, 186–187, 192, 341

Baez, Joan, 195; Institute for the Study of
Nonviolence and, 196; Sagan's partner-
ship with, 196–199; AI USA concerts
organized by, 197–198
Baker, Russell, 63
Baldwin, Roger, 30, 90, 97, 189
Bangladesh, 12, 101, 122–123
Barbor-Might, Dick, 210–211
Barre, Mohammed Siad, 256

Bayh, Birch, 226
Benenson, Mark, 91, 144, 186, 190–191, 193,
200
Benenson, Peter, 88–90, 91, 185, 301
Bengston, Nelson, 91
Benson, Lucy, 261
Bernstein, Robert, 265
Biafra, 12, 41
Bikel, Theodore, 197
Bitker, Bruno, 41
Black Panthers, 37
Blane, Andrew, 191, 194
Boettcher, Robert, 143–144, 147–148
Bosnia, 274
Boutwell, George, 277
Brazil, 47, 67, 76, 136, 145, 147, 156, 165, 228,
262; torture in, 76, 98–102, 133, 135, 171,
229, 266, 270; United States complicity
with torture in, 100–101
Brezhnev, Leonid, 106, 118, 124, 223, 265
Bricker, John, 24–26
Bricker Amendment, 24–27, 40
Brown, Edmund "Jerry," Jr., 226
Brown, Sam, 235
Brzezinski, Zbigniew, 193, 258–259, 266,
333; foreign policy suggestions outlined
by, 245–256; international human rights
interests of, 246–249; Carter influence
and relationship with, 247–248
Buchwald, Art, 70
Buckley, William F., Jr., 193
Bukovsky, Vladimir, 253
Bureau of Human Rights and Humanitarian
Affairs, U.S. State Department, 157–158
175, 259, 262
Burundi, 12
Bush, George H. W., 274
Bush, George W., 4, 112, 275

Caddell, Pat, 236, 239, 249–250
Calley, William, 62, 72, 230
Cambodia, 138
Cameron, Bruce, 180–181, 209–210
Carliner, Lewis, 91
Carlos, John, 37
Carter, Jimmy, 4, 7, 71, 76, 141, 183, 220;
human rights commitment of, 1–2, 240–
243, 251–252; human rights confusions
of, 5–6, 244, 249; moral agenda of, 15;
McGovern and, 71; campaign strategies
and success of, 74; human rights in 1976
campaign of, 215, 231–232, 236; uplifting

1976 campaign of, 222–223; foreign policy agenda of, 230, 232–233, 235–237, 245; as Washington outsider, 230–231; civil rights and, 232; Soviet Jews and, 236; administration position on torture, 236–237, 239, 251, 252, 256, 258, 261, 275; Ford debates with, 238–239; 1976 presidential victory of, 239; McGovern's morality stance compared to, 74, 240; inaugural address of, 242, 245–247; liberal displeasure with, 243, 256; as restorer of American pride, 243–244, 268; international human rights promoted by, 13–14, 15, 246–250, 266–268; Brzezinski and, 247–248; on foreign policy and morality, 252; Sakharov supported by, 253; neoconservatives congratulating, 253–254; neoconservatives opposing, 254–256; right-wing dictatorship aid and, 256–258; Holbrooke appointment by, 258; Derian influence on, 259–262; Argentina policy of, 262–264; Helsinki Final Act of 1975 and, 264; criticized for purveying guilt, 267–268; failures of, 272

CDM. *See* Coalition for a Democratic Majority

Ceausescu, Nicolae, 256

Chagnon, Jacqui, 180

Cheney, Dick, 224

Chile, 156; 163, 180, 199, 204, 206, 219; 1973 coup in, 11–12, 130, 148–151, 153, 169, 197, 217; torture in, 149, 168–169; human rights violations in, 47, 147, 149–151, 179, 194, 225, 236; foreign aid restrictions on, 150, 169, 171; Ford/Kissinger foreign aid policies towards, 167–171, 173; Kissinger on political prisoners in, 171; Carter policies toward, 237–238, 255, 266

*The Chronicle of Current Events*, 108, 195

Church, Frank, 68, 101, 227, 228–229, 310

Churchill, Winston, 18

Civil rights, 6, 47, 67, 78, 86, 89, 109, 124, 161, 216, 218, 227, 229; human rights compared to, 7, 33, 36; human rights as, 33–34; terminology of, 36–38; King on human rights, 38; Malcolm X on human rights compared to, 38; Soviet dissident movement for, 106; Henry "Scoop" Jackson's support of, 113–114, 117; Carter's history with, 231–232. *See also* Civil rights movement; Human rights

Civil rights movement, 3, 7, 10, 27–29, 31, 32–47, 56, 63, 93, 104, 111, 272; connections to human rights movement, 86, 111, 178, 180, 193, 197, 231, 254, 260; human rights language in, 33–46, 159, 233, 246; Carter and, 231–232. *See also* Civil rights

Civil liberties, 6

Clark, Bronson, 131

Clark, Joseph, 235

Clinton, Bill, 274

Coalition for a Democratic Majority (CDM), 179, 218, 234, 239, 248, 333; Henry "Scoop" Jackson and, 115–116; Vietnam War views of, 116; Carter congratulated by, 253–254

Coalition for a New Foreign and Military Policy, 180

Colby, William, 61

Cold War, 2, 3–4, 7, 10, 12, 13, 26, 52, 68, 76, 89, 143, 159, 233, 239, 245, 255, 270; effects on human rights of, 17, 21, 31, 34, 88, 177, 179, 212, 225, 273; end of, 16, 274; Vietnam War leading to reassessment of consensus on, 51, 76, 228; Fraser and, 79, 145, 147; Jackson and, 103–104, 113–115, 226. *See also* Vietnam War

Commission for the Observance of Human Rights Year, 46

Commission on Human Rights, of United Nations, 21–22, 36, 147

Communism, 2–3, 10, 13, 49, 51, 79, 81, 138, 224, 243, 252, 264, morality and containment of, 51

Congress, United States, 8, 10, 18, 23, 24, 40, 45, 56, 61, 68, 77, 86, 99, 118, 122, 128–131, 138–139, 142–143, 148, 157–161, 166–168, 171, 176–177, 206, 225, 231, 270

Conservatives, 59, 115, 128, 139, 143, 172, 236, 238–239, 241, 252–253, 255, 271; human rights views of, 3–4, 10, 12–13, 68, 113, 213, 215, 224–225; United Nations and UDHR fears of, 17, 23–26; Soviet dissident movement inspiring, 105, 153; AI USA relationship with, 193–194, 199. *See also* Coalition for a Democratic Majority; Henry "Scoop" Jackson; Neoconservatives

Conte, Silvio, 225

Convention against Genocide, of United Nations, 27, 110

Convention for the Elimination of All Forms of Racial Discrimination, 41

Conway, Jack, 87
Conway, LuVerne, 87, 341
Coughlin, Charles, 16
Cranston, Alan, 165, 173, 175, 209
Crown, Joseph, 131
Culver, John, 82
Curtis, Carl, 132

Dassin, Jules, 87
Declaration against Torture, United
    Nations, 183, 190
Decolonization, 39, 43
Dellums, Ron, 60
Demetracopoulos, Elias, 86
Democratic Party Convention of 1972,
    68–69, 230
Development aid. *See* Foreign aid
Dewey, Thomas, 24
Dobrynin, Anatoly, 108–109, 253
Drinan, Robert, 61, 121, 155, 227
Du Bois, W. E. B., 35
Dulles, John Foster, 23, 26

Eagleton, Thomas, 70
"East-West Trade and Fundamental Human
    Rights" amendment, 120–126. *See also*
    Jackson-Vanik amendment
East Timor, 130, 258
Edwards, Don, 65, 86–88, 96
Edwards, Harry, 36–37
Ehrlichman, John, 64
Eisenhower, Dwight D., 26
Eizenstat, Stuart, 236
Eldridge, Joseph, 146, 172, 182
Elections. *See* Presidential election of 1972;
    Presidential election of 1976
Ellsberg, Daniel, 64
Emotions, 3–4, 8, 49, 51–52, 57, 68, 70, 74,
    101, 109, 114, 117, 127, 132, 137, 216–217,
    218, 223, 231, 236, 237, 240, 255, 272, 348;
    Amnesty International and, 190, 203, 212.
    *See also* Anger; Guilt; Shame
Ennals, Martin, 89, 94, 147, 207
Ensign, Todd, 60
Equal Rights Amendment, 215–216
European Commission on Human Rights,
    85, 96
Evers, Medgar, 37
Evers, Myrlie, 37
Export-Import Bank Extension Act of
    1968, 83

Fallows, James, 251
Fascell, Dante, 146, 149, 150, 172, 258,
    266
Feith, Douglas, 103
Fitzpatrick, William, 25
Fonda, Jane, 137
Ford, Gerald, 2, 15, 130, 138, 175, 176, 183,
    214–215, 222–225, 232, 233–234, 242, 253,
    264; foreign policy problems of, 216–217,
    221–224; Solzhenitsyn meeting refused
    by, 217–218; uplifting campaign of,
    222–223; Reagan battles over foreign
    policy platform with, 223–225; Carter
    debates with, 238–239
Ford Foundation, 82, 92, 191, 220, 265
Foreign aid, 26, 125, 138–142, 155, 270–271;
    Fraser on morality and, 80, 269, 271;
    Fraser's goals with, 81–82, 164; morality
    and, 135–140, 176–177; early 1970s criti-
    cisms of, 138–139; Edward Kennedy's
    demands on Chile and, 150, 169; Fraser's
    demands on Chile and, 150; Humphrey's
    criticism of, 159; Kissinger's policies
    with Chile and, 166, 168–171; Amnesty
    International lobbying and, 208–211;
    Carter policy toward, 267, 268. *See also*
    Abourezk, James; Right-wing dictator-
    ship aid
Foreign Assistance Act: Title IX of, 81–83,
    141, 164; Section 32 of, 133, 136, 140,
    161–164, 165; Section 502B of, 165, 168,
    173–175, 184, 207, 209
Foreign Military Sales Act of 1968, 83
Foreign policy, United States: human rights
    and, 2, 7–8; Vietnam War and changes
    in, 7–8, 49, 52; morality in, 14, 66, 155–
    156; anticolonialism in, 43; toward South
    African apartheid, 44; toward Rhodesia,
    44–45; Nixon's, 52; New Politics and,
    53; McGovern's, 53–54; McGovern and
    morality in, 66–68, 71; Fraser's ideas
    about, 76–80, 83–84; liberal concerns
    about, 101–102; Kissinger's moral stan-
    dards and, 132; Fraser's platform for,
    142–143; Fraser's report on human rights
    in, 156–157; Ford's problems with, 216–
    217, 221; Moynihan's proposals for, 218–
    219, 235; Reagan on morality and, 223;
    Ford and Reagan battling over platform
    issues, 223–225; Carter's, 230, 232–233,
    235–237, 245; 1976 presidential election
    debates on, 232–235, 238; Brzezinski

suggestions for, 245–256; Carter on morality and, 252
Fosdick, Dorothy, 117
Four Freedoms, 17–18, 117
Fraser, Donald, 5, 65, 68, 78, 125, 147; Democratic convention reforms of, 69, 77–78; liberal foreign policy agenda of, 76–80, 142–143; shortcomings of, 77; political career rise of, 77–78; internationalist outlook of, 78, 80; civil rights and, 78; women's rights and, 78; Vietnam War changing opinions of, 78–79, 81; on foreign aid and morality, 79–80, 269, 271; United Nations and, 80, 143–144; Title IX "political development" aims of, 81–82, 164; foreign aid goals of, 82, 139, 164; on foreign policy dilemmas, 83–84; on South Africa, 84; on Greece, 87–88, 96–97; Kissinger confirmation testimony of, 128–130; right-wing dictatorship aid fought by, 140–141, 160–164; human rights hearings of, 145–147; international human rights efforts of, 141, 143–148; Rhodesia boycott and, 143; Chile and, 150; human rights reports and, 156–157; Section 32 of Foreign Assistance Act strengthened by, 163–164; legacy of, 165; Section 502B amendment offered by, 165, 168, 173–175, 184, 207, 209; Kissinger's opposition to efforts of, 166–167, 170; work with AI USA, 87, 144, 184, 207
Freedom, 5, 6, 16, 18, 23, 36, 38, 47, 50, 78–79, 81, 84, 96, 104, 123, 124, 220, 222, 229, 235, 237, 247, 254, 258, 273, 274, 276
Freedom House, 30, 179, 219, 248, 258; Amnesty International distanced from, 213
Fulbright, J. William, 54, 87, 158, 159, 310
Fundamental freedoms, 17, 19, 20, 21, 160, 161, 163, 258, 264

Galbraith, John Kenneth, 86
Geneva Conventions, 56, 58, 61, 131
Genocide Convention, 40
Genovese, Eugene, 51
Globalization, 10
Goldberg, Arthur J., 45, 65
Goren, David, 208
Grant, Frances, 90
Greece, 12, 43, 53, 67, 108, 132, 133, 136, 144, 145, 149, 152, 165, 171, 186, 270; 1967 coup in, 75–76, 84–85; human rights abuses in,

85, 96; United States position on junta rule of, 86; liberals against junta rule of, 86–88; AI USA's opposition to junta in, 94; anti-junta groups and, 95; Fraser and, 97, 156, 160; torture committed by junta in, 98–99, 101–102, 191, 193, 196; Henry "Scoop" Jackson position on junta in, 124
Greider, William, 71–72
Gross, H. R., 164
Grossman, Jerome, 64
Gruening, Ernest, 56, 131
Guilt, 3, 4, 9, 63, 68, 71–74, 102, 104, 116, 126, 136, 154, 159, 183, 218, 230, 235, 252, 255, 259, 267–268
*Gulag Archipelago* (Solzhenitsyn), 153, 217, 222

Haeberle, Ron, 59
Hague Conventions, 56, 58
Haig, Alexander, 273
Haiti, 43, 147, 210
Halsted, Anna Roosevelt, 46
Hammarberg, Thomas, 211
Harkin-McGovern-Abourezk amendment, 171–173
Harriman, Averell, 41, 65, 234, 237
Harris, Fred, 226
Hauser, Rita, 31, 33, 111, 194, 341
Hawk, David: civil rights and antiwar background of, 32–33, 63–64; Moratorium demonstration and, 64–65; AI USA and, 65–66, 183, 187, 188, 199–200
Hayden, Tom, 137
Hehir, J. Bryan, 163
Helms, Jesse, 139, 217, 224
Helsinki Final Act of 1975, 213, 215–216, 224, 238, 253, 264–265, 266
Helsinki Watch, 179, 213, 265
Hersh, Seymour, 58–59, 169–170
Hinckley, David, 196
Holbrooke, Richard, 236–237, 260, Carter appointment of, 258–259; Derian clashing with, 261–262; human rights views of, 266
Holman, Frank, 23–26
Holocaust, 11, 19, 102, 117; growing awareness of, 28–29, 108; silence as complicity lesson from, 125
Holt, Pat, 168
Horman, Charles, 150
Hovet, Thomas, 144

Human rights: Carter's commitment to, 1–2, 240–243, 251–252; idealism and, 1–2; foreign policy and, 2, 7–8; United States identity and, 3; Vietnam War healing through promotion of, 3–4, 271–272; conservatives' views of, 4, 12–13; liberals' version of, 4–5, 12; Carter's confusions with, 5–6, 13, 244, 249; contemporary understanding of, 5–7; conceptual development of, 6–7; civil rights compared to, 7, 36; confusion surrounding, 13–14; Atlantic Charter lacking, 18–19; United Nations Charter referencing, 20–21; fundamental freedoms and, 21; as civil rights, 32–47; Hubert Humphrey on, 35–36; as domestic issue, 36, 246; definitions of, 6–7, 36–38, 277; domestic issues tied to, 37–39; King's vision of, 38; Malcolm X's use of, 38; New Politics and, 52–53; Greece junta violations of, 85, 96; neoconservative aims with, 104; liberal position at odds with neoconservatives on, 126; Kissinger's record on, 128–133, 148, 153–155, 166; Fraser's identification with, 147; Chile's violations of, 149–151; Fraser's report on, 156–157; liberals' strategies with hearings on, 176; AI USA's activities for, 184; Carter's campaign adoption of, 215, 231–232, 236; Holbrooke's testimony on, 266. *See also* Human rights movement; International human rights; Universal human rights

Human Rights Bureau. *See* Bureau of Human Rights and Humanitarian Affairs

Human Rights Commission, of United Nations, 27–28

Human Rights Day, 41–42, 45

*Human Rights* journal, 37

Human rights movement: importance of torture to, 2, 12, 22, 40, 53, 76, 165, 170, 171, 172, 176–177, 191, 202, 212, 271; United States and 1970s rise of, 2–3, 178–179; diversity of, 179; groups within, 180–181, 205–206; Lister aiding, 181–182; Vietnam War's end as trigger for, 182–183; liberalism in, 183; as "industry," 206; Section 502B aiding, 207; lobbying and influence of, 209–211; racial makeup of, 211; goals of, 212. *See also specific groups*

Human Rights Party, 37

*Human Rights: Unfolding of the American Tradition*, 41

Human Rights Watch, 179, 213, 265–266, 273–274

Human Rights Working Group, 180–181

Human Rights Year, 1968, 41; failure of, 42–43; Commission for the Observance of, 46

Humphrey, Hubert, 69, 77, 115, 119, 121, 158, 165, 172, 175, 209, 210; on human rights, 35–36; Omnibus Human Rights Act of 1959 and, 36; foreign aid criticism of, 159

Humphrey, John, 28

Huntington, Samuel, 81

Idealism, human rights and, 1–2

ILRM. *See* International League for the Rights of Man

Indonesia, 12, 130, 136, 168, 173, 180, 210, 257

Indo-Pakistani War, 12, 129, 136, 144, 308

Ingersoll, Robert, 161

Initiative Group for the Defense of Human Rights, 108

Institute for Human Rights and Freedom, 258–259

Institute for the Study of Nonviolence, 196

Interdependence, 11, 101, 125, 202, 245, 270

International Commission of Jurists, 144, 145, 151, 189, 207

*International Concern with Human Rights* (Moskowitz), 152

International Covenant on Civil and Political Rights, 27

International Covenant on Economic, Social, and Cultural Rights, 27

International Development and Food Assistance Act of 1975, 171–173

International human rights: Vietnam War influence on, 7, 9; influences on development of, 10–12; jet travel highlighting issues of, 11; United States early engagement with, 15–16; post-World War II rise of, 17, 30–31; Christians' post-World War II attention on, 29–30; Johnson's achievements in, 46; Vietnam War debate without, 50–51, 56; Vietnam War violations of, 56, 58; in McGovern campaign, 67; Soviet-bloc dissident movement appeals for, 107–108; Fraser subcommittee hearings

advancing, 141, 143–148; Cold War framework challenged by ideas about, 145;
Fulbright's views on, 159; Abourezk's
views on, 162; morality in accusations
of violating, 174, 176–177; liberal agenda
with, 176–177, 270–271; Moynihan and,
220; Kissinger's reversal on, 221–222;
presidential elections of 1976 promoting,
239–241; Brzezinski's interest in, 246–
249; Carter promoting, 246–250, 266–268;
Reagan adopting, 273–274. *See also*
Human rights; Universal human rights
International League for Human Rights.
*See* International League for the
Rights of Man
International League for the Rights of Man
(ILRM), 12, 30, 90, 206–207; Vietnam
War statements of, 57–58; formation of,
189; elite makeup of, 189–190; AI USA
compared to, 190
"International Protection of Human Rights"
hearings, 145–148
International Rescue Committee,
258
International Security Assistance and Arms
Export Control Act of 1976, 175
Iranian hostage crisis of 1979, 244
Israel, 78, 108–109, 117, 119, 191, 194, 236,
263

Jackson, Henry "Scoop," 4, 80, 103, 154,
226; legacy of, 103, 113; staff of, 103–104;
anticommunism of, 104–105; universal
human rights embraced by, 105, 113,
119–120, 123–124, 152; as critic of détente,
118; Nixon cabinet offer for, 113; upbringing of, 113; defense priorities of, 114; emotional toughness of, 114; Vietnam War
positions of, 114–116; CDM and, 115–116;
civil rights supported by, 113–114, 117;
Israel supported by, 117; rejection of liberal guilt by, 116; Soviet Jews supported
by, 117–126, 269–270; SALT I opposed
by, 118; Soviet Union linked to Nazi
Germany by, 120–121, 125; conflict with
Kissinger of, 122–124; and Greek junta,
124
Jackson, Jesse, 45
Jackson-Vanik amendment, 120–126, 151,
154, 164, 180, 230, 266
Jara, Victor, 169

Javits, Jacob, 111–112, 119, 121, 132, 150, 165,
173, 194
Jewish Labor Committee, 28–29, 110
Jews. *See* American Jews; Soviet Jews
Johnson, Lyndon, 29, 35, 40–41, 44–46, 65,
68, 78–79, 86, 233
Jones, Tom, 192

Kagan, Robert, 277
Kemble, Penn, 255
Kennan, George, 123
Kennedy, Edward "Ted", 113, 122, 140, 154,
157, 158, 166, 261; Kissinger confirmation
hearing questions of, 133; Chile and, 150,
169
Kennedy, John F., 40, 44, 68, 74, 181
Kennedy, Robert F., 74, 115
Kerry, John, 60
Khrushchev, Nikita, 106
King, Martin Luther, Jr., 50, 196, on human
rights, 38; on South African apartheid,
44; on Soviet Jews, 111
Kissinger, Henry, 59, 118, 127; Nixon
discussing My Lai massacre with, 62;
conflict with Henry "Scoop" Jackson,
122–124; liberal criticism of, 128–129;
Fraser's testimony on confirmation of,
128–130; human rights record of, 128–133;
media love affair with, 129–130; Clark
on record of, 131; moral critiques of, 131;
foreign policy morality standards of, 132;
Soviet Jewish emigration stance of, 132,
167; Edward Kennedy's questions in confirmation hearing of, 133; Fraser on human
rights compared to, 148, 166; Nobel Peace
Prize controversy with, 151; human rights
legislation resulting from policies of, 153–
155; right-wing dictatorship aid and, 155;
Chile foreign aid policies of, 166, 168–171;
Argentina policies of, 166–167; opposition to Fraser human rights efforts, 166–
167, 170; Section 502B fought by, 168, 173;
on political prisoners in Chile, 171; 1976
presidential elections influence in, 215;
international human rights reversal of,
221–222; Solzhenitsyn opinion reversal
of, 222; Helsinki Final Act of 1975 and,
264
Koch, Ed, 110, 112, 208–209
Koning, Hans, 67
Korean War, 26

Kosovo, 274
Kundera, Milan, 1

Laber, Jeri, 211
Laird, Melvin, 59, 62
Lake, Anthony "Tony," 254, 258
Lauterpacht, Hersch, 28
Lawyers Committee on American Policy
 Toward Vietnam, 131
League of Nations, 19
Lefever, Ernest, 273
Lewis, Anthony, 47, 137, 171, 187
Liberals: human rights views of, 4–5, 12;
 Vietnam War views of, 8, 52–53, 86; foreign policy agenda of, 76–80; Greece
 junta rule opposition of, 86–88; AI USA
 influence of, 89–90, 198–199; foreign
 policy vision, 101–102; Soviet-bloc dissident movement supported by, 125; neoconservative vision of human rights at odds
 with, 126; Kissinger criticisms of, 128–
 129; right-wing dictatorship aid opposed
 by, 133, 154, 160, 171–172; "new internationalists" group of, 159–160; human rights
 hearings strategies of, 176; international
 human rights agenda of, 176–177, 270–
 271; Human Rights Working Group priorities of, 180–181; and human rights
 movement, 183; Carter displeasing, 243,
 256. *See also* New Politics
Liberation theology, 29
Liskofsky, Sidney, 110
Lister, George, 158, 181–182
Lord, Mary, 31
Lord, Winston, 173
Lowenstein, Allard, 64–65, 254
Lyons, Maryanne, 92
Lyons, Paul, 87, 91, 193; fundraising of,
 92, 185–186, 200; on AI USA's purpose,
 93; London office friction with, 93–94,
 186; Greece anti-junta efforts of, 87,
 93–96

MacBride, Séan, 151–152
MacDermot, Niall, 145
Malcolm X, 38–39
Mankiewicz, Frank, 197
Marchenko, Anatolii, 108
Marcos, Ferdinand, 261–262
Marsh, Norman, 189
Maw, Carlyle, 174
*Matchbox*, 189

McCarthy, Colman, 187
McCarthy, Eugene, 64, 115
McCarthy, Joseph "Joe," 24
McGill, Ralph, 41
McGovern, George, 4, 119, 122, 171–172,
 199, 259, 260, 268; Nixon's reaction to
 Vietnam War photograph compared to,
 48–49; foreign policy agenda of, 53–54;
 New Politics of, 66; morality in foreign
 policy of, 66–68, 71; 1972 campaign of,
 66–74; international human rights in
 1972 campaign of, 67; Soviet Jews supported by, 67, 119, 122; background of,
 68; Democratic Party Convention of 1972
 rules aiding, 68–69; grassroots mobilization in 1972 campaign of, 69; 1972 electoral defeat, 66, 69–70; Vietnam War
 views of, 70–72; rhetoric of guilt, 71–74,
 126; alienation of public by, 71–74; on
 failures of campaign, 73; Henry "Scoop"
 Jackson and, 114, 116; Abourezk compared
 to, 134–135; legacy of, 154, 183, 227, 253–
 256, 271; Carter and, 230, 240
Meadlo, Paul, 59
Meany, George, 69, 217, 234
Medical Committee for Human Rights, 36
Members of Congress for World Peace
 through Law, 78
Mercouri, Melina, 67, 87, 197
Methodist Church Board of Missions, 41
Mindszenty, József, 21
Mississippi Freedom Summer, 32, 36
Morality: Vietnam War and, 4, 9, 49, 51,
 54–55; in foreign policy, 14, 66, 155–156;
 Carter's use of, 15; containing communism and, 51; of New Politics, 52; in
 McGovern's foreign policy, 66–68,
 71; Fraser on foreign aid and, 80, 269,
 271; Kissinger criticized on lack of, 131;
 Kissinger's foreign policy and, 132; for-
 eign aid and, 135–140, 176–177; interna-
 tional human rights and, 174, 176–177; in
 presidential elections of 1976, 214; Reagan
 on foreign policy and, 223; Carter's stance
 compared to McGovern on, 240; Carter
 on foreign policy and, 252
Moratorium to End the War in Vietnam,
 64–65
Morgan, Thomas "Doc," 141–142
Morris, Ivan, 90, 186, 195
Morse, Bradford, 81
Moskowitz, Moses, 152

Moynihan, Daniel Patrick "Pat," 147, 217, 226, 273; political rise of, 218; at United Nations, 218–219, 220; and CDM, 218, 234, 330; and Henry "Scoop" Jackson, 226; controversies generated by, 219; international human rights and, 220; drafting of 1976 Democratic platform, 234–235; Carter and, 252–253

Muravchik, Joshua, 255

Muskie, Edmund, 52, 69

My Lai massacre, 9, 58–60, 62–63, 72, 230, 272

NAACP. *See* National Association for the Advancement of Colored People

Nader, Ralph, 37

National Association for the Advancement of Colored People (NAACP), 20, 41; 1946 international appeal written by, 34–35; Eleanor Roosevelt struggle with direction of, 35

National Council of the Churches of Christ of the U.S.A. (NCC), 29–30, 44, 55, 96, 137, 146, 180, 182, 288

National Peace Conference, 19–20

NATO. *See* North Atlantic Treaty Organization

NCC. *See* National Council of the Churches of Christ of the U.S.A.

Neibuhr, Reinhold, 63

Neier, Aryeh, 265

Neoconservatives, 115, 218, 243, 258; human rights views of, 4, 14, 104, 147, 177, 213, 273, 277; liberal vision of human rights at odds with, 14, 126; Carter opposed by, 254–256. *See also* Conservatives

New Deal, 16, 24

New Left, 4, 44, 116

New Politics: morality of, 52; human rights issues in, 52–53; foreign policy agenda of, 53; and McGovern, 66

*New York Times*, 6, 34

Nicaragua, 264

Nigeria, 12, 41, 145

Nixon, Richard, 2, 13, 15, 24, 27, 60–61, 76, 86, 97, 118, 119, 127, 129, 131, 132, 139, 158, 216, 234, 242; McGovern's reaction to Vietnam War photograph compared to, 48–49; foreign policy agenda of, 52, 106; Kissinger discussing My Lai massacre with, 62; 1972 electoral victory of, 66, 69, 70; Soviet Jews advocacy by, 110; Henry

"Scoop" Jackson receiving cabinet offer from, 113. *See also* Watergate

Nobel Peace Prize, 2, 151, 188

North Atlantic Treaty Organization (NATO), 97, 124, 274–275

Nuremberg principles, 56

Obama, Barack, 275

Olympic Project for Human Rights, 36–37

Omnibus Human Rights Act of 1959, 36

Orlov, Yuri, 265

Ottaway, David, 183

Pakistan, 12, 122, 136, 308. *See also* Indo-Pakistani War

Papadopoulos, George, 85

Papandreou, Andreas, 86

Paraguay, 257–258

Paris Peace Accords of 1973, 127, 134

Paris Peace Treaties of 1947, 21

Peace Corps, 82

Peers, William, 62

Perle, Richard, 103, 117, 119, 123, 255, 256, 258

Perlmutter, Nathan, 91

Peters, Mason, 276

Philippines, 75, 147, 152, 173, 180, 210, 252, 275

Phoenix program, 9, 138, 140, 272; controversy over, 61, 131; development of, 61

Phúc, Phan Thj Kim, 48

Pinochet Ugarte, Augusto, 130, 148, 150, 166, 169, 238, 274

Plant, Roger, 210

Podhoretz, Norman, 115, 116, 218, 256

Political development, 81–84

Political prisoners: tiger cages and torture of, 9, 131, 135, 137, 152, 172; Section 32 of Foreign Assistance Act and, 136, 140; in Vietnam, 137–140; Abourezk's fights for, 161–162; Kissinger on Chile and, 171

Popper, David, 170

Portugal, 43, 53, 108, 132, 156

Powell, Jody, 244

Presidential election of 1972, 4, 48, 52–54, 66–73, 115, 252, 259, 260; human rights and, 53–54, 67, 119–120

Presidential election of 1976: morality in, 214; Kissinger's influence on, 215; voter priorities in, 216; uplifting campaigns of, 222–223; foreign policy debates of, 232–235, 238; Carter's narrow victory in, 239; international human rights promotion in, 239–241

Racial discrimination, 39; as crime against humanity, 43; in Rhodesia, 44–45, 146. *See also* Civil rights movement

Racism, 9, 22, 34, 39, 40–46, 71, 76, 80, 218, 277; Vietnam War and, 49, 56; in Rhodesia, 44–45, 146; Zionism as form of, 219

Reagan, Ronald, 4, 103, 214–215, 222, 239, 244, 254, 270–271; on morality in foreign policy, 223; Ford battles over foreign policy platform with, 223–225; Vietnam War and, 272; international human rights adopted by, 273–274

Reeves, Richard, 77

*Refuseniks. See* Soviet Jews

Religion, universal human rights and, 16, 19. *See also specific religions*

*Report on Torture*, 1973, of Amnesty International, 137, 194

Reuss, Henry, 83

Reuther, Victor, 87, 88, 91, 94, 97

Reuther, Walter, 65

Rhodesia, 44–45, 53, 67; Fraser on boycott of, 143; racism in, 146

Ribicoff, Abraham, 112, 121

Ridenhour, Ronald, 58–59

Rifkin, Jeremy, 60

Right-wing dictatorship aid: liberal opposition to, 133, 154, 171–172; Abourezk opposition to, 135, 139–140; Vietnam War's end and issues with, 135–140; Fraser opposition to, 140–141, 160–164; Kissinger and, 155; Carter and, 256–258

Rogers, William D., 167, 170

Roosevelt, Eleanor, 21–22, 24, 27, 35

Roosevelt, Franklin Delano, 17–19, 24

Rosenthal, Benjamin, 87, 112, 142

Rumsfeld, Donald, 111, 218

Rusk, Dean, 58, 96

Russell, Bertrand, 58

Rwanda, 274

Sagan, Ginetta, 187, 195; AI USA impact of, 196; Baez partnership with, 196–197; fundraising appeals of, 199, 203–205, 211

Sakharov, Andrei, 12, 107, 122–123, 132, 154, 201, 265; legacy of, 105; fame of, 109; Nobel Peace Prize of, 152; Carter support of, 253

SALT I, SALT II. *See* Strategic Arms Limitation Treaty

Salzberg, John, 144, 146–148, 174, 207, 261, 262

San Francisco Conference, 20, 28

Schmidt, Helmut, 266

Schneider, Mark, 150, 261

Schorr, Norman, 200

Section 32, Foreign Assistance Act, 133, 136, 140, 165; Abourezk and, 133, 136, 140, 161–162; weakness of, 136, 140, 161; impact of, 140, 161–162, 165; Fraser strengthening, 163–164

Section 116, International Development and Food Assistance Act, 171–173

Section 502B, of Foreign Assistance Act, 165, 184, 209; Kissinger opposed to, 168, 173; strengthening, 173–175; human rights movement and, 207

Segregation, 39. *See also* Civil rights

Shame, 3, 9, 58, 61, 63

Sheehan, Neil, 61

Shestack, Jerome, 37

Shlaudeman, Harry, 169

Shoup, David, 55

Shriver, Sargent, 69, 73

Shuttlesworth, Fred, 36

Simon, William, 206

Smith, Griffin, 252

Smith, Ian, 44

Smith, Tommie, 37

Smuts, Jan, 20

SNCC. *See* Student Non-violent Coordinating Committee

Snyder, Ed, 172

Solzhenitsyn, Aleksandr, 12, 21, 123, 125, 132, 153–154, 224, 234; legacy of, 105; Nobel acceptance lecture of, 106–107; Henry "Scoop" Jackson and, 107, 125; fame of, 109; inspiration and leadership of, 154; Ford refusing to receive, 217–218, 238, 253; Kissinger reversing opinion on, 222; 1976 Republican party platform, 224

South African apartheid, 28, 33, 38, 41, 43–44, 53, 67, 84, 145, 222, 257

Southern Christian Leadership Council, 38

South Korea, 12, 47, 147, 167, 173–174, 210, 219, 225, 235–238, 245, 252, 262, 273

Southwest Georgia Project, 32

Soviet dissident movement, 8, 12–13; conservatives inspired by, 105; mission and aims of, 106; *pravozashchitniki* and, 106–107; origins of, 106–108; international human rights appeals of, 107–108; *refuseniks* and,

109, 111; liberal support of, 125. *See also* Sakharov; Solzhenitsyn; Soviet Jews

Soviet Helsinki Watch, 265

Soviet Jews, 12–13; McGovern advocating for, 67; emigration struggles of, 108–110, 118–119; *refuseniks*, 109, 111; American Jews advocating for, 109–112; Nixon and, 110; King on struggles of, 111; Henry "Scoop" Jackson advocating for, 117–126, 269–270; exit tax issues facing, 118–119; UDHR used to defend, 121–122; Kissinger's stance on emigration of, 132, 167; Carter advocating for, 236

Soviet Union: UDHR objections of, 22–23; UDHR violated by, 108; most favored nation status issues with, 118–120; Henry "Scoop" Jackson linking Nazi Germany to, 120–121, 125; Kissinger's policies compared to Henry "Scoop" Jackson's on, 122–124; Carter's stance against, 253, 256. *See also* Cold War; Soviet Jews; Stalin

Soysal, Mumtaz, 211

Spaceship Earth, 11

Spanish-American-Cuban-Filipino War, 275–277

Stalin, Joseph, 22–23, 106

Steel, Ronald, 3

Stettinius, Edward, 21

Straight, Michael, 88, 90–92, 94, 195

Strategic Arms Limitation Treaty (SALT I, SALT II), 118, 124

Student Non-violent Coordinating Committee (SNCC), 39

Styron, Rose, 168, 206

Supplementary Slavery Convention, 40

Sussman, Leonard, 258

Taft, Robert, 24

Talmadge, Herman, 72

Television, 10–11

Teruggi, Frank, 150

Tho, Le Duc, 127, 151

Thurmond, Strom, 139

Tiger cages, 9, 131, 135, 137, 152

Timerman, Jacobo, 265

Title IX, Foreign Assistance Act, 141; mandate of, 81; Fraser's aims with, 81–82, 164; changes made to, 82–83; impact and criticism of, 83

Tonkin Gulf Resolution of 1964, 68, 78

Torture, 13, 40, 67, 225, 265, 266, 277; as driver of human rights movement, 2, 12, 22, 40, 53, 76, 165, 170, 171, 172, 176–177, 191, 202, 212, 271; in Vietnam War, 8, 49, 55, 58, 60; of political prisoners in tiger cages, 9, 131, 135, 137, 152; in Greece, 98, 191, 193; in Brazil, 76, 98–100, 171, 229; United States complicity in Brazil's use of, 100–101; post-Vietnam War and, 137–138; in Chile, 149, 168–170, 179, 236, 274; in Uruguay, 208; Amnesty International and, 178, 183–185, 187, 189–191, 193, 194, 196–197, 202–203, 205, 212; in Argentina, 167, 262; Lefever on, 273; Carter administration position on, 236–237, 239, 251, 252, 256, 258, 261, 275. *See also* Report on Torture, 1973, of Amnesty International

Trade Reform Bill of 1973, 120

Tree, Marietta, 31

Truman, Harry, 15, 17, 22, 26, 39

Tuchman, Jessica, 227, 251, 254, 260

Tunney, John, 165

Tyson, Brady, 135, 254

Udall, Morris, 65, 87, 192, 226–228, 239, 254, 260

UDHR. *See* Universal Declaration of Human Rights

Uganda, 12, 219, 225

United Auto Workers, 65, 87, 91, 208

United Nations, 17, 19, 20, 22–23; Charter, 19–21; human rights in Charter of, 20–21; Commission on Human Rights of, 21–22, 36; conservative fears of UDHR and, 23–26; Bricker Amendment against, 24–27; Convention against Genocide of, 27, 110; Human Rights Commission of, 27–28; Third World participation growth in, 28; "International Protection of Human Rights" hearings for, 145–148; Declaration against Torture of, 183, 190. *See also* Universal Declaration of Human Rights

United States: human rights and, 3; international human rights early engagement of, 15–16; civil rights movement in, 32–47; Malcolm X on genocide committed by, 39; Vietnam War and reputation of, 49, 55; Vietnam War debate over interests of, 55–56; anticommunist dictatorships and, 75; development aid and, 75; Greece junta and, 86; torture in Brazil and complicity of, 100–101; Holocaust prevention failure of, 117; human rights movement 1970s rise in, 1–14, 178–179; Carter restoring pride

United States (*continued*)
of, 243–244, 268; Carter and guilt of, 267–268. *See also* Foreign policy; Vietnam War

U.S. Committee for Democracy in Greece, 87–88, 94–95

Universal Declaration of Human Rights (UDHR), 5–7, 53, 57–58; drafting of, 17; revolutionary importance of, 22; Soviet Union objecting to, 22–23; conservative fears of United Nations and, 23–26; Bricker Amendment against, 24–27; postwar marginality of, 31; Soviet Union violating, 108; free emigration in, 121; Soviet Jews defended with, 121–122. *See also* United Nations

Universal human rights: postwar marginality of, 15–31; property rights and, 16; religion and, 16, 19; post-World War II rise of, 17, 30–31; Henry "Scoop" Jackson embracing, 105, 119–120, 152. *See also* International human rights

Uruguay, 171, 180, 208–210, 225, 256, 262, 266

Ut, Huynh Cong "Nick," 48

Vance, Cyrus, 245, 249–251

Vatican, Second Council, 28–29

Vicariate of Solidarity, 179

Vietnam Coordinating Committee, 65

Vietnam Veterans Against the War, 55, 60

Vietnam War: human rights as healing from, 3–4, 271–272; emotional repercussions of, 3–4, 8, 51–52, 57, 101–102; international human rights influenced by, 7, 9; foreign policy changes influenced by, 7–8, 49, 52, 101–102; liberal views of, 8, 52–53; atrocities of, 8–9; morality and, 9, 49, 51, 54–55; My Lai massacre in, 9, 59–60, 62–63; iconic photograph of, 48–49; Nixon's and McGovern's divergent reactions to photograph of, 48–49; United States reputation and, 49, 55; international human rights absent from debate over, 50–51, 56, 57; opposition to, 54–66; Geneva Conventions violations in, 56, 58; inter-

national human rights violations in, 56, 58; racism in, 56; ILRM statements on, 57–58; war crimes in, 58–60; My Lai, 58–60; media interest in war crimes hearings on, 60; Winter Soldier Investigation of, 60; propaganda supporting, 63; violent protests against, 64; Moratorium demonstration against, 64–65; McGovern's views and promises on, 70–72; Fraser's changing opinions of, 78–79; Henry "Scoop" Jackson's positions with, 114–116; CDM opinion on, 116; ending of, 127; right-wing dictatorship aid and end of, 135–140; torture post-, 137–138; human rights movement and end of, 182–183

Vyshinsky, Andrei, 22–23

Wallace, George, 226

War Powers Act, 138

Washington Office on Latin America, 146, 172, 180, 182

Watergate scandal, 3, 116, 130, 148, 155, 158, 168, 181, 214, 216, 222, 240, 272

Wattenberg, Ben, 72

Welles, Sumner, 18

White, Theodore, 272

White, Walter, 35

*Why Not the Best?* (Carter), 233

Wicker, Tom, 152

Wilkins, Roy, 44–46

Williams, John, 83

Wills, Garry, 72

Wilson, James, 259

Wilsonianism, 7, 15

Winter Soldier Investigation, of Vietnam War, 60

Wipfler, Bill, 182

Wolfowitz, Paul, 103

Women's rights, 17, 19, 25, 27, 28, 34, 40, 78, 178, 266

World Day of Peace, 29

Wren, Christopher, 98

Young, Andrew, 254, 256, 260, 268

Zablocki, Clement, 172